THE RACING FIFTEEN-HUNDREDS

A HISTORY OF VOITURETTE RACING
FROM 1931 TO 1940

TRANSPORT BOOKMAN PUBLICATIONS

THE RACING FIFTEEN-HUNDREDS

A HISTORY OF VOITURETTE RACING FROM 1931 TO 1940

David Venables

PHOTOGRAPHIC ACKNOWLEDGMENTS

Eduardo Andreini: 40a, 53a, 88a, 127a, 127b.
Autocar: 15b & c, 27, 38a, 64a & b, 91d, 97, 104c, d & e, 114a, 121c, 130c & d, 183b.
Alfa-Romeo S.A.: 157a & c, 158a & b.
A.C. Gard-Lozere: 24b.
A.C. de l'Ouest: 4a, c & d.
A.C. di Palermo: 100a.
B.B.C. Hulton Picture Library: 2b, 4e, 5a, b & c.
T.P. Cholmondeley-Tapper: 35c, 46b, 55a, b & c, 67a & b, 157a & b, 183a, 206.
Daimler-Benz AG: 139, 194.
Chris Draper: 203b.
Geoffrey Goddard: 5e, 25a, 35a, 44a & b, 46c, 49a & c, 57c, 65a & b, 67c, 69c, 71a & b,
   78b, 80b, c & d, 83a & d, 103, 106a, b, c, d & e, 108a & b, 121b, 130b, 142b, 145b,
   149b, c & d, 167, 170, 172, 173, 178, 180a & b, 189, 212, 215, 217.
Earl Howe: 24c & d, 28a, 34a, 80a, 98, 112a & b.
Sidney Maslin: 40c & d, 83f.
M.G. Car Club: 34b, 44c, 62a, 197.
George Monkhouse: 24a, 69a & b, 78a, 83b, 91e & f, 127d & e.
Museo dell 'Automobile Carlo Biscaretti di Ruffia Torino: 11, 19a, b & c, 28b, 73b,
   104a & b, 110, 114b, 142a, 159.
Musées de l'Automobile du Mans et de Chatellerault: 13, 40b.
Omnia: 19d.
H. von. Perkhammer: 17b.
Cyril Posthumus: 4b, 5d, 15a, 17a, 25b, 34c, 35b, 46a & d, 48, 49b, 53b, 54a, b & c,
   57b, 62b & c, 69d, 70, 71c, 73a, 77, 80e, 83c & e, 88b, c & d, 90a & b, 91a, b & c, 93a
   & b, 100b, 121a, 127c, 130a, 132, 138, 141a, b, c, d & e, 145a & c, 146, 149a, 151,
   153, 154a, b & c, 157b, 164, 203a, 220.
Wide World: 42a, 57a.

The quotations from Autocar, Motor, Light Car, Motor Sport, Omnia and "The Grand
   Prix Car" by Laurence Pomeroy (The Temple Press) are acknowledged with thanks.

CONTENTS

Photographic Acknowledgments	vi
Preface	vii
PROLOGUE 1895–1930	1
YEAR – 1931	9
1932	21
1933	32
1934	45
1935	60
1936	76
1937	95
1938	119
1939	136
1940	156
EPILOGUE	161
THE CARS AND THE MAKERS	163
THE DRIVERS	209
THE RESULTS	227
MAPS	247
Bibliography	262

© Transport Bookman 1984

First published 1984 by Transport Bookman Publications

ISBN 0 851 84024 8

Designed and typeset by Columns, Reading
Printed and bound in Great Britain by
Chanctonbury Press Ltd, West Chiltington, Sussex

PREFACE

I MADE the first notes for this book in 1977 but the real seeds began to grow in 1947 and 1948, when as a teenager, I watched the first sketchy post-war racing in England. The ERAs and Maseratis, which made most of the running, were cars that had already made their mark in 1500cc racing more than ten years earlier, and many of them still had the same drivers. My imagination was fired by their earlier feats, and the more I learnt about this era of the sport, the more I felt it justified an attempt to record it in one book.

I have had much help in the preparation and research, and I am very grateful to the following for their advice, information and guidance:

The late Dr. Robert Andreae, Sgr. Eduardo Andreini, Messrs. Basil Bowman, T.P. Cholmondeley-Tapper, Hugh Conway, William Court, Chris Draper, Mrs. Elisabeth Harden, The Earl Howe, Mr. Denis Jenkinson, Count Giovanni Lurani-Cernuschi, Messrs. David Mark, Sidney Maslin, T.A.S.O. Mathieson, the late Raymond Mays, Mme. A. Saissi, Mr. R.E. Tongue, Herr Erwin Tragatsch, Dr. Ing. Rudolf Uhlenhaut, Alfa Romeo S.p.A., Autocar, Automobil Revue, A.C. de France, A.C. Gard-Lozere, A.C. di Lucca, B.B.C. Hulton Picture Library, British Library, Daimler-Benz AG, Motor Sport, M.G. Car Club, Musees de l'Automobile du Mans et de Chatelleraut, Museo dell 'Automobile Carlo Biscaretti Torino, Pirelli Ltd.

Finally, I give my especial thanks to Geoffrey Goddard, Brian Joscelyne and Cyril Posthumus, without their kindness, help and support, this book would not have been written or published.

London
May 1984

David Venables

PROLOGUE 1895–1930

THE RACING voiturette is as old as motor racing. The first real motor race, the 1895 Paris – Bordeaux, was won by Emile Levassor driving a 1200 cc Panhard et Levassor which, by the most exacting standards, must be regarded as a voiturette, the first of a long and honourable lineage. The term "voiturette" was the invention of another French designer and constructor, Leon Bollée, who patented a three wheeled vehicle in December 1895 with that title. Leon Bollée was declared by the French Courts to have the exclusive right to the use of the word, but it was so admirable and effective that despite the feelings of its proprietor it passed into general usage. Although having little in common with the voiturettes of the future apart from the name, Bollée's vehicle was remarkably successful, as in July 1897 it won the Paris – Dieppe race and three weeks later repeated this victory in the Paris – Trouville race.

At the beginning of 1898, the keen enthusiasts who possessed small cars were protesting that they stood no chance in competition with the larger vehicles, so for the Paris – Nice event in March 1898 the organisers included a class for cars weighing less than 400 kgs and more than 200 kgs. The winner of this first officially recognised class for small cars was a 4 h.p. Georges Richard driven by its constructor.

Although a voiturette class had now been established, the size of racing cars continued to grow and by the beginning of the new century the capacity of the larger cars had exceeded 10 litres. With the expansion of motor racing there was a need for further classification and in 1901 four classes were established based upon weight.

"A" Over 650 kg	"C" 250-400 kg "voiturettes"
"B" 400-650 kg "light cars"	"D" Under 250 kg

The distinction between classes "B" and "C" soon became blurred and was perhaps never clearly defined, but the smaller classes developed rapidly and in 1902 Louis Renault driving a 3.7 litre Renault (albeit a light car) won the Paris – Vienna race.

The booming sport was about to change dramatically though, as the disasters of the Paris – Madrid race in 1903 ended the era of town-to-town racing, and the development of motor racing thereafter lay on closed circuits. The shock of Paris – Madrid reverberated through the voiturette class and only one race in 1904/5, the Circuit des Ardennes, included a small car class. 1905 continued the evolution that had begun in 1903 and marked the effective end of the first chapter of the sport. The Gordon Bennett races had been abandoned, as manufacturers, rather than nations, wanted to race their products and in 1906 the new era was recognised by the Automobile Club de France which instituted the Grand Prix which thereafter was the top echelon of the sport. The French magazine L'Auto realising that the sport needed a secondary racing class presented a trophy, the Coupe de L'Auto, in 1905 which was intended to encourage the growth of the racing voiturette. The 1905 event was to have been for cars limited to a capacity of 1 litre. This was a fiasco, and in 1906, the rules were changed and a bore limit of 120 mm was imposed for single cylinder engines and 90 mm for twin cylinder engines with a maximum weight limit of 700 kg. The 1906 event was a great success and the following year voiturette racing to the Coupe de L'Auto rules spread to Italy, and as a greater spur to the success of the class, the regulations were changed in 1908 to permit 4 cylinder engines.

While the new voiturette class had been expanding rapidly its big brother of Grand Prix racing had suffered a slight relapse after three successful seasons. In 1909, mainly at the instigation of the French, who had been humiliated by Mercedes and Benz in the 1908 G.P. de L'A.C.F., the principal competitors signed an agreement not to participate in G.P. racing for two years, thus bringing to a halt the development of the principal branch of motor racing. This setback acted as an even greater encouragement to the lesser light and during the

(a)   (b)

a. 23rd July 1911: G.P. de France: Ernst Frederich awaits the start with his T10 Bugatti.

b. 13th July, 1913: Cyclecar G.P. Amiens: Violet (Violet-Bogy) is followed by Samuelson (Marlborough) through the S-bend at Boves.

next three years the voiturette was effectively the backbone of European racing. With the revival of G.P. racing in 1912 the voiturettes once again took a back seat, but in the 1912 G.P. de L'A.C.F., a voiturette class was included in order to ensure a full field of entrants. This class had a capacity limit of 3 litres and remained at that size until Europe went to War in 1914.

While the fortunes and dimensions of the voiturettes had ebbed and flowed between 1906 and 1914, attempts were made between 1909 and 1912 to revive Grand Prix racing. Although the A.C.F. was not enthusiastic, in 1911, it permitted the A.C. de la Sarthe to promote a race which was to have the fine sounding title of Grand Prix de France. A motley entry was given distinction by the appearance of a new marque, Bugatti. This car had a 4 cylinder 1456 cc engine with dimensions of 65 × 110 mm, and as it was not heavy enough to run as a light car, it had to run in the Grand Prix which was virtually a formula libre event, although there was a sub-classification for cars with engine dimensions exceeding 110 × 200 mm. The race was won by a 10 litre Fiat and the tiny Bugatti driven by Ernst Frederich was in second place at the finish and was awarded the first prize in the 110 × 200 mm class.

Motoring had been spreading rapidly and was no longer the prerogative of the rich, and with this spread, came the demand for a smaller car altogether which could be the first step into motoring for the enthusiastic motorcyclist. From this need came the cyclecar which flourished greatly in the years leading up to 1914. Recognising this, the organisers of the 1913 G.P. de L'A.C.F. which was held at Amiens, promoted a 170 mile cyclecar Grand Prix on 13th July, the day after the Grand Prix. For reasons that history does not reveal, the capacity limit for the race was 1100 cc, thus creating a capacity class that has remained in motor racing ever since. The victor was a three wheeled Morgan, but this was excluded by a quirk of the regulations as it lacked the essential element of a fourth wheel, becoming the first British machine to fall foul of French race regulations and establishing a precedent which has been maintained over the years. With the exclusion of the Morgan, the prize was awarded to a four wheeled 2 cylinder Bedelia. Cyclecar racing was clearly a success and three weeks later a similar event was run at Le Mans as a preliminary to the 1913 G.P. de France, which the A.C. de la Sarthe was still promoting. This time, however, victory went to a 4 cylinder Ronteix.

All this ended in July 1914, and for the next four years the Grand Prix cars, the voiturettes and the cyclecars were silent. The world that began to recover in 1919 was a very different place, and while there had been no racing for four years, the demands of war had encouraged tremendous technical and metallurgical advances which were now to be adopted with alacrity by the motor racing world. It had been the intention of the A.C.F. to resume the Grand Prix in 1920 with a capacity limit of 3 litres; the Coupe de L'Auto voiturette of 1913 now becoming the Grand Prix car of 1920, but the world had not yet made a sufficient recovery and the race was postponed until 1921. With the enterprise that it had shown before the war, the A.C. de L'Ouest, as the Sarthe Club had become, decided that if 1920 could not have a Grand Prix it would have a voiturette race for cars under 1400 cc. It had been intended to hold a cyclecar race and a race for 1400 cc voiturettes at Le Mans in 1914 – so it

3

a. 30th August, 1920: Coupe Internationale des Voiturettes Le Mans: Charles Faroux is about to start Baccioli (Bugatti (12)) and Violet (Major (11)). Dumoulin (Tictac (13)) waits his turn.

b. 30th August, 1920: Coupe Internationale des Voiturettes Le Mans: Baccioli (Bugatti) enters Mulsanne corner.

c. 16th September, 1922: Cyclecar G.P. Le Mans: The winner Robert Benoist stands between his own Salmson and that of his team mate Desvaux.

d. 16th September, 1922: Coupe des Voiturettes Le Mans: The winner Kenelm Lee Guiness (Talbot-Darracq).

e. 20th September, 1924: JCC 200 mile race Brooklands: On the Byfleet Banking, Segrave (Talbot-Darracq (14)) passes Hawkes (Salmson (35)) and Hendy (Austin (43)) while Coe (Horstman) comes up behind.

a. 26th September, 1925: JCC 200 mile race Brooklands: The 1500cc class lines up at the start. Nos. 11, 12, and 14 are the victorious Talbot-Darracq team, 15 is Morgan's Thomas-engined Aston-Martin.

b. 10th October, 1927: British G.P. Brooklands: The start with the Delage team together on the left.

c. 13th July, 1926: German G.P. Avus: The start of the 1500cc class. Kimpel (Bugatti (24)) is level with Muller (NSU (29)). The class was won by Kloble (NSU (32)).

d. 1927 G.P. de l'Overture Montlhery: The Salmsons head the field at the start of th 1100cc race.

e. 9th September, 1928: G.P. d'Europe Monza: Count Brivio in one of the "Invincible" 1500cc Talbot-Darracqs.

was run eventually, six years later. The race attracted 26 voiturettes and 22 cyclecars; Violet's Major won the cyclecar race on the 29th August, and the following day the team of three T 22 Bugattis dominated the voiturette race. These cars had been built for the 1914 race and stored throughout the War but were none the worse for that experience. Although Viscaya's Bugatti was disqualified, the remaining cars finished first and second thus establishing the pre-eminence of Bugatti as a manufacturer of 1500 cc racing cars, a state of affairs that was to last for the next fifteen years.

In 1921 motor racing began to recover momentum and 1500 cc now became the recognised capacity limit for the voiturettes while cyclecars were limited to 1100 cc. At the end of the season there was a flurry of activity which began with a clean sweep for Bugatti with the T22 in the Italian Voiturette Grand Prix at Brescia on September 8th. These cars took the first four places and thus became the renowned "Brescia" model. A fortnight later the A.C. de L'Ouest again ran the voiturette and cyclecar races at Le Mans and the balance of power was disturbed decisively. The Anglo-French combine of the French Darracq concern and the English companies of Sunbeam and Clement Talbot had entered Grand Prix racing in 1921 with a car using an 8 cylinder twin overhead camshaft engine inspired by the great Ernst Henry. Half the straight 8 Sunbeam engine made a superb 1500 cc voiturette engine and this fitted to an efficient chassis set new standards for voiturettes; racing as Talbot-Darracqs the new cars dominated the Le Mans event. In the cyclecar class another new marque appeared, Salmson also with a twin ohc. 4 cylinder engine and this, too, won its class as effectively as the Talbot-Darracqs, and established a superiority that was to last for several years. The English, seeing the growth of the voiturette, could not be left out and the Junior Car Club promoted the first long distance race to be held in England, the 200 mile race at Brooklands. This was run on 22nd October and was limited to cars of 1500 cc with a class for the 1100s. The race was another triumph for Talbot-Darracq but the 1100 class was won by a GN, a British victory for a true cyclecar.

The following year the Grand Prix formula was changed to a 2 litres capacity limit but this did not affect the growth of 1100 and 1500 cc racing and new marques such as Aston Martin and Alvis appeared, despite the discouragement of the S.T.D. invincibility. The R.A.C. promoted the first British road race for 1500s on the famous motorcycle T.T. course on the Isle of Man, an experiment which unfortunately was not repeated. A pattern had now been established for the voiturette classes which provided racing for those drivers and manufacturers who were unable to enter the Grand Prix field, and also as an additional outlet for the Grand Prix competitors. Grand Prix racing was changing, however. The major technical innovation was the introduction by Fiat of the supercharger in 1923, and by 1924 this had appeared on almost every Grand Prix car except Bugatti, and had also spread to the best 1500s. These technical advances came with the inevitable accompaniment of increased costs, and after the high point of 1924, the number of manufacturers supporting Grand Prix racing began to decline. In the hope of reviving interest, the A.I.A.C.R. announced in the middle of 1925, that in 1926 the capacity limit for Grand Prix racing cars would be reduced to 1500 cc, thus making the voiturette a Grand Prix car. If it was

6

hoped that the decision would encourage more manufacturers to enter the sport, it was a dismal failure, as the only major firms who felt it was worth while to race teams of new cars were Bugatti Delage and the S.T.D. combine. The 1500 formula was dominated by Delage whose remarkable straight 8 was the apogee of racing car design in the 1920s. Any hope that the new formula would make cheaper G.P. racing was illusory and the expense of competing, combined with increasing economic difficulties, saw Grand Prix racing almost dying on its feet by the end of the 1927 season. With the introduction of the 1500 cc Grand Prix formula, the 1100 cc class now became the voiturettes and this class was also dominated by one marque, Amilcar, whose C6 model was a miniature Grand Prix car and a far cry from the cyclecars that had raced in the class five years before.

Realising the need to reduce the cost of Grand Prix racing, the A.I.A.C.R. embarked in 1928 on a formula based on a sliding weight scale. The complications of this formula were virtually ignored by race organisers and Grand Prix racing became formula libre with cars which had been competing in the 2 litre formula of 1922-1925 as well as the 1500s of 1926-1927. With this sketchy racing, sports car racing now boomed, as many manufacturers considered that as their economic problems increased, the racing of production models was the only racing that could be justified. This, of course, provided an ideal outlet for the amateur driver particularly in the smaller capacity classes. Despite the world economic crisis that was looming in 1928, Grand Prix racing did not die and a new element now entered the sport. In 1928/29 the Fascist Party had gained complete control of the Italian government and Mussolini realised that motor racing could promote the image of the new Italy. Italians were now exhorted to race for the glory of their country, apart from other considerations, and the Alfa Romeo team received a measure of government support for its racing activities. Grand Prix racing had now become a three cornered fight between Alfa Romeo using the 2 litre P2 of 1924, Bugatti with the supercharged derivatives of the 1924 T35 and the new marque, Maserati with the 2500cc Tipo.26M. During 1930 both Alfa Romeo and Bugatti realised that new designs would be needed to deal with Maserati so Vittorio Jano designed the 8 C 2300 cc Monza Alfa Romeo, while Ettore Bugatti, inspired by the American Miller 91, announced his twin-cam T51. As a result of these developments, at the beginning of 1931, Grand Prix racing was ready to enter a new era with three full factory teams and with the new designs which were also available for any rich amateur. This healthy revival now promoted new interest amongst those who preferred to drive racing cars but could not afford the expense of the full Grand Prix machines. After the collapse of the 1500 formula in 1927, racing in the 1500 cc class had continued in a limited form encouraged mainly by Bugatti whose T37 was the ideal car for the keen amateur, so with the renaissance of Grand Prix racing at the beginning of 1931, the scene was also set for the revival of the voiturette.

1931

THE MOTOR racing enthusiast of the 1980s accepts, without question, that international motor racing takes place all over the world throughout the year. There are seasonal shifts of emphasis between the northern and southern hemispheres, but the professional racing driver can attempt to earn his living without any break. This has not always been so. In the early days of motor racing the sport was divided into two separate forms, the American style of track racing and the European style of road racing which took place either on public roads or on a purpose built road circuit. By 1931, the split between Europe and America was almost complete and there were virtually no links between the two branches of the sport. It was not until after the 1939/45 War that the Atlantic was gradually bridged by motor racing again.

The sport of road racing in the 1930s was almost exclusively European at the international level and although road racing took place in South America, South Africa and Australia, this was a pale and amateur imitation of the European original. The sport, being strictly European was also seasonal. The season began at the end of March, reached a crescendo in August during the holiday month and finished abruptly at the end of September. There was a close season of about six months which enabled factory teams and private entrants alike to prepare for the next season. In the winter of 1930/31, the voiturettes upon which mechanics worked and designers pondered came predominantly from France and Italy. Although the greater number of these were of French origin, during the winter of 1930, no new designs were being built by the French factories. The backbone of French racing was Bugatti as it had been throughout the 1920s and was to be until the mid 1930s. Voiturette Bugattis came in three types, though the same size (1500cc) and almost always in the same colour. The quickest was the T39A, the supercharged straight 8 single cam which was the short-stroke derivative of the T35 which had first appeared in the French Grand Prix at Lyons in 1924. The T39A was produced by Bugatti for the $1\frac{1}{2}$ litre G.P. formula of 1926/27 and raced by the works. It was still catalogued and available from the factory in 1931. In addition, Bugatti produced an alternative design for the 1926/27 formula which was primarily intended for the private entrants. This was the famous 4 cylinder T37 which appeared in supercharged form as the T37A and was virtually mass-produced at Molsheim in the late 1920s. Bugatti was designing a new car for grand prix racing in 1931, the T51 which was a

9

twin cam version of the T35 and this he intended to produce in short stroke form as the T51A for voiturette racing, but this variant had gone no further than the drawing board at the beginning of the 1931 season.

The other principal 1500cc challenger from France made up in quality what it lacked in quantity. The $1^1\!2$ litre straight 8 Delage had been virtually invincible in the Grand Prix races of 1926/27. After this the factory team had been sold off to private owners and by 1931 the only Delages still active in voiturette racing were in the hands of Earl Howe, the English motor racing peer and Robert Sénéchal, a French professional. Easily the fastest voiturette racing at the beginning of the 1931 season, the Indian summer of the Delage still lay in the future. Another French product of the 1926/27 formula still racing at the beginning of 1931 was the $1^1\!2$ litre supercharged straight 8 Talbot produced by the Sunbeam Talbot Darracq combine. Not particularly successful in their prime, the Talbots, somewhat modified had all found their way to Italy and were manifestly inferior in design to the Delage. In the 1100cc class, France offered one principal marque, Amilcar, which like Bugatti and Delage was really a leftover from the 1920s. The 6-cylinder Amilcar had been designed in 1925 as a sports racer and voiturette and was remarkably fast being almost a match for the T37A Bugatti. The Amilcar factory although declining rapidly in the economic depression was still supporting two works cars for José Scaron the Amilcar agent at Le Havre. Scaron's cars were both offset single seater MC0 models, but there were many of the 6-cylinder C6 models in amateur hands. The great rival of the Amilcar in the 1920s was the Salmson and although a slower car, some of the 4-cylinder twin cam 8 plug San Sebastian models were still being raced by amateurs in 1931 together with the rarer and quicker 8-cylinder 1100. The Amilcar and Salmson were joined in the 1100 class by various French specials, some of remarkable design and unremarkable performance often powered by the proprietary 4-cylinder Ruby engine.

The other centre of voiturette manufacture was the rival seat of motor racing power, Italy. Only two marques were significant. Alfa Romeo had for several years been producing a most successful 6-cylinder twin cam supercharged sports car in 1500cc and 1750cc form, which had won many important international sports car races between 1928 and 1931. Although not supported by the factory at Portello, which was busy developing the new 8-cylinder 2.3 litre G.P. car, a number of enthusiasts had seen the potential of the sports 1500 6C Alfa as a voiturette and various cars had been prepared as racing cars.

The other Italian marque, was a relative newcomer, Maserati, built by the Maserati brothers Alfieri, Bindo and Ernesto at Bologna. The voiturette Maserati was offered at the beginning of 1931 as the 1100cc Tipo 26c and the 1500cc Tipo 26. Each was supercharged straight 8 and inclined to overweight in the chassis being a small version of the $2^1\!2$ litre Tipo 26 M Grand Prix car.

Beside the profusion of strength of the French and Italian designs, the other countries of Europe had little to offer. Germany, still suffering from the aftermath of the hyper-inflation and currency collapse of the 1920s, could only field 750cc and 1100cc DKW.s and the 750cc BMW. The DKW., a 2-stroke, was derived from a production car and the BMW was the English Austin 7 built under licence.

England, as befitted a country where road racing was illegal, had little to offer. The 1100cc Brooklands Riley 9 was a quick and successful sports racing car which could be stripped easily to make an "instant" voiturette, and the Ulster Austin 7, a supercharged 750cc car, had dominated the 750 class in sports car races between 1928 and 1931. Both showed their sports car backgrounds in many ways and it was perhaps easy to dismiss these cars as "quasi" voiturettes.

The 1931 motor racing season opened, not in Europe, but in North Africa in the French colony of Tunis where the Tunis Grand Prix was held outside the ancient city of Carthage. The race took place on the flat, rather featureless 8 mile (12.7 km) Bardo circuit on the 29th March and presumably, was held early in the season to prevent the heat of the north African summer playing havoc with racing engines. The voiturettes ran with the Grand Prix cars over 37 laps and 15 starters came to the line. The race was an easy victory for Ernesto Maserati driving one of his own 1500cc Tipo 26 cars which saw off an early challenge from Count Castelbarco with one of the "Italian" Talbots, which soon fell out with gear box trouble. Eleven minutes behind Maserati, Pierre Veyron finished second with one of the eight Bugattis in the race and, a portent of his form throughout the season, José Scaron was third with his 1100cc MCO Amilcar. The Grand Prix race was won overall by Achille Varzi, giving the new T51 Bugatti its first victory, and the speed of the new model must have made some hearts beat faster in expectation of the T51A.

After the Tunisian dust had settled there was a lull of four weeks which was broken only by the G.P. Bordino at Alessandria in northern Italy on the 26th April when an 1100cc race saw Gianfranco Comotti (Salmson) leading home a mere three finishers by more than a lap. Whether Scaron left his Amilcar in north Africa after Tunis, history does not relate, but both he and the car were in superb form at Casablanca on the 17th May where a new race was held on the main streets of the town over a 3.75 mile (6 km) course. There were twelve voiturettes competing in the 1500cc class and Scaron and the little Amilcar slew the giant 1500s in winning by two minutes from Galba, a local boy who almost made good, with his T37A Bugatti, having led for the first twenty laps. Scaron and Galba completely outclassed the rest of the field as the third man home, Platé (Alfa Romeo) was 24 minutes behind.

24th May, 1931 Italian G.P. Monza: Sénéchal (Delage) at the start of the 10 hour race. The chequered flag is an unusual starting signal.

As previously related, in the hope that grand prix racing would revive, a European championship series had been instituted in 1931. To qualify for this series, a grande epreuve had to be of ten hours duration and eventually only three events were organised to this marathon formula. The Italian Grand Prix had been planned to take place at Monza on the 6th September, but at very short notice, it was brought forward to the 24th May to ensure more day-light hours and declared to be a ten hour event. Perhaps realising that a long race would produce a short entry, the organisers included a 1500cc class. Despite the attractions of being in the Grand Prix limelight, the long distance scared away most of the voiturettes and only five 1500s appeared on the starting grid at 8 a.m. to keep company with the small Grand Prix field. Easily the fastest car and an almost certain class winner was the $1\frac{1}{2}$ litre Delage of Robert Sénéchal, called the "Winged Star", the Delage had been fitted with De Ram semi-hydraulic dampers to aid its suspension on the long banked curves of Monza. Two of the ex-patriate 8-cylinder Talbots were to be driven by Ruggieri, who was sharing his car with Balestrero, while the other car was to be driven by De Vecchi. As complete outsiders, the Milan Alfa Romeo agents, Count Lurani and Nino Pirola, had entered Pirola's stripped sports 1500cc Alfa Romeo and were joined by another 6C Alfa Romeo entered by the Scuderia Ferrari and driven by Caniato and Torlini.

In motor racing nothing is certain and the "Winged Star" lost its sparkle within three laps as Sénéchal was forced to stop with magneto trouble which put him right out of the running. Altogether he changed three magnetos during the race and was in the pits "for hours and hours" according to "The Motor". With the Delage stricken, the Talbots and the Pirola Alfa Romeo began an evenly matched battle which lasted for the full ten hours and was not finally resolved until several days later! Ruggieri led for the first six hours hotly pursued by De Vecchi and the Alfa Romeo which had been delayed with dirt in the fuel lines but then both Talbots slowed with minor troubles and the Pirola car caught up again to take second place, the speed of the little Alfa surprising the onlookers who were also diverted by Lurani's large Mickey Mouse signal board. Eventually De Vecchi retired, and at the end of the ten hours, the Talbot of Ruggieri and Balestrero had apparently beaten the Alfa by just under a lap. When the organisers checked the lap charts after the race it was found that the declared result was incorrect and the Alfa Romeo had won by about 50 yards! The victory must have helped sell Alfa Romeos in Milan but what Ruggieri thought about it is not recorded. Sénéchal, who had been very fast while running, was rewarded with third place for his perseverance in the longest voiturette race to be held in the 1930s, an event five times the duration of a modern F.1. World Championship round.

A fortnight after Monza, Lurani took his own 6C Alfa Romeo to Geneva where, rare for 1931, the local Grand Prix clashed with the Rome Grand Prix on the same day. However, while the Roman race was only for 1100s, the Swiss offered something for everyone with both 1100 and 1500 voiturette races. Happily for the 1100s, Scaron had decided that all roads led to Rome but despite his absence an Amilcar still won the small capacity race driven by "Benoit", otherwise Benoit Falchetto, who came from Nice. He had a lead of $2\frac{1}{2}$ minutes

1931: José Scaron with his MCO Amilcar, seen here in a formula libre race at La Baule in September, was virtually unbeatable throughout the season.

at the end of the 200 kilometre race although another driver from Nice, Manet, led at the start with his Salmson. In second place came an historical rarity, a T36 Bugatti driven by Romano, this being one of the cars built in 1926 for the Alsace Grand Prix at Strasbourg, the smallest Grand Prix Bugatti ever built and it made motor racing history as the first-ever single seater road racing car. The 1500cc race was a straight Alfa/Bugatti contest and a T37A Bugatti came out on top driven by Pierre Veyron with a foretaste of the form he was to show over the next four years;* behind him came Roux with another T37A Bugatti while Kessler was third with the best Alfa Romeo. Lurani finished fifth and in sixth place was a new driver Jean-Pierre Wimille then at the start of his illustrious career.

There was a Roman triumph for Scaron. He led from start to finish and won by 3½ minutes in the 62 mile (100 kilometre) curtain raiser for the Prix Royal which inaugurated a new circuit built around Rome's Littorio Airport. The 2½ mile (4 kilometre) circuit, was unusual with two steeply banked curves with radii of 330 and 500 metres and a sharp hairpin at the entrance to the start/finish straight. It was fast, as Scaron did his fastest lap at 96.6 mph (155.5 kph), which also gives an indication of the remarkable performance of the Amilcar when it is compared with Varzi's best lap of 101.6 mph (163.6 kph) in his T51 Bugatti during the Grand Prix event.

The unevenness of the 1931 racing calendar then became evident as after the Rome/Geneva clash, the voiturettes had no races for four weeks, and June was almost an empty month. The next engagement was on the rolling plains of the Champagne district where the Grand Prix de la Marne took place on the 7th July on the classic road racing triangle of the Rheims-Gueux circuit. The scars of 1914/1918 were disappearing and the poplars planted along the RN 31 Rheims-Soissons road, the fastest leg of the circuit, although still young were becoming a feature of the landscape again. At Rheims, the voiturettes ran with the G.P. cars over 50 laps making a distance of 250 miles. The class was up to 1500cc and predominantly Molsheim, with 11 Bugattis facing a lone Amilcar and a Caban.

Veyron's Bugatti was owned by Andre Vagniez, an industrialist from Amiens who sponsored Veyron's early career.

250 miles was a long way on such a fast circuit and at the end of a processional race, 3 Bugattis survived to take the first 3 places led by Auber's T37A, the third Bugatti was driven by a lady competitor Madame Rose Itier who had kept ahead of the C6 Amilcar driven by Devaud. The local newspaper, "L'Eclaireur de L'Est" held a champagne party for the competitors at the finish. The wretched Devaud was flagged off nearly an hour after the winner of the Grand Prix had finished, and had by then only covered 45 laps; perhaps some champagne was left for him!

During May 1931, an event of some significance had taken place in England when the Junior Car Club held its annual Double 12 hour race at Brooklands on the 8th/9th May. This was a handicap race for sports cars and although international in name, in 1931 it attracted hardly any foreign entries. The race had seen the debut of the 750cc C-type Montlhery MG Midget and this won the race easily taking the first 5 places on handicap. The MG Car Company had been producing sports touring cars since 1923 but these had been based, very obviously, upon the touring car range made by the parent Morris Company. The C-type was the first MG to be intended as an out-and-out sports racing car and had followed up the Brooklands win by victory in the Irish Grand Prix which was another sports car handicap. To help the sale of production cars, Cecil Kimber the managing director of MG was most anxious to see his cars win the Ulster Tourist Trophy (yet another handicap) in August, but realised that the earlier successes would mean a severe re-handicap for his unblown 750 MGs. He recognised that to supercharge the car, would give it a considerable advantage in the T.T. so two experimental cars were fitted with superchargers, and to give these a practical test under racing conditions, both cars were entered for the German Grand Prix on the 19th July.

The German Grand Prix was to take place at the Nurburgring, in the Eifel mountains, in western Germany. Although opened in 1927 and used for the German Grand Prix in 1927, 1928 and 1929, these races had been for sports cars and 1931 was the first year that the German Grand Prix was to be held for racing cars on the legendary "Ring". The race had not been held in 1930 and its revival indicated the continuing improvement in the economy of the Weimar Republic. The event, as the regulations made clear was two separate races. There was a race for grand prix cars over 22 laps, and running concurrently with it, was the 1100cc German Grand Prix over the shorter distance of 18 laps (256 miles). As S.C.H. Davis emphasized in "The Autocar", the shorter race was not merely a class of the Grand Prix but a separate Grand Prix for the small voiturettes in their own right, and as such was probably the premier event of the year for the small capacity cars.

The race attracted most of the best 1100ccs in Europe. 23 entered and 14 came to the line. 5 Amilcars led by the inevitable Scaron, were matched against 2 Salmsons and 4 German two stroke DKWs, 3 of which had front wheel drive. As mentioned, the race also marked an English interest that had previously been lacking in the voiturette class in 1931. The 2 C-type MGs were to be driven by Francis Samuelson* and the Czech Hugo Urban-Emmerich who had the

*Samuelson had driven a Marlborough in the 1913 Cyclecar G.P. at Amiens.

14

a. 19th July, 1931: German G.P. Nurburgring: The rear wheel drive DKW driven by Gerhard Macher. This had two supercharged two-stroke engines in line and independent front suspension. It finished 6th in the 1100cc race.

b. 19th July, 1931: German G.P. Nurburgring: Francis Samuelson in his C-type MG which finished 5th in the 1100cc race despite delays with a loose float chamber.

c. 19th July, 1931: German G.P. Nurburgring: Dudley Froy (black belt on overalls) stands beside his victorious Riley. Rupert Riley who drove the car from Coventry to the circuit is on the left. Note the early Leica camera on the bonnet.

reputation of being a "Ring" specialist. In addition, there was a works Brooklands Riley running stripped which was to be handled by Dudley Froy, and had, in fact, been driven on the road to Germany from the Coventry factory. In practice, Scaron was easily fastest but the speed of the Riley impressed observers; Following Urban-Emmerich's advice, Froy had spent a week learning the circuit in a 14/45 Talbot saloon. Before a crowd of 150,000, the race began in the rain and at the start Scaron, as usual, went straight into the lead. At the end of the first 14 mile (22.7 km) lap he led by 39 seconds but in a surprising second place was Froy's un-supercharged Riley itself 20 seconds in front of the Amilcar of the German, Count Arco. On the second lap, Urban-Emmerich over-specialised and crashed his black MG into a 40 foot ravine but was unhurt. Rudi Steinweg however did the same thing with his white Amilcar and suffered slight injuries. Meanwhile, Scaron went on his winning way and was so fast he was keeping up with the Grand Prix cars, even passing Earl Howe with his new T51 Bugatti, while Froy still held a secure second place. The result was almost inevitable and at the start of the last lap, Scaron had a 2 minute lead but he slowed and pulled into his pit with a misfire. By the time this had been traced to a blocked jet, Froy had gone past and so had Count Arco. The rain had stopped and the pea-green Riley★ completed the final lap and to the delight of the British spectators was flagged off as a completely unexpected victor some 9 minutes ahead of Arco after nearly 4½ hours racing. A frustrated Scaron had restarted and finished third. The other 750 MG driven by Francis Samuelson had stalled on the line and then stopped with a loose float chamber, but still came in fifth, in front of Macher's rear wheel drive DKW which had caused much alarm with flapping wheels when braking. The MGs were to be seen again, and moreover, the basic Riley engine design had given a foretaste of its suitability for voiturette racing.

A week later the 1500s had their turn at the Dieppe Grand Prix, where there was a voiturette sub-division, racing concurrently with the big cars, in a race of 4 hours duration. Although the circuit was only at the other end of the Newhaven ferry only one English driver, Earl Howe, with his Grand Prix Delage, was drawn by the 4,000 Franc first prize. Perhaps the lack of suitable cars discouraged the others. At this stage of the season, Howe was the only Delage driver competing as Sénéchal had damaged himself and his car when he crashed in the Lorraine Grand Prix, a handicap race, held earlier in July. At Dieppe, the Delage showed its speed and on this classic triangular circuit, Howe had a lead of 40 miles (65 km) at the end of 4 hours racing. He had problems, for a tyre burst on lap 1 and as a cut was found in the side wall there was dark talk of sabotage. While Howe was changing a wheel and making up lost time, the lead was taken yet again by the inevitable Scaron, followed by the Rheims winner Auber, but he crashed and Howe soon caught Scaron who stopped on the course, restarted, and then retired. History does not relate if the jet was blocked again. There were showers of rain during the race and many cars

★Works Rileys were normally raced in red or their own shade of blue but for the German Grand Prix, perhaps recognising the importance of this international event, Froy's car was painted pea-green.

16

a. 26th July, 1931: Dieppe G.P.: Early Howe (Delage) entering Maison Blanche corner on his way to win the 1500cc class.

b. 2nd August, 1931: Avusrennen: Decaroli's Salmson which came 2nd in the 1500cc class is push-started.

crashed so that of the 16 voiturette starters, only 4 finished. Jean Delorme was second on what appears to have been a new T37A Bugatti, the last delivered by the factory.

There was obviously a new-found German enthusiasm for voiturettes, as on the 2nd August, a meeting was held at the unique Avus track in the Berlin suburbs. This was the first race meeting held at the Avus for 5 years and was a further pointer to improved German economic health; other signs were to follow. 200,000 Berliners turned up to watch and saw 8 Bugattis, 2 Amilcars and 2 Salmsons battle in the 1500 class. Clearly the return to the high speed Avus track of two 6 mile straights, linked by 180 degree turns at each end, caused a rush of blood to the head of the competitors. A local report said "one after another was reported as retiring with molten bearings, magneto and other defects", one caught fire. After 122 miles (196 km), only two remained, Lewy's T37A Bugatti winning from Louis Decaroli's Salmson. In the 750cc class, Macher obviously relieved by the need for less braking, won with his DKW.

While the mechanical mayhem of the Avus was taking place, on the same day at the foot of the French Alps, Scaron had obviously cleaned the jets of the Amilcar properly and secured another runaway win in the 1100cc class of the Circuit Dauphine at Grenoble. Conditions were grey and wet, but this did not deter the two lady competitors, Madame Itier and Madame Helle-Nice whose T37A Bugattis finished fourth and seventh in the 1500 class behind the winner Toselli, again T37A Bugatti mounted.

As soon as the Grenoble meeting finished a convoy set out to traverse France from the South East to the South West. The destination was Comminges within sight of the Pyrenees where, a week later, a big meeting was to be held on the St

Gaudens circuit running along both sides of the valley of the River Garonne. This had been the venue of the French Grand Prix in 1928. The weather at Comminges was a complete contrast to Grenoble, being hot, dry and sunny. One of the attractions for the competitors was the 90,000 Franc prize fund which was distributed between the grand prix cars and the voiturettes with separate classes for the 1100s and 1500s. The meeting drew a crowd of 15,000 and the 1100 race produced the almost monotonous sight of Scaron pulling out an impressive lead right from the start. Perhaps however, the Amilcar was getting tired at last, for it fell by the wayside leaving the spoils to a rather motley collection in which the Caban of Gustave Lemoine, the aviator who was later to achieve distinction by capturing the world altitude record, won from the BNC of Rougieras. The 1500 race running concurrently with the Grand Prix event was much more vigorous. The Tunisian Joly, who had finished 5th at Grenoble in his Tipo 26 Maserati, understandably preferred the sunshine of St Gaudens and "did a Scaron" taking the lead at the start and holding it all the way to finish $3^1{}_2$ minutes in front after 196 miles (315 km). Behind him there was a stirring battle in which Veyron continued to show the form that he was to maintain for the next four years. Battling with Veyron was Antonio with another Maserati and Madame Itier, who perhaps emboldened by her good results at Rheims and Grenoble, managed to overturn her Bugatti fortunately without injury.

After Comminges, the voiturette season began to fade. On 2nd August there was a farcical interlude at Livorno when the Coppa Ciano meeting was held on the 12.5 mile (20 km) Montenero circuit. The winding course ran from sea level for 3,000 feet into the mountains and had the reputation of being particularly hard both on men and machines. The cup for the winner had been presented by Count Ciano, Mussolini's son-in-law. In front of the donor of the cup and members of the Italian Royal Family and Government, Count Premoli's Salmson and Gerolamo Ferrari's Talbot Special managed to collide 600 yards from the finishing line after duelling over the whole distance of 100 miles (160 km). Of the embarrassed pair of drivers, Premoli was slightly quicker to recover and won the dash to the line by 2 seconds*.

A fortnight later another 1100 race was the preliminary event in the Coppa Acerbo meeting at Pescara on the hard 16 mile circuit with its long sea-level straight and the back leg rising into the mountains. The race was started by Marshal Balbo, the Italian Atlantic record-breaking aviator, who received a popular ovation from the crowd. Count Premoli, the favourite, was left on the line and got away after a minute's delay while he and his mechanic struggled to make the Salmson's engine run properly. The lead had been taken meanwhile by Dourel's monoposto CO Amilar, pursued by Louis Decaroli's Salmson and Ferrari's Talbot. At the end of the first lap, the Amilcar led by 2/5 of a sec, and Ferrari was only another 2 secs. behind Decaroli. While Premoli retired, the

*Some sources have credited the successes of the Talbot Special at Pescara and Livorno to Enzo Ferrari but this is incorrect. Gerolamo Ferrari built the special in Florence using a Bugatti chassis and a 4 cylinder Talbot engine, reduced to 1100cc, that had originally been used in one of the Brooklands 200 mile races, and was later used by Brivio in the Italian Grand Prix in 1928 (letter from Count Lurani to the author 1978).

a. 16th August, 1931: Coppa Acerbo Pescara: Decaroli's Salmson is flagged off to win the 1100cc class.
b. 6th September, 1931: Monza G.P.: Umberto Klinger sits on the rear wheel of the 1100/4CTR Maserati which was making its debut. Alfieri Maserati (in cap) is on the left.
c. 6th September, 1931: Monza G.P.: the 1100cc class waits for the start. Scaron's Amilcar which won is on the outside of the front row.
d. 6th September, 1931: Monza G.P.: Jose Scaron looks rather bashful as he stands beside his MCO Amilcar after his runaway victory.

battle went on but the pace was too much for the Amilcar and Dourel retired too, which left Decaroli pulling away from Ferrari and Matrullo with another Salmson. The leading Salmson was now unchallenged and Decaroli ran on to win the 63 mile race over 4 laps, by 46 secs, while Ferrari's Talbot gained its second place in two weeks.

When the Italian Grand Prix was brought forward to May it left an empty date at Monza on the 6th September and this was filled by the Monza Grand Prix over the full circuit with all the usual racing classes. The 1500s ran in the 2 litre class so are outside the scope of this work, but the 1100s had their own race at 10 o'clock in the morning for a 50,000 lire prize, 25,000 lire being for the winner. Scaron had obviously profited by the 4 week break after Comminges and this time left the result in no doubt. The blue off-set single seater Amilcar ran away from the rest of the field to win the 85 mile race by 2 mins 16 seconds averaging 85.40 mph and did a best lap of 2 min 58.8 seconds, 5.4 seconds better than the previous class lap record. Behind him the German and Italian nobility represented by Counts Arco (otherwise Count Englebert Arco-Zinneberg) and

19

Premoli fought with Decaroli's Salmson but Premoli led the group on the last lap to take second place from Arco and win the Italian 1100 championship for 1931. When reporting Scaron's victory, Henri Blanc writing in the French periodical "Omnia" observed with delightful naivety that the Amilcar had won, "because it showed, without effort that it was quicker than the others"; a fact that had been depressingly obvious to his competitors all season. Perhaps the most significant feature of the Monza race was the appearance of a new Maserati. This was a supercharged 4 cylinder 1100 the 4CTR/1100 model. Driven by Umberto Klinger, it had finished a creditable fifth. W.F. Bradley commented favourably upon it in the "Autocar" but observed that it had a very heavy chassis which was an unnecessary handicap. However, this problem was already being solved at Bologna. After Monza only one event remained and not many voiturettes went to Brno in Czechoslovakia on the 27th September to run in the 1500 race held concurrently with the Grand Prix on the long and tough Masaryk circuit. The race produced high drama as Fagioli leading the Grand Prix field on his $2\frac{1}{2}$ litre Maserati managed to collide with the supports of a foot-bridge over the course which collapsed leaving his pursuers to plough through the wreckage. By the time the 1500s arrived at the scene there was a path through the chaos so none was involved and the class went to the Czech Florian Schmidt with a T37A Bugatti followed by Count Arco with his white Amilcar. The 1500 places were completed by a local Bruno Sojka running as a team with Schmidt who came third with another T37A.

The 1931 season had seen an almost equal number of races for 1100s and 1500s and it had been noticeable that organisers had not felt the voiturettes could provide enough spectacle on their own but only as a sideline to a Grand Prix race or to pack a thin Grand Prix field. The season had produced the remarkable combination of Scaron in his Amilcar which, when running well, established standards that set him apart from all his competitors. So potent was this combination that it was a match for all but the quickest 1500s, but in that class, the honours had been evenly spread and no driver or marque had been pre-eminent.

The day before Scaron's Monza victory, the British hill climb meeting had taken place at Shelsley Walsh, the leafy lanes of Worcestershire being a complete contrast to the hot plains of Lombardy. In the 1100 sports car class, an eighteen year old Cambridge undergraduate driving a Riley in his first speed event took second place of the two runners in the class. His name was Richard Seaman.

1932

DURING THE WINTER OF 1931/1932 the motor racing world abounded with rumours as usual, which were not substantiated by the start of the season. The most popular rumour in the English press was the suggestion that MG was to launch a team of 1100cc Magnas for sports car and voiturette racing. A brief look at the brakes, crankshaft and cylinder head of the F-type Magna would have shown that this was wishful thinking and eventually the MG Car Company issued a statement to the press which denied the rumour but confirmed that the model was to be developed. However, voiturette racing was obviously being considered at Abingdon as Cecil Kimber lobbied the English motoring press in January suggesting that a voiturette race with classes for 750s, 1100s and 1500s should be held in the Isle of Man on the motor cycle TT course. The press was not impressed. "Grande Vitesse" of "The Motor" doubted if the race would attract enough entries to make it of interest and in "The Autocar" S.C.H. Davis perhaps more practically inquired who would pay for it. Rumour had not quite finished with MG however, as "The Motor" reported in March 1932 that Cecil Kimber had announced at a dinner in London that MG was to produce not just a voiturette but a full Grand Prix car. As this was the only mention this project ever received it must presumably be attributed to the quality of the wine list rather than Cecil Kimber! It was evident that the English press, echoing the sentiments of many enthusiasts, was very anxious to see a successful British voiturette but they were to wait a bit longer. The key to the future though, appeared in March 1932 when the Riley Company announced a new 1500cc 6-cylinder competition car which was declared to be both a sports and racing car. Eventually it only appeared as a competent sports car in 1932 but the design had possibilities that were not lost on some people.

On the Continent, the rumours also flew, the strongest being that Delage was to race again perhaps with a voiturette. In March 1932, it was sadly no rumour when the death of Alfieri Maserati was reported following an operation. For a time, it seemed that the future of the Maserati firm was in the balance, but happily the surviving brothers decided to carry on, led by Ernesto who had much of Alfieri's flair, both as a business man and designer. At the time of his death Alfieri had been developing a single seater chassis to take the new 4 cylinder engine and this now went into production as the 4 CM, and was to be the driving force of Maserati in voiturette racing for the next four years. The engine went into production both as an 1100 and a 1500, and a wider chassis was also developed to take a two seater body, becoming the 4CS.

The driver who went shopping for a voiturette in the Spring of 1932 had a reasonable choice. Bugatti could offer a new T37A for £700 and a new T39A for £1475. The T51A was still not catalogued but the first car reached the customer in March 1932. For the driver who could not afford a new Bugatti, a second (and a probably more) hand T37 could be bought for £195 in London. For the Italian driver, Maserati did not yet quote a price for the 4 CM but the 1100cc Tipo 26C was still available at £1100 in its rather heavy chassis form. In England, a new Brooklands Riley was £425 while an ex-factory racer was offered for £350. For the driver who preferred his voiturette to be small, a new C-type MG could be had with supercharger for £575.

History is supposed to repeat itself, the first time as tragedy, the second time as farce but in April 1932 it did almost a straight repeat. The season began as in 1931 at Tunis, the weather was very hot, the sun brilliant, and the voiturettes ran with the Grand Prix cars over 292 miles of the Bardo circuit. As in 1931, Varzi won the big car class with his T51 Bugatti and yet again, an elderly Tipo 26 8-cylinder Maserati won the 1500 class this time driven by the local driver Joly. To complete the repeat performance Veyron finished second as in 1931 but this time he had forsaken the T37A Bugatti for another Tipo 26 Maserati which had been bought by Andre Vagniez. Joly had an easy victory and led throughout, Count Castelbarco was in second place with his T39A Bugatti* but then he stopped twice for plugs and fuel and was passed by Veyron. Scaron proved that the MCO Amilcar was as quick standing still as when racing by taking only 40 seconds for a stop for fuel and finished fourth while Mesdames Itier and Mareuse finished three laps behind the rest of the field in their Bugattis.

A fortnight later on the 24th April, most of the Tunisian competitors went along the Mediterranean coast to Oran where Scaron showed that he was still in a different class to the other 1100 competitors when he won the small car class of the 3-hour race by 17 minutes. Joly and Veyron repeated the Tunis finishing order in their Tipo 26 Maseratis in the 1500 class while poor Madame Mareuse was slightly hurt when she crashed after a wheel broke up on her Bugatti. While Oran had been hot and sunny, Rome, on the same day, was wet and a field of nine 1100s ran in the 100 kilometre race which started the Prix Royal meeting on the partially banked Littorio airfield circuit. It should have been an easy win for Tuffanelli with a new 4CM Maserati but the drying though slippery circuit got the better of him and he spun off twice and finished second behind Decaroli's old GP Salmson.

The continuing success of the Monaco Grand Prix had been noted in a number of French towns and several staged imitation "Round the Houses" races which however, lacked the style and setting of the original. The old Roman city of Nimes staged such a meeting on the 16th May and as well as a full length Grand Prix in the afternoon, the morning was occupied with motor cycle races and short voiturette events for both 1100s and 1500s. The circuit was not

*Some sources have suggested that the Count had a T51A for this event. Count Lurani confirms it was a T39A, however. See "Racing round the World".

very enterprising being two parallel carriageways of the Boulevard Jean Jaures running through the centre of the town linked by a hairpin at each end and enlivened by various straw bale chicanes on the two straights. The small car race, only 28 miles (45 km), was led all the way by Scaron, but in the 1500 race, a small piece of motor rcing history was made. Madame Itier, undeterred by the wet conditions led right from the start to win in her T37A Bugatti and recorded the first voiturette win by a woman.

Scaron cannot have tarried for long at Nimes after his victory as he was entered for the 1500 class in the Casablanca Grand Prix the following Sunday. The voiturettes were to run concurrently with the GP cars in the 254 mile (409 km) event. It is possible that one of the Amilcars was sent direct to Casablanca but if he used the same car it was not affected too much by the sea voyage. It must have seemed to Veyron that he was doomed yet again to finish second behind Joly's Tipo 26 Maserati. But Joly dropped out after holding the lead in the voiturette class from the start and Veyron went on to win with his Tipo 26 ahead of Durand's T37A Bugatti, whilst Scaron came third. While this race was being run in the sun and heat of Morocco, 200,000 Berliners were thronging the Avus track, perhaps hoping to see the same mechanical disasters as the previous year. The Avus race marked the first British entries in voiturette racing in 1932. Earl Howe had entered his Delage, carried all the way from England in his new Commer Invader van,★ and there were two works single seater 750 Austins driven by Stanley Barnes and Charles Goodacre. Howe dominated the race and he lapped the field of 17 starters in 6 laps. He ran on to an easy victory setting a pace which left the rest of the field breathless. Barnes' Austin ran very well and kept up with Steinweg's white Amilcar, taking second place when the Amilcar had a fuel blockage on the last lap. The other Austin finished fourth ahead of the Czech, Zdenek Pohl, whose T37A Bugatti was the only other finisher.

Amongst those who had fallen out at the Avus was the Swiss Henry Tauber with his 1500 6C Alfa Romeo. However, the trouble must have been repairable, as a week later Tauber had taken the car some 350 miles west to the Nurburgring where he gained a good victory in the 1500 class at the Eifelrennen. The weather was dull and sometimes wet and it was a good day for Alfa Romeo, as Caracciola won the Grand Prix event with his 2.3 Monza. Tauber took the lead in the 1500 class straight from the start and was never challenged. In an equally unchallenged second place was the Hungarian Lazlo Hartmann with his T37A Bugatti. Until half distance, Steinweg upheld German honour by retaining third place with his Amilcar but then dropped out with "motor defect" as the "Frankfurter Zeitung" described it. To the surprise of the Germans, Barnes and Goodacre who were entered with their 750 Austins, did not turn up. Without the two English favourites, it became a clean sweep

★This van had a remarkable history. It was used to carry Earl Howe's cars to races from 1932 to 1939, and covered an enormous mileage. It broke down only twice, with a stripped crown wheel and with big end failure, and was repaired on both occasions by Lord Howe's mechanics on the road side. When Lord Howe rejoined the Royal Navy in 1939 the Commer went with him driven by Sidney Maslin, his mechanic, and it served throughout the War being demobilised with Lord Howe and Maslin in 1945. Its subsequent history is not known. (Conversation: Sidney Maslin with the Author – November 1978.)

a. *1932: The T26 Maserati owned by Andre Vagniez and driven successfully by Pierre Veyron during the season. The car is seen here at Dieppe in 1933 driven by Vagniez.*

b. *17th May, 1932: Nines G.P.: Chambost, winner of the unsupercharged 1100cc class with his Salmson passes de la Rochette's 750cc Rosengart.*

c. *22nd May, 1932: Avusrennen: Earl Hower (Delage) talks to Reichsverkehrs-Minister Treviranus before the start. Thomas, his head mechanic looks on.*

d. *22nd May, 1932: Avusrennen: Earl Howe supervises Thomas as he loads the winning Delage into the Commer Invader van.*

a. 5th June, 1932: Picardie G.P.: The start of the 1100cc class. Armand Girod (Lombard) has taken the lead.

b. 17th July, 1932: German G.P. Nurburgring: A 750cc DKW is unloaded from the train.

for DKW in the 800cc class; Macher, Simons and Stoll stayed in that order during the entire race.

After the flurry of activity at the end of May, June was a fairly quiet month for the voiturettes. The Grand Prix de Picardie was held on the narrow triangular circuit outside Peronne, a race that was to continue throughout the 1930s and become a voiturette classic. The first winner was Marcel Lister with a T37A Bugatti. Lister joined a number of the "Regulars" at Nancy on the 26th June for the Lorraine Grand Prix which was run on the Seichamps circuit where the back leg was a very narrow country lane passing through farm yards. It was a comparatively short race, only 79 miles and Scaron, as ususal, led at the start but retired after 4 laps with a broken piston. As he was then leading Veyron's Maserati it seems likely that the Amilcar was running with the oversized engine so perhaps the larger pistons were less durable. Once Scaron retired, Veyron's Tipo 26 8 cylinder Maserati went on to win by 2 minutes but for second place there was the motor racing rarity of a deadheat between the young and promising Marcel Lister and Pierre Guilbaut★ also with a T37A Bugatti.

Guilbaut later became famous for his adventures with small boats.

Unfortunately the race was not a happy one as there was a bad accident when Toselli crashed his T37A Bugatti into the crowd killing two spectators and suffering a broken leg himself.

There was another lull after the Nancy meeting while everyone drew breath and prepared for the most important and the longest voiturette race of the year. The ADAC, organising the German Grand Prix at the Nurburgring had decided to include a full 1500cc class in the 1932 event together with an 800cc class which was intended for the small German cars. Unlike 1931, the regulations made it clear that a win in these classes was a class win only. To win the Grand Prix outright, a voiturette would be required to record the fastest time over the full Grand Prix distance of 25 laps, 354 miles (570 km). The 1500cc class were only required to cover 23 laps, 325 miles (523 km), while the babies had 4 fewer laps to do. The organisers wanted to encourage British entries as an English translation of the regulations had been published in April with a Union Jack on the cover. Unfortunately, there were only five takers which indicated that British drivers still lacked suitable cars, certainly in the 1500 class. This was to change, but not yet.

Predictably, leading the English entries was Earl Howe; Howe was now the only driver still racing the G.P. Delage in International events as he had bought Robert Sénéchal's car during the winter. Joining Howe, were the unusual entries of two supercharged works Frazer Nashes, one with an Anzani engine, driven by the violinist Eric Siday who played with Jack Hilton's band, the other with a Meadows engine, driven by A.F.P. Fane. Facing this small British brigade, was a field of 13 other 1500s of whom the most prominent was Tauber with his Alfa-Romeo and the Berlin driver Ernst Burggaller with a new T51A Bugatti. In the 800cc class, two works C-type MGs driven by Urban-Emmerich and Hugh Hamilton were competing against a motley collection of DKWs and BMWs. The English press described the Frazer Nashes as being of much interest to the Germans and "The Light Car" said "nothing like these had been seen in Germany before." With their quarter-elliptic suspension and chain drive, it is perhaps understandable if the Germans showed more incredulity than interest when looking at the Frazer Nashes in the Nurburgring paddock.

The voiturettes lined up behind the Grand Prix cars in a bitterly cold wind. At the start, Tauber took an immediate lead and proved that he and the 6C Alfa Romeo were a formidable combination as Howe, despite his experience and the speed of the Delage, was unable to get past. Tauber held onto his lead and after 6 laps Lord Howe stopped with no fuel pressure. By the time this was remedied he had fallen to the back of the field. Burggaller, meanwhile, had retired with his new Bugatti and Fane's green Frazer Nash stopped with transmission trouble, a fate which the Germans probably considered to be inevitable! To be fair, the transmission had been damaged in a collision in Brussels on the way to the course. The other Nash, the red painted car of Siday, also fell out with a leaking fuel tank. By the finish, with a drive that had taken nearly five hours, Tauber had shown his domination by extending his lead to 13 minutes over Lazlo Hartmann who was second with his T37A Bugatti, repeating the finishing order of th Eifelrennen. Finishing third after an impressive performance was the Works single seater 4CM 1100 Maserati. This had started the race driven by

26

17th July, 1932: German G.P. Nurburgring: A tired-looking Mme Itier (T37A Bugatti) makes a pit-stop. The exhaust manifold is a modification. The aero-screen is broken.

Ernesto Maserati but Ruggieri took the car over at half distance after his own 2½ litre Grand Prix Maserati had retired from the principal event. Clearly the central gear lever which had worried "The Autocar" was no handicap. Madame Itier finished in eighth place driving her usual T37A Bugatti and her polished performance brought favourable comment from the press.

The sensation of the day among the voiturettes was in the 800cc class where Hugh Hamilton's handling of his Montlhery MG was remarkable. So well did he go that he was keeping up with the battle for the lead between Howe and Tauber and was well up among the G.P. cars. At the end he won his class with a margin of 13 minutes to earn with Caracciola and Tauber a golden "Nurburgring" award.

As a reflection on Tauber's performance in the 6C Alfa Romeo in the Germand Grand Prix, it is interesting to note that about a month before the German G.P., Tauber and Count Lurani who had been gaining many successes with his own 6C Alfa in hill climbs, approached Vittorio Jano, the Alfa Romeo designer. They suggested that the Portello factory should produce a pure racing 6C with an alloy cylinder block, short chassis and larger brakes. Unfortunately, the factory feeling that voiturettes were all right for the boys, dismissed the proposition as it was fully occupied with the development of the new Tipo B for the men in Grand Prix events. This was a pity as a lightweight 6C would have been a formidable voiturette, but the time would come when Alfa Romeo would think differently of the 'boy's class'.

A week later it was the turn of Nice to stage its "Round the Houses" race using part of the Promenade des Anglais in the 2 mile (3.2 km) circuit. The 2 voiturette races were very short, each being 10 laps. A Salmson driven by Raymond Chambost won the 1100 class and Frederic Toselli having recovered from his broken leg, led all the way in his T37A Bugatti to win the 1500 race from Veyron's Tipo 26 Maserati and an over-bored Amilcar. This was a

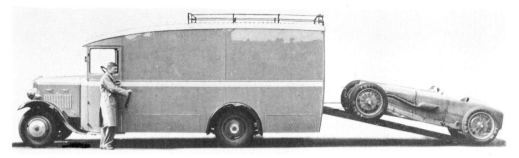

a. 1932: Early Howe's Commer Invader van. Thomas is winding the Delage in on the winch.

b. 14th August, 1932: Coppa Acerbo Pescara: The 1100cc class assembles on the grid. Scaron in the middle of the front row is about to gain his last international victory with the MCO Amilcar.

satisfying win for Toselli as he lived in Nice. It would hardly have been worthwhile for any driver to travel far for such short races and this emphasized a problem which confronted many drivers in the early 1930s, namely how to get a racing car to a race. Earl Howe had been one of the pioneers in building a workshop into the van body on his Commer Invader and this example was quickly followed by others. Before the days of the racing transporter, cars had either been driven to races, towed or carried by freight train. This had its problems, as the Works Frazer Nash had found in Brussels; very soon though, the driven or towed racing car would be a thing of the past and cars would travel by van, lorry or trailer.

The distance did not deter a handful of voiturette drivers from making the journey to the foot of the Pyrenees on the 31st July where a 1500 class was again included in the Comminges Grand Prix. As in 1931, the race was run on the 16 mile (26 km) St Gaudens circuit and from the three-abreast start, Dourel led the voiturettes with his 1100 Amilcar until he was passed by Veyron's Maserati. Once he was in front, Veyron went on to win the class by over 6 minutes from Dourel and was unaffected by the showery conditions which caused Wimille (Alfa Romeo) and Dreyfus (Bugatti) to crash on the last lap when in first and second places overall in the Grand Prix. Another Tipo 26 Maserati was third, driven by Antonio and fourth was Pierre Guilbaut who had been driving steadily in his T37A Bugatti throughout the season and gaining a number of places for his efforts.

July 31st was a good day for Maserati voiturettes for while Veyron had been winning at Comminges, Count Cerami with a new 4CM/1100 Maserati had been winning the 1100 class in the Coppa Ciano meeting at Livorno. This win helped him to become Italian 1100 champion for the season. The race was again honoured by the presence of Count Ciano himself. Matrullo was second in his veteran Salmson although he too had taken delivery of a new 4CM/1100 Maserati but perhaps he had decided not to risk it on the dangerous Montenero circuit. To prevent accidents, the organisers did not have a massed start but released the cars in groups of three.

At least Count Ciano had a cup to present to the winner at Livorno but a trophy was denied to the victor at Pescara a fortnight later as the Coppa Acerbo for the Grand Prix cars was stolen two days before the race. However, the thief left behind the cup for the voiturettes and this was duly received by Scaron who had a good victory in his true 1931 style with the MCO Amilcar. Scaron won the 63 mile (102 km) race by 25 seconds and behind him came Raymond Chambost, showing that the old San Sebastian Salmson was till a car to be reckoned with by beating Francesco Matrullo, who this time, had decided to use his new Maserati. The Salmson led by 4 seconds at the end, Matrullo possibly wished he had brought out the old Salmson again. Sadly, Pescara was the last victory for the formidable Scaron/Amilcar combination. The car was as quick as it had been in 1931 but no quicker and the opposition was speeding up. New 1100s were appearing, though there were fewer 1100 class events. The Amilcar factory was going through hard times and had lost interest in racing. Scaron however, was to return to the 1100cc class some years later when he joined Amédée Gordini in developing the Simca Gordini.

Only two more voiturette races remained on the 1932 calendar; the Masaryk Grand Prix at Brno had a 1500 class to make up the field on the 4th September. The race was run in a downpour which caused much dampening of ignition. The spirits of the Bugatti supporters cannot have been dampened however, as the voiturette class gave the T51A its first victory driven by the portly Ernst Burggaller.★

The race was led at the start by Ernesto Maserati with a 4CM, but he was delayed when the car caught fire so the T51A then showed it was a car to be reckoned with, as Burggaller finished 14 minutes in front of Veyron's Tipo 26 Maserati which itself had proved to be quicker than most throughout the season. The Brno race demonstrated the international appeal of voiturette racing. A German won, a Frenchman was second, the Czech, Bruno Sojka was third with his red painted T37A Bugatti, Lazlo Hartmann the Hungarian was fourth and Ernesto Maserati who had restarted was fifth for Italy. At the tail of the field were two local built Wikovs driven by the unpronounceable Szcyzycki and Konechnik. The later finished some 51 minutes behind the victorious

★Burggaller who owned a driving school in Berlin had been a member of the Richtofen Circus in the 1914/18 War. He joined the Luftwaffe on the outbreak of war in 1939 and was reported to have been killed in action in 1940.

Burggaller. The T51A's first victory must have made the day for Molsheim particularly as the Masaryk Grand Prix had been won outright by Chrion's T51 which was the first occasion that the Tipo B Alfa Romeo had been bested in 1932.

The season ended on the Riviera at Cap d'Antibes where the Circuit de la Garoupe was run on September 11th on the wooded headland between Juan-les-Pins and Antibes. Perhaps the race was held late in the season so that the summer visitors would not be disturbed, but it only attracted a small entry. The circuit, which ran through the woods, was narrow, and this brought tragedy for the voiturettes. Marcel Lister had bought a new Tipo 26 1500 Maserati, having collected it from Bologna only 10 days before the race. Lister who had been noted by the British press for his promising driving, may have been impressed by the speed of Veyron's Tipo 26 car which had beaten him at Nancy and his car was the last 8 cylinder voiturette made by the Maserati brothers.★ Sadly almost as soon as practice started, the Maserati struck the bank on the bend after the pits and Lister was killed instantly when he was thrown out of the car. With the accident to Lister, there were only 6 starters in the 63 mile (101 km) voiturette race. Scaron's Amilcar soon fell out and only 4 finished in a small procession led by Toselli's T37A Bugatti. The circuit which was narrow even by the standards of the early 1930s was not used again.

No driver or car had established supremacy during the season. Veyron had shown that the obsolescent Tipo 26 1500 Maserati was a quick car and he was a promising driver, but equally, the 6C Alfa Romeo had been fast on the few occasions it had raced. It was evident though that times were changing. The Tipo 26 Maserati, the Alfa and the T37 Bugatti were all relics of the vintage years of the 1920s. The designs of the 1930s, exemplified by the T51A Bugatti and the 4CM Maserati were in the ascendant. In the 1100 class, the old Amilcars and Salmsons were being pressed by the new Maseratis and all the 1100s were under pressure. It was noticeable in 1932 that more 1500cc races were being organised. In 1931 there had been an almost equal number of events for both classes but in 1932 the larger class predominated. This is easy to understand, as some of the slower 1100s were very slow indeed and must have offered little spectator interest. The 1500s were not only quicker, but larger cars also, and offered more for the spectator to look at, and the driver of a fast 1100 like Scaron, could still find glory racing against the bigger cars. The tide was turning against the 1100 voiturette although it would linger for several seasons and was about to have a powerful new recruit. In England, the rumours of an 1100 MG which had started in the Autumn of 1931 finally bore fruit. In October, just before the London Motor Show began at Olympia, the M.G. Car Company announced that it would build a supercharged sports racing 1100 for 1933, the K3 Magnette model. In fact, the announcement was premature as the prototype only existed on paper but for British drivers who sought a home-grown voiturette, the prospects were hopeful.

★Lister's car differed in many respects from the earlier Tipo 26s. It had a cast iron block and electron crankcase and the chassis, body and radiator had been used previously in the Tipo T26M GP car raced by Klinger in 1931.

Meanwhile, amidst speculation about the new MG, an English driver, Raymond Mays was considering how he could re-capture the course record for the home of English hill climbing, Shelsley Walsh. Mays, probably the foremost exponent of the peculiarly English pastime of the short sprint, wanted to take the Shelsey record, then held by Hans Stuck with an Austro-Daimler, with an English car, and also wanted the car to be under 1500cc, a class in which Mays had made his name in the 1920s with Bugattis and ACs. Mays had been impressed by the 6-cylinder 1500cc Riley which had run quite well in sports car races in 1932, so he went to have a discussion with Victor Riley of the Riley Company. Their conversation was to bear far more fruit than either could ever have realised at the time.

Other moves were to disturb the voiturette scene, as in October 1932, the International Sporting Committee announced that the Grand Prix formula would change at the end of the 1933 season. The new formula for 1934 would permit grand prix cars of unlimited engine capacity. The only restrictions being a maximum weight limit of 750kg and certain body dimensions. The new formula brought a stream of protests in the press and much apparent scorn from the principal racing car manufacturers, who, having expressed their views, immediately began to design new cars. It was significant perhaps that the new formula aroused interest in Germany also.

The voiturette world too was on the move, and another event, wholly unconnected with the world of motor racing was about to have a decisive impact.

31

1933

On THE 30TH JANUARY 1933, Adolf Hitler came to power in Germany. This event was to have just as dramatic and far reaching effect on the history of motor racing as it was to have on the history of the world. The first signs of a change were not long in coming. In February, Hitler opened the Berlin Motor Show and promised in his opening speech that motor racing was to be encouraged and furthered in Germany. This speech was duly reported in the European motoring press but it is unlikely that the political significance of his remarks was appreciated at the time.

At the beginning of 1933 motoring racing was still an amateur sport at heart. Admittedly, there were factory teams with paid drivers who sought starting money and raced for prize money and bonuses, but the attitude of those concerned was not particularly professional. The rivalries lay more between individual drivers than between the factory teams, and drivers of the calibre of Chiron and Caracciola raced as private entrants with cars purchased from the factories which were quite as potent as the works cars. It was possible for the skilful and rich amateur to keep up at the front of the Grand Prix field while for the lesser lights with Grand Prix ambition there were plenty of events in which to exercise their talents and machines. S.C.H. Davis writing in "The Autocar" during the 1933 season referred to the "rash of events" all over Europe.

The majority of these races were small events organised by local motor clubs where the circuit was made up of roads closed for the two days of practice and for race day itself. Sometimes the circuit was outside the town, but quite frequently, following the growing fashion for "Round the Houses", in the streets of the town itself. Maybe it is still possible to feel some of the atmosphere of those events 50 years after. The circuits varied in length but were made up of roads that were often narrow and sometimes with an indifferent surface. The more obvious hazards were rather inadequately protected with straw bales and the walls and hedges around the circuit were decorated with advertising banners. Nothing was permanent, it was a 3 day circus which came to town and disappeared again as soon as the performance was over. The pits, often only a line of trestle tables beside the road, faced a makeshift grandstand usually open, for the comfort of the local dignitaries. The race officials, pressed into service, often with little knowledge of the sport, varied from the efficient to the farcially incompetent. The flag marshal, with an internationally recognised code of flag signals, was now accepted as a feature of the sport, but frequently the marshals were to be found sitting at a table under an umbrella with a bottle of wine, the flags lying unattended on the ground!

The field itself was a mixture. There was the regular "Circus", a hard core of works and works supported drivers, backed by dedicated amateurs with the latest cars. With these were also the dilettantes and the playboys who would race occasionally when the mood took them, and making up the field, the inevitable local drivers to whom their local event was the big occasion of the year and who often made up in dash and bravura what they lacked in skill. The predominating colours were red and blue, green being still a rarity. For the enthusiast there was the noise and the smell while, looking back at those races now long ago, the sun usually seemed to be shining.

The voiturette world was a mirror image of this grand prix picture, but in 1933, the voiturettes suffered a slight but perceptible setback. From the dark ages of 1929 and 1930, the grand prix work had suddenly broken out into a warm and sunny prosperity. Cars were easily available, events were plentiful and Europe was starting to recover from the Depression. Organisers of races such as Tunis, Nice and Comminges who had included a voiturette class to make up the size of the field in 1931 and 1932 now found that the grand prix field could stand by itself and put on an acceptable show without the voiturette adulteration.

Despite these setbacks it was clear, by the time the 1933 season began, that voiturette racing was still alive and fit. British racing had received two distinct filips. The MG Car Company entered a team of three K3 Magnettes in the 1100 class of the Mille Miglia on the 8th April and this team swept the board, winning their class and the overall team prize. The K3 with its supercharged 6-cylinder single overhead camshaft engine and a Wilson preselector gearbox perhaps looked a bit heavy to continental eyes, but here at last, was a British car which with its road equipment removed, was a competitive voiturette. The other event, which was to change the face of British racing, and exercise a great influence on the future of voiturette racing, was the opening of a genuine road circuit at Donington Park in Derbyshire. Until now the only place on the British mainland where British drivers had been able to race was at Brooklands, and the only British road races had been held occasionally in Ireland and the Isle of Man. Brooklands, despite its traditions and atmosphere had immense shortcomings as Sir Henry Birkin had pointed out most forcefully in his autobiography "Full Throttle" which was published in the Autumn of 1932.

The usual rumours abounded before the season started. Veyron was announced as a Maserati driver which he immediately disproved by turning up at the first big meeting with a works supported Bugatti, while Raymond Sommer was alleged to have obtained the Maserati agency for France with the intention of racing both grand prix cars and voiturettes, but he too disproved the rumours by settling for an Alfa Romeo. Despite the waning interest of the Amilcar firm, Jose Scaron declared his intention of racing again in 1933 and was reported to be building two new MCO single seaters with works support, a support which was to be shown as very limited.

With the reduction of the number of voiturette races, the season did not start

33

a. 21st May, 1933: Avusrennen: The start. Howe's Delage is behind the 750cc Austins of Barnes and Goodacre which have registration nos. Burggaller's T51A Bugatti is on the extreme left of the field.

b. 21st May, 1933: Avusrennen   R.T. Horton's special bodied C-type MG (seen here at Brooklands) which won the 800cc class.

c. 21st May, 1933: Avusrennen: R.T. Horton and Earl Howe share a joke.

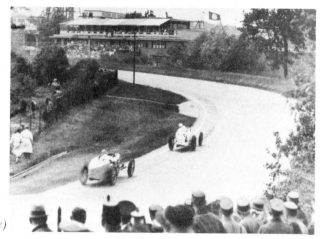

a. 21st May, 1933: Avusrennen: Pierre Veyron is about to pass Burggaller and take the lead on lap 2.

b. 21st May, 1933: Avusrennen: Veyron (T51A Bugatti) Burggaller (T51A Bugatti) and Earl Howe (Delage) on their lap of honour.

c. 21st May, 1933: Avusrennen: Successful seat. The cockpit of Veyron's T51A Bugatti. The clock is prominent.

properly until the later half of May, though the first voiturette race was held on the 25th March at the inaugural Donington meeting. With true British caution and an apparent fear of genuine motor racing, the regulations required mechanics to be carried in the cars and banned single seaters which were unacceptable to the insurers of the circuit. The fastest race of this first meeting over a mere 10 laps of the 2.25 mile (3.6 km) circuit was won by Ken Hutchinson with a T37 Bugatti. With the reduced number of races it was ironic that the continental season should start on the 21st May with a clash of events. The Avusrennen took place in Berlin in front of the usual huge crowd, while in complete contrast the Grand Prix de Picardie was run at Peronne in Northern France on the rural circuit on the edge of the Somme battlefield, still showing its scars. The Peronne meeting was overshadowed by fatal accidents to Guy Bouriat and Louis Trintignant, the brother of the later-to-be-famous Maurice, in the main Grand Prix event, but the 1500 race, with a rather thin field of 8 starters, was another victory for Madame Rose Itier whose new T51A Bugatti, which was delivered to her in March, was much faster than the rest and led throughout. The race was not much of a spectacle as Madame Itier finished $7\frac{1}{2}$ minutes in front of the second place Tipo 26 Maserati of Andre Vagniez, now driving his own car in the place of Veyron, and nearly 14 minutes in front of Devaud who was third with another Maserati. Armand Girod who had bought the two 8C 1100 Salmsons from the factory and refurbished the cars, started with one, but soon retired.

Although Peronne was disappointing, the 200,000 crowd who went to the Avus had their fill of excitement. The sun shone and the event was honoured by the presence of Der Fuhrer himself. In the 1500 race which started the meeting at 1.30 p.m. the two T51A Bugattis of Veyron and Burggaller fought throughout the 122 mile race. Burggaller led the field of sixteen at the start but was pursued by Veyron who took the lead with his works supported car on the second lap. After that despite all the efforts of the German driver he could not regain the lead, although at the finish they were only 0.4 seconds apart. Earl Howe finished a disappointing third in the Delage. The engine had been rebuilt before the race and was still stiff, and a change of carburettor had resulted in a slight loss of power. In the 800cc class which ran with the 1500s there was another dramatic finish which produced a British victory; Ron Horton's odd looking single seater C-type MG passing Barnes' works Austin on the last lap to win by 1.2 seconds. Goodacre with the other works Austin was fourth behind Macher's DKW which had omitted huge clouds of smoke throughout the race and now sported two twin cylinder 2-stroke engines geared together and fed by a Zoller supercharger. In these circumstances, the smoke was understandable!

As in 1932, a week later, the Eifelrennen were held at the Nurburgring. Most of the Avus competitors took part in the 252 mile, 1500 cc race and this time, Earl Howe had his revenge. In unpleasant slippery conditions, the 49 year old peer led from the start. Throughout the race, he was hounded by Burggaller who was never more than a few lengths behind, but despite a sticking clutch race and failing fuel pressure, the Delage went on to win by one length after 212 miles. Howe said afterwards that he thought that it was the hardest race of his career. Pierre Veyron could not match the pace of the leaders and finished third,

5^{1}2 minutes behind. While Howe and Burggaller were having their fifteen lap duel, Hugh Hamilton was doing equally heroic things in the 800cc class which had to cover 12 laps. Hamilton had a new 746cc J4 MG, the improved C-type with larger brakes. He took the car to Cologne on the train and then drove it to the circuit. During the race he kept up with the 1500s and even held on to the slower GP cars and finished with the enormous lead of 24 minutes over the second car, Kohlrausch's 750cc Austin.

The following Sunday the second French voiturette race of the season was held at Nimes on the simple circuit in the centre of the town. The 1100s and 1500s ran together as a sub division of the 2 litre race and the significant feature was the speed of Chambost's old 1100 Grand Prix Salmson which was quick enough to lead all the 1500s. The other interest of the race was the appearance of an American Miller "91" in the 1500 class, driven by the French driver Boucly. While the two long straights along the Avenue Jean Jaures were probably to the Miller's liking, the hairpins at each end were not, and the car retired.

The lure of "round the houses" racing had already spread as far as Poland the previous year when the Lwow Grand Prix was staged and this was now repeated on 11th June. A number of regular competitors considered it worthwhile to make the long journey to Eastern Europe★ including Veyron, Burggaller (who only had to travel from Berlin) and Madame Itier who towed her T51A Bugatti on a trailer behind a Bugatti touring car accompanied by one mechanic. The circuit which ran through the centre of the town was only 1.8 miles long and very slow which was perhaps as well as there was no protection for the spectators who lined the circuit. It took Veyron nearly 4 hours in leading from start to finish to beat Burggaller who thus finished second, for the third time in 4 weeks. The race had further interest inasmuch as of the ten starters, three were women. Madame Itier was fifth with her Bugatti, Madame Kozmian was ninth in another Bugatti while Madame Orsini retired in her Maserati. It was reported that the Polish crowd was jubilant that a French driver had beaten a German into second place.

With the Polish race over there was a lull for over a month until 12th July when the British held an international voiturette road race, the first in the British Isles for 11 years. For this event, the Mannin Beg, the R.A.C. had uncharacteristically followed international fashion and picked as 4.6 miles (7.6 km) circuit through the streets of Douglas in the Isle of Man. Sadly, there the similarities with continental practices ended. With the extraordinary insularity of British race organisers between the wars, the regulations were drawn up in a form which not only precluded any worthwhile foreign entries but even kept out the best British based voiturettes as well. Entries were invited from supercharged 1100s and unsupercharged 1500s only. The supercharged 1500s such as the Delage and all the blown Bugattis were expected to race in the Mannin Moar for Grand Prix cars which was to take place 2 days later. Worse still, riding mechanics were to be carried so that all single seaters were disbarred. The regulations were derided on all sides, but the R.A.C. self-righteously made no changes, even though Earl Howe, then the doyen of British drivers, declared

★So far east that Lwow was incorporated in the USSR in 1945.

a. 12th July, 1933: Mannin Beg. Douglas: The start. Dixon's Riley (7) is surrounded by K3 MGs.

b. 12th July, 1933: Mannin Beg. Douglas: Dixon on his way to victory. Les Ainslie his mechanic appears unmoved.

in an open letter to "The Motor" that "the races were bound to be second rate affairs". It is sad to record that so far as the entry was concerned they were. An all-British field of 10 MGs, 2 Rileys, a Frazer Nash and a Morris, fought themselves almost to a standstill over 250 miles and at end only 3 cars were running, Freddie Dixon won with his black 1100 Riley as befitted a former motor cycle T.T. winner and to maintain the motor cycle theme, Mansell, whose 746 cc MG was second, was the son of the managing director of Norton Motor Cycles. All the K3 MG Magnettes which were expected to sweep the board fell out, the majority with broken differentials. Kaye Don with a K3 MG led the race at the start, which was situated on the Central Promenade in Douglas. After 3 laps Hugh Hamilton took the lead with his K3 MG and held it for the next 34 until he retired with the fashionable differential failure.★ Dixon had always been up with the leaders, as his "Brooklands" based car was remarkably quick, even without the benefit of a supercharger, and with Hamilton gone there was no challenge left to the Riley.

It was evident that 1933 was a lean year for voiturettes as there was no event on the European mainland for seven weeks after the Lwow race, but with the start of the holiday season, at the end of July, a rather moribund season livened. The Coppa Ciano, on the Montenero Circuit outside Livorno, was one of the few which catered only for 1100s, and this was run on the 30th July, over 8 laps of the $12^{1}2$ mile (20.1 km) circuit, which ran from sea level to 3,000 ft in the mountains. Earl Howe who had received an eye injury while driving his Bugatti in the French Grand Prix on the 11th June, had recovered sufficiently to enter a K3 MG for which he had high hopes, but the car slid off the road in practice on some loose gravel and overturned, and Howe was lucky to escape with a shaking. Although there were Salmson, Amilcar and Miller entries (Boucly's 91 model reduced to 1100 cc) the race was a clean sweep for Maserati and Ferdinando Barbieri driving a 4 CM entered by the Scuderia Capredoni of Genoa led throughout and finished 54 seconds in front of Guido Landi with Giuseppe Furmanik in third place. Furmanik used his 4CM Maserati as relaxation from his occupation as principal tester of parachutes for the Regia Aeronautica. Boucly's Miller lasted for 5 laps which was good going for a car which had never been intended for tough mountainous road circuits.

A rather poor season sank to its nadir at La Baule in Brittany 2 weeks later. The traditional sand racing meeting organised for the benefit of the holiday-makers included a 1500cc class running with the GP cars. Despite quite generous prize money, only 3 cars started the 58 lap race over the 3 km circuit. José Scaron made a rare racing appearance with the MCO Amilcar. Despite his pre-season announcement, Scaron's racing with the Amilcar had been dictated by economic stringencies and had been restricted to hill climbs in which he had been very successful. Running against him was Madame Itier with her T51A Bugatti and a 750cc Rosengart. The Amilcar led but soon retired with the old bogey of a broken piston, then Madame Itier with the prize as good as hers, was pushed off the course by another competitor. All this excitement was too much

★The K3 MGs were fitted with a 2-star differential, similar to that fitted to the production cars. After the Mannin Beg this was changed to a 4-star on the K3s and was fitted to the mass-production MGs about a year later. A good example of racing improving the breed.

(a)

(b)

(c)

a. 30th July, 1933: Coppa Ciano Livorno: Furmanik's 4CM Maserati with the white-edged grille has a slight advantage at the start. On his left and behind him are the 4CMs of Landi and Barbieri.

b. 13th August, 1933: La Baule G.P.: Desbois (750cc Rosengart) is lapped by Williams (T54 Bugatti). The sand is being cut up on the outside of the corner.

c. 15th August, 1933: Coppa Acerbo Pescara: Whitney Straight is jubilant after his victory in his K3 MG.

d. 15th August, 1933: Coppa Acerbo Pescara: Straight's MG rests after its win and waits to be taken back to Milan by Earl Howe's mechanics.

for the Rosengart's clutch and so the 1500 race was over long before the 68 laps were completed. Luckily, the regulations provided for the prize money to be paid out to all competitors if there were only 4 finishers, or none at all! 2 days after the debacle at La Baule, the Coppa Acerbo Veturetta took place at Pescara and proved to be a much more virile event, of some significance. During the 1932 and 1933 seasons, the name of Whitney Straight had become prominent in motor racing. Straight, who was a 21 year old millionaire, was an American by birth but had lived in England since his childhood. He started racing in 1931 and raced a 2.5 litre GP Maserati mainly in British events in 1932. As a driver of great talent he quickly made his mark and during the 1933 season he drove the same Maserati in several Continental GPs and showed himself to be the equal of most of his opponents. Straight had been impressed by the performance of the K3 MG so he bought a car which was re-bodied with a lightweight racing body and prepared by Thomson & Taylor, the Brooklands tuners. The car was entered for the 1100 race at Pescara and from the start, Straight took the lead. Despite being slightly under-geared for the long Pescara straight, the black MG could not be caught; to the astonishment of the Italian crowd it was flagged off as the winner, ten seconds in front of Barbieri's Maserati which had chased it throughout the race. More Maseratis finished third, fourth and fifth, and once again, the Millers of Boucly and Marret retired. The Italians did not look kindly on the speed of the MG and, perhaps misled by the large external appearance of the engine, a protest was made that the car was over 1100cc. Immediate measurements showed the validity of the engine and thus Straight won the first ever victory for a British racing car on an Italian road circuit. The black MG had taken 1 min. 13 secs. less than Scaron's Amilcar to cover the same distance the previous year which was an indication of the performance of this newcomer to voiturette racing. More successes were to await this particular MG in the future in other hands, but meanwhile Straight's victory had given a new vitality to voiturette racing and an increase in the international interest of the class.

The promotion of a new event at Albi in the south west of France near Toulouse was perhaps another indication of better prospects for the future. A 1500 race preceded the Albi Grand Prix on 27th August and this was to be the first of a series which was to become a voiturette classic up to 1939. The circuit was approximately $5^{1}2$ miles (8.9 km) and was a narrow and bumpy triangle. The race was an easy win for Pierre Veyron with his T51A Bugatti. Behind Veyron was Andre Vagniez with his Tipo 26 Maserati, Durand with his T37A Bugatti and the reliable Madame Itier with her T51A.

Just when it seemed that a rather mediocre season was to fade away, the final event produced what could perhaps be regarded as one of the more heroic voiturette drives of the 1930s and one which, if it had ended successfully might have become a legend. The scene of this feat was the Masaryk Grand Prix on the Brno circuit on the 17th September. The 1500 class ran together with the Grand Prix cars over 15 laps of the difficult circuit, a distance of 272 miles (437 km). Unlike earlier events this final fling produced quite a respectable entry and 16 cars came to the line; 7 Bugattis faced 2 Masseratis, 2 Millers, 3 local specials and single entries of Hans Ruesch's Alfa Romeo and the J4 MG of Hugh Hamilton. Hamilton had had a frustrating season. He had been second in the

17th September, 1933: Czechoslovak G.P. Brno: The 1500cc start. Boucly's Miller is making smoke and obscuring the view of Ruesch (Alfa-Romeo (63)).

1100 class in the Mille Miglia and although he had won the 800cc class at the Nurburgring, he had seen the Mannin Beg slip from his grasp, and had lost a certain victory in the Ulster Tourist Trophy through inept pit work. The Czech race started in appalling conditions of wind and driving rain and in places the rain had carried mud across the road. Veyron took the lead at the start but the slippery road was his undoing and he crashed with slight injuries, so after 4 laps Guido Landi led the race, driving his 4CM Maserati, from Ernst Burggaller and Hamilton who was coming through the field very fast after a slow start. Hamilton was going spendidly and after 7 laps he had passed Landi, and caught up with Burggaller, when both cars stopped for fuel. This time Hamilton had his pit staff properly drilled and he restarted before Burggaller, just as Landi went past. Immediately the MG gave chase and his excitement, coupled with the terrible conditions, Landi spun and Hamilton was leading the 1500 class with a car half the size of the rest and found himself, remarkably, in third place in the Grand Prix overall. The 746cc M.G. was even gaining on Fagioli who was in second place in the Grand Prix. Landi recovered quickly from his indiscretion and realising the humiliation of being led by such a small car speeded up and on the 10th lap he passed Hamilton again but the Englishman was not giving up. The crowd was urging him on as it realised that there was the extraordinary possibility that the 750 MG could be placed in the Grand Prix overall, and could even win, as it was so much better suited to the conditions than its larger opponents. At the start of the 11th lap Hamilton had caught up with Landi again, and was only a few lengths behind, and anything seemed possible but then fate took a hand. Hamilton had been wearing a waterproof poncho to keep out some of the rain, and this blew up over his face, causing him to lose control. The car slid wide, left the road, and overturned several times and Hamilton received severe injuries. After the meteoric drive of the MG, and its equally spectacular exit, the voiturette race assumed more normal proportions. Landi was still leading but he now crashed in his turn on the next lap and it was left to Ernst Burggaller to gain a victory which had so narrowly eluded him all season. Only 4 cars finished; Bruno Sojka was second now driving a T51A Bugatti which he shared with Florian Schmidt and Hans Ruesch was third with his 6C Alfa Romeo, maintaining the successful Swiss tradition established by Tauber with these cars. Altogether 6 of the voiturette drivers were hurt in crashes but the unfortunate Hamilton came off worst with several broken ribs and other injuries. He made a speedy recovery however, and celebrated his return to fitness by journeying to India and shooting tigers.

In a lean season, the car to beat had been the T51A Bugatti. There were not enough 4CM/1500 Maseratis around to make a great impact but Earl Howe had shown the veteran 8 cylinder Delage was still as fast as any other car available. The continuing decline of the 1100 class was most marked. Only the Italian race organisers had any real interest in the smaller cars and even one of their principal events had been stolen away by a British interloper. The K3 MG Magnette was certainly a match for the best 4CM/1100 Maseratis and it was a pity that more K3s had not been entered for voiturette races as a good one would certainly have been better than a lot of the 1500s.

Pierre Veyron, aided by his works Bugatti, had been the most successful driver, but probably the most significant feature of the 1933 season had been the increase of British interest. British cars were coming onto the scene and the MGs had shown that they were fully competitive in the right hands. Whitney Straight had opened the door for the British with his Pescara win, much as Tony Brooks was to do with his Connaught victory at Syracuse 22 years later, and many would follow after him.

During the summer, an indication of the future had been shown in England. Raymond Mays had been working hard on his supercharged Riley and at the end of July the car was ready. It made its first appearance at Brooklands on the 1st August for the Bank Holiday meeting and its speed was impressive despite some initial bothers. The "White Riley" then went to Shelsley Walsh on the 30th September where Mays kept his promise to Victor Riley and broke the course record only to lose it again before the end of the meeting to Whitney Straight with his 2.5 GP Maserati. The Riley finished the season by winning a Mountain Handicap at Brooklands. Mays was so encouraged by the promise of the Riley that he decided to produce a series of cars based on it, when he was approached by Humphrey Cook, a rich English amateur driver, who offered to sponsor the development and production of the car. Much of the engine design work on the Riley had been done by Mays' friend Peter Berthon, who had been helping Mays with his sprint cars for some years, and Berthon now began a much more radical development of the engine, assisted and guided by Murray Jamieson, the supercharger expert. Meanwhile, Mays had enlisted the help of Reid Railton of Thomson & Taylor who had designed a number of successful record breaking cars. Railton was commissioned to design a chassis for the new car which was to be a single seater, and inspired by the contemporary 8CM Maserati and Tipo B Alfa Romeo, Railton produced a neat but conventional chassis in a very short time. In November 1933 the British motoring press announced that Mays and Cook were to produce the car for sale to the public and it was named ERA, which stood for English Racing Automobiles, a most suitable title for a car which Cook intended to be a patriotic symbol. During the next 6 years, those initials were to become synonymous with voiturette racing.

a. 7th August, 1933: Brooklands: The White Riley makes its debut. Raymond Mays smiles happily at the wheel. Peter Berthon in shirt sleeves pushes on the far side of the car and Murray Jamieson looks on critically.

b. March, 1934: The first E.R.A. R1A. Raymond Mays is at the wheel and Peter Berthon stands beside the car which still has the original rising sun ERA badge.

c. Spring 1934: K3 MGs are prepared in the competition department of the MG factory at Abingdon.

1934

IN MARCH 1934, the first ERA to be completed was shown to the press. The neat and businesslike appearance of the car evoked an enthusiastic welcome. The car was a conventional single seater, with a narrow chassis frame, mounted on semi-elliptic springs all round. The Riley-based 6-cylinder engine had a Jamieson supercharger driven vertically from the front of the crankshaft while the Riley system of valve operation with 2 camshafts mounted high in the cylinder block, operating the valves through short push rods and rockers, was retained. The transmission continued the fashion set by MG, incorporating an Armstrong-Siddeley preselector gearbox. No attempt had been made to lower the transmission line so the driver sat rather high over the propeller shaft and the steering-wheel was slightly off-set in the cockpit to allow for the placing of the column on the side of the chassis frame. By the standards of 1933 the car, although conventional, was right up-to-date but, as very few of those who first saw the ERA, could have realised, at the end of 1933, the standards of motor racing and racing car design had changed overnight completely and irrevocably.

On the 1st January 1934, the 750 kg Grand Prix formula came into force and in the Autumn of 1933 the motoring press began to carry rumours of secret and remarkable new German cars. It was not long before rumour became fact, and it was evident that the new German cars were quite unlike anything that had been seen in motor racing before. The W25 Mercedes Benz had all-independent suspension and a streamlined body, while the P-Wagen Auto Union, although sporting the independent suspension and streamlined body of the Mercedes, had the revolutionary feature of the engine behind the driver. The effect of the German cars was to condemn the existing Tipo B Alfa Romeo, 8CM Maserati and T59 Bugatti to instant obsolescence. The effect on Grand Prix racing was to be dramatic and this change was to be reflected in a similar and complete change in the character of voiturette racing. However, this is to look further ahead than the beginning of the 1934 season, and so far as the voiturette classes were concerned, little had changed since the Autumn of 1933. The ERA had been announced, but would need development before becoming an effective force and so far, Raymond Mays and Humprey Cook had only declared their intention of running single cars in the 1100 and 1500 class. There were no new cars from Bugatti; Salmson and Amilcar were now a spent force, though Maserati continued to produce a tiny handful of cars which gained results out of

a. 27th May, 1934: Avusrennen: Fork (modified K3 MG) leads Simon (T37A Bugatti).

b. 27th May, 1934: Avusrennen: The engine of the 1500cc supercharged 2-stroke Zoller which made a disappointing debut.

c. 27th May, 1934: Avusrennen: Pierre Veyron sits in his T51A Bugatti after his victory. The car is running on track Racing tyres.

d. 27th May, 1934: Picardie G.P.: Louis Decaroli looks tired after his win in his modified T37A Bugatti.

all proportion to their number. In England, apart from ERA, the K3 MG was still in production and was being sold with a pointed tailed body and improved brakes for 1934. Earl Howe had fitted a Wilson preselector gearbox to his Delage which by now had almost become a naturalized British subject. The calendar of voiturette races was still rather thin, and this was deplored by Sammy Davis, writing in "The Autocar" at the beginning of the season, who commented that most race organisers only wanted to support the Grand Prix cars. This was to change much sooner than anyone could have anticipated.

As in 1933, the Continental season began at Chimay in Belgium on the 20th May where an 1100 class was included in the GP des Frontieres which, on a narrow circuit over country roads, would now be regarded as little more than a club event. The race produced the now rare outcome of an Amilcar victory when Marcel Rouleau won with his old C6. His continuing loyalty to the marque was perhaps justified as he was still the Belgian agent. In England, the season had started in March with a minor meeting at Donnington Park but the short voiturette events still only attracted an entry comprised mainly of stripped sports cars. However, all these were to seem insignificant in comparison with the events a week after Chimay. On the 27th May, a huge crowd of Berliners flocked to the Avus, excited by the prospect of seeing both Der Fuhrer and the debut of the new German Grand Prix cars. Much to the crowd's disappointment the W25 Mercedes-Benz were declared to be unready and were withdrawn, but 3 V-16 Auto Unions appeared. Before the Avus Grand Prix there was the usual preliminary voiturette race and 16 starters formed up in their balloted starting places, under ominous black clouds. Earl Howe had decided not to run the Delage as he was already engaged to drive his new 2.9 Maserati in the GP race later in the afternoon. The race was to be the debut of a new German voiturette of which much was expected; the Zoller, a 6 cylinder 1500cc supercharged 2-stroke which was rumoured to develop 200 bhp, though practice times had belied this. From the start, Pierre Veyron took the lead with his T51A Bugatti pursued, as always, by Ernst Burggaller whose white single-seater T51A had started from the sixth row. At the end of lap 1, Burggaller was 9 seconds behind while Gerhard Macher and von Delius retired with the Zollers whose alleged 200 bhp had caused a great excess of heat. Veyron continued on his way and gradually drew away from Burggaller to win by 33 seconds. Before the race, the MG Car Co. had sold the Magic Midget 750 class record car to the German MG distributor, Robert Kohlrausch. He started the race well, with great hopes of winning the 800cc class prize, but after 4 laps, the tiny cockpit of the Magic Midget took its toll, and the unfortunate Kohlrausch had to be lifted from the car and given emergency massage on the pit counter, to relieve acute cramp. What Hitler thought was not recorded! As usual the Avus was hard on the cars as well as the drivers and there were only 8 finishers. Count Castelbarco's 4CM Maserati was third while Adolf Brudes, driving Kohlrausch's white J4 MG, won the 800cc class as the only survivor. "Motor Sport" reported, rather gloomily, that "the race was not an interesting one". In winning, Veyron had averaged 113.52 mph an increase of only .62 mph over his winning average in 1933. It was clear that Bugatti had done little or no development on the T51A in the past 12 months though it is likely that there was not much more that could

47

4th June, 1934: Eifelrennen: Count Castelbarco winner of the 1500cc class in his 4CM Maserati.

be done with the design. With the preoccupation of making the T59 GP car race-worthy and going into production with the T57 touring car, Molsheim now had little time for voiturettes and sadly, the great racing days of Bugatti were coming to an end. It is unlikely that these matters were pondered upon by many at the Avus that day, or if anyone cared particularly, for the crowd had come to see greater things. When the GP event started, in pouring rain, Hans Stuck took the lead with his Auto Union and soon extended this to 85 seconds. Minor problems forced him to retire as did Prinz zu Leiningen with another Auto Union but Momberger managed to gain third place with the third car of the team. The Avus crowd had seen the birth of a motor racing legend and the growth of another, for Tazio Nuvolari had driven his Maserati into fifth place with his leg in plaster; the result of a crash at Alessandria on the 22nd April.

While legends were being made at the Avus, on the same afternoon, the Picardie GP was being held at Peronne. Apart from the voiturette and GP races, the meeting had various sideshows, the principal one being the opening of the course by "La Petite Rosalie" the Citroen world record holder, and the collapse of the main grandstand during the racing. The circuit had been slowed down by introducing straw bale chicanes on the straights, perhaps prompted by the 2 fatal accidents in the previous year and the voiturette race with 7 starters had an unusual entry. This was the appearance of the rare 1100cc 8 cylinder Salmson which was to be driven, as in 1933, by Armand Girod. The Salmson now showed it was a quick car and took the lead at the start from Cattaneo's T51A Bugatti. These two swopped places for 15 laps until the Bugatti broke a piston, and the Salmson had a clutch problem, then Louis Decaroli took lead with his rebodied single seater T37A Bugatti and went on to win. Girod, however, was able to get going again and held second place to the finish, keeping ahead of Madame Itier, who did not reproduce her 1933 form.

If Mercedes-Benz had been unprepared for the Avusrennen, the problems were soon rectified, for on the following Sunday, the new W25 cars were produced for the world to see at the Nurburgring. As usual, the Eifelrennen had subsidiary classes for the 1500cc and 800cc cars which started in their separate groups after the GP cars had been flagged away. Count Castelbarco obviously

a. 30th May, 1934: Mannin Beg. Douglas: Walter Handley K3 MG (9) leads at the start from Dixon's 1500cc Riley (20) Hamilton's K3 MG (4) and Eyston's K3 Magic Magnette (8).

b. 30th May, 1934: Mannin Beg. Douglas: Handley is having problems with his MG while in the lead on lap 2.

c. 30th May, 1934: Mannin Beg. Douglas: Eyston's Magic Magnette leads Hamilton's MG and Victor Gillow's Riley round the Bray Hill hairpin.

preferred the corners of the "Ring" to the straights of the Avus and won comfortably from Florian Schmidt with his T51A Bugatti while Burggaller had to be content with third place. Unfortunately, the Viennese driver, Emil Frankl, was killed instantly when his Bugatti overturned just after the start, caused allegedly by the breaking up of a wheel. In the 800cc class Kohlrausch, perhaps now with a remedy for cramp, led for 3 laps until the engine of the MG Magic Midget failed and again the class was won by Brudes with Kohlrausch's J4 MG. The hot Zollers were still too hot, but this probably did not worry the huge crowd, for the race had shown that not only did the German teams mean business, but they were now in business. Two W25 Mercedes-Benz had started the race and one driven by Manfred von Brauchitsch had won, while to spread the German joy, Stuck's Auto Union had finished second. The outcome of one race had changed the face of grand prix racing though the effect on the voiturette class was to take a little longer to appear.

Unlike previous years there had been no British competitors at the Nurburgring. This was not due to any political undertones, but during the week between the events at the Avus and the "Ring", the British had been competing in their own International voiturette race. Despite local criticism and reports of a big financial loss in 1933, the RAC had decided to repeat the Mannin Moar and Mannin Beg races in the Isle of Man. The circuit used in 1933, was reduced to $3\frac{1}{2}$ miles (5.6 km) and the RAC had listened to some of the criticisms of the previous year, for now, single seaters were permitted, though the Mannin Beg still only provided for blown 1100s and unblown 1500s. The supercharged 1500s were again required to run with the Formule Libre cars in the Mannin Moar. The race only attracted a National entry but much interest was aroused by the entry of an 1100 ERA for Humphrey Cook, while a $1\frac{1}{2}$ litre ERA was entered for Raymond Mays in the Mannin Moar. As it turned out, the ERA hopes were premature, as Cook's car could not be finished in time, but Mays' car appeared for practice and showed impressive acceleration, but the spring rates were wrong and the car was withdrawn after giving its driver a very bumpy ride. "The Motor" observed prophetically "When this chassis has been modified we shall see fireworks". Unfortunately there was a fatal accident in practice when Kaye Don crashed his K3 MG while testing the car on the public roads after practice had finished. At the time, he was carrying Frank Tayler, an MG works mechanic, who was killed. This mishap had an unhappy sequel, for Don was subsequently convicted of manslaughter in the Isle of Man courts and served a 4 month prison sentence. This action caused much disquiet and feeling among his fellow competitors. Without Cook's ERA, 19 cars faced the starter comprising 12 MGs, 5 Rileys, a Singer and the McEvoy, a Wolseley Hornet-based special. Walter Handley a motor cycle TT winner★ led for 2 laps until he crashed his K3 MG, whereupon George Eyston went to the front with the "works" single seater K3, variously known as the Magic Magnette or the "Humbug" because of its striped finish. After 10 laps, Eyston was passed by Freddie Dixon's $1\frac{1}{2}$ litre Riley and Dixon was running away with the race until lap 45, when he stopped with fuel starvation, while leading by $2\frac{1}{2}$ minutes. With Dixon gone, there was

★Winner 1925 Ultra Lightweight TT, 1925 Junior TT, 1927 Lightweight TT and 1930 Senior TT.

a MG walkover and Norman Black's K3 led 4 similar cars home. It had been a better race than 1933, but the lack of foreign entries and the supercharged 1500s, had diminished its appeal.

After 4 voiturette races in 8 days, there was now an extraordinary lull for 7 weeks while no voiturette races were held. However, despite the lack of races, the voiturette competitors were not inactive. Madame Itier went to Le Mans and drove a "PA" MG, while most of the continental "regulars" went to the Kesselberg Hill climb in the Tyrol, where Count Castelbarco, fittingly perhaps, as the son-in-law of the conductor, Arturo Toscanini, hit his own high note and won the 1500cc racing car class, and Kohlrausch, at last succeeded in gaining a class win with his Magic Midget MG. Ernst Burggaller also went to Kesselberg and perhaps hoping for the win which always seemed to elude him, decided to run his T51A Bugatti with road equipment in the sports car class, but yet again, he was out of luck as he was beaten by Lurani's Maserati by the impossible margin of .01 sec! Burggaller had his reward however, for he went one better than all the other voiturette competitors, as he was given a drive by the Auto-Union team in the German Grand Prix at the Nurburgring on the 15th July. Unhappily though, he did not cover himself in glory as he broke the gearbox after a few laps.

The British voiturette racers were also busy during the enforced lull. With the casualties of the Isle of Man made good, most of the faster 1100s and 1500s were at Brooklands on the 23rd June for the British Empire Trophy a class handicap race held on an artificial road circuit marked by straw bales and sand banks. George Eyston beat his handicap to win with his multi-striped K3 MG, but the most interesting entry was the $1\frac{1}{2}$ litre ERA which Raymond Mays and Humphrey Cook drove steadily throughout the race, and despite stops for adjustments, the car was still running at the end. The black K3 MG which had carried Whitney Straight to victory at Pescara the previous August, appeared again, driven by its new owner Richard Seaman. Bothered by minor troubles, he made little impression in the race.

With remarkable lack of foresight, when the voiturettes raced again on the 22nd July, there was a clash of events. The Italians, still faithful to the 1100 class, held the annual event at Livorno and on this long, difficult circuit, Romano Malaguti led all the way with his 4CS Maserati. Federico Matrullo was second with a 4CM Maserati while a stripped "Balilla" Fiat, a rare interloper, was third. The other race was down in the South West of France on the $5\frac{1}{2}$ mile (8.9 km) Albi circuit. Much to the annoyance of the competitors, the start was delayed and most of the cars overheated on the line. When released, Veyron took the lead on his T51A Bugatti but after the delay, the car was not running well and he was being pressed by Leoz Abad who took the lead with a T37A Bugatti when Veyron stopped to change plugs. The plug change effected a cure and Veyron chased Abad, passed him and went on to win. The only British competitor was Richard Seeman who had a most unhappy race with his K3 MG. The car boiled on the line and then stalled. For receiving a push start from the eager spectators, Seaman was fined 100 Francs by the unsympathetic organisers and he retired with a very hot engine.

After Albi was over, Seaman towed his MG on a trailer behind an old

51

Lagonda tourer across France and into Italy, as far as Pescara, where the Coppa Acerbo meeting was held on Tuesday 15th August. The voiturette race began at the unpleasantly early hour of 8 a.m. and the early start cannot have been improved by the wet showery condition. The organisers had moved with the times and the race was now open to cars up to 1500cc. There were only 8 starters and 3 were K3 MGs. It was an indication of the rise of Britain in voiturette racing that these MGs took the first three places. Matrullo took the lead at the start with his 4CM Maserati but was passed by Hugh Hamilton's silver single seater K3 on the second lap after Hamilton had made up for a very bad start. After Matrullo retired with a burnt piston, Rafaele Cecchini, an Italian printer who was also racing an MG and Seaman, took over second and third places and completed the 4 laps of the race in that order. Although the Pescara meeting had been a happy one for the British contingent, it was marred by the death of the Algerian driver Guy Moll who crashed his Tipo B Alfa Romeo while trying to catch Luigi Fagioli's leading Mercedes in the G.P. race. Moll who was 24 years old had indicated that he was a driver of great promise having already won the Monaco Grand Prix and the Avusrennen earlier in the season.

The next voiturette race on the calendar was undoubtedly the premier event of the season. Following the increased interest in grand prix racing, a grande epreuve had been organised in Switzerland, and a fast and difficult circuit had been chosen for the first Swiss Grand Prix which ran through the Bremgarten, the thickly wooded park on the northern outskirts of Berne. The circuit was 4.5 miles (7.28 km) long with no proper straights but very fast corners. Part of it was surfaced with smooth stone setts. As a preliminary, a 1500 race was to be held in the morning of 26th August, starting at 10.30 a.m. The race attracted 28 entries, drawn perhaps, by the generous first prize of 6000 Francs, and the list contained most of the best cars and drivers in Europe. The starting grid was arranged by ballot and in pouring rain the lead was taken by the Swiss Kessler with his 4CM Maserati. He did not last long however as the engine blew up much to the disappointment of the crowd, and Malaguti with his 4CS Maserati headed the field, Hamilton, who had been the fastest in practice, had the misfortune to start from the back row, as did Seaman but Hamilton's MG had a bad misfire so he was not able to show his Pescara form. Seaman however, driving his MG magnificently began to work his way through the field and, passing Veyron and Burggaller, took second place behind Malaguti. The Maserati began to misfire and Seaman swept past it on lap 11 and went on to win. This was a completely unexpected victory by a relatively inexperienced and almost unknown driver; furthermore, Seaman had beaten all the best 1500s with a car of only 1100cc. Veyron and Burggaller were second and third while Lord Howe, who had given the Delage its first voiturette race of the season, was fifth although the car was not running well. Seaman's delight at his first victory was to be cut short, however. He had purchased the MG from Whitney Straight at the beginning of the season, but for domestic reasons, Seaman still had the car entered in Straight's name and it appeared to the world at large that the car was a part of the Whitney Straight team which had been entering a pair of 8CM Maseratis in most GP events during the season. At Berne, Hugh Hamilton, a regular member of the team, drove one of the Maseratis in the Grand Prix race

a. 22nd July, 1934: Coppa Ciano Livorno: At the start the stripped sports Balilla Fiats bring up the rear of the field.

b. 15th August, 1934: Coppa Acerbo Pescara: The 4CM Maserati are out in front as Hamilton (K3 MG) the eventual winner is push-started at the rear of the field.

(a)

(b)

a. 15th August, 1934: Coppa Acerbo Pescara: The winner, Hugh Hamilton with his re-bodied K3 MG.

b. 15th August, 1934: Coppa Acerbo Pescara: Rafaele Cecchini who was second with his single-seater K3.

c. 15th August, 1934: Coppa Acerbo Pescara: Seaman who came third with the K3 which gave Straight victory the previous year.

a. 25th August, 1934: Practice for the Prix de Berne: Veyron's T51A Bugatti arrives on a trailer with a spare rear axle.

b. 26th August, 1934: Prix de Berne: Richard Seaman after his first victory.

c. 25th August, 1934: Practice for the Prix de Berne: Bruno Sojka stands between his T51A Bugatti and Cholmondeley-Tapper's T37A. Tapper sits on the pit counter with Eileen Ellison and Mme. Sojka smiles happily.

in the afternoon. Sadly, on the last lap of the race, the car skidded and struck a tree and poor Hamilton was killed instantly. His death was a great shock to the British motor racing community as his pleasant manner and exuberant racing style made him a popular figure, and he was considered by many to be the most able British driver at that time.

Seaman was not the only newcomer to voiturette racing to win a race, for a week after Berne, a small meeting was held in the streets of Biella, an Italian industrial town about 50 miles north of Turin. There was every justification for the meeting as it was the home town of Count Brivio and Count Trossi. The race included a 1500 class running with the GP cars in 3 heats, and the voiturette winner was Giuseppe Farina with a 4CM Maserati. Behind Farina, Count Lurani finished second with his 4 CS Maserati ahead of his team mate in the Scuderia Subalpina, Count Castelbarco, while last in the class was "Tino" Bianchi, Castelbarco's mechanic who was given a drive in the team's old T39A Bugatti.

Sammy Davis had been right, when he commented on the limited number of voiturette races in 1934. Only 3 races were held in France, and the third, at Montlhery on 9th September was one of the events in the impressive sounding Grand Prix de France, which however, was only a club meeting. For a small meeting though, it had some interesting technical aspects. Armand Girod showed what might have been achieved with the 8-cylinder Salmson, when he won the 1100 class after a hard fight with Maurice Mestivier who now owned one of Scaron's MCO Amilcars. Girod's results with this car during 1934 had demonstrated what a pity it was that the Salmson factory had been unable or unwilling to develop the design properly as it could have been a worthy successor to the Grand Prix model. The Dutchman Harry Herkuleyns won the 850cc class with a new "Q" type MG. Although extremely fast, this design had exaggerated the inherent defect of the J4, for the engine performance had far outstripped that of the chassis.

Farina had shown that he was a man to watch, by his ability to keep up with the GP cars at Biella, and he maintained this form at the end of the month, when he went to Brno and led the 1500 class of the Masaryk G.P. from start to finish. The race, unlike previous years, was run in intense heat in front of a crowd estimated at 350,000. Yet again, Ernst Burggaller finished second of the 20 starters while Bruno Sojka was third. The 2 British entries were George Eyston, who had forsaken his Magic Magnette for a normal road racing bodied K3, and Dick Seaman and they finished fourth and fifth respectively. Seaman's MG was slightly outclassed for speed on this occasion but his driving brought favourable comments from no less an observer than Tazio Nuvolari. As soon as the Czech race was over, Seaman and Jim Burge, his mechanic set off across Europe for England towing the MG on a tow rope behind an old Fiat 520. ★ Their destination was Donington Park where the final meeting of the season was being held 6 days later. The organisers, the Derby & District C.C. had been presented with a trophy by Lord Nuffield, for a race to be held for voiturettes,

★The Fiat was borrowed from Whitney Straight's workshop in Milan after Seaman's Lagonda had broken down on the way to Brno.

56

a. 30th September, 1934: Czechoslovak G.P. Brno: The start of the 1500cc class, No. 46 is George Eyston's K3 MG.

b. 14th October, 1934: Circuit of Modena: Cecchini winning the 1100cc race with his modified K3 MG and thus becoming the 1934 Italian 1100cc champion.

c. 6th October, 1934: Nuffield Trophy Donington Park: The Leyland Cub transporter of the new ERA team. Behind it is Raymond May's Riley Kestrel saloon which had an ERA engine.

and this was to be the longest race yet held on this, the only British road circuit. Unfortunately, the race, like almost all British long distance races in the 1930s, was held as a class handicap, which considerably reduced its stature, but despite the handicap, it produced a very satisfactory result for British enthusiasts as Raymond Mays had an easy and convincing victory with the $1^1\!2$ litre ERA in most unpleasant weather conditions. Seaman justified the dash across Europe by finishing second on handicap, and being the first 1100 car home. This was not the first ERA victory as Humphrey Cook had won a Mountain handicap at the Brooklands August Bank holiday meeting with the 1100 car, but the Donington win showed that the new car not only had speed but was also finding reliability.

The Autumn rains at Donington did not quite mark the end of the season, as the last event was held on the 14th October, in the streets of Modena the home of the Scuderia Ferrari. To start the meeting there was a 50 mile 1500cc voiturette race and this saw a tremendous battle throughout between Farina with his 4CM Maserati and Raffaele Cecchini with his single seater K3 MG. These two fought so hard that contemporary reports commented on their "ragged and dangerous driving" but it was clearly safer than it looked, as both cars finished the race and Cecchini scored an unexpected and clear-cut victory beating Farina by 5.8 seconds. By doing so, Cecchini became the Italian 1100 champion for 1934, and this success for a British car, in the class which the Italians regarded as their especial preserve, must have caused much feeling as the regulations were changed in 1935, so that only Italian cars were eligible for the National championships.

Although the season was finished, the voiturette world was still active. Giuseppe Furmanik removed the front brakes from his veteran 1932 1100 4CM Maserati and aided by wheel discs and some streamline fairings, set up new 1100cc (International class G) records over the flying mile and kilometre at 138.344 mph which showed how quick even an 1100 voiturette could be. It was reported that for the record attempt the engine was boosted to give 152 bhp at 6,700 rpm which was a much higher figure than MG's were getting even for the Magic Magnette. At that time, 124 bhp was being quoted by the Abingdon factory. As a more direct comparison, Hamilton's K3 had been timed at 122 mph over a measured kilometre during the Coppa Acerbo at Pescara.

Emboldened by the Donington win, ERA Ltd. announced in November that limited production of the car had started at the Bourne factory. £1,700 was the listed price for the 1500 and £1,500 the price of the 1100 which was a lot more than the price quoted in "Motor Sport" for the 1100/4CM Maserati, 55,000 lire, or £915, at the rate of exchange then current. In November a rumour circulated that Mercedes-Benz had an eye on the 1500 class and intended to build a car for the 1935 season. Perhaps it was as well for the subsequent history of voiturette racing that the rumour had no apparent foundation at that time.

No driver had been pre-eminent in the 1934 season though the established figures such as Pierre Veyron had found that they had been forced to work hard for their successes. It had been noticeable that a new generation of drivers was appearing and some, particularly Seaman and Farina, were above the usual level of competence; both had shown much promise and they would confirm this in full measure. Of the cars, Bugatti sadly was fading and towards the end of the

58

season even the best T51As had been well beaten by both Maserati and MG. The handful of Maseratis continued to produce results out of all proportions to their numbers while the K3 MG had proved to be both fast and durable, a worthy competitor among the 1500s and clearly the best 1100, as Cecchini's championship in the spiritual home of the 1100s had shown. At the end of the season the unknown quantity was still ERA. It was fast, it was becoming reliable, but it had not yet shown its form in a scratch race. But the car was now in production, and a number of British drivers had been to Bourne to talk to Raymond Mays. All this however, was far away from the problems of a young Siamese prince living in London. He was doing his best during the winter of 1934 to persuade his cousin, who was also his guardian, that he would be unlikely to come to any harm if he was allowed to race his Riley Imp in some minor events at Brooklands.

1935

ALTHOUGH much interest had been shown in the ERA, and a number of drivers had discussed the car with Raymond Mays, the little factory at Bourne had only two firm orders in the Spring of 1935. One car, an 1100, was for Pat Fairfield who had returned to England in 1933 after spending many years in South Africa, although he was English by birth. He had been entered for a number of races in 1934 by Freddie Dixon in one of the Dixon Rileys and had earned the nickname of "Skidder" Fairfield, the result of his very fast but rather eratic driving. The three cars built in 1934 had been called A-types, as was Fairfield's car, but the second scrics, which were now being laid down, were the production models intended for sale and had slightly stiffer frames and altered spring rates so were to be called B-types. The first B-type, a 1500, had been ordered by Richard Seaman. Seaman had admitted privately to his friends that his ambition was to become a professional grand prix driver and he had shown an intelligent and deliberate approach to his career in pursuit of his goal. It was interesting therefore that such a driver was prepared to stake the furtherance of his career on a relatively untried car. It must be remembered though, that in finishing second behind Raymond Mays at Donington the previous October, Seaman had been given a better opportunity than most to evaluate the new car and assess its potential.

The 1934 season had finished with the German teams dominating grand prix racing but many people thought that this was merely a phenomenon and expected the grand prix world to rever to an Italian/French monopoly in 1935, with the expectation of new and competitive cars from Alfa Romeo, Bugatti and Maserati. Added to this, was much speculation about the grand prix formula which would take effect when the 750 kg formula expired at the end of 1936. In the Spring of 1935, there was already some lobbying by those with vested interests. As he had done in the past, Cecil Kimber aired his views in the British motoring press and declared his preference for a 1500cc formula, probably hoping he could persuade Lord Nuffield to finance a team of MGs. Kimber did not get much support as the RAC suggested 2 litres, but "Motor Sport" in its editorial in January 1935 considered that the 1500cc proposals had some merit. That 1500cc could even be considered as a possible GP formula, was a clear indication of the rising prestige of the voiturette class, and with the possibility of a successful contender in the ERA, British enthusiasm for a small capacity grand prix formula was understandable. The controversy and rumour about new formulae was to continue until the Autumn of 1935, when the AIACR decided to extend the 750 kg formula for another year until the end of 1937. This postponement of the decision was to be significant as by the time the new rules were drawn up, the character of grand prix racing had changed entirely and many new influences had become important.

Although the ERA was in limited production, on the other side of the English Channel there were no signs of any new voiturettes. There were strong rumours that Pierre Veyron would be driving a new or improved Bugatti, but all the Molsheim factory could produce for him was his veteran T51A now entering its fourth season with a twin cam engine although it has been suggested that the chassis of this particular car dated back to 1928. In Italy, Maserati were still producing 4CM and 4CS models and six new cars were delivered to customers in the Spring of 1935 which was a further indication of the progress of the voiturette. The fastest small Maserati of all, the Furmanik record holder, was bought by Gino Rovere for the Scuderia Subalpina and he proposed to share the driving with Giuseppe Farina, and to make the car more competitive, a new 1500 engine was bought from the Bologna factory. The previous December, Luigi Della Chiesa had arranged with the Maserati brothers that he would enter the works Maseratis during the 1935 season under the banner of the Scuderia Subalpina which he ran with Rovere. Maserati were thus in much the same position as Alfa Romeo with the Scuderia Ferrari. The biggest technical advance in the voiturette class however was produced in England which was rapidly becoming the natural home of the small capacity racing car. On 25th April, the MG Car Co. mindful of the shortcomings of the chassis of the Q-type, unveiled their new 750 in the showrooms of University Motors, the London distributors of MG. The new car, the R-type designed by H.N. Charles, was in many ways as advanced in the voiturette field as the German cars had been in grand prix racing a year before. It had independent suspension on all wheels using torsion bars as the springing medium, while the chassis frame was a "Y"-shaped fabricated steel 'backbone' structure with the engine mounted between the arms of the "Y". MG were very confident and were happy to confide in the press that a monoposto K3 was likely to be marketed in 1935 and pointed out that an extended R-type chassis would take a K3 engine. Furthermore, there was talk of a K3 engine extended to 1500cc which was a perfectly feasible proposition with the various MG racing components available. A 1500cc engined R-type had already been given the provisional factory appelation of S-type. It was sad that all this confidence and technical innovation at the Abingdon factory was to be brought to naught within a few months.

As an indication that the independent driver in grand prix racing was under pressure, the Association Generale Automobile des Coureurs Independants was formed in Paris in January. This was an association of amateur drivers which aimed to obtain better starting money for the independents and to assist them to get entries. Prominent among the Officers of the Association were Jean Delorme and Madame Itier. Despite these admirable aims, the private entrant was being squeezed out of grand prix racing. The cost could not be met from a private purse and race organizers did not want the elderly machinery offered by

a. Spring 1935: The prototype R-type MG is run up in the competition department at Abingdon.

b. 28th April 1935: Targa Florio: Nando Barbieri (1500 4CM Maserati).

c. The Q-type MG of Harry Herkuleyns who modified it with a single seater body for the 1935 season.

most amateur entrants. For the amateur who wanted to race a single seater, the voiturette door was open and the prospects beckoned alluringly.

In 1935, the voiturette season started at a new venue, though in terms of motor racing history, one of the oldest of all. This was the short Madonie circuit in Sicily, the home of the Targa Florio. Sadly, by 1935 the once great race, which had seen such heroic struggles in earlier years, had declined until it was little more than an Italian National event. It seemed that it was to suffer a further indignity in 1935 by losing its proud title in being renamed the Targa Primavera Siciliana, but two weeks before the race, it was announced that the famous old title would be retained. In order to pad out a thin entry, the organizers included an 1100cc class but perhaps it was the hard nature of the circuit, or 28th April was too early in the season, for the class only attracted a handful of entries, and after 6 laps and 267 miles (430 km), there were only two finishers in the voiturette class, both stripped sports Balilla Fiats; the winning car being driven by Troia who finished only 5 minutes in front of Gerolamo Ferrari in the second car after over $6^{1}2$ hours racing. Barbieri's 1500 4CM Maserati achieved a notable success in the general classification finishing third behind the Tipo B Alfa Romeos of Brivio and Chiron.

After the early start on such an untypical circuit, the next event was a return to normality and also a nostalgic return to the past. On 26th May, the Circuit of Orleans was organised on a course which ran through the streets of the City and along the banks of the River Loire. It provided classes for all the voiturettes, running together. Leoz led the start of the 25 lap race in his T37 Bugatti but was soon passed by Maurice Mestivier in the ex-Scaron MCO Amilcar, now starting on its eighth racing season. The car was still quick, and Mestivier went on to win outright, beating all the elderly 1500s in the true Scaron fashion.

The season was gradually building up and three days after the Orleans event, the first major contenders showed their hand. Despite stories of great financial losses in previous years, the RAC persevered and once more ran the Mannin races in the Isle of Man. However, the plunge into the competitive world of a full 1500 race still could not be faced, and again, the Mannin Beg was restricted to supercharged 1100s and un-supercharged 1500s. The circuit was slightly altered from 1934, with a 180° turn on the seafront and practice showed that the course was now very bumpy. The majority of the 13 starters were MGs, but Dixon had entered his 1500 Riley again, and most interesting of all were the ERAs. Raymond Mays was driving a works entry and Pat Fairfield his new white painted 1100 car. Already, ERA Ltd had decided that the factory car should be made faster than the customers' machines and Mays' car was therefore fitted with a Zoller vane supercharger which gave about 10 lbs more boost than the Jamieson supercharger fitted to the production cars. At the start, Fairfield led but was passed by Eddie Hall's K3 MG during the first lap. On lap 2, the extra power of the Zoller showed itself, and Mays passed Hall and Fairfield and led for 3 laps until an oil pipe broke, and he retreated to the pits for repairs. Fairfield, meanwhile, had repassed Hall and went on steadily to win. His pace and the bumpy circuit soon thinned out the field, and the only two cars were classified as finishers, with Dixon in second place. Two MGs were still running, one being a new R-type. Mays had restarted after his repairs, but gave up after

a. 29th May, 1935: Mannin Beg. Douglas: On lap 5 Mays leads in his ERA but is laying a trail of oil from a broken pipe. Hall (MG) and Fairfield (ERA) avoid it while taking the seafront hairpin.

b. 29th May, 1935: Mannin Beg. Douglas: George Eyston (R-type MG) leads Raymond Mays (ERA) round the turn off the seafront.

(a) (b)

a. 29th May 1935: Mannin Beg. Douglas: Raymond Mays cleans up after being sprayed with oil by his ERA.

b. 29th May 1935: Mannin Beg. Douglas: Pat Farfield's victory is toasted in champagne. Humphrey Cook, Raymond Mays and Peter Berthon are on the left.

the oil pipe broke again, blinding him momentarily and nearly causing him to drive off the front into the sea! Such was the excitement of the press photographers after the race that the roof of Fairfield's pit collapsed from the weight of those wanting a better vantage point. The ERA now had both speed and stamina and was obviously going to be a hard car to beat.

Voiturette racing was passing through a period of transition and the races during 1935 were falling into two divisions of quality. At Montlhery a week after his Orleans win, Mestivier did it again in the minor Grand Prix de France meeting, while in the 750cc class at this meeting, Maillard-Brune gave the R-type MG its first victory.

So far, there had been no voiturette races on the Italian mainland, but on 9th June, the Biella meeting was repeated and despite the small entry the all-Maserati field produced a dramatic race. Rovere led with the record breaking car at the start, but had to contend with Siena for the lead. On lap 13 they collided, letting Count Lurani through. Undeterred, Rovere restarted and re-passed Lurani only to spin off on lap 20, leaving Lurani's two seater 4CS to win. In second place came Count Castelbarco with his 4CM which he had modified extensively during the winter, the principal change being a new light-weight chassis and torsion bar independent front suspension.

Although everyone suspected the ERA was bringing a new concept to voiturette racing, it had still to prove itself in the tough arena of racing in Continental Europe. This question was likely to be answered by the entry of four cars for the Eifelrennen on 16th June. The three apple-green* works cars were to be driven by Mays, Humphrey Cook and Tim Rose-Richards who had much experience racing sports cars, while Richard Seaman had entered his new

*A colour called liberty green.

black painted B-type car which was maintained for him at the Bourne factory. Perhaps the opposition was not as strong as some would have wished for a true test of the British car, but there were two 4CM Maseratis of the Scuderia Subalpina, backed by several private entries and the usual supporting cast of Bugattis and MGs. Once again, the Zollers appeared despite the death of their creator Arnold Zoller the previous January. As he had not raced at the 'Ring before Mays spent every spare moment during the week before the race, driving round the circuit in his $3^1\!2$ litre Bentley saloon, to familiarise himself with the innumerable corners. The morning of the race was wet, but the weather cleared by 11 a.m. when the cars were released by a new traffic light starting system. Mays took the lead immediately, followed by Rose-Richards and Seaman, who were ahead of the Maseratis of Hans Ruesch and Della Chiesa. At the end of the first lap Seaman passed Mays, and began to pull away leaving Mays to battle with Ruesch whose 2-seater 4CS Maserati was going very quickly. The Maserati challenge was soon blunted as Ghersi with one of the Subalpina 4CMs stopped with a badly cut eye, while Della Chiesa retired when the engine of the other Subalpina car blew up, after battling with Rose-Richards for fourth place. Seaman kept his lead for 6 laps but the ERA was losing oil and when he stopped to top up the dry sump tank, Mays took the lead again and despite having to maintain fuel pressure by hand pumping, went on to score the first ERA victory in a Continental scratch race, a most fitting reward for all his efforts to establish the marque. Ruesch was second, $^1\!2$ a minute behind, while Rose-Richards, Seaman and Cook were the next finishers. To complete the British domination, MGs took the first three places in the 800cc class. Kohlrausch won with the Magic Midget now with a new, conventional and perhaps, less cramping body! In second place was a Q-type MG which had been entered for DudleyFroy who had driven his Riley so well four years earlier. Froy was unable to drive, so the car was handled by Jack Wren, a Thomson & Taylor mechanic who had been with Froy in 1931.

Hans Stuck was so impressed with the ERA that he asked Mays if he could try the car. The next day he drove it on the now deserted circuit and afterwards said that it was much superior to any 1500 car he had driven before.

Running at the rear of the field in the Eifelrennen 1500 race were two English amateurs driving T37A Bugattis, Stanley Smith and T.P. Cholmondeley-Tapper.★ Tapper had an entry for the Lorraine GP on the Seichamps circuit outside Nancy on 30th June and as his T37A had lubrciation problems he was loaned Smith's car. With this, Tapper had a stirring drive; the 3 hour race on the 3.4 mile (5.5 km) circuit had a small voiturette entry running with the GP cars and was notable for the presence of Veyron with his T51A Bugatti. On the first lap, Tapper was rammed by Mestivier's MCO Amilcar but was undeterred and after $2^1\!2$ hours racing had a lead of 10 minutes over Veyron. Unfortunately, he then spun off with braking problems and by the time he had restarted, Veyron had caught up and was uncatchable again. Tapper finished second followed by another T37A by Miss Eileen Ellison, the only Englishwoman to compete in

With a more modern car, Cholmondeley Tapper could have been a prominent competitor in the 1500 class. His ability was recognised by Mercedes-Benz who offered him a trial at the end of the 1936 season.

Continental voiturette races during the 1930s.

The young Siamese Prince who wanted to go motor racing, finally prevailed upon his cousin H.R.H. Prince Chula Chakrabongse that no harm would come to him, if he raced his sports Riley Imp at Brooklands so the car appeared at the opening Brooklands meeting in March; the driver raced under the pseudonym of "B. Bira" which concealed his true identity of H.R.H. Prince Birabongse. Although the Riley was slow, subsequent races at Donington showed that Bira was a driver of great promise, so Prince Chula bought the last K3 MG to be built at Abingdon, and with this car, Bira finished fifth in the Nuffield Trophy at Donington on 15th July. Once again, this was a class handicap for cars up to 1500cc and the winner was Pat Fairfield's 1100 ERA. Already, before the Donnington race, Chula and Bira had decided that the young driver's future lay in 1500cc racing, so after much urging from the keen Bira, Chula ordered an ERA, the second B-type to be built, which was partly assembled at Bourne awaiting a customer.

The reputation of the ERA was spreading and it was probably a source of satisfaction to the entrants for the Albi Grand Prix, run the day after the Nuffield Trophy, that all the ERAs were either engaged at Donington or resting in

(a)

(b)

(c)

a. 14th July, 1935: Albi G.P.: Nando Barbieri (4 CM Maserati) takes the lead at the start of the first heat.

b. 14th July, 1935: Albi G.P.: Eileen Ellison with the T37A Bugatti in which she came fifth.

c. 13th July 1935: Nuffield Trophy Donington Park: Percy Maclure on his way to second place in his works-supported 1100cc Brooklands Riley.

England. The Albi entry had the appearance of a race from a bygone era, although the event had an innovation that was to be much copied in later years, for all the cars ran in 2 heats and their times in both heats were to be added together to determine the final order. It was also noteworthy that the organizers had abandoned the full Grand Prix event held in previous years, and the race was now solely for voiturettes. In the first 20 lap heat, Nando Barbieri led all the way in his 4CM Maserati, finishing over a minute in front of a Bugatti trio of Pierre Veyron, Leoz and Durand with Earl Howe back in fifth place in his Delage which was slightly off-form. In the second heat, Barbieri, determined to repeat his performance led for 3 laps until his engine failed and Veyron then drove steadily through to win the heat and the overall classification. The Delage was now fitter and came second ahead of Durand. Eileen Ellison who had been in fourth place until a fuel line broke, finished fifth in her T37A Bugatti. Once again, one of the Miller 91s ran driven by Jouve, and showed a lack of speed and durability for road racing. Veyron had shown remarkable consistency, for his time in the first heat was 1 hour 17 minutes 34.2 seconds and the second heat his time was 1 hour 17 minutes 35.8 seconds. During his steady drive Veyron had unwittingly, and perhaps sadly ended an era of motor racing history, for the Albi race was the last voiturette race of any significance that was to be won by a Bugatti. The great days of Molsheim were over.

Having received his ERA as a 21st Birthday present from Prince Chula, Bira did not have long to wait before he was able to use it, and it was at the Dieppe meeting on 20th July that he was able to make his debut with his blue-painted car. The organisers were anxious to encourage the revitalised 1500 class and a prize fund of 40,000 Francs was a lure for the drivers and entrants with 15,000 Francs for the winner (approximately £180). In addition to the financial reward, "The Motor" presented a trophy for the winner, which had previously been awarded to the winner of the voiturette race at the successful Boulogne meeting in the 1920s. The race was run on Saturday, as a preliminary to the Dieppe Grand Prix the following day. When the cars lined up for the 4 p.m. start, the complete change in national fortunes was plain to see, for the 4 fastest cars in practice were ERAs, with Seaman, Mays and Fairfield on the front row and the new boy, Bira on the second row. With the fall of the flag, Mays led the 19 starters, closely followed by Seaman. For 5 laps, the green and black ERAs were little more than a length apart while on lap 3 Bira, with scant regard for reputation despite his inexperience, passed Earl Howe to give the ERAs the first 3 places. Seaman's race was over after 5 laps when, to his disgust, the blower drive sheared and he stopped on the backleg of the course. Mays continued to increase his lead driving at such an impressive pace that "Motor Sport" was inspired to say "The ERA places an entirely new aspect on voiturette racing". The pace however was too hot, and after 16 laps, Mays retired with a burnt piston, but he had caused much grief among his pursuers, for Bira had to stop for new plugs and Earl Howe retired with erratic brakes. This left the consistent Pat Fairfield in the lead from Pierre Veyron in his now old-fashioned looking T51A Bugatti, who must have wondered if Fairfield would have trouble like the other British cars and thus enable him to restore the old order of things. Alas for Veyron, it was not to be, for Fairfield carried on steadily in his 1100 car and

68

a. 20th July, 1935: Dieppe G.P.: Charles Faroux stands in the middle of the road with the Tricolour under his arm. On the right Seaman wriggles in his ERA cockpit. Mays gives last minute instructions to his mechanic and Fairfield, the eventual winner, sits and waits patiently.

b. 20th July, 1935: Dieppe G.P.: Pierre Veyron holds his T51A Bugatti (30) on the handbrake and Robert Aumaitre his mechanic looks for the flag. Next to Veyron are the two chief backers of 1500cc racing. Gino Rovere holds the handbrake of his 4CM Maserati (52) while Humphrey Cook (ERA (6)) checks that he has preselected first gear.

c. 20th July, 1935: Dieppe G.P.: Bira (ERA) Leeds Rovere (4CM Maserati) on the back leg of the course.

d. 20th July, 1935: Dieppe G.P.: Earl Howe (Delage) leads Bira (ERA) round Maison Blanche corner. This was Bira's debut with the car.

won, having covered 243.44 kilometres during the 2 hour race. Bira had restarted with new plugs and chased Veyron with great determination, catching him just before the end to gain a most creditable second place for such an inexperienced driver. Just before the end of the race, a large van drove onto the course and blocked it momentarily at Maison Blanche corner, but outraged officials shooed it away without mishap.

Now indeed, ERA dominated the voiturette classes and on the form shown at Nurburg and Dieppe it did not seem likely that Maserati and Bugatti would have any immediate answer to the British car. Sadly, ERA now stood alone in defending British fortunes, for at the beginning of July, Lord Nuffield who had been the sole proprietor of the MG Car Company transferred his interests to Morris Motors Limited in the reorganization of the Nuffield Corporation. The first fruit of the transfer was an announcement by Lord Nuffield that all MG racing activities were to cease immediately and the racing department at Abingdon was closed virtually overnight; no more development was to be carried out on existing designs and no support was to be given to private entrants. In future it was announced that MG would only produce sports cars. Perhaps, on strictly commercial grounds, Lord Nuffield was right. The 750 and 1100 classes were dying, and the development of the proposed S-type 1500 capable of beating the ERA, would have been costly, and probably not justified commercially. From the point of view of the racing world, the decision was most unhappy. With the rapid development taking place among the voiturettes, the MG soon became an also-ran, and it was the end for the fertile and capable design team at Abingdon which had such shown impressive vision with the R-type.

With half the season over, Seaman was very disappointed with the results he had achieved with his ERA. The car was being prepared under contract by the ERA factory, and Seaman felt that the resources of the small works were not able to give his car the attention it needed, so he terminated the arrangement and employed his own mechanic to overhaul and prepare the car. His next engagement was at Pescara, on 15th August, but this was preceded by another

August 1935: Seaman tests his ERA at Monza before going to Pescara.

a. 15th August, 1935: Coppa Acerbo Pescara: Richard Seaman puts his tongue out at the photographer as he waits by his ERA before the start.

b. 15th August, 1935: Coppa Acerbo Pescara: Moris Bergamini considers his 1100 4CM Maserati while his mechanics seem to have better things to look at.

c. 15th August, 1935: Coppa Acerbo Pescara: Tuffanelli (4CM Maserati (21)) leads the field followed by Ettore Bianco (4CM Maserati (5)) at the 8.20 a.m. start. Seaman's ERA (26) is beside Tongue's R-type MG.

Italian event, the Coppa Ciano on the demanding Montenero circuit at Livorno. Once again, it was for 1100s, over 8 laps of the 20 km circuit; no K3 MGs were entered, so the Maseratis had it their own way. Ghersi, his eye now recovered, led for 3 laps but then retired leaving the race to Tuffanelli who despite stopping to cure a misfire won from Ettore Bianco who somehow managed to hurt his arm during the race. Reggie Tongue's R-type MG had been third for much of the race, but retired,★ and the third place at the finish went to a newcomer, Luigi Villoresi driving a Balilla Fiat. Dudley Froy retired with his Q-type MG when the crankshaft broke.

The Coppa Acerbo at Pescara started at the usual early hour of 8.30 a.m. and Seaman, despite a fast practice time, was on the back row of the balloted grid, behind the other 11 starters. Tuffanelli led the field away but his engine blew up at the beginning of the long straight, and at the end of the first lap, Seaman led by the remarkable margin of 30 seconds. Thereafter, the black ERA had no challenger and Seaman eased off to finish nearly $1^1\!2$ minutes ahead of Ettore Bianco. Steinweg was third in the white single seater T51A Bugatti that he had brought from Burggaller during the previous winter, and Pietro Ghersi was fourth, winning the 1100 class while Reggie Tongue was third in the small car class having mended his MG after Livorno. Enrico Platé had entered two of his old straight eight Talbots but it was a sign of their age and obsolescence that Platé, in the only car to finish, was just one place in front of the R-type MG. After the race, the organizers asked for the head of the ERA to be lifted so that the capacity could be checked. To general astonishment, including that of Seaman, it was declared to be 1300cc, until someone pointed out that the piston in the measured bore was not at bottom dead centre!

The speed and vitality the ERA had brought to the 1500 class had a remarkable effect. Voiturette racing was now being regarded in an entirely different light and this was shown when Rudolf Caracciola was interviewed by Henry Heck and was reported in "The Motor" as saying that there was now justification for a full International 1500cc formula as a recognised training class. A week later, reflecting on the ERA successes, "The Motor" expressed the editorial view that "It would not be surprising to find that more and more 1500cc races will be run".

Conscious of their improved status, the best of the 1500 competitors assembled at Berne for the Prix de Berne, which was to precede the Swiss Grand Prix on 25th August. Run again on the Bremgarten circuit, the race attracted 18 starters and in practice, Raymond Mays was fastest, having again used his Bentley saloon to learn the circuit. Bira was on the front row with Mays, while Seaman shared the second row with Ghersi. Seaman had felt during practice, that his car was not giving its full power and suspected that the fuel supplied by the organizers for the 1500 class differed from its declared specification. He had a sample analysed by a chemist in Berne who confirmed

Practice had been eventful for Tongue ". . . the Grand Prix cars and the Voiturette cars practised at the same time. I remember very well Nuvolari coming to me in the hotel and laughing at the fact that when passing me on a mountain road with a sheer drop of several thousand feet he had pulled over and left me little room. He could quite easily have put me over the side and thought it was very funny." – *Letter R.E. Tongue to the Author October 1978*

the suspicion. Seaman had some fuel made up to the correct formula so his ERA was the only one which came to the line with the right mixture. With the benefit of his front row position, Mays took the lead at the start, pursued by Seaman, Lord Howe with his Delage and Bira, but the works ERA began to misfire, and Seaman swept past, half way round the first lap, and as far as the lead was concerned, the race was over. Seaman pulled away from his pursuers by about $2\frac{1}{2}$ to 3 seconds a lap and went on to win after a most impressive drive. Mays, despite the misfire and oil breather problems held second place for 2 laps but then stopped for urgent attention to his ERA which let Bira through, now followed by Ghersi. The hot pace set by the ERAs was too much for the Maserati and it fell back, being passed by Earl Howe. Bira and Howe held onto their places and finished exactly one minute apart. It had been a bad day for Bugattis for Pierre Veyron had fallen out with a blocked fuel line, while Sojka's car had a slipping clutch.

a. 25th August 1935: Prix de Berne: On the grid are Kohlrausch (Magic Midget MG (54)) Evans (R-type MG (64)) and Tongue (R-type MG (70)). No. 88 is Ruesch's 4CS Maserati which went so well in the Eifelrennen.

b. 15th October, 1935: Circuit of Modena: Tuffanelli (1100 4 CM Maserati) who won the 1100cc class and came second overall is leading Rovere (1500 4CM Maserati).

With his professional approach to his racing, now that his car was prepared immaculately, Seaman was becoming the man to beat and it was probably much to the relief of the wholly Italian entry at Modena, on 15th September, that neither Seaman or any other ERAs were entered. Of the 10 starters 8 were Maseratis, the interlopers being Cecchini's MG and Platé's ancient Talbot. The race provided all the drama that seemed inevitable on the short Italian circuits. Berrone's 1500 4CM Maserati led all the way, chased by Bianco who then crashed, after which Barbieri took up the class, until he, too, retired, and the 1100 4CM Maseratis of Tuffanelli and Bergamini finished second and third, the old Talbot came fourth but 2 laps behind, while Cecchini was out of luck and gave up in the early laps.

If the Continental drivers hoped for a respite from the British onslaught, this was to be denied to them even in the only race left in the calendar, the Masaryk Junior Grand Prix at Brno on 29th September. Seaman made the long journey from England and his efforts were richly rewarded for despite a practice crash which bent the ERA's front axle, he was able to start and he led the race for the whole distance. Despite all his efforts, Pierre Veyron could only urge his T51A Bugatti into second place nearly 3¾ minutes behind Seaman. Keeping up his consistent record in this race, Bruno Sojka finished third, his fifth consecutive place in this race. Sadly, right at the end of the season Rudolph Steinweg was killed in his Bugatti at the Mount Gugger hill climb in Hungary. A cafe owner from Munich, at 47, Steinweg was one of the oldest voiturette drivers and had been a regular entrant for several years, at first with his C6 Amilcar, and then with the Bugatti.

The 1935 season had seen a complete reversal of fortunes in voiturette racing. The ERA had wholly fulfilled the hopes and expectations of its supporters and had won every 1500 race in which it had started. Probably most significant of all, the British car had given an entirely new look to the class. The car was reliable, impressive to watch and above-all very fast. The average race speeds recorded by the cars would have been creditable for a grand prix car 3 years earlier. Race organizers could now be confident that a voiturette race would have enough appeal for most spectators and this was summed up nicely in the editorial of "Motor Sport" in August 1935. "The revival of 1500cc racing has been largely brought about by the British enterprise behind the construction of the ERA. When the car was first planned the chief argument against it was the dearth of races for which it could be entered. Now most of the Continental organizers are considering running 1500cc races. Production has created a demand." This was echoed in France by the great Charles Faroux, the doyen of motoring journalists, who issued a virtual directive in saying that the promoters of small events would now be wise to run 1500 races. The impact of the ERA had left the other manufacturers breathless; MG was a spent force and Bugatti was in ever-deepening shadow. There were rumours of a new car, but only rumours. Maserati had resolved to meet the British challenge however, and reports came from Bologna in the Autumn of 1935 of a new 6-cylinder 1500.

With the rise of the new British marque came a new generation of drivers, British or British-based. The dominant driver of the season had been Richard Seaman, and his decision after Dieppe to have his car prepared by his own mechanic was the turning point in his season and perhaps justifies the speculation, that if the car had been properly prepared, Seaman would probably have won at Nurburg and Dieppe as well. Raymond Mays had been dogged by the same problems of preparation at the Bourne factory as Seaman, but while he had only won at the Eifelrennen, he had been leading at Dieppe and Berne when the car misbehaved. Mays was now one of the major competitors, though before 1935, he had had relatively little road racing experience and his competition driving had been restricted to the particularly English pastimes of the short sprint and sand racing. Of the other ERA drivers, Pat Fairfield had lived down the "Skidder" reputation and become a model of rapid consistency, with his victories at Douglas, Donington and Dieppe, while Bira was already being tipped as a man who would be bound to win a race before long. The Continental drivers were overwhelmed by their British rivals, but poor Pierre Veyron had struggled with an uncompetitive car and had gained most of his results by skill and tenacity. The Italian hope, Giuseppe Farina had already been lured away to the heady world of grand prix racing; the voiturette world would see him again but in very different circumstances.

In the Autumn of 1935, the Maserati brothers toiled in Bologna to perfect their new car, and at Bourne Raymond Mays and Peter Berthon looked with mesmerised fascination at the power offered by the Zoller supercharger. In London, Richard Seaman had long discussions with Giulio Ramponi, Whitney Straight's former chief mechanic, who had now joined him, and then went to visit Earl Howe.

1936

O N 30TH OCTOBER 1935, Italian forces invaded Abyssinia, a substantial step towards embroiling Europe in the Second World War, and one which polarised the countries of Europe into pro- and anti-Italian camps. The League of Nations, outraged by the Italian action, immediately voted in Geneva for the imposition of economic sanctions upon Italy, although these sanctions were not supported by Germany, Austria, Switzerland and Hungary. However, in order to soften the blow (and make the sanctions virtually useless) the League decided that there should be no embargo upon oil supplies to Italy, thus leaving the Italian economy virtually unharmed, and merely leaving Italian national feelings suitably outraged.

The effect upon the motor racing world was immediate, as it was declared that no Italian team would race in a country which had voted in favour of the sanctions. This was perhaps less impressive than it sounded, as the only major motor racing country affected was France, for Great Britain virtually did not exist as far as the Italian teams were concerned. France on the other hand, had already taken steps to deal with such a move by the Italians. Dispirited by the French failures in grand prix racing in 1935, and the inability or disinclination of Ettore Bugatti to produce a new grand prix car, the Automobile Club de France announced in the Autumn of 1935 that the 1936 French Grand Prix would be held for sports cars. Most major French race promoters followed the lead given by the National Club and it was soon apparent that a grand prix event would be a rarity in France in 1936. For those organizers who still wished to see racing cars on their circuits, the 1500cc voiturette was the obvious solution and it was now clear that the status of the voiturette was fully recognised. A meeting was held in Zurich on 7th December 1935 of the Bureau Permanent International des Constructeurs des Automobiles, attended by all the major European grand prix car manufacturers and as a sign of the respect that the marque had gained, Raymond Mays was invited to attend on behalf of ERA. The object of the meeting was to discuss and put forward proposals for the new grand prix formula to take effect when the 750 kg formula expired on 31st December 1937.★ Not much came out of the meeting but there was some support for the idea that the next formula should be for 1500cc cars. Mays prudently suggested

★The formula had been extended for another year in October 1935 by the AIACR.

that before such a proposal was adopted, the existing formula should be continued for three years and a 1500 race should be held as a preliminary event before each Grande Epreuve, thus giving time for the public reaction to the smaller cars to be assessed. Mays' view was supported by Alfred Neubauer who represented probably the strongest voice at the conference table, that of Mercedes-Benz. Nothing came of Mays' proposal and the discussions as to the nature of the next grand prix formula dragged on into 1936, but it was clear that although the future of grand prix racing was somewhat uncertain at the beginning of 1936, the growing and active 1500 class was ready to meet any calls to be made upon it.

Spring 1936: Prince Chula has bought a new Ford V8 van to carry Bira's ERA "Romulus".

The successes of 1935 had resulted in a satisfactory demand and the ERA factory at Bourne was busy in the Spring putting new cars together for eager customers, by the end of April, seven new cars had been delivered to private owners. The Works fitted a 1500cc engine to the 1935 2 litre car for Mays and also built up a new car for the Algerian driver Marcel Lehoux* who had previously raced for Bugatti, Maserati and the Scuderia Ferrari and who had signed up with ERA when the dearth of French racing cars and racing was apparent. Following the experiments of 1935, Mays and Peter Berthon had decided that the Works cars should have Zoller superchargers for the 1936 season; despite technical problems, the lure of the extra power had proved irresistible, and perhaps essential, with the threat of the new 6C Maseratis.

The 1935 Season had been a total disaster for the Maserati factory, Their V8RI GP cars had been completely outclassed and the 4CM voiturette could offer no resistance to the ERA. The links between the Scuderia Subalpina and

*Another works car was completed during the 1936 season but did not run in voiturette events.

the Bologna factory had become stronger as the season had passed and Gino Rovere, who was a manufacturer of American cloth from Turin, provided some essential financial support. The Maserati concern was receiving no financial aid from the Italian government and the brothers decided that their participation in GP racing during the 1936 season would be very restricted. In January 1936, Gino Rovere became President of the Maserati Company, and with his renewed support, a complete programme was prepared for a works Team for the new season. Rovere bought back the cars of the Scuderia Subalpina as a basis for the 1936 works Team and signed up Count Trossi and Omobono Tenni the Italian motorcycle champion as his drivers. Luigi Della Chiesa had reformed the Subalpina Team meanwhile, as the Scuderia Torino, with Siena, Ghersi and Dusio as his drivers. These changes renewed the enthusiasm at the little Bologna factory and a completely new design was being prepared. The new car, the 6C, had a 6-cylinder twin ohc engine of 65mm × 75mm fed by a Roots type supercharger driven from the nose of the crankshaft. Power output was said to be 175 bhp at 6500 rpm. Electron had been used extensively both in the engine and the chassis in order to keep the weight down and the chassis was a considerable step forward in voiturette design. The front suspension was independent, using double wishbones and torsion bars, although at the rear there were the conventional semi-elliptic springs. The car had a neat single seater body with a streamlined cowl over the radiator and front suspension and it was clearly the fore-runner of the next generation of voiturettes.

From France, rumours still came of a new Bugatti, but even the British motoring press, which had a very soft spot for Ettore Bugatti and his cars, was beginning to be rather sceptical about any new car appearing. Voiturette racing was still to have a French car however, albeit with a very strong English accent. In the Autumn of 1935, Richard Seaman suspected that the 1936 works ERA would be much quicker than the earlier cars and began to consider a quicker car

a. Spring 1936: The rebuilt engine of Seaman's newly-acquired Delage being bench-tested in Ramponi's workshop.

b. Spring 1936: Ernesto Maserati hoped the torsion-bar independent front suspension of the new 6CM Maserati would enable it to beat the ERAs.

to replace his own ERA. Seaman discussed the matter with Giulio Ramponi who, to Seaman's astonishment, said there was a 1500 racing car in England which would be capable of matching anything that ERA Limited could do; this was the 1927 GP Delage belonging to Earl Howe. At first, Seaman dismissed the suggestion as he felt that the Delage was too old and outdated, but Ramponi pursued his arguments convincingly, pointing out that the Delage could be lightened considerably, and with the advances in fuels and metallurgy which had taken place since the car was built, the engine could now give much more power with reliability. Seaman, who had great respect for Ramponi's knowledge and ability, was persuaded that he should approach Earl Howe who reluctantly agreed to sell the Delage for £1500, prompted partly by his wish to race an ERA. Ramponi stripped the Delage completely and the engine was rebuilt with a higher compression ratio and the valve timing was restored to its original setting. It appeared, when the engine was stripped, that the marks by which the engine had been timed by Earl Howe's mechanics, had been wrongly inscribed on the timing gears and there had been an appreciable power loss. Ramponi paid much attention to detail fitting, as it was the intention that the engine once rebuilt, should last at least half the racing season without a major overhaul. The chassis was lightened and braced with wooden blocks inside the channel section and the front springs were outrigged. Large brakes were fitted and a new and lighter body was built, which had the significant feature of a steel fuel tank with a 40 gallon capacity which comprised the tail of the car. The heavy ENV preselector gearbox used by Earl Howe was replaced by a lighter 5-speed box from a 1925 V12 2-litre Delage. The reaction of the motor racing world to Seaman's purchase was much as Seaman's reaction had been to Ramponi's original suggestion. Although too polite to say so, it was clear that many felt Seaman had made an error of judgment.

An inspection of the racing calendar showed that the quality of the races in 1936 was likely to be high. The minor "second division" events were gone and all the races gave the promise of a high class competitive entry, furthermore the 750 and 1100 classes had been almost universally abandoned, even in Italy. It was therefore rather a pity that in March 1936, the Austin Motor Company announced the most advanced 750cc racing car yet built. The new Austin, which had been designed by Murray Jamieson under the personal direction of Lord Austin, and allegedly at his own expense, had a supercharged twin ohc engine in a neat chassis with transverse leaf semi independent front suspension and a rigid rear axle on quarter elliptic springs. The power output was said to be 116 bhp at 8500 rpm and when the car was announced, it looked and was finished, like a miniature grand prix machine. It made a great impression on the opposition for Raymond Mays in a letter to "The Motor" described the car as "the most wonderful machine designed for a long time" Immediately, there were rumours that the design was to be the basis of a 1500cc V8 with a rear engine, but a more lasting effect of this new car was to make British race organizers renew their commitment to the class handicap for most long distance events. The British motor industry had so little interest in racing that organizers felt obliged to give full support to any manufacturer who took the plunge. The little Austin proved to be such an effective car that it is perhaps permissable to

a. 10th April 1936: Coupe de Prince Rainier, Monaco: The cars line up before early morning practice. Two of the 4CM Maseratis are in the foreground.

b. 11th April, 1936: Coupe de Prince Rainier, Monaco: The cars assemble behind the pits. No. 44 is Frank McEvoy's 4CM Maserati. Behind it is the new 6CM Maserati (66) making its debut. Bira and Gino Rovere engage in earnest conversation behind the 6CM.

c. 11th April, 1936: Coupe de Prince Rainier Monaco: Raymond Mays strolls nonchalantly past the works ERAs. No. 58 is Marcel Lehoux's car later to be destroyed at Deauville.

d. 11th April, 1936: Coupe de Prince Rainier Monaco: Lehoux takes the Tabac corner followed by three Maseratis.

e. Spring 1936: Hans Ruesch converted his 4CS Maserati with Dubonnet front suspension and a new body.

surmise that a 1500 Austin would have been a most formidable machine.

Demonstrating how important the 1500 class had now become, the very first race of the season on Saturday, 11th April was a new event, the Coupe de Prince Rainier which was to be a preliminary event the day before the Monaco Grand Prix, on the original classic round-the-houses circuit in Monte Carlo. The organizers, perhaps unrealistically, had intended to invite only 3 cars from each country to compete, but it was soon obvious that this was impractical. A very good entry was received and 18 cars came to the line to compete for the 30,000 Franc prize. The principal contenders were 6 ERAs matched against 9 Maseratis, one being the new 6CM prototype driven fittingly by Gino Rovere; these were supported by single entries of Bugatti, Amilcar and Alta – the latter an enterprising British car, making its first entry in a Continental voiturette race. Notable absentees were Richard Seaman, whose Delage was not yet ready, and Pierre Veyron, while Robert Kohlrausch had the misfortune to wreck the Magic Midget MG in a collision while driving through the streets on the way to the start. In practice, Earl Howe with his new blue ERA had profited from his previous experience of the circuit and had been equal fastest with Raymond Mays and Omobono Tenni, the Italian motorcycle champion who shared together the front row of the 3 × 3 grid. There had been some doubts if Bira would be able to start, as his eye was cut when his goggles were shattered while driving in the British Empire Trophy, the usual handicap event at Donington the previous Saturday, but his vision had recovered sufficiently for him to make the third row of the grid. Immediately before the start Peter Berthon gave instructions that the carburettor needles in the works ERAs of Mays and Lehoux, and also Howe's car, were to be changed. This inexplicable decision had a considerable influence on the result of the race. The disappointingly small crowd, perhaps deterred by the cold, dull weather, saw Howe take the lead at the start, closely followed by Mays and Tenni. This order was maintained for 3 laps then Bianco, who was fourth with his 4CM Maserati, spun entering the Casino Square. The cars following him spun in attempts to avoid a collision, and one of the victims was Pat Fairfield who stalled and was unable to restart his engine on the handle, as the regulations required, as that vital component was bent underneath the front of the white ERA, as a result of a collision. Fairfield received a push start, and was instantly disqualified, although he was not to know this until after the race. Perhaps in sympathy with Fairfield's predicament, but more certainly as a result of the carburettor adjustment, the ERAs of Howe and Mays started to misfire, and both made for the pits on lap 4, where, after a plug change Mays' car could only be restarted with a push, thus being disqualified like Fairfield. These dramas left Tenni's 4CM Maserati in front, and he made the most of his opportunity, and started to pull away from Bira who was now in second place, having passed Luigi Villoresi's 4CM Maserati after dodging his way through the spinning cars. At 25 laps, Tenni led Bira by almost a minute, but his brakes were failing and under pressure from the Siamese, he hit the sandbags lining the Gasworks hairpin on lap 35, and his race was over. Bira now led easily from Nicholas Embiricos, a Greek driver, who had bought one of the 1935 ex-Works A-type ERAs which had been painted grey, and had worked his way steadily up the field. For a while, Freddie Zehender, who had

81

had much Grand Prix experience, had taken over the new 6CM Maserati from Rovere, and looked as if he would challenge Bira, but the new engine, perhaps not yet appreciating what was required of it, blew up on lap 43 at Ste Devote, and another multiple crash followed as cars spun on the oil. This time the 4CM Maserati of McEvoy the Australian★ and the 4CS of Hans Ruesch★★ were eliminated and a shaken Villoresi continued after hitting the sandbags. Bira completed the 50 laps and was the worthy winner of a dramatic race, thus gaining the first of many victories to come. Behind him Lehoux had passed Embiricos in the closing laps to take second place, having climbed up through the field after delays in encountering the straw bales, and stopping for plugs on his works ERA. The pace and the drama had eliminated all but 6 cars.

There was now to be a long break before the next International 1500 race, but some of the British competitors took the chance of keeping their hands in, by competing in a minor club meeting at Donington on 9th May. The meeting was important, for Ramponi had finished work on the Delage and it appeared for its first race, looking slightly sinister in its new black paint. After winning a handicap, the Delage ran in a 5 lap 1500 scratch race where Seaman had little difficulty in disposing of the ERA opposition and showed that the Delage was likely to be a formidable competitor. Ramponi had obviously done his work well, for after the Donington meeting, the only modification the Delage needed was a change in the size of the front wheel brake cylinders, as Seaman had found the front braking too powerful.

Despite the criticisms and the financial losses, the RAC had decided to persevere with motor racing in the Isle of Man and at the fourth attempt, the race seemed to be what everyone wanted, a straightforward 1500 race with no restrictions. Unfortunately, the Isle of Man was too far away from Italy to draw the 6CM Maserati and none of the Continental independents was attracted, so the entries were confined to British-based cars, though the foreign element was added by the presence of Bira and Lehoux. For the race on 28th May, a new 4 mile (6.4 km) course had been chosen which used the motor cycle TT pits. The course was criticised for being too narrow and bumpy, with a poor surface and Freddie Dixon withdrew his Riley after practice stating that he considered the course was too dangerous, though perhaps, the lack of enthusiasm that the Riley had shown for the new Centric supercharger fitted to it was a contributing factor. It was reported in "The Motor" that Seaman had been offered a works 6CM Maserati for the race but had declined, feeling that the Delage was more suitable. Perhaps it was the threat of the Delage that stimulated ERA to invite Earl Howe to join the works team with his new car, which was repainted pale green like the other two cars of the team. Howe's car had been practised by Lehoux who had put it on the front row of the grid and with this to encourage him and in front of a large crowd, Howe led the 18 starters away pursued by Seaman, Bira and Cyril Paul in a new ERA. On lap 4 the black Delage passed its

★Although an Australian, McEvoy had represented Great Britain in the Winter Olympic Games in 1936 as a member of the four-man bobsleigh team which won the bronze medal.
★★During the winter this car had been rebodied with a radiator cowling reminiscent of an Auto Union and had been fitted with Dubonnet i.f.s.

a. 28th May, 1936: R.A.C. International Light Car Race Douglas: Earl Howe (ERA (16)) and Bira (ERA (17)) lead the field away from the start. Seaman's Delage can just be seen behind Bira.

b. 14th June, 1936: Eifelrennen: Seaman stands behind the Delage (68) and looks thoughtfully at the MG Magic Midget (54).

c. 28th May, 1936: R.A.C. International Light Car Race Douglas: Seaman, on his way to victory follows Howe and Briggs (K3 MG) round Parkfield Corner.

(a)

(c)

d. 28th May 1936: R.A.C. International Light Car Race Douglas: Seaman (Delage) leads Briggs (K3 MG) into Onchan village.

e. 21st June, 1936: Picardie G.P.: At the start of the final the tar is melting on the road surface. Trossi (Maserati 6CM) and Pat Fairfield (ERA (14)) slide down the camber.

f. 21st June 1936: Picardie G.P.: Earl Howe (ERA) takes the corner before the pits. The road surface is melting in the heat of the day.

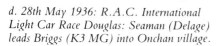

(d)

(f)

former owner, as Howe began to slow, troubled by excess air pressure in his fuel tank. Once Seaman took the lead, the race was decided, for the opposition realised that not only was the Delage too fast to catch, but it became obvious Seaman was intending to complete the 200 mile race without refuelling, whereas all the ERAs would need to stop. Bira and Paul held their places behind Seaman although Paul was led briefly by Lehoux who then had a brush with a stone wall and fell back. The other Works ERAs had an unhappy race. Howe's fuel tank swelled with the pressure until it touched the back axle and then split, while Mays who was driving the only Zoller supercharged car then built, appeared to find it unsuited to the circuit and then retired with a broken half shaft after 35 laps having run no higher than fourth.★ Charlie Dodson driving the new 750 twin cam Austin showed that it was remarkably fast, and held fourth place until a flying stone shattered a plug insulator and caused a long stop. Seaman drove on steadily, reeling off the 50 laps and finished 1 minute 17 seconds in front of Bira to gain a most sensational victory. The lone Delage had beaten 10 ERAs and in doing so had averaged 7 mpg and finished with 7 gallons in the tank. During the race, Seaman had heard a crunch from the rear axle but the car seemed unaffected. When the axle was stripped later, however, Ramponi found that teeth were missing from the crown wheel and the pinion! Seaman's victory was hailed by the popular press, which gave the impression that the race had been won by a rebuilt wreck, driven by a penniless undergraduate, though the truth could not have been a greater contrast on both counts. After the race there was a uproar over the award of the prize money. The sums stated in the race programme were up to £100 more than those set out in the regulations, but the regulations also provided that the prizes could be increased at the organizers' discretion. The RAC tried to pay out the smaller sums and the subsequent row lasted for several weeks until the larger sums were eventually paid under threat of legal action by the outraged drivers.

With a new crown wheel and pinion fitted, Seaman set off with the Delage to the Nurburgring, to complete in the Eifelrennen on 14th June, where his main opponents were to be the works ERAs and Bira, and the 6CM Maserati supported by many 4CMs. After two hot days of practice, race day was cool with rain and mist. As an indication of the growing sophistication of voiturette racing, the works ERAs and Bira's car were started on the line by portable electric starters. From the start, Seaman took the lead, but half way round the first lap, he made an error of judgment and spun off; the Delage was bogged down in mud at the side of the road, and he was only able to restart long after all the field had gone by. The works ERAs were in their usual difficulties, Mays and Howe stopping with misfiring while Lehoux's car lacked revs, so at the end of the first lap Count Trossi led with the new 6CM Maserati, pursued by Tenni with the older 4CM while Bira worked hard to keep up in third place. Behind Bira was the new 750 Austin driven by Walter Baumer which was again

★The ERA team had been experimenting with a ZF limited slip differential and an initial error in the design of the ZF had resulted in seizure and fracture of the half shafts. When first tested on a road circuit the ZF gave little advantage over the standard type and made the car more difficult to control which may have indicated another manufacturing fault. (Letter: Peter Berthon to Earl Howe 12th August 1936.)

showing the speed that had already been impressive in the Isle of Man. Seaman, having lost so much time, toured round to the pits and retired. At half way, 4 laps, the order was unchanged and the 6CM was 53 secs in front of Tenni and a whole 2 minutes in front of Bira who was still being chased by the Austin. The independent front suspension of the Maserati was paying great dividends on the bumps and swerves of the Nurburgring and there was nothing the ERAs could do about it. With the race in his pocket Trossi eased off and won by 46.2 secs from Tenni, Bira kept third place and Baumer eventually had to yield fourth place to Lehoux.

The ERA supporters were now totally deflated, for they had been beaten first by the Delage and now by the 6CM Maserati, but a week later, the chance came to gain revenge at Peronne in the Picardie Grand Prix. The Works ERAs had increased supercharger pressure to take advantage of the long straights, and it was also reported that the road holding of the Zoller cars had been improved, as fitting the big Zoller supercharger behind the engine had previously affected the weight distribution and handling. The race was to be in two heats and a final with half the entry running in each heat. The works Maserati team suffered a cruel blow in practice when one of the mechanics crashed while testing Rovere's 6CM and received severe head injuries when the car went through a barbed wire fence. The damaged car was withdrawn and Rovere had to use a spare 4CM, but Trossi grasped the Trident and led the first 10 lap heat until he was passed by Fairfield who had now joined the ERA team as Howe had done earlier. Trossi regained the lead on lap 4 and finished 8 secs in front of Fairfield, with Bira and Lehoux close behind. The second heat looked as if it would offer more excitement, for Seaman led at the start followed by Mays and Howe. Mays, using the Zoller power to the full, passed Seaman on the straight and estimated that the car was reaching 150 mph. Seaman commented that it was like being passed by an Auto Union, so May's estimate was probably accurate. The season was continuing to be a disaster for the ERA team, for the speed and the power of the Zoller over-excited two con-rods after 5 laps, and Mays stopped with two large holes in the crankcase. His short drive had not been an easy one, for the ERA road-holding was still troublesome and the car had been understeering badly. Afterwards, Mays said "Heaving it out of corners was a most unpleasant pastime." With Mays gone, Seaman ran on steadily to win the heat from Howe and Tongue but the Delage's time was nearly a minute slower than Trossi in the first heat, and during the lunch break, Prince Chula noticed that Seaman was very preoccupied and wondered if he was affected by the intense heat of the day. Only 8 cars left the line in the final for Lehoux's Zoller ERA did not get away as a con-rod broke at the start. Fairfield led from Trossi and Bira, but the Maserati was running erratically and Bira soon passed it. Seaman disputed third place with Trossi but on lap 4 the Delage ran off the road on the 90° turn in the village of Brie. The car struck a wall and the steering arm, rear wheel and brake drum were damaged. Seaman was unhurt but very shaken as the steering had failed. Inspection showed the steering box had split, almost certainly as the result of the crash at Nurburg the previous week.* Bira closed up on Fairfield and the two

*In his book "Dick Seaman, Racing Motorist", Prince Chula stated that the crash was caused by

Inspection showed the steering box had split, almost certainly as the result of the crash at Nurburg the previous week.★ Bira closed up on Fairfield and the two ERAs changed places several times in a stern struggle, until the last lap, when Fairfield attempted to out-brake Bira on the Brie corner, overshot, and struck the bank. By the time he had recovered, the Siamese had gone and á disappointed Fairfield had to settle for second place 31 secs behind. Lord Howe came home third while the Australian Frank McEvoy was the only other finisher in a new 6CM Maserati, the first to be delivered to a customer, some 2 laps behind, for Trossi had fallen back and stopped after 10 laps with clutch failure.

Trossi and Rovere now returned to Bologna with their cars and a new clutch was fitted to the 6CM before its debut in front of the home crowd at Milan the following week. The 1500 race was a preliminary·to the Milan G.P. on a new 1.6 mile (2.6 km) circuit round the Sempione Park in the City. An all-Italian entry turned up for the 40 lap race which was an easy win for the new car, and at the end, Trossi was 1 min. 18 secs in front of a newcomer, Emilio Villoresi, the younger brother of Luigi who was now returning to the sport, having finished his military service, and was sharing the 4CM that Luigi had been driving earlier in the season; Luigi had entered the old family Fiat Balilla. Rovere elected to drive a 4CM 1100, perhaps as the 1500 had not recovered from Peronne, and finished fifth, 3 laps behind Trossi. The Baronessa Avanzo who had raced sports Alfa Romeos for the Scuderia Ferrari some years before finished 9th in her Maserati. While the Italians were indulging in a National event, the British drivers were preparing for their own 1500 race, the Nuffield Trophy at Donington on 4th July. Yet again, this was a class handicap and the scratch ERAs overwhelmed the 750s and 1100s to take the first 3 places. The winner was Charles Martin, followed by Arthur Dobson and Peter Whitehead. Bira appeared in an unfamiliar car, a side valve 750 Austin entered by the Austin Motor Co. but it did not run well.

The damage to the Delage took Ramponi longer to repair than he and Seaman expected, and they were forced to borrow a steering box from Capt. J.C. Davis, the owner of the other G.P. Delage in England. The delay prevented Seaman from making the long trip to the South West of France for the Abi G.P. Raymond Mays was detained in England by business affairs so the ERA team was to be Lord Howe, Lehoux and Fairfield. Another 6CM Maserati now appeared, to be driven by the Hungarian Lazlo Hartmann, while a car entered by the Swiss, Luciano Uboldi had a 6C engine in a special chassis allegedly designed by Vittorio Jano, the famous Alfa Romeo designer. A rare return was made by Pierre Veyron, still with his veteran T51A Bugatti, although it was said that his new Bugatti would have been ready, had the Molsheim factory not been closed by the strikes which crippled France during the summer of 1936. At the beginning of the season, Prince Chula had bought another new ERA for Bira, to back up the original car. Bira immediately named the cars "Romulus" and "Remus", his heavenly twins. "Romulus", the original car, had been used in all the International 1500 events so far, while "Remus" had been kept for British and Irish events, with rather indifferent results. Albi was to see

86

the first appearance of "Remus" in a voiturette race with a doubtful reputation to redeem.

As in previous years, all the cars ran in two heats of 20 laps with the final result found from the aggregate times of both heats. In front of a large crowd, Lehoux led the 13 starters using the power of the Zoller blown ERA. Bira held second place in front of Fairfield and after 16 laps was able to pass Lehoux whose car was losing its tune. Bira went on to win from Lehoux and Fairfield. It was not a good Maserati day as Ettore Bianco with a 4CM was fourth nearly $2^1{}_2$ minutes behind Bira while Veyron's old Bugatti managed to hold off Hartmann's 6CM for fifth place. The heat had its drama when Frank McEvoy spun his 6CM Maserati on the bend before the pits and rolled the car on the straw bales lining the circuit. Luckily, he was thrown clear unhurt but the car caught fire and was extensively damaged before the blaze was extinguished. In the second heat, only 6 cars left the line as the Works ERAs maintained their expected form. Lehoux's supercharger seized at the start and Fairfield had gearbox trouble, a problem which had stopped Earl Howe in the first heat. With the collapse of the opposition, Bira won the heat and thus the overall race much as he pleased. After following Bira for 10 laps, Reggie Tongue with the only other ERA, retired with a puncture, and a rather surprised Veyron finished second in front of Hans Ruesch's rebodied 4CS Maserati. After his great feats three years earlier, it was sad that this was the end of Veyron's career as a voiturette driver. He never raced a 1500 again though he was to gain equal fame driving Bugattis in sports car races during the next three seasons.

A week after Albi, Marcel Lehoux was entered for the Deauville G.P., a formula race run in the streets of the fashionable French resort. His car was fitted with a 2 litre engine, and while holding third place, near the end of the race, he had a collision with Farina's Alfa Romeo which was leading. The ERA overturned and caught fire and Lehoux was killed instantly. He was a cheerful, popular man, older at 48, than most drivers and his death greatly upset the racing world, and was a considerable blow to ERA where his experience had been of much value to the team. The Deauville meeting was ill-starred, for Raymond Chambost was also killed when his G.P. Maserati overturned. Chambost had gained some notable successes in voiturette races with a G.P. Salmson some four years before.

In the latter half of July, the small Seaman equipe crossed the English Channel and the team's Dodge lorry set off across France, in the direction of Italy, with the Delage aboard. The car had been repaired, and Ramponi had changed the engine for another, which he had been rebuilding during the early part of the season. The new engine developed about 10 bhp more than the previous one. With half the season over, Seaman's fortunes had been mixed. Apart from a notable victory in the Isle of Man, the Delage had not been very successful and Seaman's critics felt their predictions had been right and the Delage had been a mistake. During the next four weeks, not only Seaman would silence the critics for ever, but he and the Delage would make a motor racing legend.

The first stop for the Dodge was at Livorno, where on 2nd August, the Coppa Ciano meeting was being run on a new circuit in the southern suburbs of the town replacing the Montenero mountain course. The race attracted all the

87

a. 25th July, 1936: Practice for Coppa Ciano Livorno: Seaman passes the tribunes in the final session. The hastily painted number is evidence of the car's late arrival after delays at the Italian customs.

b. 26th July, 1936: Coppa Ciano Livorno: Trossi is about to take the lead from Seaman whose Delage is suffering from fuel starvation.

c. 26th July, 1936: Coppa Ciano Livorno: Trossi in his 6CM rounds the tribune loop on his way to victory.

d. 26th July 1936: Coppa Ciano Livorno: McEvoy (6CM Maserati) leads Rovere (4CM Maserati) round the tribune loop.

(b)

best Italian voiturettes, and Seaman, whose luck did not yet seem to be turning, had the misfortune to be held up at the frontier by the Italian Customs so he was only able to reach Livorno for the last practice session. As a result, the Delage could not be given final adjustments and the air pressure pump was not working properly. At the start, the Delage took the lead and held it for three laps, until the air pressure fell in the tank and the engine began to misfire with fuel starvation. The Delage gradually dropped back down the field, and Trossi delighted the crowd by taking the lead. He was not caught though he did not have an easy win as he was chased very hard by Nicholas Embiricos in his grey ERA. It was clear that the ERA was faster than Trossi's 6CM Maserati, but the greater experience of the Italian told and as a local report put it, the Greek's ERA "was less docile and less prepared". Eventually Trossi won by 58 seconds, while Luigi Villoresi who was gaining experience steadily, finished third with his 4CM Maserati. A very disappointed Seaman brought the Delage, popping and banging, into sixth place.

After Livorno, Seaman's little team had nearly a fortnight to make a leisurely journey to Pescara for the Coppa Acerbo, an event with happy memories for Seaman for the past two years. At Pescara, the Maserati team appeared again, and were joined by Bira and Tongue with their ERAs. Now at last, all went well for the Delage and Seaman dominated both practice and the race. The Delage took the lead at the 8 a.m. start and was quite unbeatable. Trossi did his best, but was 1 minute 23 seconds behind at the finish, while Bira whose ERA (Romulus) had lost oil pressure in practice and was not running properly, retired when in a fading second place, after 4 laps. As the ERA stopped at its pit, Bira and Chula were more discomfited as the car caught fire, though it was quickly extinguished. Ruesch finished a distant third with his modified 4CS Maserati while Frank McEvoy was fourth with his rebuilt 6CM and Moris Bergmini was fifth driving a new 6CM. The Italian had hastily rebuilt his new car after spoiling it in a practice crash.

Having repeated his 1935 victory at Pescara, Seaman now had his sights set on a hat trick of victories at Berne. Run once again as a preliminary to the Swiss G.P. on 23rd August, the Prix de Berne did not attract quite such a powerful entry in 1936 principally because the works 6CM Maseratis were withdrawn, being declared "unready". It may be wondered if the knowledge that the Delage and the works ERAs would be present had made the Bologna factory a trifle dilatory in their preparation! Once again, the Zoller blown ERAs showed their tremendous speed and Fairfield made the fastest practice lap at 92.97 mph, 8 secs. faster than the previous lap record. However, the form the ERA team had been showing did not promote confidence in their prospects and "Motor Sport" summed it up saying "The history of the ERA team for winning races, or shall we say losing them, did not encourage people to believe in their chances of victory".★ Instead of appearing in their usual pale green, the works ERAs were

---

★The preparation of the works ERAs during 1936 was very poor. Furthermore, the Bourne factory seemed to be seeking problems. Some years later Peter Berthon admitted that water was being added to the lubricating oil to emulsify it. A practice of dubious value and a considerable risk. (Motor Sport June 1943)

a. 15th August, 1936: Coppa Acerbo Pescara: Seaman, Trossi and Bira are abreast at the early start.
b. 15th August, 1936: Coppa Acerbo Pescara: Giuseppe Furmanik in his uniform as President of the Sporting Commission of the R.A.C.I. with Seaman and Trossi after the race.

presented at Berne in sombre black with an announcement that it was hoped a change of colour might produce a change of fortune. The cynical suggested that as the ERAs had not been able to beat Seaman, perhaps they were hoping to join him.

At the start Seaman made his usual excellent getaway and led the field, chased by Bira and Fairfield. The engine from "Remus" had been fitted to "Romulus" after the Pescara misfortune and Bira was determined to give Seaman a run for his money. Ignoring Chula's signals, he pursued Seaman with the enthusiasm of inexperience but despite pushing the blue ERA much faster than it wanted to go, Seaman was pulling away at 2 to 3 secs. a lap and while doing so lowered the lap record to 2 mins. 58 secs. After 16 laps "Romulus/Remus" had had enough and Bira retired with a broken rocker. The works ERAs had already run true to form and retired earlier. With Bira gone, Seaman did not slacken his pace and finished the 28 laps at an average of 87.84 mph, 7.77 mph faster than his average for the previous year in his ERA. Embiricos maintained his consistent record with second place 1 min. 24 secs. behind Seaman and Tongue (who had had rather a disappointing season with his new ERA, apart from a win in the Cork G.P. an Irish handicap) was rewarded with third place, although 3 mins. 14 secs. behind Seaman. Earl Howe, Ruesch with the leading Maserati and Baumer with the 750 Austin were all a lap behind, though the little Austin had kept up well on such a fast circuit.

The British contingent at Berne was not able to tarry for long after the race was over, for they had another commitment in England only 6 days later, on the following Saturday at Donington Park. In 1921, the Junior Car Club had organized the first long distance race in England, the 200 mile race, which had

a. 22nd August, 1936: Practice for the Prix de Berne: Seman's Delage demonstrates considerable understeer.
b. 23rd August, 1936: Prix de Berne: Seaman's Delage outstrips the ERAs of Howe and Bira at the start.
c. 23rd August, 1936: Prix de Berne: Giulio Ramponi (with armband) and Jock Finlayson attach the victor's wreath to the Delage. Behind in shirt sleeves, hands in pockets, Rudolf Uhlenhaut of Daimler-Benz is perhaps wondering if Seaman should be offered a test drive.
d. 29th August, 1936: J.C.C. 200 mile race Donington: Seaman toasts his victory. On the left is Ramponi and on the right Earl Howe with Finlayson behind.

(a)

(b)

(d)

e. 29th August, 1936: J.C.C. 200 mile race Donington: Seaman laps Denis Scribbans (ERA) at Red Gate Corner.

f. 1936: The view that most competitors had of Seaman's Delage during the season.

(f)

been a "Flat-out" event on the outer circuit at Brooklands for racing cars up to 1500cc. It was a great success and continued annually until 1928, eventually leaving the outer circuit and using an artificial road circuit. The race did much to develop the small capacity racing car in England, but by 1928, interest had waned in favour of sports car racing though the last race of the series was won by Sir Malcolm Campbell driving a 1500 Delage. In 1936, the J.C.C. decided that the great interest in voiturette racing justified the revival of the "200" but with the timidity of British race organizers, it was felt that a pure scratch race for 1500 cars would not have enough appeal, so the race was to have an up-to-1500 class, and an over-1500 class, running together for the Andre Gold Cup which would go to the first car home, irrespective of capacity. The race attracted a good entry, though wholly British based, but the over 1500 class was small and interest centred on the 1500s where Seaman with the Delage was to challenge a mass of ERAs once again. The voiturette class drew 13 entries with an 1100 as well, and yet again, the fastest car in practice was Fairfield's Works ERA. In bright sunshine, the field was led at the start by Peter Whitehead's ERA, but after 2 laps, as was inevitable, the black Delage was in front, pursued by Earl Howe. To the surprise of the crowd, Howe passed Seaman on lap 13, with Bira now third, ahead of Fairfield. Mays' ERA had run true to form again and was already in trouble with oil leaks. Lord Howe was driving superbly and was trying hard to pull out enough lead to make a refuelling stop without letting the Delage through, but Seaman was driving a thoughtful race and however hard Howe pressed on, the Delage was never more than 15 secs. behind. On lap 41, Fairfield retired with engine bothers and then, after 50 laps, Howe made his stop and was away after 39 secs. It was too late though, the Delage had gone by and was never to be seen again, Seaman completed the 77 lap race and finished 51 secs. ahead of Earl Howe, with the ERA of Briault and Evans in third place, 2 laps behind. The over 1500 class had made no impact on the race at all, which had become almost a pure voiturette event. Seaman had won 3 races within 15 days and in doing this, the Delage had received no maintenance apart from routine checking and a change of sparking plugs. As the flag fell on that hot afternoon at Donington, the black Delage and its owner secured for themselves motor racing immortality. 10 years before in 1926 and 1927 the Delage had no peers and now, with an amateur driver who had developed the car intelligently and driven it brilliantly, it was still unbeatable. Astonishingly however, despite its total domination of the class, the Delage would never again win a voiturette race. Events, as much as the passing of time, would prevent Seaman's feats with the car being equalled' or even attempted. All this could not be known to the crowd at Donington who congratulated Seaman after this third victory, though the more percipient must have realised that Seaman could well have driven his last voiturette race, for the Grand Prix world already beckoned to a driver of his talent.

As far as the English were concerned, the JCC 200 had ended the voiturette season, but the Italians had other ideas. On 7th September the second Coppa Edda Ciano, presented by Mussolini's daughter, was held on a very tight circuit in the medieval city of Lucca, which ran through narrow gateways into the old city and along the ramparts. General Vaccaro, the President of the Royal

Automobile Club of Italy, dropped the flat at 3.30 p.m. precisely, and Ettore Bianco leapt into the lead with his 4CM Maserati and held it "at the price of most virtuosity", as "Il Giornale d'Italia" described it, for 9 laps. Trossi had started slowly with his 6CM and first had to pass Vittorio Belmondo with another 4CM, before chasing Bianco and taking over the lead on the ninth lap. After that, it was all over, Bianco having lost his lead and his virtuosity, now lost several places and fell back to fourth place by the end of the 30 lap race while Belmondo finished second, 43 secs. behind Trossi.

a. 7th September, 1936: Circuit of Lucca: Count Trossi (6CM Maserati) pursues Vittorio Belmondo (4CM Maserati) in the early laps. The smoking tyre shows how hard Belmondo is trying.

b. 7th September, 1936: Circuit of Lucca: Trossi cruises home to an easy win in the closing laps.

A fortnight later on 21st September the Modena G.P. was run through the streets of the Italian town where the Scuderia Ferrari had made its home and Count Trossi in the preliminary 1500 race made a better start this time and showed that his 6CM Maserati was still quicker than all the others. He led all the way in the 50 mile race and finished 1 min. 48 sec. in front of Biondetti's 6CM; Maseratis took the next 3 places while Enrico Platé came sixth in his old straight-eight Talbot. True to historic form, the Talbot had been no match for the Delage in 1926/27, and now, 10 years after, rebuilt much as the Delage had been, the Talbot was still not as quick.

The honours of the season had been shared between three drivers, Seaman, Trossi and Bira but although Seaman had only won 4 races, he had dominated them completely and neither Trossi nor Bira had been able to offer any effective challenge to him; Seaman had only been beaten by misfortune in those events he did not win. As far as Seaman was concerned, voiturette racing had served its purpose, for as soon as the 1936 season was over, he received an invitation to trials with Mercedes-Benz and at the close of the year it was announced that he would join the Mercedes G.P. team for 1937. Although his judgment in buying and rebuilding the Delage had been justified, it may perhaps be permissible to speculate that his results might have been just as good, or even better, if he had kept his ERA for another season. With Ramponi's skill in preparation and development, the ERA would probably have been nearly as quick and just as reliable as the Delage, while Seaman's fears about the works ERAs were not realised; however without his intervention with the French car, the history of motor racing would be much poorer in being deprived of one of its more romantic stories.

Trossi and Bira had both shown themselves to be most competent drivers but the 6CM Maserati had been rather a disappointment after its brilliant start at the Eifelrennen, and it seemed that by the end of the season, the works Maseratis were content to seek out those races where the opposition was less formidable. The 6CM however had shown the advantages of independent front suspension in a voiturette. Power and cart-springs would soon no longer be enough. For ERA, the story could have been most dismal. Without the efforts of the Siamese Princes, the results would have been sadly mediocre after the brilliance of 1935. The works cars had had a tragic and disastrous season, with truly pathetic results, despite their obvious speed. Perhaps the only bright spot for the Bourne team had been the remarkable efforts of Earl Howe. Now 52 years old, and old enough to be the father of most of his rivals, he had been prominent in every race in which he had started and was still one of the fastest drivers in the class. Perhaps, if he had been 20 years younger, he too would have received an invitation from Stuttgart! It was noticeable that the dominance of the three principal drivers had completely overshadowed the lesser lights, and the other independents driving both ERA and Maserati had made little impact on the season.

In the Autumn of 1936, Richard Seaman sold the Delage to Prince Chula who looked proudly at it and began to make plans for it to go even faster, while at Bourne, Raymond Mays and Peter Berthon used every power of persuasion to convince Humphrey Cook that the Zoller ERA could be both fast and reliable and was worth financing.

The GP Delage had won its last race, but another 8-cylinder voiturette would appear. This car, in the fullness of time would achieve a glory surpassing even that of the Delage, for at Modena, Enzo Ferrari realised that if Alfa Romeo was to regain former glories, a new approach was needed.

1937

THE ABYSSINIAN WAR was over and although the League of Nations' sanctions still existed, in practice, no one was now much concerned, for the nations of Europe had a new war in which some were dabbling enthusiastically. The Spanish Civil War had begun in June 1936, and the Italians and Germans both gave their prototype war machines a trial run in supporting the Nationalist cause in Spain. The more perceptive began to realise another European war was perhaps nearer then many wished to believe. Discussing the new G.P. formula, Grande Vitesse had written in "The Motor" of 20th October 1936 "It should be highly interesting in 1938 if the World War holds off until then".

The voiturette world was not dismayed by the distant prospects of war, and in England and Italy, work proceded furiously to prepare for what was to be the most active season of 1500 racing in the 1930s. With the trouncing of Alfa Romeo and Maserati in G.P. racing, most race organisers in Italy now saw the 1500 class as the obvious choice for their events, with the additional attraction of a possible home win. At Bourne, Raymond Mays and Peter Berthon realised that the B-type ERA had limitations, and could not guarantee to defeat the 6CM Maserati under all conditions. The Zoller supercharger had given all the power needed, though at the expense of reliability, but the semi-elliptic front springs and beam axle of the ERA were no match for the wish-bone and torsion bar independent front suspension of the Bologna car. Berthon solved the reliability problem by designing new connecting rods capable of taking the higher revs and power output that the Zoller gave so readily. The ERA team could now hope for a reliable 225 bhp with the Zoller giving a boost of 25lbs per sq.ins. which was a considerable advance on the 185/190 bhp of the Jamieson supercharged B-type. The chassis was redesigned, and the front axle replaced with Porsche designed trailing arm suspension, operating short transverse torsion bars. The cost of fitting the team cars with the new suspension was £500 apiece, a very high figure for 1937. Ken Richardson, the ERA chief mechanic said many years later, "We paid Dr. Porsche a lot of money for his suspension and I don't think we ever really understood how it worked". Despite the possible failure to appreciate the finer points of the Doctor's design, the new car was quicker round corners, and to slow it down, hydraulic brakes were fitted, using a Lockheed system to operate a Girling mechanism. The revised ERA was called the C-type, and 2 B-types were re-built to the new specification for Mays and Fairfield. It is surprising that no attempt was made to produce the C-type for sale, or even to offer the existing B-type chassis with the Zoller supercharged engine. With the increasing interest in the 1500 class, there were a number of drivers who would have liked to buy a new ERA for the 1937 season, but the Bourne concern was not interested in producing any more cars for sale. Every ERA built had been sold at a loss, so Humphrey Cook was reluctant to see any more money spent in this way. Surprisingly, the Factory only received one inquiry about the possibility of uprating a B-type to C-type specification. This came from Prince Chula.★

Another new British car also appeared in January 1937. The little firm of Alta had been making sports and racing cars for about five years in a tiny factory at Tolworth, on the Kingston-by-Pass, the direct route from London to Brooklands. The first Alta had been an 1100 sports car but Geoffrey Taylor, the proprietor and designer of the firm had developed the prototype, and by 1936, a conventional racing car with a 4 cylinder twin-cam engine was being produced at the modest price of £850 for the supercharged 1500. The Alta was quite fast, and was sold to a number of drivers, but unfortunately it was not very reliable, so the car had rarely appeared in International voiturette racing. During the winter of 1936/37, Taylor designed and produced a completely new car which although it still used the 69 mm × 100 mm, 4 cylinder engine, had a new chassis with independent suspension on all wheels using coil springs on vertical pillars. This new car had a neat well-faired single seater body and was offered for sale at £1,250.

At Bologna, the Maserati brothers had decided that as the 750 kg formula had only 12 months to run, there was no point in building a new G.P. car in the hope of beating the German teams. They would wait until the new formula began in 1938, and for 1937, they would concentrate on voiturettes; they were quite content with the 6CM, but as an insurance against the threat posed by the C-type ERA, they looked once again at the old 4C engine and at the rear suspension of the 6CM. A number of 6CMs were sold to drivers who might have bought an ERA if it had been available; meanwhile, 60 miles away at Modena, 1500cc racing cars had suddenly become of much interest to the Scuderia Ferrari.

Although there was no prospect at all of a new French voiturette, it seemed likely that a French car would still be in the forefront in 1937, and would gladden French hearts by being painted blue as well. When he bought the Delage, Prince Chula immediately commissioned Albert Lory, the car's original designer, to design a new chassis with independent front suspension. Lory decided that the car was powerful enough but would need to corner better to keep up with the C-type ERA. His new design was similar in layout to the 1926/27 original, but used a transverse leaf front suspension identical to that fitted to the current Delahaye and Delage sports cars. Although the plans were drawn in France, the new frame and suspension were made in England and the car was being built up by Prince Chula's mechanics in the work shops of the White Mouse Stable in Hammersmith.

Letter from Raymond Mays to the author February 1979.

29th January, 1937: A mechanic works on a 6CM in the Maserati factory at Bologna. In the background is a 4CS.

It was very fitting that as Italy had now embraced 1500 racing so enthusiastically, the season should start in Turin, the heart of the Italian motor industry. The race was to be held on 18th April in the Valentino Park in the middle of Turin, alongside the River Po. Much to the disappointment of the organisers, the ERA team did not enter although the C-type had already scored its first victory, the first the team had gained since the 1935 Eifelrennen, when Mays had won the British Empire Trophy handicap at Donington, 8 days earlier. At Turin the works 6CM Maseratis were entered for Ettore Bianco and for the GP driver Rene Dreyfus, who had previously driven for Bugatti and the Scuderia Ferrari; there were 10 other Maseratis. The opposition was to come from the ERAs of Bira, Reggie Tongue and Eugen Bjornstadt, a Norwegian with much ice racing experience in Scandinavia; his car, painted red, was R1A, the original ERA now starting its fourth season of racing. Chula had hoped to take the Delage to Turin but it was not ready. On a very hot afternoon the race was started by Crown Prince Umberto and Bianco took the lead from Dreyfus and Bira. On lap 2 Bjornstadt who had been fifth spun and fell back. His technique clearly owed much to the ice racing and was described by "The Autocar" as "Quite unorthodox". After 5 laps, Bira passed Dreyfus and set off after Bianco; By lap 10, he had caught up and was looking for an opening to pass, but on the tight circuit, Bianco was not giving way, despite Bira's shaking first. Bianco's tactics so angered Trossi and Farina who were watching the race, that they complained to the organisers but meanwhile, Bira had passed, as Bianco had lost his goggles and was suffering from oil being sprayed into his eyes. Bira's lead did not last for long as on lap 30 "Romulus" was out of the race with a loose prop. shaft so Bianco led again. Meanwhile, Bjornstadt had recovered from his spin, passed Dreyfus and then passed Bianco on lap 35 and kept in front for the remaining 5 laps, to gain an unexpected victory with his veteran car. Dreyfus was second and Tongue who had driven steadily was third ahead of Rocco who had taken over Bianco's oily car.

England, which for so long had lacked any road circuits at all, gained two additional circuits to support Donington in 1937. The more interesting of these circuits had been constructed in the park in the heart of S.E. London, where the Crystal Palace, built to house the Great Exhibition of 1851, had subsequently been rebuilt. The circuit was 2.0 miles (3.2km) long and was twisting and sinuous, partly to get a reasonable length lap in a small site. Well appointed, with a good paddock and grandstand, it was the equal of any European park circuit. The other new road circuit came from the realisation that Brooklands, built in 1907 had such limitations that it was becoming an anachronism in the racing conditions of the mid-1930s. As a result, a 2.26 (3.63 km) artificial road circuit was built within the track, which used part of the Outer Circuit. This brave attempt to bring Brooklands up-to-date suffered from the limited space available. Brooklands, despite its unique charms, had, by 1937, drifted completely away from the main stream of European racing and almost every race held there was a handicap, catering only for British drivers. If a road circuit had been built 10 years earlier, perhaps the story of Brooklands would have been very different, but sadly, the Campbell Circuit, named in honour of Sir Malcolm Campbell was too little and too late.

The Crystal Palace was the first of the new circuits to stage a race. In honour of the impending Coronation of King George VI, the race was called the

24th April, 1937: Coronation Trophy Crystal Palace: The start of the final. May's C-tye ERA (17) is smoking heavily.

Coronation Trophy, and was run on Saturday 24th April in front of a crowd estimated at 30,000. It was to be a scratch 1500 race of two 40 mile heats and a 60 mile final and although no foreign entries were received, the ERA team entered, together with most of the better English private entrants. The works ERAs dominated the event, for Pat Fairfield won the first heat by 21 seconds from Charles Brackenbury, driving the 4CM Maserati owned by E.K. Rayson. In the second heat, Mays had a hard fight but won by 1.2 seconds from Arthur Dobson, while Peter Whitehead was third. In the final, Dobson, who was being tipped by the press as a promising driver, led the works ERAs for 2 laps then Mays went past. The C-types were not quite right yet for Mays only lasted for 7 laps when he retired with serious brake problems. With Mays gone, Fairfield who had also passed Dobson went on to win by 49 seconds from Dobson, while Robin Hanson was third with a new 6CM Maserati. The new circuit was a success but the organisers were worried that the rather processional final was not to the taste of the crowd.

The English 1500s raced round the Park on Saturday, and the Italian proceeded to race round another Park on Sunday. After the Turin race most of the competitors went south to Naples where a short race was to be held on the following Sunday, 25th April on a hilly 4 km circuit at Posillipo the attractive wooded headland about 9 miles (15 km) south west of the city where the competitors had magnificent views over the Bay of Naples. The feelings of the competitors had already been aroused by the short time given for practice, and their tempers and their cars became overheated when the Crown Princess of Italy, in whose humour the race was named, held the flag up for nearly 2 minutes before starting the race. Franco Cortese with a works 6CM Maserati led, chased by Trossi with the other works 6CM, Bira's ERA and Bianco. After 5 laps, Cortese stopped to change plugs, and Bira led for a lap but Trossi, his car cornering noticably better than the beam axle ERA, took the lead on lap 6 and then pulled away steadily by 2 to 3 seconds a lap. Behind Bira, Bianco was being chased by Tongue and Bjornstadt with their ERAs, but Tongue was forced to stop for plugs and then Bjornstadt passed Bianco. The Norwegian's ERA responded valiantly to his ice-racing techniques but by the end of the race, the rear tyres were showing canvas and the oil tank was hanging loose, so Trossi won, followed home by Bira and Bjornstadt.

The Siamese team and Reggie Tongue had no time to enjoy Naples after the race, as 6 days later they had an engagement at Brooklands for the inaugural race on the Campbell circuit. The race was for the Campbell Trophy, and had classes for cars up to, and over 1500 cc. Surprisingly for Britain, and even more so for Brooklands, it was a scratch race. The 1500 class with an all British entry had 7 ERAs, including a works car, being shared by Mays and Fairfield, competing against 3 Maseratis. The second works ERA had been withdrawn with incurable brake problems in practice. From the start, the 1500 class and the whole race was led by Earl Howe. Driving with enormous spirit on his 53rd birthday, he had a great struggle with the leader of the over 1500 class, Bira's 3 litre 8CM Maserati. Howe led the class for 26 laps, until he made a slight error of judgment and the ERA struck the parapet of the bridge which carried the course over the River Wey. The car overturned and the Earl suffered severe

99

head injuries. After this unhappy incident the 1500 class lead was taken over by E.K. Rayson, driving his veteran 1933/34 4CM Maserati, and he kept this lead for the rest of the 100 lap race. The race had been unhappy for the ERAs generally and only one other car, Denis Scribbans' ERA, was classified as a finisher in the 1500 class while 3 other survivors were flagged off. The works ERA had been particularly disappointing.

For some years, the fastest road race in the world had been held on the Mellaha circuit in the Italian province of Tripoli. This race had always attracted the best Grand Prix field drawn by the kudos of the fastest race and also by the abundant prize money which was boosted by an Italian lottery on the result. In 1937 the race was still promoted for Grand Prix cars but with the new-found Italian enthusiasm of 1500 racing, a class for the small cars was included. Racing with the G.P. cars on 9th May, the voiturettes had to cover 34 laps of the 8.1 mile (13.1 km) circuit. The organizers invited Chula to enter Bira with an ERA but the Princes had to decline the invitation as they had a prior commitment to attend the Coronation of King George VI. This was a pity, as the fast smooth circuit should have been well suited to the ERA's speed and handling, and it left the 1500 class with an all Italian entry of 10 Maseratis and Castelbarco's Talbot

a. *23rd May 1937: Targa Florio: Giovanni Rocco's victorious 6CM Maserati has a last minute check before the start.*

b. *31st May, 1937: Avusrennen: Franco Cortese (6CM Maserati (17)) had a slight advantage over Charles Martin (ERA (12)) at the start.*

special. From the start, the works 6CMs of Dreyfus and Cortese fought for the lead, but eventually the experience of Dreyfus in GP racing began to tell, and he pulled away to win by 3 mins. from Cortese. The remaining finishers were several laps behind but the race had been fast, as the winning average was 107.75 mph (173.79 kph) and Ghersi made the fastest lap at 114.27 mph (183.97 kph).

After the intense activity during the first month of the season, it was probably a relief to the competitors that there was now a break for a fortnight until the next engagement. This however, was another all-Italian affair with the revival of the emasculated Targa Florio which was to be run on a short circuit in the Favorita Park in Palermo. In addition to being the 28th Targa Florio the race was also to be the first Prince of Naples Cup. The field was a mixed bag with 7 Maseratis, a 6C Alfa Romeo, a T37A Bugatti and 3 Balilla Fiats. At the start Giovanni Rocco took the lead with his 6CM Maserati and did a meteoric opening lap to pass the pits nearly 300 yds. in front of Belmondo, Severi and Bianco. Nando Barbieri stopped his 6CM to change a plug and was away again before the tail-end Fiat appeared. Rocco began to pull away steadily, and by 20 laps he was 33 secs. in front of Bianco who had been battling with Severi since the start. Just when it seemed the race was to be a dull procession, everything happened. On lap 23 Rocco stopped for fuel and new plugs and Severi passed Bianco to become the new leader; Rocco restarted after 4 mins. but had to stop again for carburettor adjustments. On lap 31, Bianco passed Severi again but next time round he came into the pits to repair a broken oil pipe and lost 6 mins. leaving Severi with a commanding lead. At the same time Rocco appeared at the pits on foot, as a piston had succumbed to the mixture defect. Bianco's stop let Count Lurani up into second place with his new car an 1100 4CM Maserati which had the 6CM chassis with a small 4C engine. Bianco had restarted and came third, but now 5 laps behind. As the 28th Targo Florio, it had perhaps been a pale shadow of its former glories, but as the 1st Prince of Naples Cup, it had been quite a lively race. ★

By the Spring of 1937, the influence of the National Socialist Party had permeated all aspects of German life and motor racing had been no exception. For 3 years G.P. racing had been used as an instrument of German propaganda but now it became clear that there had been a further change of policy, and race organisers were being encouraged to promote events only for those classes where German cars were likely to succeed. In the 1937 Eifelrennen there was to be no 1500 race; instead, great emphasis was being placed on the 2 litre sports car class in which the new 328 BMW was establishing an omnipotence akin to that of the German teams in G.P. racing. The rather lame excuse was given that the Eifelrennen would be unlikely to attract entries with the profusion of events in Italy, which conveniently ignored the fact that the race had been one of the premier events in previous years. Despite the Party line however, there was a voiturette race in Germany in 1937. The Avusrennen had been restricted to G.P. cars in 1935 and was not held in 1936 as the track had been drastically altered by the construction of a banking, 60ft. high, on the north curve of the circuit, which replaced the former shallow cambered 180° curve. This banking, with a

★Severi's victorious 6CM was the car raced by Moris Bergamini in 1936.

gradient at the top, of 1 in 1, was brick surfaced and it was expected that the GP cars would establish astonishing record speeds on the rebuilt circuit. These expectations were not disappointed as in practice, the Mercedes and Auto Unions, with all-enveloping bodies, lapped at over 170 mph (275 kph). It seemed that a new era of G P racing was dawning and the 1500 race, which was to be a curtain raiser for the titanic feats to follow, must have seemed truly puny by comparison. This was relative though, for Charles Martin driving an ERA had been fastest in practice lapping at 123.1 mph (198.2 kph) and at the start of the race, Martin took the lead from Bjornstadt with his ERA and Franco Cortese with the latest 6CM Maserati of the Scuderia Ambrosiana.★ The few British spectators present felt justifiably proud as the dark green ERA, being driven flat out, swept off the "wall of death" at the end of the first lap closely followed by Bjornstadt. Banked circuits did not suit the Norwegian's technique particularly as he was running on road racing tyres, unlike Martin who with the benefit of Brooklands experience, was using track tyres. On lap 3 the red ERA burst a rear tyre, leaving Cortese and Platé with a 4CM Maserati pursuing Martin. The ERA had a lead of 8 secs. on lap 4, and was leaving the north banking as Cortese entered it, but on lap 5, the gap had closed to $6^1\!2$ secs. and on the start of the 7th and last lap, the Maserati was only a few lengths behind. The independent suspension of the 6CM was giving it an advantage on the curves but Martin had been driving to conserve his tyres on the intensely hot day and now used the superior speed of the ERA to pull away. The heat and the pace then took their toll, and to the excitement of the spectators, the ERA appeared alone to take the flag for the Maserati had burst a tyre on the south curve and spun off. Martin had averaged 119.63 mph (192.6 kph) in one of the more heroic voiturette drives of the decade and had won the last 1500 race to be held in Germany in the 1930s.

While Charles Martin was receiving the plaudits of 380,000 spectators, some of the Italian voiturette drivers had been trying their hand on a new circuit in the streets of Genoa, modestly described as the Circuit Automobile della Superba. The 11 starters were led on the first lap by Nando Barbieri with his 6CM Maserati, who, as a local lad, probably knew the circuit better than most. After 3 laps Vittorio Belmondo took the lead but then a newcomer came up with the leaders. This was Aldo Marazza from Milan who was starting his racing career with the old 2 seater 4CS Maserati that Count Lurani had used several years before and which Marazza had bought from Giuseppe Gilera only three days before the race. On this old car, Marazza chased Belmondo for nearly 25 laps, then he took the lead and went on to win, while Belmondo had to settle for third place as he was also passed by Severi in his 6CM, in the closing laps.

On that very active Sunday most of the British voiturette competitors were preparing to load their cars onto the ferry for the Isle of Man, where the RAC had decided to promote the annual 1500 race once again. For 1937, the circuit used the TT pits as in 1936, but the back leg ran along the seafront as in earlier years. There was much interest as Prince Chula had entered both the remodelled

---

★This team had been formed at the beginning of the season by Count Lurani, Luigi Villoresi, Cortese and Minetti and had strong ties with the Bologna factory.

102

31st May, 1937: Avusrennen: Charles Martin receives his victor's laurels from Reichscorpsfushrer Huhnlein. Plate who was second in his 4CM Maserati looks on.

Delage and an ERA for Bira. Both cars were tried in practice, and although the Delage ran well and handled impressively, the ERA "Romulus" was 7 secs. a lap quicker in 2 mins. 59 secs., equalling Mays' time with the C-type ERA, so the Siamese team had no difficulty in deciding which car to race. Sadly, the practice was marred when Philip Jucker, driving the first of the new independently sprung Altas, struck a lamp post on the seafront and died of his injuries shortly afterwards. The race was started in heavy rain, and Mays took the lead but was passed on the first lap by Bira, who drove most skilfully and began to pull steadily away. Mays was having the same brake problems which had affected the works ERAs earlier in the season, and fell back being passed by Fairfield with the other works car and Luigi Villoresi with a 6CM Maserati entered by the Scuderia Ambrosiana. These two battled for the next 20 laps until the Maserati retired with engine bothers. Meanwhile, Mays who had dropped back to sixth place had come to terms with his erratic brakes and speeded up to take third place behind Fairfield. When Bira stopped for fuel on lap 31, the ERAs went past and were first and second but the remarkable Bira, revelling in the conditions, took up the chase and repassed both to take the lead again on lap 36. There was nothing that Mays and Fairfield could do and the 1935 ERA finished 42 secs. in front of Mays' works car with Fairfield, Tongue and the Peters, Walker and Whitehead who shared a car, giving ERA the first five places. In sixth place, driving an elderly 4CM Maserati was the Swiss driver Emanuel de

a. *31st May, 1937: Circuito delle Superba Genoa: Nando Barbieri (6CM Maserati) Aldo Marazza (4CS Maserati) and Vittorio Belmondo (4CM Maserati) strive for the lead at the start.*

b. *31st May, 1937: Circuito delle Superba Genoa: Aldo Marazza on the way to an unexpected victory in his ex-Lurani 4CS Maserati.*

c. *3rd June, 1937: RAC International Light Car Race Douglas: Pat Fairfield warms up the transmission of the works C-type ERA (9) in dismal conditions before the start.*

d. *3rd June, 1937: RAC International Light Car Race Douglas: A damp Bira discusses form with an inadequately sheltered Raymond Mays before the race.*

e. *3rd June, 1937: RAC International Light Car Race Douglas: Robin Hanson (6CM Maserati) is about to be lapped by Fairfield and Luigi Villoresi as he turns onto the seafront.*

Graffenried who was at the beginning of a long and distinguished career.

Most of the competitors in Douglas dried out themselves and their cars and started to make plans for the next British event, the Nuffield Trophy, which was being held at Donington nine days later on 12th June. The race was a class handicap as before, and the ERA team looked forward to it with new confidence and more important, new brake drums. Their faith was rewarded, Fairfield and Mays finished first and third sandwiching Arthur Dobson in his white B type ERA. Chula and Bira had decided to ignore the Donington race, for they had set their sights on a far bigger prize which had been proudly announced as "The 1500cc race of the decade". This was to be run in Florence, and it was a pity that the organizers, with such confidence in the importance of the race, had omitted to send regulations to most of the English 1500 competitors. The only non-Maserati entries were the four ERAs of Bira, Tongue, Whitehead and Embiricos whose A-type was prepared by Giulio Ramponi and had been modified by fitting Tecnauto independent front suspension. This proprietary system which used a single trailing arm operating in torsion on a transverse coil spring was readily available in Italy and the kit of parts to convert a Balilla Fiat was reported to cost only £15, a considerable contrast to the price of the Porsche system on the C-type ERA and perhaps as effective. De Graffenried's 4CM Maserati had been converted to the same system. The 2.0 mile (3.3 km) Florentine circuit ran round the Fortezza Di Basso and the Piazza Cavour and was thus only a few yards from the centre of the City; in honour of its declared importance, the first prize was to be 100,000 Lire. This obviously had its attractions for the Maserati team and with the clear intention of disposing of the ERAs and the 6CMs a new car was produced for Trossi. This used the 6CM chassis and body with an uprated 4C engine and quarter elliptic rear springs in place of the semi elliptics of the ordinary 6C.★ The new car was fastest in practice but one of the ERAs was eliminated when an over-zealous official moved the straw bales lining a corner during practice and the unfortunate Embiricos arrived to find the line of the corner had been changed completely since his previous lap. In the crash which followed Embiricos suffered only slight injuries but decided motor racing was too dangerous and declared his immediate intention of retiring from the sport.★★ The race was run in the intense oppressive heat that Florence can produce. Bira took the lead from Trossi but could only hold it for 4 laps as he was trying to outbrake the Maserati to compensate for the ERA's inferior cornering and not surprisingly, the brakes weakened. Bianco and Dreyfus also passed the ERA so the works Maseratis held the first 3 places but on lap 24 Trossi who was suffering from the heat, stopped and handed over to Rovere leaving Dreyfus leading from Bianco. Bira gave up the brakeless struggle on lap 30 and Trossi, now feeling better, called in Rovere

★On 3rd June, Giuseppe Furmanik had used this car, fitted with an aerodynamic body built by Viotto of Turin, to break the international class F S/S Kilometre record on the Florence-Pisa Autostrada. For circuit racing, the principal modification to the engine was an increase in the supercharger size from 115 mm to 130 mm. In its record breaking tune the 4CM gave 200 bhp.
★★Embiricos honoured a commitment to drive a Talbot with "Raph" at Le Mans the following weekend. He did not take the wheel as the car was involved in the multiple crash on lap 7. He did not race again. He was killed flying a light aircraft in the U.S.A. in 1939.

105

a. 3rd June, 1937: RAC International Light Car Race Douglas: De Graffenreid (4CM Maserati) leads Tongue (ERA) around the hairpin at the end of the seafront. The Maserati has Tecnauto independent front suspension.

b. 3rd June, 1937: RAC International Light Car Race Douglas: May's C-type ERA is ahead of Bira's B-type "Romulus" at the Onchan turn.

c. 12th June, 1937: Nuffield Trophy Donington: The start; the ERAs are Martin (9), Dobson (12), Mays (18), Scribbans (10), Fairfield (2) and Connell (8). The Maseratis are Luigi Villoresi (3), Aitken (7), De Graffenried (4), and Du Puy (at the rear).

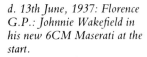

d. 13th June, 1937: Florence G.P.: Johnnie Wakefield in his new 6CM Maserati at the start.

e. 13th June, 1937: Florence G.P.: The flag is about to fall.

and took over the new car again and chased through the field in search of the lead. Dreyfus was flagged off as the winner, and after much argument about laps and times, it was declared that Trossi was second, only 7 secs. behind. As the Bianco car, which had been handed over to Rocco, finished third, the race had been a complete triumph for the Bologna factory.

The relentless series of Italian races continued, and it was perhaps a pity that the Italians, in their new-found enthusiasm for 1500 racing, had provided their drivers with a complete season without any need to cross the Alps in search of more racing. Equally, the introduction of the Crystal Palace and the Campbell circuit at Brooklands, had now made it possible for an English driver to have a complete season of racing without crossing the Channel. As a result, the two main centres of voiturette racing seemed at times, to be developing on parallel lines which only converged at occasional meetings.

There was little rest for the competitors who had raced at Florence, as most of them were engaged to race again on the following Sunday at Milan on the Sempione Park circuit. Prince Chula had doubts about the prospects of racing the ageing "Romulus" again, without an overhaul, and made discreet overtures to the Maserati team in the hope of borrowing a works 6CM for Bira, but was told politely that the factory preferred to sell cars, not to lend them!★ The entry for Milan, which was only a short race of 50 laps, was a large Maserati contingent opposed by the 3 ERAs. The ERA team much to the disappointment of the organizers, had shown no inclination to drive their Bedford vans over the Alps and during the Milan weekend, Fairfield was fully occupied, as he had taken up the offer of a drive with a factory entered 328 BMW in the Le Mans 24 hour race. During practice in Milan, the dominance of the Maseratis was very marked. The ERAs were well back on the starting grid and even Bira had been disappointing, as the brakes had been relined and had not yet bedded in. At the start, Severi led from Rovere, Siena and the two Villoresi brothers with Bira in sixth place. Severi stopped on lap 6 and Rovere with the new 4CM also retired which left Eugenio Siena with a 4CM to drive on steadily to win. Bira was bothered with his brakes and gave up when "Romulus' " engine, now very tired, lost its oil pressure on lap 18. Behind Siena, Aldo Marazza had had a most impressive drive up through the field to take second place on the ancient 4CS Maserati. Siena's win must have been nostalgic for some of those present, for more than 10 years earlier, he had been riding mechanic for Ascari and Campari, in the famous P2 Alfa Romeo team.

As the race finished at Milan, news came through which caused great distress, especially to the British contingent. Shortly after the start of the Le Mans 24 hour race, there had been a crash involving several cars at White House corner, the scene of the famous Bentley crash 10 years earlier. Fairfield's BMW had collided with an overturned Bugatti and had itself been rammed by a Delahaye. Fairfield received very severe internal injuries and died on the following Monday morning. His death was a cruel blow to the ERA team and was also a great loss to British racing. Only 29, he had become a most able driver and had played a very important part in the new-found success of the ERA team. In

★Road Star Hat-trick Page 55.

a. *27th June 1937: Picardie G.P.: Raymond Mays (C-type ERA) gets the chequered flag. The Bouriat/Trintignant memorial is in the background.*

b. *27th June 1937: Picardie G.P.: Mays relaxes after his victory. Ken Richardson, the ERA Chief mechanic, is second from the left.*

reporting his death, "Motor Sport" summoned up the feeling which prevailed, "Fairfield's death is a tremendous blow for British motor racing. He had a natural flair for cornering and thoroughly deserved the many victories which came his way. Added to this, he had a personality, a disposition, which made him universally popular."

Although they might reasonably have been excused, the ERA team turned up on the following Friday at Peronne to honour their commitment to the organizers of the Picardie G.P.; only one car was produced for Raymond Mays. The White Mouse Stable also had its problems, for "Romulus" was totally unfit and "Remus" was in pieces, so Prince Chula was forced to bring the rebuilt Delage back to the land of its birth. In practice, Bira was faster than Seaman had been the previous year and was also quicker than he had been with "Romulus".

As before, the race was run in 2 heats and a final and in the first heat, Trossi who should have driven the 4CM Maserati did not turn up as he was suffering from eye strain, but Dreyfus with a works 6CM took the lead at the start from the American, John Du Puy with another 6CM, and the Delage. Bira soon passed the Maseratis and led for 7 laps then he stopped to complain of clutch slip and a loss of power. The disappointment at the failure of the Delage resulted in an instant row in the Siamese pit, and the team's chief mechanic, Stanley Wuyts promptly resigned, together with his assistant. While all this was going on, Dreyfus won the first heat by over 4 mins. from Robin Hanson with another 6CM while Du Puy was third. The second heat showed the complete dominance of the black works ERA which led all the way. In 10 laps, Mays had almost lapped De Graffenried who was second with his old 4CM Maserati while the rest of the field was almost another lap behind. In third place was Johnny Wakefield, a young English driver who had previously raced Altas and had just bought a 6CM Maserati. Peronne was his third race with the car, as he had already finished tenth at Florence and also at Milan. To mystify the spectators, the Italian car with an English driver was painted blue! At the start of the final, Dreyfus led for barely 50 yds. then the power of the C-type ERA swept Mays past, and into the lead that he never lost again. Mays won the 20 lap final by 1 min. 43 secs. and established a new lap record of 96.5 mph for the narrow triangular circuit. In a suitably respectful procession behind the ERA came Dreyfus, Wakefield, De Graffenried and Hanson. The works ERAs had not been to Italy, but Peronne had shown that the works 6CM Maserati could offer no opposition even when driven by a driver of the calibre of Dreyfus.

A fortnight afterwards, the ERA team had another engagement at the Albi G.P. where two C-types were entered. The team had not yet found another driver, so the second car was to be driven by Humphrey Cook. Cook, who was then 44 years old, and had not raced for 2 years, gamely took over the second car of the team which he was supporting so generously. Albi differed from Peronne as the race was run in 2 heats with the whole entry running in each heat and the result was found from the aggregate time. To the chagrin of the organizers, Bira was not present, but with both ERAs and the Delage broken, he had no car available and it was clear that the previously impeccable organization of the Siamese team was in disarray. The absence of the quickest private ERA did not matter though, for it seemed, that like Peronne, the race was to be a walkover for the ERA team. Mays led from the start and pulled out a lead of 17 secs. from Emilio Villoresi with his 6CM Maserati, Tongue and Cook, who was going very well despite his recent inactivity. However, just when it seemed Mays was to win easily, he stopped on lap 17 with a broken half-shaft and Emilio Villoresi found himself winning from Tongue, Cook and his brother Luigi. In between the heats in the manner of the best continental G.P. teams, Cook handed over his car to Mays. Although the steering column and the seat on Cook's car were not set up for Mays, and he was also suffering from a twisted knee,* it did not seem to make any difference and he shot away from the start knowing that he had to finish at least 1 min. 58 secs. ahead of

*As a result of a childhood injury Mays had one arm slightly shorter than the other so the steering

109

Emilio Villeresi and 40 secs. ahead of Tongue to make up Cook's deficit in the first heat. Like Peronne, he was not seen by his pursuers again except when he lapped them. Emilio Villoresi was in second place for a while, and then he became over-excited, and his Maserati was too badly bent to continue when he spun it into the straw bales, so provided Mays kept going, it was all over, and he did. This left Charles Martin with his ERA in second place ahead of Tongue, while Righetti with the leading Maserati was fourth, but nearly eliminated himself in a tremendous spin on the bend before the pits. With fraternal loyalty, Luigi Villoresi then emulated the spin of his brother but was able to carry on with a rather battered car. With ERAs in the first three places, it was not a day to be remembered at Bologna and it was fitting that Humphrey Cook who had carried the main financial burden of ERA since its inception should have gone into the record book as the co-winner of an international 1500 race driving one of his own cars.

So far, the tempo of the season had been intense with the calendar containing more 1500 races than ever before. Now however, perhaps to the relief of the mechanics, if no one else, the pace slackened slightly; the British competitors returned to England where most of them entered for the London G.P. at the Crystal Palace, being run as a class handicap, which it was stated the spectators preferred. Some of the Italian drivers went to San Remo on the Italian Riviera, where a 1500 race was organized on the 26th July. Although only a small meeting, it aroused unusual interest as it marked the return to racing of Achille Varzi. Varzi had been regarded as one of the greatest G P drivers in the early 1930s, but he had withdrawn from motor racing in 1936, with his personal and emotional life in chaos and with dark rumours of drug addiction. Clearly, with the intention of proving his critics wrong, he had borrowed the works 4CM Maserati. The race was run in three short heats on the 1.86 km circuit with the

26th July, 1937: Circuit of San Remo: Achille Varzi stands beside his 4CM Maserati and smokes a nervous cigarette before his successful comeback.

box on his personal ERA was always mounted on the left-hand side of the frame, unlike the production cars, to compensate for the slight disability. The twisted knee was an injury received in an escapade at the Paris Exhibition which Mays had visited before travelling on to Albi.

first two in each heat going into the final. In heat 1, Dusio's 6CM easily disposed of the similar cars of Emilio Villoresi and Ettore Bianco, who had stopped to change a plug. The second heat looked more promising, for Varzi appeared to race against Aldo Marazza and Luigi Villoresi, but Marazza's car had magneto trouble and Villoresi retired with engine bothers, so Varzi won by over a lap. Cheekily, Lurani with his 1100 4CM Maserati jumped the start of heat 3 by 3 secs. but Rocco whose 6CM was only running on five cylinders managed to catch up and pass Lurani and as all the other cars in the heat retired, Lurani got into the final, despite a 1 min. penalty. Dusio led the final for 4 laps, but the G P skill and experience, or more likely, the torque of the 4C engine told, and Varzi went ahead to win while Dusio managed to keep Rocco at bay.

After San Remo, there was much speculation that Varzi would drive a Maserati again now he had proved that he was still competitive. The prospects of Varzi in a 1500 was not the only source of excitement now emanating from Italy. For over a year there had been enthusiastic rumours of a 1500cc Alfa Romeo and with equal enthusiasm, these had been denied by the Milan factory. In January 1937, John Dugdale of "The Autocar" visited the Scuderia Ferrari works at Modena, the centre of Alfa Romeo racing activities and had received from Nello Ugolini, the Scuderia manager, a direct denial that such a car existed or was proposed. Despite the denial the rumours persisted and in May, "The Autocar" reported that the car would have a 60° V12 engine designed by Vittorio Jano. Obviously, it was becoming impractical to deny such a badly kept secret any longer and in August, it was announced that a 1500 Alfa Romeo had been designed by Gioacchino Colombo, who had worked with Jano, and it was being built with the intention of competing in voiturette races in 1938; true to the racing traditions of Alfa Romeo however, the car was to be not a V12, but a straight 8. The announcement caused great speculation in the press and produced forecasts that the Alfa Romeo would be the car to beat in 1938, particularly as it appeared that the limited resources of ERA were now being devoted to building a car to compete in the new 3 litre G.P. formula for the next season.

Speculation as to the prospects for 1938 did not detract from the obvious fact that for the rest of 1937 it was very unlikely that anyone was going to beat the C-type ERA provided it kept going. With the ERA flag flying so high, it was surprising that thre was only one British entry for the Coppa Acerbo at Pescara on 15th August, particularly as this event had been dominated by British cars and drivers for the past 4 years. Reggie Tongue was the only British entrant in the field of 15. On the long hard circuit, Luigi Villoresi led from the start ahead of Bianco, Rocco and Cortese and at the first corner, in the middle of the field, Pasquino Ermini tried to force his 6CM past the similar car of Uboldi. Ermini slid wide and was struck by Tongue's ERA which was on his tail and the Maserati spun into a crowd of spectators who were lining the corner. Tragically, four were killed and Ermini was injured. Tongue escaped unhurt but was out of the race which was led for the first 3 laps by Villoresi until his gearbox broke. Ettore Bianco should then have inherited the lead, but he spun off in the excitement of the moment, and Giovanni Rocco, who had been biding his time, went past and was not caught despite all Bianco's efforts to catch up.

The result was a clean sweep for the Bologna cars, though with Ermini's accident, no one could have felt much like celebrating.

a. *21st August, 1937: Practice for the Prix de Berne: Plate is having starting problems with his veteran 8C Talbot.*

b. *22nd August, 1937: Prix de Berne: The start of the second heat: Bira (ERA) and Cortese (6CM Maserati) lead Berg (6CM Maserati), Marazza (4CS Maserati) and Dobson (C-type ERA).*

Although the ERA team was not willing to cross the Alps, it was quite prepared to go as far as those mountains and both cars appeared at Berne. The second car was to be driven by Arthur Dobson who had been very impressive in his own private ERA in British events during the season. Everyone was very surprised when the works team of Maseratis was withdrawn, the excuse given being that they could not be made ready in time. The ERA team probably drew its own conclusions, but it meant that there was not likely to be much opposition to the black cars. There was great excitement when it seemed that Trossi, deprived of his 4CM Maserati, would drive Embiricos' ERA but nothing came of the rumour and at the end of practice the hopes of the ERA marque did not seem quite as high as they should have been; Dobson had supercharger trouble, "Romulus" had broken two pistons and had cracked his cylinder block and Tongue was forced to use his spare engine which was already worn out! The race was to be run in two 63 mile heats and a 95 mile final and the ERA prospects looked even less happy when Luigi Villoresi took the lead at the start of the first heat in his 6CM Maserati and led all the way to the finish. Mays however, was only 2 secs. behind, and the more perceptive wondered if Mays had been conserving his car for the final. Behind Mays, were Charles Martin in his B-type ERA and the Hungarian Lazlo Hartmann, in a new 4CM Maserati. Walter Baumer proved that the 750 Austin was still most competitive by holding sixth place until he retired.

In the second heat, ERA fans were encouraged for Dobson emulated Villoresi and led all the way. At first Bira held second place keeping in front of Cortese's 6CM Maserati but in an endeavour to preserve his car, whose cylinder block was patched with chewing gum, he eased off letting Cortese into second place. Behind Bira was the German Herbert Berg in a new white 6CM Maserati, which had been completed at Bologna only two weeks before, and Aldo Marazza in his old 2-seater 4CS.

Although the heats had been fairly predictable, the final was dramatic. Just before the start, it began to rain lightly and at the end of the first lap, Franco Cortese and Luigi Villoresi were in the lead followed by Bira 10 secs. behind, with the works ERAs fourth and fifth. Bira closed up the gap to 2 secs. then on the third lap the rain began to fall very heavily and Bira, as in the Isle of Man, took his chance and passed both Maseratis. He pulled away, and by the fifth lap, he was 13 secs. in front of Villoresi while Cortese had dropped back to fourth behind Dobson. On lap 6, Villoresi spun off and Dobson began to catch up with the blue ERA as the rain was easing off, and on lap 9 he took the lead. Mays was still 29 secs. behind Bira but there was to be drama for on lap 12 Berg spun his Maserati in front of the pits and struck the barrier at the side of the road; the battered and now very second-hand car bounced back onto the track and caught fire. Dobson who was just about to lap Berg, stopped dead, having misunderstood the flag marshal's signals. By the time he had started again, Bira had swept past and was in the lead once more. However, the speed of the works ERA soon told and by the end of lap 14 Dobson was in front again. Two laps later, Mays also passed "Romulus" and then caught up with Dobson and passed him so that on the last lap the two C-type ERAs were only two lengths apart. A victory for the ERA team was inevitable, but still the excitement was not quite over for as Mays approached the line he eased off, and Dobson passed him to win by half a length. Bira finished third after a fine drive with an ailing car while Cortese, with the best of the Maseratis was fourth.

Even though the tide was flowing so strongly for British voiturettes, no organizer on the English mainland felt justified in staging a full length 1500 scratch race but once again, the Junior Car Club went as far as it considered was prudent by promoting the 200 mile race at Donington with separate classes for the 1500s and the larger cars. In the 1500 class there were 7 ERAs including the two C-types, 4 Maseratis and a solitary MG. There was much delight that a fully recovered Earl Howe was to drive his equally fully recovered ERA. In practice, after a dash back from Berne, the C-type ERAs were much too fast for the opposition and Mays broke the lap record unofficially in 2 mins. 03 secs. At the start, Mays led the 1500 class from Dobson and Whitehead, while Bira was leading the race outright with his 2.9 Maserati. After 13 laps, Mays and Dobson passed Bira to lead the general classification and the 1500 class while Earl Howe, driving as well as ever, was third in the class ahead of Whitehead. Howe was having braking problems and stopped for adjustments, being re-passed by Whitehead so at 50 laps, the works ERAs led with impressive ease. Two laps later, however, Howe narrowly avoided another serious accident when his brakes failed and he struck the bank entering Starkeys Corner. It looked as if the ERA team was going to repeat the Berne performance but on lap 64, with 13 to go, there was a loud crack as Mays passed the pits and he pulled off with a broken rear axle. Dobson drove on steadily to win his second race in six days ahead of Peter Whitehead and Johnny Wakefield who had driven a good race in his 6CM Maserati, now painted red. Dobson finished 5 mins. 33 secs. in front of Whitehead while Wakefield was another 1 min. 51 secs. behind; the pace had

a. 11th September, 1937: Phoenix Park Dublin: The starter checks his watch, Mays' C-type ERA is about to be started on the handle, Wakefield (Maserati (11)) adjusts his goggles and "Lofty" England stands in front of Bira's Delage (1).

b. 19th September, 1937: Circuit of Lucca: Trossi (4CM Maserati) repeats his victory of the previous year.

been hard and Charles Brackenbury who had been driving Dobson's B-type ERA was the only other finisher in the 1500 class.

Throughout the season there had been great rivalry between Raymond Mays and Bira, both of whom were anxious to win the British Racing Drivers' Club Gold Star for road racing; in effect, the British championship. After Berne, there had been a lull in voiturette racing on the European mainland and by the beginning of September, both Mays and Bira were eager for points to clinch the title. Both took an interest in the 1500 race which was to be a new event in the annual meeting organized by the Irish Motor Racing Club in Phoenix Park in Dublin on 11th September. The D-shaped road circuit was the fastest in the British Isles and Bira held the lap record at 102.3 mph (164.7 kph) which he had gained with his 2.9 Maserati during the handicap race held on the circuit in 1936. Mays was driving his black C-type ERA, and with mechanical problems still besetting his ERAs, Prince Chula was forced to enter the Delage for Bira which he felt was likely to be well suited to the fast circuit. In practice, Mays lapped in 2 min. 29 secs. but surprisingly, Wakefield was second fastest with his 6CM Maserati, re-painted yet again and now green, some 2 secs. slower while the Delage lapped in 2 mins. 32 secs. The 1500 race over 24 laps of the 4.25 mile (6.8 km) circuit took place after the handicap race in which Bira finished 2nd with his 2.9 Maserati. Mays took the lead immediately and led by 5 secs. at the end of the first lap with the Delage in second place followed by Billy Cotton, the band leader, having his first race in the ex–Seaman ERA. Wakefield who had been fourth, overtook Cotton and gradually caught up with the Delage, taking second place on lap 8. The 6CM was going surprisingly quickly and during the next 10 laps the Delage and the Maserati changed places several times. On lap 17, Bira managed to draw away by 3 secs. but the Delage was unaccustomed to such a pace after such a long layoff and on lap 19, Bira stopped with a broken near-side rear spring. Wakefield settled down to follow Mays for the rest of the race and was flagged off in second place 2 mins. 12 secs. behind the victorious C-type ERA. Mays had averaged 102.9 mph (165.6 kph) and had lapped at 104.4 mph (168.0 kph) during his impressive demonstration. Cotton was third with his ERA and Robin Hanson was the only other finisher in his 6CM Maserati, but a lap behind; the rest of the 10 starters had retired.

Although it was now September, the Italian voiturette season continued with unabated fury and the "Millecinquecentisti" returned to the anciety city of Lucca for the Contessa Ciano Cup on the tight little circuit in the city. The main interest of the 60 lap race was Varzi's decision to flirt with a voiturette again. As at San Remo, he had a works 4CM and as Trossi had a similar car there was every prospect of a fierce race.★ The race was run on the 19th September and at 3.30 p.m. precisely Giuseppe Furmanik in his capacity as President of the Sporting Commission of the RACI launched the 13 starters and Franco Cortese took the lead followed by Varzi, Luigi Villoresi and Trossi. As everyone expected, Varzi was in front on the next lap while Trossi was up into third

★Before it was known that Varzi would be driving, the AC di Lucca had agreed with the Maserati factory that 4000 lire starting money would be paid for Trossi and 3000 lire each for Rocco and a third car with an unnamed driver: (AC di Lucca archives). Presumably Varzi justified a rise for the third car.

place. On lap 7 Trossi was second and three laps later he passed Varzi and took the lead; meanwhile, Cortese and Villoresi fought grimly only yards apart for third place. Varzi now had problems and the 4C engine began to misfire and after 15 laps he had fallen back to 20 secs. behind Trossi. Cortese passed him and at 24 laps Varzi's race was run. Trossi now had no challengers but Cortese and Villoresi continued their battle and were joined by an enthusiastic Bianco who became over-enthusiastic on lap 34 and buckled a wheel while passing through the Porta di Pietro. Cortese decided that whatever Bianco could do, he could do better, and when lapping Severi in front of the Wall of the Fascist Martyrs, he spun three times and hit the straw bales hard, and was taken to hospital with slight injuries. Amidst all the excitement, Trossi won by over a lap from Villoresi and Rocco who had driven steadily up the field as the others retired.

After Lucca, Luigi Villoresi had a long drive to his next engagement, the 1500 race which was to precede the Masaryk G.P. In 1937 this was given a new title, the G.P. de la Ville de Brno. Still looking for points for the BRDC Gold Star, Bira was entered with "Romulus" who had been given a new cylinder block since Berne, and he was joined by another English entry, Charles Martin with his ERA. The 12 starters balloted for grid places and Charles Martin led at the start of the 5 lap, 95 mile (153 km) race. Bira came up to second place from the back of the grid but then overshot a corner and fell behind Villoresi and Lazlo Hartmann with their 6CM Maseratis. Undaunted, the Siamese recovered and passed both the Maseratis and was only 2 secs. behind Martin at the end of the first lap. During the next 2 laps Martin extended his lead to 11 secs. but on lap 4 Bira speeded up and took the lead, but the effort was too much for "Romulus", and a piston burnt out as it had done previously in practice. Martin looked set for a well-deserved victory but on the last lap, his ERA wet a plug and began to misfire and he was passed by Villoresi who had not only driven steadily but quickly also, as he made fastest lap in 13 mins 55 secs. Villoresi came in to win while Martin finished second ahead of Hartmann; Bira just managed to struggle home in fourth place with a very sick car in front of the veteran Sojka who once again was racing his old T51A Bugatti in front of his home crowd.*

It might be thought that this would have been enough, but while Villoresi was beating the ERAs in Czechoslovakia, on the same day, 26th September, the rest of the Italian 1500 drivers were finishing off their season in fine style. On the Eastern shore of Lake Lugano is a delightful political anachronism; Campione d'Italia which is a small town forming an Italian enclave surrounded by Swiss territory. Campione is a holiday resort, so a 1500 race made an excellent finale to the summer season, run on a diminuitive 0.69 mile (1.11 km) circuit in the town. The race had particular significance, as it was to decide the 1937 Italian 1500 championship, for Trossi and Bianco arrived there with equal points. The race was run in three 40 lap heats with the first 2 cars in each heat going into the 50 lap final. Bianco won the first heat followed by an obedient Marazza who had been given a works 6CM for the race and was obviously obeying orders. Rocco and Lurani qualified in the second heat as did Trossi and

*Sojka even reappeared with the T51A in Czech events after the War in 1949. Unfortunately he was killed driving a works monoposto Tatra special at the Ecco Homo Hill climb in 1950.

Severi in the third. In the final, Rocco led for 5 laps then Trossi went ahead and by lap 20 he was lapping the tail end of the field, but on lap 25, he emulated Cortese's feat at Lucca and spun off while lapping Lurani. Trossi re-started the 4CM himself and returned to the pits where Marazza was pulled in and ordered to hand his car over to Trossi. The car must have resented the change and promptly retired with engine troubles which left Bianco in third place and with it the championship. Although he had to retire a lap later, the system of scoring gave him the title which he had deserved as he had been a front runner in almost every Italian event. Amidst all this excitement, Rocco drove steadily on to win from Severi and Lurani.

That at last was the end of the season for the 1500s, but for the Czechs, had they but known it, it was the end of motor racing. Austria had been under great pressure from Germany to yield to demands that it should agree to annexation as part of the Greater German Reich, and Hitler now began to make claims that Czechslovakia should cede the Sudeten territories in the west of the country to Germany. The political situation in Europe was deteriorating and the more realistic knew already that there could only be one outcome.

1937 had been the most strenuous season of all for the voiturettes, for there had scarcely been a weekend from April to September without a National or International race. In some ways, it had been an unsatisfactory season, for the principal protagonists, the C-type ERAs and Trossi's 4CM Maserati had not met and while the ERAs had been able to dispose of all the 6CMs with little difficulty, there was the nagging doubt that on some circuits, Trossi would have been a tough opponent for the Bourne team. Nevertheless, the black ERAs had been invincible after solving their brake problems at the beginning of the season and Raymond Mays and Humphrey Cook must have been well satisfied with their results. Furthermore, after Pat Fairfield's death the team had found a worthy replacement in Arthur Dobson. Of the private ERA drivers, Bira had still been the best, despite many technical disasters. It was clear that the Siamese team had tackled too big a task in trying to keep the ERAs raceworthy and develop the rebuilt Delage at the same time. If his ERA had been given enough time for preparation, it is likely that Bira's results for the season would have been much better. The other ERA private entrants had not made much impact; after his excellent results at the beginning of the season, Bjornstadt had faded away but Charles Martin had shown his skill and versatility with his notable victory in Berlin and his near-miss at Brno. The 6CM Maseratis had been a mixed bunch and clearly the performance of the car depended very much on who was driving it though the Villoresi brothers and Bianco had shown how well the car could still go. The Italian Maserati "Circus" had fought magnificently amongst themselves for the whole season and the Italian 1500 races had produced some fierce and close racing of a high standard. The British ERA drivers who had driven in the Italian events had found them much harder than they had expected and on the short urban circuits favoured by the Italians, it is possible that even the C-type ERA would have found the local drivers hard to beat. There was no shortage of newcomers anxious to enter the voiturette field and some of them, notably Aldo Marazza and Johnny Wakefield had both shown ability which augured well for the future.

117

In the Autumn of 1937, British enthusiasts could consider with some pride that the ERA was still the dominant 1500 in Europe but the design, although improved and developed, was now 4 years old, and there was little scope for further progress. Time was running out inexorably for the ERA, and already there were others eagerly waiting for the chance to take its place.

1938

THE START of a new Grand Prix formula usually brings great speculation and many forecasts of the likely form. In January 1938 perhaps the interest was less fervent than it had been four years earlier, for it was known that Mercedes-Benz and Auto-Union were going to race under the new formula and on the form that had been shown during the previous season, it was unlikely that the German teams would be matched by their rivals. In theory, the new formula was opening G.P. racing to a much wider field as it encompassed supercharged cars from 666cc to 3 litres with a sliding scale of minimum weights and unsupercharged cars now entered the list from 1000cc to 4^{1}_{2} litres with a corresponding weight scale. The Germans, who by now, probably knew the business of G.P. racing better than anyone else, settled down to build supercharged 3 litre cars and it was clear that no other type was likely to have any chance although in France, Delahaye and Talbot had ready-made unsupercharged G.P. cars to hand by stripping their successful sports cars.

In Italy, Alfa Romeo were building a new V16 3 litre and initially much more emphasis was being placed on this than on the new 1500 cars. In an endeavour to make their racing organization more efficient, in January 1938, the Alfa Romeo racing department in Milan was amalgamated with the Scuderia Ferrari which had previously conducted the practical side of the business. The new organization, called Alfa-Corse, with Enzo Ferrari in command, was based in the Scuderia's works at Modena.

While Alfa Romeo and Ferrari had been giving birth to Alfa-Corse, big changes were taking place in Bologna. For some time, Commendatore Adolfo Orsi, a rich Italian industrialist with many commercial interests, had been wooing the Maserati brothers in the hope of buying their business. At the beginning of 1938, agreement was reached and Orsi acquired the Maserati factory including the profitable sparking plug business which had given the small firm its major financial backing. The Maserati brothers were retained under a service agreement and Orsi appointed his own son Omer to manage his new acquisition, which was to remain in the old factory at Bologna for the time being.

Immensely strengthened by the Orsi takeover, while they had declared that their future now lay with the 1500 class, the Maserati brothers were also building a new 3 litre. ERA, their principal rivals in the voiturette field, had declared that they would support the new G P formula and were building an advanced car in the Bourne factory. This enthusiasm was extraordinarily misguided for it was announced at first that the car would be a $2\frac{1}{2}$ litre, then a $2\frac{1}{4}$ litre and finally it was declared that the English team would take on the world with a mere 2 litre engine. The English press, starved of a national G.P. car for so long, was inclined to persuade its readers that the new car was bound to be a world beater. An immediate and unfortunate effect of the decision to make a GP ERA, was that the resources of the tiny factory at Bourne were now divided between the new project and the existing voiturette team, to the detriment of both enterprises. Humphrey Cook was still giving the team an enormous subsidy from his own private resources, and it was astonishing that no attempt was being made to find the company any other income from the sale of racing cars, or technical expertise. There were vague plans for a sports car to be designed by Murray Jamieson, but nothing had or would come of this proposal. As a clear indication of the waning interest of ERA Ltd in voiturette racing, the second C-type of the 1937 team was sold to Prince Chula during the winter and only one C-type was retained for Raymond Mays. This car was slightly modified with improved front suspension, and brakes and became known as the "D" type. To give Mays some support, Lord Howe's old B-type was rebuilt at the factory to C-type specification at his own expense and he was to run as a team with Mays on an informal basis.

For the beginning of the 1938 season, the re-vitalized Maserati brothers were content to continue their variations on the 4CM and 6CM themes. The nose of the car was dropped to give a better view for the driver, the output of both engines was increased and the quarter-elliptic springs became a production feature. From Alfa-Corse came little real news of the new 1500 car, but behind the Ferrari doors at Modena, 6 cars had been laid down to the designs of Gioacchino Colombo and the parts had been machined in the Alfa Romeo factory at Milan for assembly at Modena. The first car was already being tested in the Spring by Attilio Marinoni who had been a works driver for many years. Despite the announcement in the previous August that the 1500 Alfa would be an 8 cylinder there were still rumours early in 1938 that the car would be a 6, but one doubt about the Alfa-Corse plans was resolved when Emilio Villoresi announced that he had signed an agreement with the team to drive the new cars.

As the principal opposition to the works teams, the White Mouse Stable of the Princes Chula and Bira was in a stronger position than in 1937, with the purchase of the second C-type and this joined the stable to be named "Hanuman" after a Siamese God. Bira had suffered some personal embarrassment during the winter as he had lost his driving licence the previous November for what Sammy Davis described, rather picturesquely, in "The Autocar" as "a little bit over-much enterprise round Meriden way". As the Delage venture had been so unsuccessful, Chula offered the cars for sale with all the spares and equipment for £2,500. Not surprisingly, there were no buyers for what many felt had grown from a white mouse into a white elephant. For most buyers, a more attractive bargain would have been the 1937 6CM Maserati offered at £750 by Robin Hanson at the end of the season.

After the success of the Phoenix Park race in September 1937, the Irish MRC

120

a. 22nd April, 1938: Practice for Cork G.P.: Bira (C-type ERA "Hanuman") leads Armand Hug (4CM Maserati) at Castle Bend.

b. 23rd April, 1938: Cork G.P.: The dilapidated Fiat lorry used by Hug to carry his Maserati.

c. 23rd April, 1938: Cork G.P.: The start on the 2½ mile straight. Bira (22) with a weak first gear goes off slowly and is beaten by Arthur Dobson (ERA (24).

decided to promote another 1500 race. This was to be run as part of a motor racing festival at Cork, on April 23rd, in conjunction with the Cork and District Motor Club, and the prize fund was increased by a generous donation from Joseph McGrath, who was the managing director of the Irish Hospitals Sweep Stake. Apart from the 1500 race, there was to be a local handicap event and a full G.P. race to the new formula. The most interesting feature of the meeting was the remarkable Carrigrohane circuit, with its 2½ mile (4 km) straight, on the outskirts of the city. Much to the organizers' disappointment, the race did not attract an entry from the ERA team, but several continental drivers had felt it worthwhile to make the long journey to compete for the substantial prize money, including a works supported 4CM Maserati for the Swiss driver Armand Hug, who was giving his new car its first voiturette race.★ The first prize was to be £250 with awards down to sixth place. The race was expected to be an easy victory for Bira with the C-type ERA "Hanuman" as the long straight was ideal for its Zoller blown engine, but unknown to his competitors, Bira had a problem, for the first gear band of the preselector gearbox was almost worn out and there had not been time to replace it before the race. At the start, much to the surprise of the crowd, said to be 100,000 strong Bira crept away and was passed by almost the entire field of eleven, but once in second gear, the acceleration of the C-type ERA took Bira back through the field and he was in second place behind Arthur Dobson's white B-type ERA at the end of the long straight. Bira was handicapped by the lack of first gear in negotiating the hairpin at the end of the straight but at the end of the first lap, he was closing up on Dobson and being followed by the 6CM Maserati of Luigi Villoresi entered by the Scuderia Ambrosiana, the 4CM of Hug and Wakefield with his 6CM. On the second lap, Bira took the lead; from then on, despite all Dobson's efforts, the blue car pulled steadily away, gaining between 7-11 secs. per lap on his pursuers. Dobson seemed to be safe in second place, but behind him, a tremendous battle began between Villoresi and Wakefield with an even match in cars and probably also in driving ability. By lap 5, Villoresi was starting to pull away from Wakefield whose engine was sounding woolly, while Hug, who had stopped for plugs, was up into fourth place again. At the end of the tenth lap, Bira was 37 secs. ahead, and on the eleventh lap Dobson found he had troubles, as the filler cap of the oil tank on his ERA opened. He attempted to lean down to close it while taking the hairpin but his efforts, together with the oil mist sprayed onto his rear tyres caused him to spin and strike the bank. The car was slightly damaged but with the filler cap shut, he restarted, Luigi Villoresi was close behind him and on the last lap made desperate efforts to catch the white ERA, while Wakefield who was driving with even greater vigour to compensate for his sick engine, also realised that there were higher stakes to play for. Unfortunately, on the back leg of the course, Wakefield made an error at Hell Hole corner and the Maserati left the road, overturned and rolled down a 30 ft. slope to the River Lee. Wakefield was thrown clear and was only slightly injured. Meanwhile, Villoresi had continued his chase and failed to

★Hug's car had an experimental Memini carburettor, a modified cylinder head and a stronger crankshaft.

catch Dobson by only 0.2 sec. but Bira had passed the flag 1 min. 40 secs. earlier. There were only 6 finishers and during his victorious progress Bira had been timed on the straight at 138 mph (222 kph), nearly 18 mph faster than the best Maserati.

After the Irish race, the English competitors returned home to a round of national events and Wakefield approached Raymond Mays with a request to build him a C-type ERA. For Hug and Villoresi, there was a long journey to North Africa for the Tripoli G.P. This race, on the fastest road circuit in the world, was run in conjunction with an Italian National Lottery, and in order to give the participants a reasonable chance of a winning ticket, it was necessary to swell the thin G.P. field by including a 1500 class. This was an all Maserati entry and it was clear that the difference in speed between the G.P. cars and voiturettes was likely to cause problems. Rocco's 6CM was fastest in practice in 4 mins. 26 secs. some 9 secs. faster than the Frenchman Raph with a similar car. The race was started by Marshal Balbo and there was some confusion so that the 1500cc cars were already threading their way through the G.P. cars, still waiting on the grid for the flag to fall. Villoresi led the 1500s at the start with the Ambrosiana 6 CM but soon dropped back and was passed by Cortese driving the latest works 6 CM. The race was run in intense heat with strong cross winds blowing sand on to the course and the conditions made passing difficult for the GP cars. On the eighth lap Cortese was about to be passed by Eugenio Siena who had joined Alfa Corse and was driving the new Tipo 312 GP Alfa Romeo. Siena slid on the loose sand and struck the wall of a house beside the course, and was killed instantly. Cortese retired shortly afterwards and this left Piero Taruffi to fight off a strong challenge from Rocco with the second of the works 6 CMs. Meanwhile, there had been another accident on lap twelve when Farina driving the second of the Tipo 312 Alfas collided with Lazlo Hartmann's 4 CM Maserati. Both cars overturned and while Farina was lucky to escape with slight cuts, the Hungarian, a veteran of so many voiturette events, suffered very severe injuries from which he died the following day. At the end of this unhappy race Taruffi came home to win the voiturette class by a mere 8 secs from Rocco after 327 miles (526 km). Lurani was third with his 4CM now with a 1500 engine. This car had been fitted with Tecnauto units replacing the rear semi-elliptic springs during the winter.

The all-Maserati circus had only a short sea trip to get to their next engagement in the Favorita Park at Palermo on the following Sunday 22nd May where the emasculated Targa Florio was being held once more. The race had suffered a further indignity as the RACI felt the original distance of 50 laps was likely to be too severe and reduced the distance to 30 laps. Race day was unpleasant as although it was very hot, the sky was overcast, there was a squally wind, and showers kept the circuit wet. As with so many races, Bianco led the field of 16 at the start followed by Luigi Villoresi, Marazza and Pietsch. This order held for 3 laps when Bianco's efforts and perhaps his revs, proved too much for the valve springs of his 4CM Maserati and he retired. He was joined by Lurani who had spun off into the straw bales. This left Villoresi in front staving off the attacks of Marazza driving the latest type works 6CM who went past into the lead on lap 10. He and Villoresi then battled fiercely followed at a

123

prudent distance by Rocco. The duel continued until lap 26 when the two Maseratis collided; Marazza spun off and was slightly hurt while his car suffered severe damage and Villoresi took nearly 3 mins to restart. This left Rocco who was driving the earlier type 6CM with an unassailable lead and he won by 2 mins. 10 secs. from Raph. Villoresi managed to rush through the field again and gained third place.

While the Italians had been racing their voiturettes on two continents, the English drivers had been taking part in the usual handicap events in which the D-type ERA had shown fast but unreliable form at Donington and Brooklands. However, the full European season was now starting and on 12th June, there was the usual strong British entry for the Picardie G.P. at Peronne. The most fancied entry was the D-type ERA of Raymond Mays who was supported by Earl Howe's works prepared C-type. The ERA team had now reverted to their original Liberty green although Howe's car had a blue stripe along the side. Although it looked as if the works ERAs would dominate the race as in 1937, at the end of practice their prospects did not seem so good, for Mays' engine was in pieces, having seized piston rings replaced, and Howe had supercharger problems. As before, the race was run in two heats and a final. In the first heat, Howe was matched against Bira with the C-type ERA "Hanuman" and at the start, the works car led and was 2 secs. in front of Bira at the end of the first lap. Bira then went past and carried on to win by 14 secs. while Ettore Bianco with a new works 4CM Maserati was unable to do anything about the ERAs and was lapped by both Bira and Howe before the finish. There was a shower of rain between the heats, but the road soon dried, and in the second 10 lap heat, Raymond Mays took an immediate lead and although feeling unwell with a high temperature, he pressed on to win by nearly 4 mins. from Norman Wilson's ex Fairfield A-type ERA with Lanza's 6CM Maserati a lap behind in third place. Behind Lanza was de Burnay's old K3 MG which although not able to keep up with the modern 1500s was certainly durable as de Burnay had won his class with it in the Bol d'Or 24 hour race at Montlhery the previous weekend. Johnny Wakefield, who had recovered from his Cork accident, had been third for 3 laps with Ian Connell's ERA★ until a piston broke, and Armand Hug who had held second place with his 4CM Maserati, retreated to the pits with brake problems early in the race and his mechanics borrowed some brake parts from the works ERA pits before the final, hoping to rectify the defects. After the first heat the Zoller supercharger of Howe's ERA was changed but the mechanics' efforts were of no avail as the vanes of the new supercharger broke up on the first lap of the final. At the start, Mays made a meteoric start and led the field but in doing so burnt out the first gear band. Without this essential aid, Mays could not hold Bira away from the slow corners and at the end of the first lap, the Siamese led by 4 secs. and began to pull away from a frustrated Mays. By lap 7 Bira had a lead of 1 min. but he then found his oil pressure was falling and he stopped for more oil. He restarted before Mays appeared, but "Hanuman" was now a sick car and just as Mays was about to retake the lead on lap 8, one of

★There is some doubt if this was Connell's car. This matter is discussed in detail in "The History of English Racing Automobiles Ltd" by David Weguelin.

124

"Hanuman's" con rods broke and the pieces almost hit Mays as he went past. After that, Mays reeled off the remainder of the 15 laps and won by 2 mins. 26 secs. from Bianco, with Sofietti, Wilson and Lanza a lap behind.

When the victorious ERA was flagged off at Peronne, an era which had begun at the Nurburgring more than 3 years earlier was ended, for never again would an ERA win a voiturette race on the European mainland. The shadows, just as they had done for Amilcar and Bugatti before, were now lengthening for ERA.

After Peronne, the English contingent returned home to mend their broken engines and gearboxes while the Italians had a fortnight to prepare for the next race on the calendar, the Princess of Piedmont Cup at Naples on 26th June. The race was run on the hilly Posillipo circuit as in previous years and race day was intensely hot. Trossi who had entered a 6CM Maserati for a change, asked for a reserve driver in case he could not cope with the conditions. He led the 18 starters away and stayed in front for 20 laps (50 miles (80 km) until he pulled into the pits complaining of double vision. As the reserve driver could not be found Trossi did another slow lap and then stopped and the car stood idle for nearly 10 laps until Rocco, whose 6CM had retired, took it over at the tail end of the field. Before Trossi's stop, he had been followed by Pietsch in his silver 4CM and Villoresi's 6CM. Pietsch now led for 10 laps, until passed by Villoresi and Aldo Marazza, and the German then hit a kerb and damaged his suspension. The heat was affecting many drivers and several stopped to hand over their cars to hastily summoned reserves. Marazza had already refuelled and so when Villoresi stopped, he went past and carried on to win, while Villoresi, despite furious efforts, had to be content with second place.

Throughout the season, there had been rumours and counter-rumours about the debut of the new Alfa Romeo. It was reported that the cars had been tested satisfactorily at Monza early in June★ and then the rumours intensified that the cars would be at Albi on 10th July. The leading voiturette competitors journeyed to South West France but found no Alfa Romeos present. It was noticeable that only one British driver, Raymond Mays, had felt the long trip worthwhile. British participation in European events was diminishing, perhaps because the ERAs were ageing, and the British owned 6CM Maseratis were not able to match the works cars, particularly when so far from home. Albi was run in its usual form of two heats for all the cars with the best aggregate time winning the race and attracted a surprisingly poor field. Only 9 cars came to the line and although the D-type ERA was the fastest car in the field, it had been beset with such supercharger problems that Mays had done virtually no practice. At the start of the first heat, Mays leapt into the lead which he held for 5 laps but then the Zoller blower asserted itself once again, and the ERA retired, but Mays at least had the satisfaction of a new lap record of 3 mins. 24 secs., a time which would not be beaten for another 10 years. Mays had been followed by Luigi Villoresi who now took the lead which he kept for the rest of the 20 lap heat. Behind him, Armand Hug retired when his oil filler opened and all the contents of the oil tank were duly ejected; Raph broke pistons and poor Ettore

★The Motor 7th June, 1938.

125

Bianco who was in third place managed to lose control of his 4CM Maserati, which overturned, cutting down telegraph poles. Bianco was removed to hospital and was reported to be seriously injured. Villoresi finished a lap in front of the other 4 finishers with Teagno and Soffietti in second and third places. In the second heat, there were only 6 starters but Villoresi took the lead again followed by Teagno and Hug who had refilled his oil tank. Hug, although he had no chance of winning was determined to make a race of it and passed Teagno, then Villoresi, on lap 7. The Swiss pressed on and finished 1 min. 33 secs. ahead of Villoresi but his effort was of no avail and Villoresi, somewhat bothered by oil being sprayed over him from his engine, gained an all-Italian victory with Teagno second and "Gigi" Platé with his modified 1926 straight eight Talbot was third, no less than 8 laps behind on aggregate. It had been a disappointing race and it was clear that the D-type ERA, although still fast, was now very brittle; the resources of the little works at Bourne were so over-stretched that it was proving too much to develop a new car and keep even one other racing. Perhaps British supporters derived some comfort from the knowledge that both Villoresi and Hug had raced on Dunlop tyres. Luigi Villoresi must have left Albi as soon as he had collected his prize money for he had another commitment a week later as he was entered for the Circuit of Varese on a tight 2.23 mile (3.6 km) course in the little town in the Alpine foothills. The entry was divided into two heats; Aldo Marazza won the first and Villoresi was the victor in the second, but in the final Villoresi's car broke down, perhaps feeling the strain of the rapid return from Albi and Franco Cortese won, having kept ahead of Marazza who was 28.4 secs behind at the end of the 30 lap race. While Mays had been frustrated at Albi, Bira had taken the easier option and raced at Donington the previous day where he had won the Nuffield Trophy with "Hanuman". Sadly yet again, this was a class handicap; even though the golden days of ERA were ending, the organisers of English events still fought shy of a straight forward 1500 scratch race.

At last, 4 weeks after Albi, it happened. In 1937 the Livorno meeting had been elevated to the dignity of the Italian G.P. and no voiturette race had been deemed necessary, but in 1938, the G.P. went back to Monza and the Coppa Ciano was revived with its supporting voiturette race, on a circuit shortened to 3.6 miles (5.8 km). In honour of the revival, Alfa Corse produced 3 of their new cars the Tipo 158 Alfa Romeo. In hindsight, 7th August 1938 was a turning point in voiturette racing, and a true landmark in the history of motor racing, but at the time, the organizers and the Italian enthusiasts were merely relieved that at last, the cars were shown to be in existence, and were going to race. The cars were small, neat and tidy in appearance. The streamlined and well faired body covered a straight 8 twin cam engine with trailing arm front suspension using a transverse leaf spring and swingaxle rear suspension also using a transverse leaf. The chassis frame was tubular and the gearbox was in unit with the final drive. The technical specification of the car was a considerable step forward, and immediately dated all the contemporary voiturettes. For the first race, the drivers were to be Emilio Villoresi, Clemente Biondetti and Francesco Severi who had been a test driver for Alfa Romeo and raced for the Scuderia Ferrari. The race was a short one, only 25 laps and in practice, the new Alfas

126

a. *7th August, 1938: Coppa Ciano Livorno: Luigi Villoresi smiles confidently before his first works Maserati drive. His new 6CM has quarter elliptic rear suspension and a light alloy cylinder block.*

b. *7th August, 1938: Coppa Ciano Livorno: Emilio Villoresi fastens his windcap as he waits beside his Tipo 158 Alfa Romeo about to make its triumphant debut.*

c. *7th August, 1938: Coppa Ciano Livorno: The Tipo 158 Alfa Romeos out accelerate Luigi Villoresi's 6CM Maserati at the start.*

d. *7th August, 1938: Coppa Ciano Livorno: Severi is push started after spinning his Tipo 158 Alfa Romeo.*

e. *7th August, 1938: Coppa Ciano Livorno: The German Paul Pietsch in his works entered 4CM Maserati.*

showed they were cars to be reckoned with by taking the front row of the grid with Luigi Villoresi's 6CM Maserati. Villoresi had been invited to join the Maserati works Team in the place of Rocco and to cope with the opposition the Bologna factory had built a new 6CM with a lower nose, more streamlined body and a light alloy cylinder block. At the start, Severi led the field of 16 away, but brother Luigi upheld the honour of Maserati by taking the lead during the first lap. On the second lap Luigi Villoresi still led followed by the Alfa team in line ahead formation, with Pietsch trying hard to keep up with his 4CM Maserati. Ettore Bianco was racing his 4CM Maserati despite his Albi injuries but retired after one lap. It seemed as if the new cars would not be able to match the speed and experience combined in the leading Maserati but the pace was telling and Emilio Villoresi took the lead when the Maserati began to sound rough. The driving of some of the tail enders was more spectacular than skilful and two Maseratis ended up in the straw bales on the long right hand bend after the pits. After 15 laps, Luigi Villoresi was out of the race and the Alfas then settled down to complete the 25 laps and score a most convincing victory, marred slightly by Severi, who had been forced to stop for a plug change after a spin and then lost 2 laps. Over a minute behind the victorious Alfa Romeos of Villoresi and Biondetti, was Aldo Marazza's 4CM Maserati and the only other car still on the same lap was Cortese's 6CM.

The Tipo 158 Alfa Romeos were now the cars against which other voiturettes had to be judged, and their next appearance a week later, at Pescara, was eagerly awaited. As a sign of the decline in British interest in continental voiturette racing, for the first time in 6 years, the Coppa Acerbo Vetturette attracted no British entrants, though there was now little incentive for British drivers to race in Italy, as a change in the Italian currency regulations had made it almost impossible to take starting and prize money out of the country. It was a rather meagre field of 11 cars that lined up for the usual early start at Pescara. Luigi Villoresi was clearly determined to show that he and the works 6CM Maserati were a match for his brother with his new Alfa Romeo and at the start the Maserati took the lead followed closely by Severi's Alfa Romeo and Marazza with his Maserati. This time, the Alfa Romeo team found that it was not so easy. The climb into the mountains and the descent to the long sea level straight upset the carburation of the 8 cylinder engines and the team of 3 cars retreated to the pits for plug changes. This did not remedy the trouble for Emilio Villoresi and Biondetti, who both retired while Severi limped on. Marazza had also retired with his works 6CM, so this left Luigi Villoresi to drive on to win by over 3 minutes from Paul Pietsch and Guido Barbieri to give a clean sweep for Maserati, and to show that the new Alfa was not quite so invincible as it had seemed before. The Tipo 158 was fast though for Severi, while limping into 5th place, had been timed at over 141 mph on the straight, over 4 mph faster than the best Maserati, which surprisingly, was not Villoresi's but that of Pietsch.

So far the Tipo 158 Alfa Romeo or the *Alfettas* as they had become known, had met the works Maseratis twice and the results had not been wholly conclusive but the week after Pescara, the new cars were entered for the voiturette race preceding the Swiss G.P. at Berne, and as both the ERA and Maserati teams were also attending, the race was eagerly awaited in the hope

128

that it would establish who was the king of the 1500 castle. There was much disappointment when Alfa Corse announced that their cars would not be going to Switzerland. Obviously the cars were not yet perfected while furthermore, they were engaged to race at Monza on 11th September and it was understandable that it was important, for reasons of prestige, for the Monza race to be a success for the Tipo 158s. Even with the Alfa Corse withdrawal, Berne promised to be a good race for the best of the rest were there. The organizers seemed to have made some attempt to "seed" the entires in the two heats as 2 of the 3 fastest Maseratis, those of Villoresi and Pietsch, were racing against Bira's C-type ERA in the first heat while the works ERAs of Mays and Earl Howe now appearing in a new metallic blue finish only had the Maserati of Hug as their real opposition in the second heat. The first heat was to be run at 10 a.m. and at the start of the 14 lap race, a Maserati trio of Villoresi, Pietsch and Berg led an ERA trio of Bira, Wilson and Wakefield who now had a new ERA, the last car to be sold to a private customer. This was a B-type chassis with a C-type engine. Initially, Wakefield had ordered a full C-type to replace his wrecked Maserati, but as the fitting of the Porsche front suspension would have delayed delivery, he took the earlier chassis which had apparently been stored by the factory since 1936. At the end of the first lap, Villoresi led from Pietsch, with Wakefield now third, for Bira went straight to his pit and retired with a split supercharger casing. Villoresi now began to pull away from his pursuers but it was not to last and he retired with engine problems, leaving the heat to Pietsch who was followed in by Wilson and Wakefield. As the second heat started, it began to rain but this did not deter Mays who made his usual sprint start and led at the end of the first lap followed by Earl Howe and the 4CM Maseratis of Hug and Bianco. In fifth place, driving in his first major voiturette race, was a 19 year old officer cadet on leave from Sandhurst, Tony Rolt, who had bought Bira's old ERA "Remus" and had already shown much promise in small events in Britain. Rolt passed both Hug and Bianco on lap 4 and held third place behind the works ERAs until the end. 14 cars qualified for the final and it seemed unlikely that the works ERAs would be unduly troubled. Although Mays was beaten at the start by Pietsch and Bianco, he was in the lead at the end of the first lap followed by Earl Howe whose engine was misfiring slightly. This soon made the Earl an easy prey for the pursuing Maseratis, and Pietsch went past. It was not to be ERA's day for Mays, whose gearbox had disliked his getaway in the first heat, now retired both with gearbox problems and a broken supercharger. The weakness of the Zoller was due partly to the difficulty of getting the correct clearances on the sliding vanes and partly to the distortion of the casing. Overwhelmed by his unexpected fortune, Pietsch's Maserati now expired, so Earl Howe led briefly but the misfire was getting worse and despite all his efforts, Hug, Bianco and then Wakefield passed him. To the huge delight of the crowd, Hug kept his lead and became the first Swiss driver to win an international race in his own country. Bianco, now fully recovered from his Albi crash was second, but 1 min. 40 secs. behind and only just staved off Wakefield, who was 1 sec. behind the Italian at the finish. Rolt, who should have been well up after his form in the heats, stalled on the line and lost 2 laps before his car would start. After that he drove with great verve and despite the 2

a. 21st August, 1938: Prix de Berne: Johnnie Wakefield sits in his B/C type ERA at the pits; for an almost new car the seat is surprisingly scruffy.

b. 21st August, 1938: Prix de Berne: Pietsch's 4CM Maserati leaves Bira (ERA (58)) and Wakefield (ERA (12)) at the start of the first heat.

c. 21st August, 1938: Prix de Berne: In the final Pietsch is again quicker off the mark than the ERAs. No. 18 is Mays, No. 16 is Howe. Rolt (ERA (10)) has stalled his engine.

d. 21st August, 1938: Prix de Berne: Rolt is about to pass Teagno (6CM Maserati) in his efforts to make up lost time in the final. The back leg of the Bremgarten circuit was surprisingly narrow and bumpy.

lap deficit, he managed to work his way up into the tail-end of the field and finished ninth.

After the Berne meeting there were many who wondered if, by 11th September, there would be any motor race at Monza in which the Alfettas could run, for the political situation in Europe was deteriorating and war now seemed certain. In the previous March, the Austrians had finally yielded to Hitler's pressure and had submitted reluctantly to the annexation of the country by the Greater Reich. This triumph had made Hitler's insistent demands that the Czechs should hand over the Sudeten territories, even stronger. By August, it seemed to the British and French governments that if Hitler's demands were not granted, it was likely that Germany would take the Sudetenland by force. As France had guaranteed the frontiers of Czechslovakia, such an act would precipitate another European war. Such a disaster seemed unthinkable after the holocaust of 1914/18 and there was a frenzy of activity by the diplomats of Great Britain and France whose governments were determined to prevent a war for which both were so ill-prepared, despite a programme of re-armament which had begun in 1935. There was an equal frenzy of activity by their German diplomatic counterparts, who were bent on obtaining the maximum advantage for Germany, short of starting a war, for which Germany was not so well prepared as the rest of Europe believed. While both sides played their diplomatic hands, the nations of Europe waited with foreboding.

It was in this atmosphere of gloom, that the British contingent returned home from Berne, for they were to race over the Campbell circuit at Brooklands, the following Saturday, in the JCC 200 which as in previous years had a 1500 class racing against a formula libre class for the outright prize. In 1938 an 1100 class was included as well, however, the race did not attract any foreign entries and was virtually a British national event. Bira's 3-litre Maserati was the only car likely to beat the 1500s for the out-right prize, and in the 1500 class, Mays took an early lead, but the works ERA was running true to form, and stopped for plugs after 8 laps thereafter retiring with scavenge pump failure. This left Arthur Dobson in the class lead but his old ERA broke a piston on lap 22 and Johnnie Wakefield then led the 1500 class in his new B/C type ERA and after a stop by Bira, he also led the overall classification. Driving with skill and restraint, Wakefield held the lead to the end and thus scored his first major victory; behind him in the 1500 class, Lord Howe was second, 2 laps behind, followed by Tongue, Rolt and E.K. Rayson who had resurrected his 1934 4CM Maserati. The 1100 class was won by the K3 MG of Cuddon-Fletcher which had been fitted with a twin cam cylinder head and independent front suspension of Lancia type by its owner Reg Parnell. This had been the car with which Hamilton had gained his victory at Pescara in 1934. The day after Wakefield's win, Armand Hug won again, this time on the sands at La Baule where the small meeting now had a 1500 race as the main event. The Swiss, driving his usual 4CM Maserati had a struggle in the early laps with Rene Dreyfus who had returned to voiturette racing for a busman's holiday after driving for the Ecurie Bleu Delahaye team in grand prix events, but Dreyfus' 6CM did not last, and once he had retired, the excitement went out of the race and Hug had an easy win. A lap behind, came Berg in his 6CM Maserati* while in third place, as an echo of the

---

*Berg entered his car under the title of the Scuderia Altona.

past, was Jean Delorme with his T51A Bugatti. An even more poignant reminder of past glories was the appearance of Maurice Mestivier, driving the ex-Scaron MCO Amilcar, which took a gallant fourth place.

The Italians felt, perhaps with some justification, that the quarrel their partner in the Berlin-Rome Axis was having with the British and French over the fate of the Czechs, was not yet their concern, so they decided to carry on motor racing. The Lucca event for the Coppa Edda Ciano run in the old City, was held on the 4th September. No doubt to the joy of the organizers, Alfa-Corse entered two Tipo 158s, but unfortunately these did not appear and this left a field of 11 Maseratis to race in heavy rain. As seemed almost inevitable, Ettore Bianco led at the start but Villoresi passed him on lap 3 and went on steadily to win, clinching the 1938 Italian 1500 championship. Bianco held second place for 29 laps until his transmission failed, while Pietsch, who had been close behind Bianco at the beginning, spun off on lap 9 and spent the rest of the race tearing through the field trying to catch up. At the end he was up to third place only 13 seconds behind Cortese. A week later Alfa-Corse indicated that they felt the answers had been found, for the Alfettas arrived at Monza for the Milan Grand Prix, the 1500 preliminary event before the Italian Grand Prix. The Italians were very disappointed that the race only attracted one British entry, the old white ERA of Arthur Dobson. It was pointed out with some bitterness that during the four seasons they had been racing, the works ERAs had never crossed the Alps, although during that time, the Italian works and works supported teams had managed to visit the British Isles. However whatever the reasons had been in earlier years, the Italian currency regulations provided little incentive for the works ERAs to appear now. As the cars were lined up on the grid, the drivers were presented to Signor Dino Alfieri, the Italian Minister of Propaganda and

11th September, 1938: Milan G.P. Monza: Severi at Lesmo corner on his way to second place in his Tipo 158 Alfa Romeo.

the crowd shouted its delight when the august minister was greeted by an exuberant Fascist salute from Arthur Dobson. Perhaps the excitement of this reception over-excited Dobson, as the ERA broke a half shaft when the field was flagged away and so took no further part. The Alfetta team had been strengthened by the recruitment of Raymond Sommer, by then perhaps the leading French driver, who had replaced Biondetti, and at the end of the first lap Sommer's Alfa led Luigi Villoresi's 6CM Maserati, the Alfa of Severi and Pietsch's Maserati. A retreat from Berne had not quite solved all the problems, as on the next lap Sommer came into the pits for new plugs and this left Luigi Villoresi leading Severi and his brother Emilio, as he had done at Livorno and Pescara.

As on the two previous occasions, the 6CM Maserati was already being pushed along faster than it liked, to keep in front of the Tipo 158 Alfas, and on lap 4 it rebelled with a burnt piston. This left brother Emilio in the lead with Severi close behind ahead of Marazza, Marinoni with the fourth Alfa and Pietsch. The two cars ran on for the rest of the 25 lap race; Severi took the lead on the penultimate lap but was repassed by Villoresi and the two cars crossed the line 1.2 seconds apart to produce the sort of demonstration that Alfa-Corse had wanted. As an indication of the rapidity of the Alfa Romeos, Armand Hug who finished third on his 4CM Maserati was 2 min. 55 sec. behind. Sommer had restarted with new plugs and pressed on, although far behind his team-mates. Perhaps he pressed too hard, for as the car crossed the line, it emitted a great cloud of smoke, probably from a broken piston. Aldo Marazza who had lost over a lap in the pits was following the Alfa across the line and failed to see the flag, so continued at full speed, not realising the race was over. As Marazza entered Lesmo corner, it is possible that his view was obscured by the smoke from the Alfa Romeo that was still ahead of him. The Maserati slid wide and somersaulted as it touched the edge of the track, and the driver was thrown high into the air and impaled on the branch of a tree beside the track. Poor Marazza was terribly injured and died later that evening. A native of Milan, he was 24 years old, and it was perhaps ironic that one of the new Alfa Romeos should have been instrumental in causing his death as it seemed likely that Alfa-Corse would have been anxious to obtain the services of such a promising driver for the following season.

There was now only one voiturette race left in the calendar, and it began to seem likely that the season would end before a war could start, even though the political situation was still critical. The last race was to be round-the-streets of Modena, the home of the Alfa Romeo in the old Scuderia Ferrari premises. The race was expected to be a triumphant finale for the new Alfa Romeos, and 4 cars were entered for Emilio Villoresi, Biondetti, Sommer and Severi. All the best Maseratis were present, and Arthur Dobson came with his old ERA, to which he had fitted a new half-shaft. As it was to be the last race of the season, it was clear that the Alfa and Maserati teams would show no mercy. Luigi Villoresi led the 19 starters, followed by Cortese, Biondetti, brother Emilio and Severi. On lap 2, Biondetti passed Severi and then went past Villoresi on lap 4 and took the lead. On the next lap, Villoresi was in front again, and the pace was already too fast for some, for 3 cars had already retired, and on lap 4, Biondetti stopped at

133

his pit. A lap later, perhaps exulting in the failure of the first Alfa, Villoresi broke the gear lever on his 6CM Maserati and retired. This left Emilio Villoresi in the lead, and at 10 laps he led by 2 seconds from Cortese, who had Severi only 1 second behind him. Meanwhile, Sommer had also stopped at his pit and the Alfas were in serious trouble with oil pressure and bearing problems. The order held until lap 20, but Pietsch had stopped on lap 17 and handed over his 4CM Maserati to Luigi Villoresi, who set off to catch up the leaders who were now over a minute in front of him. Severi then stopped with a misfire, but restarted again, as had Biondetti and Sommer, and the 3 Alfas ran together at the tail of the field. At the front of the field, Emilio Villoresi was now having troubles with his brakes, and on lap 27, Cortese went past the Alfa which then pulled up at the pits on lap 31 with the same bearing problems as the other cars. Villoresi did not restart and he was soon joined by Biondetti and also by Severi whose rear suspension was broken. Sommer kept going for another 8 laps then he too stopped and that was the end of Alfa-Corse hopes. Cortese who was driving the 6CM used by Pietsch at Monza was now able to ease up, there being no one left to challenge him, for Luigi Villoresi had retired on lap 34. Of the 19 starters, there were now only 4 survivors and Cortese won by a lap from Armand Hug; Arthur Dobson, who had driven steadily in his ERA, although outpaced, finished third 3 laps behind the winner. The race had been a humiliation, but also an object lesson to Alfa-Corse, and had shown up the weaknesses of the Tipo 158 in front of its own home crowd.

On the Monday following the Modena race, ERA Ltd. announced that it had abandoned the project of building a Grand Prix car. This had been tested at Donington during the summer and was totally uncompetitive so the decision was taken to use the new chassis with much modification for a 1500 with a redesigned and improved engine. It was clear that the little firm stood no chance at all in Grand Prix racing and with the appearance of the Tipo 158 Alfa Romeo, even an ERA revival in voiturette racing was not likely to be easy. The decision to abandon the Grand Prix car, was the start of a crisis that was to simmer at ERA for the next few months. As the crisis in the life of ERA Ltd. began, so the European political crisis was apparently ending, for on 29th September, Britain, France, Germany and Italy signed the Munich Agreement which dismembered Czechoslovakia and gave Hitler all that he had demanded; this being considered a cheap price to pay for "peace in our time". Despite the apparent satisfaction that war had been averted, the main signatories of the Munich Agreement now settled down to rearm at an even quicker pace, for it was clear that sooner or later, war was certain.

Relieved by the knowledge that there was now likely to be a 1939 season, the motor racing world went back to its business, and soon the rumours were flying in the press that Mercedes Benz and Auto Union were building 1500s to rival the Tipo 158 Alfa Romeos. It was said that the Mercedes was to be a V12, but amidst the rumours there was one clear statment; the Tripoli Grand Prix was to be a 1500 race in 1939. Inevitably, as with so many events in those troubled times, this had a political incentive. The Italians decided that it was bad for their prestige as a colonial power, that the fastest road race in the world, held in their principal colony, should be an annual German benefit, so the change was made

134

with the confident prediction that this would secure an Italian victory. To those who could pause during a troubled autumn to reflect on the past season, it was clear that the advent of the Tipo 158 Alfa Romeo had overturned the existing world of voiturette racing which was now divided into two divisions of quality.

The first division events were those in which the Alfas competed, and the rest were relegated to the second division. Although the new cars were not quite perfect, their design and performance, and the professional approach of the Alfa-Corse team with its massive industrial backing, made the other competitors appear amateurish. The difference between Alfa Romeo and its competitors, was as marked as it had been for ERA and its rivals in 1935. For ERA, beset by internal problems and increasing financial stringencies, the good days were over. It was clear that the resources of the little factory at Bourne could not hope to rival even the Orsi-backed Maserati brothers, let alone the potential of Alfa-Corse. It is perhaps a source of regret that the ERA team in decline did not meet the rising star of Alfa Romeo, for it may be conjectured that such a conflict would have been very evenly matched in 1938. The D-type ERA and even the C-type were certainly faster than Luigi Villoresi's 6CM Maserati, and this car had the speed to hold the Alfettas, so perhaps the British car could have left the arena in glory, had the chance come its way.

At Maserati, the future still looked bright. In Luigi Villoresi they had a driver of great skill, as had been manifested by his victory in the Italian 1500 championship. He was, moreover, the only driver to keep ahead of the Alfa Romeos with a car that had been designed nearly 3 years before. With a new design in hand, the prospects were promising and perhaps anything was possible. However, if Luigi was Italian 1500 champion, there were those who declared that Emilio was the finer driver. The other bright star for Maserati had been Armand Hug, who had started the season being placed well in races, and ended it by winning them. In England, the fading of the ERA had also faded the hopes of some drivers. Bira and Mays had only one victory each to show for their efforts, but there were other young drivers, particularly Wakefield and Rolt, with promising prospects for the future. The coming season augured well for Alfa Romeo, but there were others who had plans in the new, politically influenced world of the voiturette.

1939

B Y THE OPENING OF 1939, International politics were profoundly affecting the sport. The tension between the European nations had grown to a point where every action was deemed to have a political and nationalistic motive, and at the centre of the tension, both geographically and actively, were Germany and Italy, the two partners in the Rome-Berlin Axis. Relations between France and Italy had been deteriorating, as France suspected Italian intentions concerning the French colonies in North Africa. Italy had declared that a 1935 agreement between the two nations on the subject was no longer binding, and demanded that the whole matter of colonial frontiers should be given proper consideration by the French. As this was not forthcoming, the Italian government decreed that amongst other things, no Italian drivers or factory teams should race in France in 1939. This caused less anguish to the French than to the Germans, who were relying upon Tazio Nuvolari as the leading driver in the Auto Union team. As a further blow for the cause of Italian nationalism, it was decreed that the Italian manufacturers should only pick Italians for their works teams. As a result, Armand Hug who had hoped to sign up with Maserati, found himself out of a job, and there were no more Alfa Romeo drives for Raymond Sommer. The future of Grand Prix racing was now a subject of constant discussion and it seemed clear that if the 3-litre formula was allowed to run its full course, it would be followed by a 1500cc formula, thus elevating the voiturette to full grand prix status, as it had been before in 1926/27.

As Italy had virtually dropped Grand Prix racing in favour of the 1500s in order to regain lost national prestige, it was almost certain that the German teams would enter the voiturette field, and the rumours of a 1½ litre Mercedes-Benz proliferated. Between January and March 1939 it was variously reported in the British motoring press that the 1500 Mercedes would be a six, a straight-8 and a V12, but from Daimler Benz, there came no word.

While the world waited for Mercedes, Alfa Romeo had been improving the Tipo 158 by altering the lubrication system, and fitting needle roller big-ends, a direct consequence of the failures at Modena. This was despite rumours in the British press that the whole team of Tipo 158s was to be sold to a British driver while Alfa-Corse developed a new V12. The Maserati brothers, with Orsi support, had been developing an entirely new design during the winter. This used the wishbone and torsion bar front suspension of the 6CM and the quarter elliptics which had been adopted for the 6CM in 1938. The whole car was much lower however, and had a neat well-faired body. The biggest change was in the engine where a 4 cylinder "square" 78mm x 78mm layout was chosen with 4 valves per cylinder fed by a Roots supercharger from the front of the engine.[*] When asked why the 6 cylinder design was not favoured Bindo Maserati said that although the 6CM probably had greater potential for development, the 4 cylinder car was more accessible, robust, easier to maintain, cheaper to build, and hence to sell, and the Maseratis and the Orsis were in business to sell racing cars, which did not seem to leave much scope for further discussion. Despite these comments though, development of the 6CM continued.

As Alfa Romeo and Maserati prepared their cars, British enthusiasts waited with increasing impatience for a chance to see the new ERA. Unlike the Italian firms with almost unlimited industrial resources, the English company was forced to rely on outside suppliers for almost every component. British industry was now working at top speed to fulfil lucrative armament contracts, and "one-off" work for a small private customer had no priority, so the new car was held up by continuous delays. At last, the car, the E-type[**] was shown to the world at the beginning of April and it was seen to be a low, shapely machine, with a long tail. The front suspension was the well-tried Porsche system, while at the rear, the De Dion principle was used, like the current W163 Grand Prix Mercedes-Benz. The frame was built of parallel steel tubes, which had already proved too flimsy on test, and an extra tube had been roughly welded to the top of the existing tube. The 4-speed synchromesh gear-box was in unit with the final drive, while the driver sat astride the propeller shaft which had been lowered by using drop gears. The engine was perhaps the biggest surprise, for it was still a 6-cylinder using the Riley lay-out of two camshafts set high in the block, with short push rods and rockers, and was fed by a very large Zoller blower mounted alongside the block. The use of the Riley valve gear had been unusual in the original car, but had been prompted by the need to get commercial support from Rileys, but its retention in a pure racing design nearly six years later, was remarkable. The new car had been designed by Peter Berthon and Arthur Barratt and its debut was promised in the British Empire Trophy Handicap at Donington on April 1st.

The considerable interest that the new ERA had promoted, was largely over-shadowed a few days later by an announcement from Daimler Benz, that a $1\frac{1}{2}$ litre Mercedes Benz had been built, and two cars would be entered for the Tripoli Grand Prix on the 7th May. This was to be the first major event of the season, but some of the voiturette had already raced when the new year was only two days old. For several years, there had been a short season of South African races in December and January, and although these had been handicaps, they had attracted large European entries and even Auto Union had felt it worthwhile to send a car in 1936/37. The majority of entrants in these handicaps had driven voiturettes, and the organizers, realising that 1500 races would be

---

[*]The car was tested with 2 superchargers positioned alongside the cylinder block but this arrangement was abandoned.

[**]As an indication of its ancestry it had the chassis number "G.P.I."

2nd January, 1939: South African G.P. East London: The works 6CM Maseratis of Luigi Villoresi and Franco Cortese dominated the race. Cortese has a slight lead from Villoresi at the start.

fully supported, decided to promote two scratch events in January 1939. The first race, on 2nd January, had the full dignity of the title of South African Grand Prix, and attracted quite a good entry, headed by the works 6CM Maseratis of Luigi Villoresi and Franco Cortese. These were supported by Taruffi with his 6CM and Hug and Pietsch with their 4CMs. Lord Howe and Peter Whitehead had also made the long sea voyage with their ERAs. The race was run over 18 laps of the 11 mile (17.7 km) Prince George Circuit, outside East London, and in front of a crowd of 50,000, the two works Maseratis took the lead from the start, and were never headed. Villoresi was the winner 1 min. 40 secs. in front of Cortese. Behind the Maseratis there was a lively battle involving Howe, Hug, the Hon. Peter Aitken (ERA)* and the local drivers, Roy Hesketh with an ERA, and Dr. Massacurati, an ex-patriate Italian dentist with another works supported 6CM Maserati. Howe stopped to change a plug on lap 4 and then lost oil pressure while Hug fell back with various problems and the good doctor took third place with the fastest lap of 104.27 mph (167.8 kph), which was only proper, as he was a cousin of Tazio Nuvolari. A fortnight later, the second race of the series, the Grosvenor Grand Prix, was held at Cape Town and this time, Cortese won from Aitken and another local, Steve Chiappini with a 6CM Maserati. Villoresi and Lord Howe fell by the wayside.

    The South African races had been more of an epilogue to the 1938 season, than the start of 1939, and the proper season was to begin on a truly heroic scale in Tripoli on 7th May, in a meeting of the giants where the Tipo 158 Alfa Romeos were to face the new 4CL Maseratis and the unknown quantity of the new Mercedes-Benz. When the new Mercedes arrived in Tripoli, it was seen that they resembled small replicas of the W163 Grand Prix cars. The new

★The ex R.E. Tongue car.

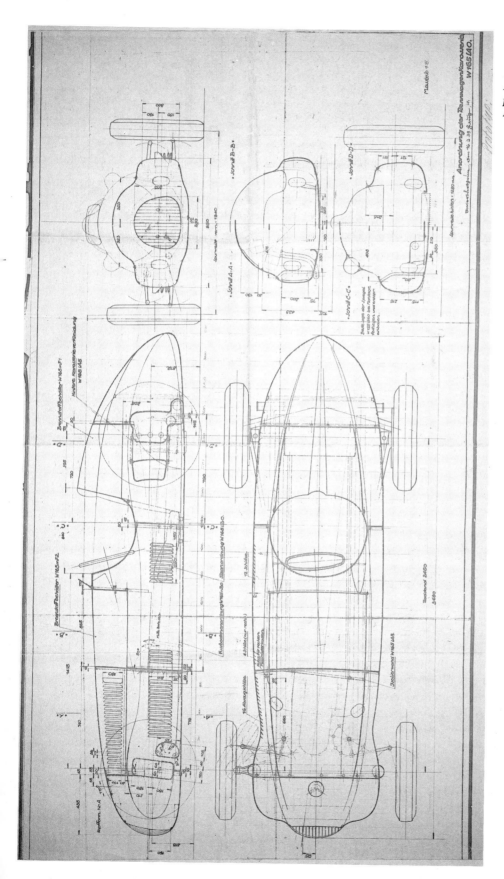

16th February 1939: Preliminary body drawings are prepared for the W165 Mercedes-Benz.

models, designated W165, were V8s, a configuration that none of the rumours had considered. The chassis of the new cars were scaled-down versions of the grand prix models, with wish-bone and coil spring front suspension and De Dion suspension at the rear, using torsion bars. Each bank of cylinders on the V8 engine had two camshafts and there was a large Roots supercharger driven from the front of the engine. The chassis was tubular, and there was a 5-speed gearbox mounted in unit with the differential. It was reported that the new engines were developing 240 bhp at 10,000 rpm. The Mercedes-Benz team arrived as for a Grand Prix with 40 personnel and over 200 tyres.

For this great showdown of the new age of the voiturette, the Maserati brothers, appreciating the need for flat-out speed on the Mellaha circuit, had fitted Luigi Villoresi's new 4CL with an all-enveloping body, built by Stabilamente Farina under Jaray patents and with this aid Villoresi, made the fastest practice time, in 3 min. 41.8 sec, an astonishing average speed of 134 mph (215 kph). The Maserati was reported to be attaining 170 mph (274 kph) emphasising that voiturette racing had come a long way since the struggles of the Amilcars and Bugattis of 1931. Although Villoresi had been fastest, even the most optimistic Italian cannot have been entirely confident, for Lang, with the faster of the two W165s was only $\frac{1}{2}$ a second slower than Villoresi, with Rudolf Caracciola 1.3 seconds slower, having done 3 mins. 43.1 secs. The race had attracted no entry from Britain, as apart from the deterrent of the Italian currency regulations, the new E-type ERA was unready and there was no place for a B-type ERA in the brave new political world that was emerging. Of Auto Union there was no sign. A new car was being developed but was planned to appear in 1940.

Traditionally the race was started by Marshall Balbo, Governor of Tripoli and at once, the Mercedes did as their larger brothers had done countless times before, and surged into the lead. Immediately, Italian hopes were shattered for on the first lap the Maserati team was a spent force. Villoresi had difficulty in selecting gears on the start line and retired his 4CL at the end of the lap with a burnt piston; Trossi's 4CL went out with the same trouble and to complete the fiasco Cortese, who was driving the latest 6CM almost identical in appearance with the 4CL, also retired with piston failure. At the end of the first lap, Lang whose car had higher gearing, led Caracciola who was pursued by Farina, heading the Alfa Romeos on which the honour of Italy now relied. On lap 5, to the delight of the crowd, Farina passed Caracciola though he was now 70 seconds behind Lang, while the other Alfettas of Biondetti, Emilio Villoresi, Pintacuda, Severi and Aldrighetti showed no signs of keeping up with Farina. Just as Luigi Villoresi had broken his Maserati keeping up with the Alfa Romeos nine months before, now the Alfa Romeos broke trying to hold the silver Mercedes. At ten laps, the heat of the day and the astonishing high speeds took their toll and Farina was out with an overheated engine and he was quickly followed by Biondetti and Pintacuda both suffering from the same complaint. Emilio Villoresi was now left alone and running at a reduced pace to keep down the engine heat; with no hope of victory he settled for third place while the Mercedes-Benz reeled off the remainder of the thirty laps in one of the most remarkable demonstrations motor racing had ever seen. In front of an unusually

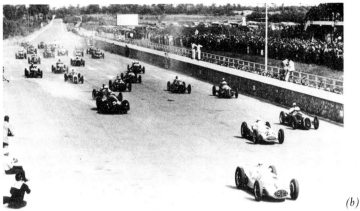

a. 7th May, 1939: Tripoli G.P.: Luigi Villoresi's 4CL Maserati with all-enveloping body by Stabilamente Farina.

b. 7th May, 1939: Tripoli G.P.: The W165 Mercedes-Benz of Lang and Caracciola leave the T158 Alfa Romeos and the 4CL Maseratis behind at the start.

c. 7th May, 1939: Tripoli G.P.: Alfred Neubauer stands beside the mechanic signalling to Lang the extent of his lead.

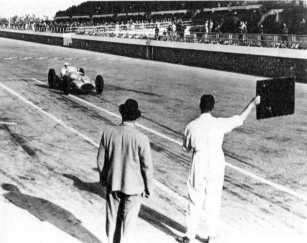

d. 7th May, 1939: Tripoli G.P.: Caracciola's W165 is refuelled.

e. 7th May, 1939: Tripoli G.P.: The Italians are glum or disinterested as the jubliant Mercedes-Benz team greet the victorious Lang.

silent and undemonstrative crowd Lang was flagged off to be greeted by a jubilant Neubauer having averaged 122.90 mph, some 13 mph faster than Taruffi had averaged the previous year. Rudolf Caracciola finished second 3 mins. 36 secs. later to complete the Germany joy. The mighty were truly fallen for Emilio Villoresi was 7 mins. 13 secs. behind at the end and the course stayed open for another thirty minutes while the rest of the field straggled in.

Stunned by this further display of German invincibility and total mastery of the art of motor racing, the world took stock, for voiturette racing now had a new division. If before, races with the Tipo 158 Alfa Romeos had been first division events, this was no longer so, for the presence of the Mercedes was needed to ensure this quality. There was much speculation as to the next race when the W165s would appear, and after the drama and action of Tripoli, the Targa Florio on the Favorita Park circuit in Palermo, the following Sunday must have seemed an anti-climax.

The works 4 CLs were clearly past immediate repair, so the works Team was represented by the 6CMs of Villoresi and Cortese. As an indication of the problems caused by the Tripoli debacle, Villoresi was driving the car sold to Mike Boyle of Chicago and raced in the Indianapolis 500 in 1938, which had recently returned to the Bologna factory.

Villoresi led at the start while Ettore Bianco went straight into the pits and retired with his 4 CM. After five laps Villoresi was 29 secs. in front of Cortese who was followed by Taruffi, Pietsch and Hug, but Hug then fell out of the race and Villoresi continued to draw away so that at thirty laps he was over a minute in front of Cortese. The strain of pursuing Villoresi was too much for Cortese's gearbox and he retired on lap 32, which left Villoresi to lead home an

a. 14th May, 1939: Targa Florio: Luigi Villoresi's 6CM Maserati is on pole position as the flag falls.

b. 6th May, 1939: J.C.C. International Trophy Brooklands: The debut of the new 4CL Maserati driven by Reggie Tongue seen here leding Percy Maclure's Riley onto the Member's banking.

all-Maserati field followed by Taruffi who was driving the 6CM used by Villoresi at the end of the 1938 season while Barbieri was third with another 6CM.

Following their declared policy of making racing cars for the world to buy, the Maserati firm had made the new 4 CL model available to private buyers at the same time as the cars were being produced for the factory team. There had been striking evidence of Maserati's desire to encourage the private entrant, as a 4CL had been supplied to Reggie Tongue to replace his ageing ERA, and to Tongue had fallen the honour of giving the new car its racing debut as it appeared at Brooklands in the JCC International Trophy, a class handicap race, on Saturday 6th May, the day before the Tripoli Grand Prix. Although Maserati gave much support to private entrants, and supplied a car ready to race in every respect, they imposed a curious restriction upon Tongue, as the car was sold to him on his undertaking that he would not race it in events where the works Team was appearing.* Having placed this restriction upon Tongue, the Bologna factory must have forgotten about it very quickly, for another 4CL was then sold to Johnnie Wakefield and immediately he entered for the Princess of Piedmonte Race at Naples on 28th May where his principal opponents were none other than the works cars. As was now customary in Italy when the Alfettas did not run, the 150 mile race had an all Maserati entry and from the start, Rocco led with one of the new cars. He kept his lead for 13 laps closely followed by Wakefield and Villoresi, then Wakefield went by to lead the field for the next seven laps until Luigi Villoresi asserted his superiority by passing both Rocco and Wakefield on lap 20. Although he had taken the lead, Villoresi was unable to pull away from Wakefield. The new car was proving thirsty and at half distance while only 4 seconds ahead of the English driver, and despite a 27 gallon (125 litre) tank, the works car stopped to refuel, letting Wakefield past again. His 4CL was finding it thirsty work too and he now stopped so the race then had a fourth leader in Franco Cortese with another 4CL. Wakefield's stop was a long one as his pit staff were slow but he restarted and was able to re-pass Cortese who had once more yielded the lead to Villoresi. Villoresi's car now had its problems as it had lost a gear and the carburation had become erratic so on lap 45 with 15 to go Wakefield once again took the lead. Perhaps in frustration, Villoresi spun but restarted, now with no hope of regaining the lead. Wakefield completed the course to gain a notable victory the first for the 4CL and showed that he had now matured into a competent and competitive driver; it also showed there was little difference between the cars of the customer and factory. A further development of the 6CM appeared at Naples with a 24 valve cylinder head. It was driven by Luigi Bellucci, but retired with a broken gear box.

The debut of the W165 Mercedes Benz made Richard Seaman very excited and he immediately suggested to Sailer, the Mercedes racing director, that one or both cars should be entered for the Nuffield Trophy. At last this race was to be held as a 1500 scratch event at Donington Park on 9th June and the Derby & District Motor Club hoped for a full international entry. It was ironic that it was not until the British voiturette was in decline after years of supremacy that a full

*Letter R.E. Tongue to the author October 1978.

143

1500 race was to be promoted on the English mainland. Sailer had been interested in Seaman's suggestion and initially it seemed that the W165 would race at Donington but this interest evaporated when Rudolf Uhlenhaut pointed out that the cars could not be prepared in time and the organizers also failed to attract entries from Alfa-Corse. As some recompense the new E-type ERA was entered. Since its announcement, this car had been beset with problems. It had been intended that its debut should be at the British Empire Trophy at Donington on 1st April but the car was not ready and was withdrawn. Next, it was promised for the JCC International Trophy at Brooklands on 6th May but the compulsory Brooklands silencer caused it to overheat badly in practice and it was withdrawn again. On the Monday after the race, Raymonds Mays tried the unsilenced car over the International Trophy course and its times were creditable but the next day, 9th May, it became clear that not only was the car in trouble but so was ERA Ltd. Humphrey Cook announced he felt unable to carry on supporting the Company and stated that he had spent over £70,000 (a very large sum by the standards of 1939) in promoting and sponsoring ERA since 1933. The Company was to close on 26th May and Cook invited the British Motor Racing Fund which had been established to support the ERA Grand Prix venture, to accept the E-type and the assets of the Company. At the same time, Raymond Mays announced the end of his association with Cook and with ERA Ltd. and declared his intention of racing as an independent for the rest of the season using the D-type ERA which, with the aid of friends, he had bought from ERA Ltd. Mays had little alternative, as he wanted to continue racing, and even before Humphrey Cook made his decision to close down E.R.A. it had been clear that there would be insufficient funds available to run a works team in 1939 and to develop the "E-type" as well.* The British Motor Racing Fund had high aims but low funds and declined Cook's offer so he agreed to carry on for another 4 weeks while the Fund endeavoured to raise £8,000 by public subscription. This was the sum estimated as necessary to race the car for a season. With the Fund vainly trying to raise money (only £1620 had been raised by the end of May) Cook decided to carry on for a few weeks and entered the car for the Nuffield Trophy with Arthur Dobson as the driver; once again it was in trouble and the engine blew up in practice although it had managed to make 5th fastest time in 2 mins. 25 secs., 0.4 secs. faster than Tongue's new 4CL Maserati. It was declared a non-starter. The ERA was not the only car in trouble in practice as Tongue had withdrawn his Maserati with a broken final drive. Two works Maseratis had been entered but did not appear, and the Challenger, a new 1500 of advanced design built by Reg Parnell, also failed to arrive. Seventeen cars left the grid and although Bira with his C-type ERA "Hanuman" had been fastest in practice he was third at the end of the first lap behind Percy Maclure's Riley and Robert Ansell's B-type ERA. Maclure, driving bare-headed without goggles as usual, led for five laps, when his gear-box failed, and Bira went into a lead which he never lost again. Raymond Mays held a steady second place and closed on Bira but had no chance of catching him after a refuelling stop as his black ERA then began to misfire. Bira, now racing with a Siamese

*Letter Raymond Mays to the Author February 1979

a. 9th June, 1939: Practice for Nuffield Trophy Donington: The E-type ERA stands in front of the temporary ERA works. Humphrey Cook, hands on hips is perplexed, Philip Mayne the team manager leans on a front wheel, Arthur Barratt the co-designer stands behind the car in sunglasses and Arthur Dobson puts a hand in the cockpit. On the right is one of the veteran Bedford transporters of the team.

b. 10th June, 1939: Nuffield Trophy Donington: Tongue's 4CL Maserati is partly dismantled in an abortive attempt to repair broken reduction gears.

c. 10th June, 1939: Nuffield Trophy Donington: Charles Dodson makes a pit stop. He is driving the 1500/4CM Maserati owned by Count Turani in 1937/38 and finished 5th. The Scuderia Ambrosiana badge is still on the scuttle.

145

competition licence, the ERA painted in the new Siamese colours of blue and yellow, was flagged off as the winner 1 min. 38 secs ahead of Mays after completing the 200 miles (322 km) course. Mays admitted subsequently that as an independent he now had to conserve his car particularly as ERA engine spares were becoming hard to get, a further indication of the decline of the marque and the Company. Peter Whitehead and Ansell were third and fourth while Charlie Dodson was fifth with the 4CM Maserati that Count Lurani had raced in 1938 now with a 1494cc engine. As the competitors and spectators left Donington that evening it would have seemed unbelievable to them that they had been at the last major event that would be run on that circuit for 38 years. . . .

The day after the Donington race, the usual Picardie Grand Prix meeting was held on the narrow road circuit outside Peronne. This event, had relied greatly on British entries in the past and in the clash with the Nuffield Trophy, Peronne had come off worst. There were only 10 starters so instead of the usual 2 qualifying heats and a final, all the starters were to run in a 10 lap heat and the survivors would take part in a 15 lap final. The only British competitor was Johnnie Wakefield with his 4CL Maserati and he looked a likely winner with his chief opposition coming from Raymond Sommer driving De Graffenried's 6CM Maserati and Armand Hug who now had a 4CL engine in his 1938 car, perhaps as a slight recompense for losing his works drive. To add to the disappointment of the small field, the heat was started in the rain and as expected Wakefield took the lead. He pulled away steadily from Hug while the French driver Horvilleur with a 6CM Maserati held third place until he stopped, while Sommer only ran for a few laps as his Maserati misfired continuously

11th June 1939: Grand Prix de Picardie: Armand Hug sits in his 4CM Maserati at the pits during practice.

146

with poor carburation. Wakefield won the heat by 30 seconds from Hug while the old C6 Amilcars of Tremoulet and Grignard were third and fourth. Jean Delorme had made extensive modifications to his T51A Bugatti during the winter and the car, perhaps resenting the dilution of "pur sang", disgraced itself by falling into the ditch early in the heat and took no further part in the proceedings. A damp and rather dismal band of 7 cars faced the starter for the final. Wakefield again took the lead followed by Hug and Sommer but both stopped at the end of the first lap for Hug to change a plug and Sommer to play with his carburettor. Both restarted but Hug had burnt a piston and retired and Sommer gradually fell further and further behind, he then stopped for fuel which made Wakefield's lead unassailable and he finished the 15 laps to finish a clear 2 laps ahead of Sommer and Horvilleur.

Once again, the threat of war was coming uncomfortably close. The uneasy "peace" of Munich had only lasted for 6 months as in March 1939, Germany had annexed the remainder of Czechoslovakia and the unhappy Czechs were subjugated while the rest of Europe stood aside. Emboldened by his success Hitler now directed his attention to Poland with the usual claims for territorial re-alignment. Britain had guaranteed Polish sovereignty so a direct confrontation seemed unavoiable if Hitler persisted in his claims. The International crisis was having its effect on motor racing. Crowds had been noticeably smaller in 1939 and the racing calendar had been contracting with cancellations of races for a number of reasons but all stemming from a lack of optimism for the immediate future. The voiturettes now had a lull for 4 weeks, something which had not happened for nearly 5 years and the sense of gloom intensified when Richard Seaman was fatally injured when his W163 Mercedes-Benz crashed while leading the Belgian Grand Prix at Spa on 26th June. His death was a particularly cruel blow to the British motor racing community as Seaman was the only Briton racing in grand prix events and his remarkable achievements with MG, ERA and Delage, culminating in his membership of the Mercedes team and his win in the 1938 German Grand Prix had been a source of pride to many. June had been a particularly sad month for Emilio Villoresi had been killed at Monza the previous Monday, 20th June while testing a Tipo 158 Alfa Romeo. Perhaps the most promising of the younger generation of Italian drivers, his loss was a hard blow for Alfa-Corse but a much greater grief to his biggest rival, his elder brother Luigi.

Grand prix racing was perhaps less affected than the voiturettes and the French Grand Prix which had reverted to a race for grand prix cars after its sports car flirtation in 1936 and 1937, had found a home on the classic circuit at Rheims. In a realistic appreciation of the importance of the voiturette, the race was to be preceded by the Coupe de la Commission Sportive for 1500s over 38 laps 183 miles (294 km) of the circuit. When the race was announced, the ACF expected it would attract official entries from Mercedes Benz, Alfa Romeo and Maserati but the German team, after their convincing demonstration of "Deutschland uber Alles" at Tripoli, showed no inclination to race the two W165s again and the Franco-Italian tension put paid to any hope of the Alfa Romeos or the works 4CL Maseratis coming to France. The entry for the race, which had originally shown promise of being a re-run of Tripoli on the European mainland, was beginning to look a little threadbare but there was some small consolation for the organizers as Humphrey Cook had decided that it was now or never for the E-type ERA and had entered the car for Arthur Dobson to drive. To the relief of the British contingent at Rheims, the car appeared for the first practice and proved that it had some potential by establishing the fastest practice time in 2 mins. 53 secs. an average of exactly 100 mph (161 kph); it was reported that the car was exceeding 160 mph (258 kph) on the long RN 31 straight. In the second practice session Dobson improved his time to 2 mins. 52 secs. but Bira appeared with "Hanuman" and with determination to uphold the new Siamese colours, equalled Dobson's time. This did not satisfy Bira and in an attempt to better this time, he lost control of "Hanuman" on the long fast uphill curves after Gueux village and overturned. The car was wrecked, but Bira escaped with slight cuts. There was trouble in the ERA camp as the E-type was overheating, caused by inadequate louvres to release the air under the bonnet. Three exhaust-valves had burnt out and unable to rebuild the engine in time, Cook was forced to withdraw the car. It was not lost upon the more percipient observers that although the car had been equal fastest in practice, it had been matched by a two year-old car with less power and 40% more frontal area.

A depleted field of eleven cars which included three sports Simcas faced the starter in what was to have been the Blue Riband of voiturette racing. Armand Hug who had a 4CL engine in the 1938 4CM Maserati led the field away followed by Wakefield's 4CL Maserati but the British driver was in front at the end of the first lap. Hanson's ERA was third ahead of Dipper's 6 CM Maserati* and Pollock's ex-Embiricos ERA while Raymond Sommer's 6CM Maserati was already in trouble and George Abecassis had retired with his silver all independently sprung Alta. Wakefield began to pull away having a lead of five seconds after five laps whereupon Pollock's ERA now blew up and retired. On the next lap, Wakefield stopped to seek a cure for failing brakes and Hug swept past and was twenty seconds ahead when Wakefield restarted. The 4 CL Maserati was a spent force and Hug began to build up a lead which soon widened to 1 min. 30 secs. Hanson who had started the race with a suspect engine to gain starting money had decided to carry on and took third place from Dipper only to run out of fuel as his mechanics had only filled the car with a "starting money" quantity! On lap nineteen both Hug and Wakefield stopped for fuel and Wakefield lost a further 25 secs. as his car would not restart easily. The car had to be cranked by hand as the regulations forbade push-starts. A disappointing race ran its course and Hug was flagged off to win by 1 min. 56 secs. ahead of Wakefield with Dipper two laps behind. Amédee Gordini led the Simca team home in a slow but reliable demonstration and was six laps behind the winning Swiss. The poor showing of the British contingent disappointed many people and Sammy Davis said in "The Autocar" that the British entrants had "a general air of amateur ineffectiveness".

Although Mussolini's edict prevented the Italian team being at Rheims, the

*Heinz Dipper and Leonhard Joa formed the Suddentsche Renngemeinschaft (South German Racing Association) based at Freiburg. Their 6CM Maseratis were painted silver with red numbers similar to the German GP teams.

a. *8th July, 1939: Practice for Coupe de la Commission Sportive Rheims: Arthur Dobson enters Gueux Corner with the E-type ERA.*

b. *9th July, 1939: Coupe de la Commission Sportive Rheims: Awaiting the start: on the front row are Pollock (ERA), Hug (Maserati) and Wakefield (Maserati). Pollock has cut slots around the grille of the A-type ERA to make it look like a D-type.*

c. *9th July 1939: Coupe de la Commission Sportive Rheims: One of the sports Simca-Fiats takes to the grass at the start.*

d. *9th July, 1939: Coupe de la Commission Sportive Rheims: Wakefield brings his 4CL Maserati out of La Garenne corner onto the N31 straight.*

Maserati team was not deprived of a race that Sunday for as a consolation the team went to the N.E. coast of the Adriatic as far as the coastal holiday resort of Abbazia★ where the Circuit of Carnaro was being run on a 3.7 mile (6 kilometre) circuit. This made a change from the usual Italian short circuit and nine Maseratis appeared. The Works Maserati Team comprised two 4 CLs for Villoresi and Cortese and the 24 valve 6CM for Rocco.† Rocco's 6CM led Villoresi and Cortese at the start but then fell back with engine bothers leaving Villoresi and Cortese to complete the 93 mile (150 km) course in an easy demonstration. The pace was hard as five cars fell out including those of Pietsch and Barbieri both of whom only lasted for one lap. To race so soon after his brother's death was a courageous act for Villoresi.

Bitterly disappointed by yet another failure of the E-type ERA Humphrey Cook announced after Rheims that the car would race no more in 1939. However, with the burnt valves replaced it was taken to Montlhery for high speed testing on the Monday and Tuesday after the Rheims race. So well did it go that Cook now had a change of heart and informed the AC du Midi that the car would appear at Albi on the following Sunday where a much better entry had been received. As at Rheims, the new ERA was fastest in practice ahead of Mays' D-type ERA and the 4 CL Maseratis of Tongue and Wakefield while Prince Chula had resurrected the B-type ERA "Romulus" for a sore and stiff Bira. The practice sessions had been on a wet road and this caught out Armand Hug who overturned his 4 CL engined 4 CM Maserati and suffered very severe injuries including a fractured skull which caused partial paralysis. As usual at Albi, all the competitors ran in two heats with an aggregate time to find the victor and in the first heat to the delight of its supporters the E-type ERA took the lead at the start and led at the end of the first lap followed by Wakefield and Tongue with their Maseratis and Bira and Mays with their ERAs. The pale green car held a secure lead on lap 2 while Mays passed Bira and began to threaten Tongue. The prospects for the new car began to look a lot brighter as on the fourth lap Dobson established the fastest lap of the day in 3 mins. 22 secs. albeit a second slower than Mays' record lap in 1938. Two laps later there was sudden drama as Mays passed Tongue and his horrified pit staff saw that a rear hub cap was missing from the black ERA. It was inevitable that the car would lose a wheel but it was impossible to warn Mays. Mercifully the wheel came off without disaster and Mays brought the car safely to a halt. The onlookers who had previously criticized the new ERA began to wonder if they had been unjust after all, but on lap 9 the car began to misfire and Dobson was signalled by the team manager Philip Mayne to come into his pit. The signal was given to him just before he entered the bend on which the pits were situated and instead of going round for another lap be braked, spun and struck the straw bales bending the tail of the car and damaging the rear suspension. It seemed that the new car had been eliminated by bad luck but examination of the engine after the race showed that one of the three exhaust valves not replaced after Rheims had failed

★After World War 2 the province of Venezia Giulia was ceded to Yugoslavia and now forms part of the province of Istria. Abbazia has been renamed Opatija.
†This was the 4 CL used by Villoresi at Tripoli now fitted with the 24 valve 6C engine.

150

16th July, 1939: Albi G.P.: Before the start of the first heat, Wakefield, Dobson and Mays discuss prospects beside Mays' D-type ERA (18). No. 14 is the E-type ERA and 32 is Wakefield's 4CL Maserati. On the second row are Tongue's 4CL Maserati (22) and Bira's ERA Romulus.

and the car was the victim of bad preparation instead. With Dobson and Mays gone and an unfit Bira driving an obsolete car there was little opposition for the two 4 CL Maseratis. Wakefield kept his lead to the finish despite a stop for fuel which seemed remarkable in a heat of only 110 miles (178 km). Tongue was second and an off form Bira was third ahead of George Abecassis' Alta. With most of the opposition gone, the second heat was completely uneventful with Wakefield leading all the way although he stopped to refuel his thirsty 4 CL yet again on lap 16. Tongue was second after passing Bira who finished third thus establishing the overall order for both heats. Abecassis was unable to repeat his form of the first heat as the Alta's engine seized and the car was struck from behind by Leslie Brooke's Alta-engined special both drivers escaping unhurt.

Following their humiliation at Tripoli, Alfa Corse had been working hard on the Tipo 158s and had modified the cooling system and fitted a new body which enclosed the front suspension. With a larger driver's head-rest the appearance of the car was to change little during the rest of its legendary career. As previously related, Emilio Villoresi had been killed while testing the modified car at Monza on 20th June, but despite this tragic setback the cars were now deemed to be satisfactory and the team was committed to three races in three weeks. The first was at Livorno on 30th July where the meeting was now entirely devoted to voiturettes. The Coppa Ciano over 60 laps (216 miles 348 km) was the premier event and there was a "junior" race over 20 laps (72 miles 116 km) for the also-rans. In the main event, the full team of four Alfa Romeos were opposed by seven Maseratis. Before the start the drivers and the crowd observed a one minute silence in memory of Emilio Villoresi, and there must have been much sympathy for Luigi Villoresi who courageously appeared again with the Maserati team. Farina took the lead at the start pursued by Cortese, Villoresi and Pietsch. Villoresi passed Cortese on the second lap, but clearly Farina was going to be uncatchable and was pulling away by 2½ secs. a lap. Behind Villoresi, Cortese and Taruffi with their 4 CL Maseratis began a fierce battle with Biondetti for third place, until the Alfetta lost its breath after passing them and stopped at the pits on lap 23. While the Alfa Corse mechanics looked at Biondetti's car, Pintacuda, who was running sixth was brought into the pits and was told to hand over his car to Biondetti who then set off in pursuit of the Maseratis. Meanwhile, the mechanics had repaired the Biondetti car and this was offered to Pintacuda who perhaps, somewhat piqued, declined it. By now, the car was over four laps behind and eventually Severi, the reserve driver, took it back into the race. Taruffi now slowed and was caught by Biondetti but he was unable to get to grips with Cortese who was now a lap ahead and who moved up into a safe second place, after Villoresi retired on lap 43 with a broken halfshaft, a fate which had already overtaken Rocco's 4 CL. This left Farina to run on to an impressive win, but despite the development work, the Alfa Romeos were still not quite right as Giordano Aldrighetti, the new member of the team and the 1938 Italian 500 cc motor cycle champion had retired on lap 32, but the cars had redeemed themselves by Farina's win which was at almost the same average as Von Brauchitsch had recorded with his 3-litre W 154 Mercedes in 1938. The preliminary "junior" race was an all-Maserati benefit and Teagno beat Lami by 0.4 sec. after a hard struggle.

The Italian voiturette circus now had a fortnight to prepare for the next event, the Coppa Acerbo at Pescara. As at Livorno, the organisers had abandoned Grand Prix cars and the principal race was for the best of the 1500s, with the rest running in a junior event. With one car written-off in Villoresi's fatal accident, Alfa Corse now had five left and as a demonstration of confidence all these were entered. Tragically, the team was reduced to four when Aldrighetti crashed his car outside Spoltore village in practice. The unfortunate driver was trapped when the car overturned into a ditch and caught fire, and by the time he was released he had suffered burns from which he succumbed soon after. Despite this misfortune, Alfa Corse decided to race the team and perhaps as some small consolation the race became a demonstration of the superiority of the Alfettas and the Alfa Corse organisation. The "Junior" race was run before the main event with an all Maserati entry and the first three finishers were to qualify to run with the first division cars. The race, over 4 laps, was led all the way by Nando Barbieri with his 6 CM closely followed by Teagno and Brezzi with similar cars, Lami was held back with a misfiring engine in his 6 CM but

152

took third place just before the finish when Brezzi dropped out. The three "juniors" were refuelled and joined the "big boys"; at the start, Villoresi hotly pursued Farina's Alfa but lost his chance when the 4 CL was reluctant to restart after refuelling. By the time Villoresi was under way again, Biondetti had gone past and he now took the lead for Alfa Corse when Farina stopped to change a plug and was himself passed by Villoresi and Cortese. The works 4 CLs were firmly established in second and third places but with little hope of catching Biondetti when they began the last lap. Then, when about 10 kms from the finish, amid scenes of astonishment and consternation both Maseratis ran out of fuel, leaving the Alfa Corse team a clean sweep. Pintacuda, presumably mollified, was second, followed by Farina and Severi. The only English competitor was Con Pollock, with his ex-Embiricos A-type ERA, which was some nine minutes behind at the finish in fifth place. Of the three junior qualifiers Barbieri and Teagno had retired at the pits at the end of the first lap while poor Lami did not complete the lap as he ran off the course at Ospedaletti corner and was killed when his 6 CM overturned. There was perhaps some small crumb of consolation for the Maserati team, as Villoresi's 4 CL was timed on the long straight at 147.14 mph., a speed unequalled by the Alfas and an indication that the 4 CL was a very rapid car.

The Alfa Corse team had little time to reflect upon their sweeping victory at Pescara, for the team had entered two cars for the Swiss Grand Prix at Berne, a week later on the 20th August. The Swiss, recognising the potential of the new generation of voiturettes, had arranged that they should run in a 20 lap race in the morning, and the best would qualify to race on level terms against the Grand Prix cars in the afternoon. The two Tipo 158 Alfa Romeos were to be driven by Farina and Biondetti, but the works 4 CL Maseratis had not entered with the rather implausible excuse that they did not wish to race against the full GP cars. Despite the lack of official entries, 4 CLs were to be driven by Rocco and Wakefield, supported by Pietsch's 4CM. It must be speculated on how "private" was Rocco's entry! Farina led the field of ten from the start, followed by Rocco, Pietsch, Biondetti and Wakefield. So fast was the Alfetta, that Farina's time for his standing lap broke the previous 1500 lap record established by Arthur Dobson in 1937. This pace was too much for the only French entrant, Horvilleur, whose 6 CM Maserati retired after only a lap. Biondetti meanwhile, clearly feeling that reputations had to be maintained, passed Pietsch on lap 2 and then did the same to Rocco on lap 5, to take second place behind the leader. Farina continued at his record speed and lapped the two ERAs of Bob Ansell and Con Pollock on lap 7. By half distance, Farina led Biondetti by 28 secs. and Wakefield, showing once again that he was probably as good as a works entry passed Pietsch. To prove his point, Wakefield then passed Rocco on the next lap and held third place to the end of the race. After lunch, the best half dozen voiturettes were wheeled out to take their place on the grid with the Grand Prix cars which had run in their own heat meanwhile. The wheel had come the full circle since the beginning of the decade and the voiturettes were making up the Grand Prix grids again, no more as humble retainers though, but now as profit-sharing partners. There was astonishment at the end of the first lap, for while Hermann Lang led with his W 163 GP Mercedes, in second place, Farina was

153

a. 13th August, 1939: Coppa Acerbo Pescara: Biondetti is given the chequered flag in his victorious Tipo 158 Alfa Romeo.

b. 20th August, 1939: Prix de Berne: Farina (hand on steering wheel) and Biondetti wait with their mechanics for the start of the 1500cc heat.

c. 20th August, 1939: Prix de Berne: Biondetti in his Tipo 158 Alfa Romeo is about to pass Rocco (4CL Maserati (60) to take second place in the 1500cc heat.

only two seconds behind, with a comfortable lead over Caracciola in the second of the GP Mercedes. It took Caracciola six laps to get past the Tipo 158 Alfa Romeo and although Farina gradually lost ground to the full Grand Prix cars, the point had been made, and he finished the race in sixth place. The W 165 Mercedes-Benz had humbled Alfa Corse at Tripoli, but now Italian honour was redeemed by the ability of the Alfa Romeo to live with a Grand Prix car of twice its capacity. Biondetti finished second in the voiturette class, having covered 28 laps, in front of the British trio of Wakefield, Ansell and Pollock.

After Berne, the British contingent wasted little time in returning home because it was becoming clear that no second "Munich" was likely to prevent war and already German troops were massing on the Polish frontier and the Polish army had been mobilized. They did not have long to wait; at dawn on Friday, 1st September, the German forces crossed the Polish frontier and the Second World War had started.

There was to be no more voiturette racing in those countries already contesting the War, and in Italy, who maintained a belligerent neutrality, all racing ceased, with an almost complete ban on private motoring. The 1939 season had been enigmatic as well as incomplete, and it had left one question which could never be answered. Would the Tripoli result have been repeated if the W 165 Mercedes and the Tipo 158 Alfa Romeo had met once more? The Mercedes-Benz would never race again; they had won the only race in which they ran, and in doing so, had gained motor racing immortality. For the British, the decline which had started in 1938 had continued, and the E-type ERA had given little encouragement to its supporters. With the honourable exception of Johnnie Wakefield, the British efforts had been summed up succinctly by Sammy Davis as "a general air of amateur ineffectiveness". Apart from the humiliation of Tripoli, the Alfettas had been unbeatable and while the other nations of Europe now turned to a sterner and more brutal contest, for the Italians there was to be just one more voiturette interlude.

1940

WHEN THEY had recovered from the initial shock of the war around them, the Italians decided that it would be "business as usual" and a full calendar of races was drawn up for the 1940 season. The 3-litre formula was discarded and all the principal racing car events were to be held for 1500s culminating in the Italian Grand Prix at Monza on 8th September. During the winter, Alfa Corse and Maserati busied themselves preparing for what was to be a season of "National" events. As the team had been reduced to four cars by the accidents to Emilio Villoresi and Aldrighetti, Alfa Corse built a new series of six cars the Tipo 158C which were similar to the later 1939 versions. Under the direction of the Orsis, the Maserati factory was moved from Bologna to Modena in October and November 1939 and the Maserati brothers made detailed improvements to the 4 CL and found a ready market for the car still existed in Italy.

Despite the prospect of a voiturette Grand Prix in September, the race which really mattered was Tripoli, for honour had to be redeemed and the German defeat of 1939 avenged. In April a team of BMWs had been victorious in the Brescia Grand Prix which had taken the place of the Mille Miglia and indicated that although at war, Germany did not regard motor racing as totally "verboten". This encouraged the rumours that Daimler Benz would send the W165 to Tripoli again, but no move came from Unterturkheim. The British press smugly suggested that the proximity of the British base at Malta to the shipping lane to Tripoli had prevented the entry, as the Germans did not wish the team to run the risk of capture and internment. Whatever the true reason, the race was an all Italian event and had already been overshadowed by much more serious matters for on Friday 10th May, two days before it was held, Germany had invaded Holland, Belgium and Luxembourg, the blitzkreig in the West had begun and apart from the Italians, few people had thoughts for motor racing any more.

Marshal Balbo flagged away the 22 starters. In practice, Farina had been fastest, while Tazio Nuvolari, who had decided to return to the Trident after six years, had rejected a works 4 CL as being too slow and inadequate for his talents, so the car was taken over by Franco Cortese. Villoresi's 4 CL, perhaps as a mild retort to Nuvolari, led at the start and kept its place at the end of the lap pursued by Farina's Alfa Romeo, Cortese with the rejected 4 CL and Biondetti with the second of the Alfas. On the second lap, Farina took the lead

156

a. 12th May, 1940: Tripoli G.P.: 4 secs to go; Marshal Balbo is about to drop the flag.

b. 12th May, 1940: Tripoli G.P.: Villoresi's 4CL Maserati leads the Tipo 158 Alfa Romeo of Farina and Trossi and the 4CL of Cortese at the start.

c. 12th May, 1940: Tripoli G.P.: Farina concentrates hard as he drives onto win.

a. 12th May, 1940: Tripoli G.P.: Farina takes the chequered flag.

b. 12th May, 1940: Tripoli G.P.: Farina holds an amphora as he stands beside Marshal Balbo and waves to the crowd after his victory.

and extended this to 10 seconds by lap 5, while Villoresi held second place, 2 seconds ahead of Biondetti who was now just in front of Trossi with another Tipo 158. Cortese had slipped back to fifth place which perhaps confirmed Nuvolari's views. Farina's lead was short lived though, for on the next lap, he slid wide and by the time he had recovered, Villoresi was in front again and he stayed there until lap 10 when once more, he was passed by Farina. On lap 14, Biondetti also managed to pass the 4 CL but even so, only 17 seconds covered the first three cars after 16 laps. On the next lap, all the leaders came into the pits to refuel and here, the efficient team management of Alfa Corse ultimately decided the outcome of the race, for while Farina was able to start after a 24 second pause, the Maserati mechanics took 57 seconds to replenish their machine and Villoresi's hopes were now gone, for by lap 20 he was 1 min. 30 secs. behind Farina and had also been passed by Trossi. Despite these setbacks, he did not give up and continued his vain pursuit of the Alfettas. At the finish, Villoresi had cut the gap between himself and Farina to 1 min. 7 secs., but Biondetti and Trossi were still ahead of the Maserati which came fourth, only 14

23rd May, 1940: Targa Florio: The all-Maserati field is lined up at the pits before the start. No. 20 is Plate, 28 is Ascari and 14 is Rovere, all with 6CMs.

seconds behind the third Alfa Romeo. Franco Cortese was fifth and Carlo Pintacuda who had not been able to match the speed of his team-mates, was sixth with the fourth car of the Alfa team. In ninth place, driving the 6 CM Maserati used by Villoresi in 1938, in which he had bought a half share from Piero Taruffi just before the race, was a promising new driver named Alberto Ascari, son of a famous father, who would in the fullness of time, surpass all that his father had achieved.* Italian honour had been satisfied, for Farina had been made to work quite hard for his victory, and in doing so, had averaged 128.21 mph, over 5 mph faster than Lang had averaged in 1939. As a small comfort for the Maserati brothers and Count Orsi, Villoresi's time also bettered the Mercedes figures.

On that Sunday morning, at about the time when the mechanics in Tripoli were checking over the cars before the race Flying Officer Garland and Pilot Officer Gray of the Royal Air Force were winning posthumous Victoria Crosses in their vain attempts to bomb canal bridges in Belgium and stem the German advance. Europe was now in the grip of total war and the Alfa Romeo victory at Tripoli received scant attention from the rest of the world. Ten days later, Villoresi, as he had done in 1939, gained some small consolation at Palermo when he led the Targa Florio from start to finish in his 4 CL. The main interest in the race lay in a fierce battle between Cortese and Rocco who finished second and third in their 4 CLs, while Bianco was fourth in his 4 CM. The rising star, Alberto Ascari, had an undistinguished race as he spun off. Luigi Villoresi had been one of the most devoted and consistent supporters of voiturette racing since his debut with his Balilla Fiat five years before, so perhaps it was fitting that he won the Targa Florio once again, for there was to be no more voiturette racing. On 10th June, Italy declared war on Britain and a stricken France, and for another six years motor racing would only be a happy and poignant memory.

*Ascari had already achieved success racing motor cycles and had ordered a new 4 CL for the Tripoli race. This could not be delivered in time and he persuaded Taruffi to sell a half share in the 6 CM so that he could compete.

EPILOGUE

WHILE THE ITALIAN drivers were indulging in their Indian summer of motor racing during May 1940, the War for some of the former competitors had already become a real and brutal event. Ernst Burggaller had already been killed in action, and within a few days of the Targa Florio, Tony Rolt serving with his regiment, the Rifle Brigade, had become a prisoner of war while defending Calais and barring the German path to Dunkirk. Pierre Veyron, an army reservist, had been called to the colours as Quartermaster in an artillery regiment, and was now an unwilling participant in the disintegration of the French Army. Within a few months, Whitney Straight and Reggie Tongue were flying as fighter pilots in the Battle of Britain. As the War continued its course for the next five years it took its toll of those drivers who had raced voiturettes, and among those who would never go motor racing again, were Tim Rose-Richards, E.K. Rayson, Johnnie Wakefield and Norman Wilson.

Within a month of the War ending, in August 1945, a motor race had been held in the Bois de Boulogne in Paris and in the spring of 1946, motor racing started again upon the mainland of Western Europe, but in England, still suffering from the national indifference to the sport, it was another story. The German grand prix teams had disappeared in the holocaust that enveloped Germany, but in Italy, Alfa Romeo and Maserati had not only survived the War, but had continued to develop their cars, so to the satisfaction of race organisers, and the delight of the large crowds which flocked to the races, there were two works teams to provide the backbone of the racing, backed up by many independents. The Italians offered 1500s, the British still had ERAs so it was universally agreed that the main events should be for these cars. A year later, in 1947, the first post war Grand Prix formula was launched, and this was the happy and inevitable merger of the blown 1500s and the lesser light of the 1938 formula, the unblown $4\frac{1}{2}$ litre. The scene was then set for seven years of Italian domination, and the Tipo 158 Alfa Romeo lived up to the promise it had shown in its voiturette infancy and became one of the great immortals of grand prix racing. For the British, the deterioration which had been showing in 1938 and 1939 came to full flower and truly Sammy Davis had been prophetic in his observations of a "general air of amateur ineffectiveness". The amateur ineffectiveness was not to last though, because the small workshops and the limited budgets of the 1930s were to be the foundations upon which British endeavours in grand prix racing survived in the early post war years, and these were to be the seeds from which British domination of grand prix racing eventually grew. From these humble beginnings came the British racing car industry with the world as its customer.

Joining the pre-war voiturettes as the backbone of postwar racing were the pre-war voiturette drivers. The domination of the Italian cars gave an immediate advantge to the Italian drivers and this was assiduously seized upon. Farina was the first to shine, becoming world champion in 1950 and was rivalled in the early postwar years, by Luigi Villoresi who had lost none of his old panache and was perhaps only held back by the cars he drove. The other great Italian star, who had come late to the voiturette field, was Alberto Ascari who was to outshine his contemporaries and his illustrious father in becoming world champion in 1952 and 1953. There were others too, Bira returned, perhaps not quite as fast as he had been in the mid-30s but still a force to be reckoned with, and Raymond Mays continued to race his black D-type ERA until he found that his new project, the BRM, left no more time for competition. Most of the drivers who competed in grand prix races in the early postwar years had been racing in the previous decade and the majority had driven a voiturette in those years. Under the paternal guidance of these "veterans" a new, young generation of drivers grew up and matured, nurtured in the traditions which had been honoured in the voiturette races of an earlier era.

Truly the voiturettes of the 1930s and their drivers were the foundation stones upon which modern grand prix racing has been built.

THE CARS AND THE MAKERS

ALFA ROMEO (*S.A. Alfa Romeo, Milan*)

The Alfa Romeo was born at Portello in the suburbs of Milan from two ventures, A.L.F.A. (Anonima Lombarda Fabbrica Automobili) and S.A.Ing. Nicola Romeo & Co. By the early 1920s, Alfa Romeo had become an acknowledged constructor of motor cars and a keen supporter of motor racing. With the introduction of the P2 Model in 1924, the firm became one of the leading lights of Grand Prix racing and this model gained for the firm, the first World Championship in 1925. The P2, a supercharged 8 cylinder, with a conventional chassis, was designed by Vittorio Jano and following this success, Jano turned his hand to designing a small capacity production touring car. This appeared as the 6 cylinder 6C Model with a single overhead camshaft engine and went into production in 1927 in a long chassis form with touring coachwork. Within a year, Jano had developed a twin-camshaft for the 6C and this car was raced by the factory and by many private owners in super sports form during 1928 and 1929. The car was an instant success and gained many victories, the most important being the 1928 Mille Miglia. In 1929, the car grew to 1752 cc and became known as the immortal "1750" which won innumerable races between 1929 and 1931. Although raced as a sports car it was not long before private owners realised that a stripped 1750 made a perfectly good racing car and when fitted with a sleeved block to reduce it to the original capacity of 1487cc, it made an excellent voiturette.

Although only a few cars were developed as 1500cc voiturettes these had a fine record. In 1931 Jano's next masterpiece, the 8 cylinder 2.3 litre was introduced and in full racing trim as the "Monza" it was a formidable Grand Prix car. The bodies fitted to some of the racing 6C 1500s were very similar to the "Monza" and with the 2.3 radiator cowl, the 1500 had the appearance of a small G.P. car. The works support given to these voiturettes was minimal, but nonetheless, they gained notable class victories at Monza in the 1931 Italian G.P. and at the Nurburgring in the 1932 Eifelrennen and the 1932 German Grand Prix. As previously related, Henry Tauber and Count Lurani tried to persuade Jano to produce an outright racing version, but he showed no interest. This was a pity for on the evidence of the results obtained with the comparatively modest converted sports car, it is likely that a full racing version would have been a

163

The engine of the Tipo 158 Alfa Romeo in 1938 form.

formidable machine in the early 1930s. The 1750 ceased production in 1933 and after this, the 1500 Alfa voiturette faded away. The last important success was a third place in the 1500 class of the Czech G.P. in 1933.

For five years, the voiturette class lacked Alfa Romeo and despite the effort of Maserati, the palms of victory passed to England with the dominance of ERA. Meanwhile, in the Grand Prix field, the once all-conquering Alfa Romeo was now humbled and at the end of 1936, Enzo Ferrari decided that if Alfa Romeo could not win Grand Prix races any more the only alternative was to win voiturette races instead. With the encouragement of Ferrari, Gioacchino, Colombo, who had worked with Jano, began designs for a 1500 Alfa. This was to be a supercharged straight 8, the engine broadly comprising one bank of the V16 Type 316 3 litre Alfa Romeo Grand Prix car. The major components were made in the Alfa Romeo factory at Milan, but the cars were assembled in the Scuderia Ferrari workshops in Modena where Colombo had executed the designs. At the beginning of 1938 Alfa Corse was formed from the racing department of the Alfa Romeo factory and the Scuderia Ferrari, so the testing and development of the new car, known as the Tipo 158, proceeded under the Alfa Corse management during the Spring and early Summer of 1938. An initial batch of six cars was built and three of these made their debut at Livorno for the Coppa Cianoi on 7th August. The cars achieved the dream of every designer and constructor by winning their first race, taking first and second places. For the rest of the 1938 season the cars had mixed fortunes. They were eliminated by carburation problems in the Coppa Acerbo at Pescara and by bearing failures in the final race of the season at Modena, but gained another victory at Monza in the 1500 race before the Italian Grand Prix.

For the 1939 season, the plain big-end bearings were replaced by needle roller big-ends to cure the only engine defect of the design, and Alfa Corse now expected the cars to be masters of the 1500 class. There was a shattering setback for the team at the first race of the season in Tripoli when the new W165 Mercedes-Benz outran the Alfa Romeos and took first and second place. The Alfas were outpaced and overheated badly and the surviving car of the team could only manage a weak third place. Work was put in hand immediately to revise the cooling system and further modifications were also made to the lubrication. Before the cars raced again, new bodywork was fitted and the revised shape was retained by the car for the rest of its career. Unfortunately, when the revised car was being tested at Monza by Emilio Villoresi, he crashed and was killed, but despite this setback, the cars were raced in three more events at Livorno, Pescara and Berne before the abrupt end of the 1939 season, and were quite unbeatable. With the death of Emilio Villoresi, Giuseppe Farina was now the leading driver of the team and in a particularly heroic drive in the Swiss Grand Prix at Berne, he showed that the Tipo 158 was capable of holding the full 3 litre G P Mercedes–Benz in the wet, which indicated that the car had brought a new dimension to voiturette racing and had rendered all its rivals obsolete with the exception of the W165 Mercedes.

With the loss of Villoresi's car and another machine when Giordano Aldrighetti was killed in practice at Pescara, the original batch of cars was reduced to four so a second series of six cars, the Tipo 158C, was built during the winter of 1939. With the start of the Second World War, the 1940 racing season was an Italian national affair and the Alfa Romeo team only appeared once at Tripoli, where the humiliation of 1939 was at least partly avenged when the cars took the first three places at a record speed.

When racing was resumed in Europe in 1946, the Tipo 158 Alfa Romeo reappeared and then dominated Grand Prix racing until the rise of the unsupercharged Ferrari in 1951. The Alfas raced until the end of the 1500cc S 4½ litre GP formula in 1951 and gained the World Championship for Farina and Fangio in 1950 and 1951 respectively. During their post war racing career the Tipo 158 Alfa and the Tipo 159 derivative started in 33 Grand Prix events, and won 29 of them. This is a record which will probably never be equalled. The design had an active life of eight racing seasons spread over thirteen years, so the car which began as a voiturette ended its career as one of the greatest Grand Prix cars of all time.

ALFA ROMEO 6 C/1500 SS T F

Designer: VITTORIO JANO
Wheelbase: 9' 0" (2.74m)
Front track: 4' 6" (1.37m)
Rear track: 4' 6" (1.37m)
Unladen weight: 1450 lbs (estimated) (659 kg)
Bore: 62 mm
Stroke: 82 mm
Number of cylinders: 6
Capacity: 1487 cc
BHP: 84★
RPM: 5000★
Cylinder head: Cast iron integral with cylinders

Valve no: 2 per cylinder
Valve angle: 90°
Cylinder block: Cast iron one piece
Carburettor: Memini
Supercharger: Roots
Ignition: Marelli or Bosch magneto
Plugs no: 1 per cylinder
Crankcase: Aluminium split on centre line upper half carrying main bearing housing
Crankshaft: One piece counter-balanced.
Main bearing no: 5
Main bearing type: White metal

★ These are the figures for the production car. The racing version must have developed considerably more power.

165

Big end type: White metal
Lubrication: Wet sump
Camshaft no: 2
Camshaft location: In head driven from rear of crankshaft by vertical shaft and bevel gears.
Clutch: Multi plate.
Gearbox and location: 4 speed in unit with engine
Transmission: Torque tube to bevel drive rear axle

Frame: Channel
Front suspension: Semi elliptic
Rear suspension: Semi elliptic
Shock absorber type: Hartford type friction
Brake system: Mechanical, rod operated.
Wheel type: Rudge
Number produced: 10
Price: £850 (production chassis)

ALFA ROMEO T 158

Designer: GIOACCHINO COLOMBO
Wheelbase: 8′ 2¹⁄₂″ (2.50m)
Front track: 4′ 2″ (1.27m)
Rear track: 4′ 2″ (1.27m)
Unladen weight: 1792 lbs (814 kg)
Bore: 58mm
Stroke: 70 mm
Number of cylinders: 8
Capacity: 1479 c.c.
BHP: 195 (1938), 225 (1939)
RPM: 7000 (1938) 7500 (1939)
Cylinder head: Aluminium integral with block
Valve no: 2 per cylinder
Valve angle: 100°
Cylinder block: aluminium with steel liners.
Carburettor: Weber
Supercharger: Roots
Ignition: 2 Marelli magnetos
Plugs no: 1 per cylinder
Crankcase: Cast magnesium split on centre line of crankshaft.

Crankshaft: One piece
Main bearing no: 9
Main bearing type: Plain
Big end type: Needle roller (1939)
Lubrication: Dry sump
Camshaft no: 2
Camshaft location: In head: gear driven from front of crankshaft
Clutch: Multi plate dry
Gearbox and location: Unit with final drive 4 speed
Transmission: Open propeller shaft to gear box. Swing axle with enclosed half shafts.
Frame: Tubular.
Front suspension: Trailing arm with transverse leaf.
Rear suspension: Swing axle with transverse leaf.
Shock absorber type: Hydraulic
Brake system: Hydraulic 2 leading shoe
Wheel type: Rudge
Number produced: 6 (1938) 6 (1940)

ALTA (The Alta Car and Engineering Co., Tolworth Surrey.)

The Alta began life as an 1100 cc sports car designed and hand-built by Geoffrey Taylor, a young engineer from Kingston Hill, Surrey, who wanted a car which embodied his ideas. The first Alta, a "one-off", appeared in 1929 and was an advanced design with a twin overhead camshaft engine and a low chassis with semi-elliptic front and quarter-elliptic rear springs. Taylor developed the car and in the early 1930s went into limited production in a small workshop which he built himself on the Kingston-by-Pass. The basic engine design was enlarged to 1500cc and then to 2000cc and in supercharged form was a very potent machine. In 1935, the car was marketed with an off-set single seater body as a 1500 voiturette and a number were sold in 1936-37. One of the attractions was the very reasonable price of £850 but unfortunately the car developed the reputation

166

The 1938/39 1500cc Alta seen here driven by George Abecassis at the Crystal Palace. The twin rear wheels are a local custom.

of being very fast but fragile and only suited to sprints and short races. It is clear that the machine needed development which Taylor's small concern was unable to give it, and Johnnie Wakefield was one driver who abandoned his Alta in favour of the 6 CM Maserati.

In the spring of 1937, Taylor produced a new design. This had the previous 69mm x 100mm engine now boosted to give a claimed 180 bhp, but the chassis was entirely new, with independent suspension all round, operated by coil springs on vertical pillars, a design that had superficial similarities with the classic Lancia system. The first car was sold to Philip Jucker and was said to have exceeded 140 mph when tested at Brooklands. Unfortunately, Jucker crashed the car and was killed when practising for the Isle of Man event in May 1937 and although another 1500cc car was built to the new design, this was raced only in English National events. The Jucker car was rebuilt in 1938 for George Abecassis who showed that it was very fast and capable of beating the ERAs in short races, although it still lacked reliability, which it demonstrated by its failures at Rheims and Albi in 1939.

It was a great pity that the Alta was not cultivated by a team of the calibre of Seeman/Ramponi or the White Mouse stable, as with proper development, it could have been a force to be reckoned with in voiturette racing, and capable of being the equal of the ERA and 6 CM Maserati.

The Alta firm survived the War and built engines for some of the small British racing teams who were struggling for a foothold in postwar motor racing, HWM and Connaught in particular. The greatest victory for an Alta engine was gained when Tony Brooks won the Syracuse Grand Prix for Connaught in 1955 and started the run of successes which carried Britain to the top in Grand Prix racing.

ALTA 1½ LITRE 1936

Designer: GEOFFREY TAYLOR
Wheelbase: 8' 0" (2.43m)
Front track: 4' 2" (1.26m)
Rear track: 4' 2" (1.26m)
Unladen weight: 1568 lbs (712kg)
Bore: 69mm
Stroke: 100 mm
Number of cylinders: 4
Capacity: 1496cc
BHP: 140
RPM: 5800
Cylinder head: Detachable light alloy
Valve no: 2 per cylinder
Valve angle: 68°
Cylinder block: Alloy integral with crankcase
  with cast iron liners cast in pairs
Carburettor: S.U.
Supercharger: Roots
Ignition: Lucas magneto
Plugs no: 1 per cylinder

Crankshaft: One piece
Main bearing no: 3
Main bearing type: Plain
Big end type: Plain
Lubrication: Wet sump
Camshaft no: 2
Camshaft location: In head chain driven from rear
  of crankshaft
Gearbox and location: In unit with engine 4
  speed Wilson T110 preselector
Transmission: Open propeller shaft to bevel drive
  rear axle
Frame: Channel
Front suspension: Semi elliptic
Rear suspension: Quarter elliptic
Shock absorber type: Hartford friction
Brake system: Girling mechanical
Wheel type: Rudge
Number produced: 6
Price: £850

ALTA 1½ LITRE 1937/8

Designer: GEOFFREY TAYLOR
Wheelbase: 8' 4" (2.54m)
Front track: 4' 4" (1.32m)
Rear track: 4' 4" (1.32m)
Unladen weight: 1484 lbs (675kg)
Bore: 69 mm
Stroke: 100 mm
Number of cylinders: 4
Capacity: 1496 cc
BHP: 180
RPM: 6300
Cylinder head: Detachable light alloy
Valve no: 2 per cylinder
Valve angle: 68°
Cylinder block: Alloy integral with crank case.
  Cast iron liners in pairs.
Carburettor: S.U.
Supercharger: Roots
Ignition: Lucas magneto
Plugs no: 1 per cylinder

Crankshaft: One piece
Main bearing no: 3
Main bearing type: Plain
Big end type: Plain
Lubrication: Wet sump
Camshaft no: 2
Camshaft location: In head chain driven from rear
  of crankshaft
Gearbox and location: In unit with engine. 4 speed
  Wilson T110 preselector
Transmission: Open propeller shaft to bevel drive
  rear axle with open half shafts
Frame: Channel
Front and rear suspension: Vertical slides with coil
  springs. Twin slides at rear.
Shock absorber type: None
Brake system: Girling mechanical, rod operated
Wheel type: Rudge
Number produced: 3
Price: £1,250

AMILCAR (*Société Nouvelle pour l'Automobile Amilcar, St. Denis*)

The French motoring historian Jacques Potherat, has written of the Amilcar, "more robust than a Bugatti, less aesthetic perhaps, it was born of the simple logic of a French blacksmith"* which may be a rather harsh epitaph for one of the most exciting racing cars of the vintage era and one which still dominated its class in the early 1930s. The Amilcar arose out of the failure of the Le Zèbre firm which had made light cars before the 1914/18 War. It is alleged that two Le Zèbre engineers, Edmond Moyet and André Morel met in the Excelsior Restaurant in Paris in 1920, decided to set up their own firm to build cycle cars and drew out the first design on the tablecloth. The result was the Société Nouvelle pour l'Automobile Amilcar, financed mainly by Emil Akar and Joseph Lamy, hence perhaps, the name. Moyet became chief engineer of the new company and Morel the works driver, and right from the start there were competition successes. The first model was a sophisticated cycle car with a 4 cylinder side valve engine which was soon enlarged to 1100cc for competitions. The greatest competitor and commercial rival of the Amilcar was the Salmson, and the twin cam Salmson was much too good for the side valve designs of Edmond Moyet. For several years, the Amilcar played second fiddle, but in 1925, Moyet designed a new 6 cylinder model, intended to beat the Salmsons at their own game.

The new model was the C0, which had a twin overhead camshaft engine of 55mm x 77mm, (1096cc) with a Roots supercharger driven from the front of the crankshaft. A low chassis with semi elliptic front springs and quarter elliptic rear rear springs was clothed with a conventional two seater racing body. As well as driving Amilcars, André Morel was a member of the Grand Prix Delage team in 1924/25, and it has been suggested, perhaps rather unkindly and probably inaccurately, that the basic design of the C0 Amilcar was acquired from Delage by André Morel and was one half of the 2 litre V12 G.P. Delage engine of 1924/25, with which it shared some common features. Pierre Chan, Morel's assistant, has said they were joined by a draughtsman from Sunbeam-Talbot-Darracq who brought drawings of the 1924 G.P. Sunbeam with him.** Plagiarism has been a very respectable feature of racing car design since the earliest days, so it is likely that Moyet considered both the Delage and the Sunbeam designs, and adapted their best features. Racing has always shown that it is not difficult to copy a design, but it takes a clever man to make it work, particularly if it is only one half of a design.

Three prototypes of the C0 model were built during the winter of 1925/26, and in 1926, the car went into production as the C6 model which was intended to be a very advanced sports-racing car with dimensions of 56mm x 74mm (1094cc). The C0 and C6 achieved all that had been expected of them and were quite unbeatable in the 1100cc class and the previously all-conquering Salmsons now found that they were relegated to a supporting role. At the beginning of 1927, the Amilcar factory built three off-set single seaters, with roller bearing engines, the MC0 model. These three cars together with another ten C0 models built between 1927 and 1931 were raced extensively and were still very active in 1931. Two of the MC0s were taken over by the Amilcar Agent in Le Havre,

---

* L'Automobiliste No. 14.
**Thoroughbred & Classic Car: Dec. 1974.

The engine of the C0 Amilcar 6.

José Scaron, and were run by him with considerable works support, so can be regarded as factory entries. A larger engine of 59mm x 77mm (1262cc) was built and was used by Scaron on a number of occasions when running in the 1500cc class. In 1931, the MC0 was invincible, and was still very potent the following year, but the Amilcar factory was having economic problems, the support for Scaron diminished, and so, as a result, did his racing activities. Some of the C0 series were fitted with offset single seater bodies and had many successes with private owners, but there was a wide gap between the performance of the MC0 and C0 models and the "production" C6. Development of the design finished in 1927/28, so the ability of the MC0 to stay ahead of the opposition until the end of 1932 was a great credit to the original design of Edmond Moyet. Old age, new designs and the eclipse of the 1100 class finally removed the Amilcars from front line voiturette racing, but they still appeared in second line events and as tail-enders in the bigger races until 1939.

AMILCAR C6, C0 AND MC0

Designer: EDOUARD MOYET
Wheelbase: C6 and C0 7′ 3″ (2.20m)
   MC0 7′ 0″ (2.13m)
Front track: 3′ 6″ (1.06m)
Rear track: 3′ 6″ (1.06m)
Unladen weight: C6 and C0: 1244lbs (565kg)
   MC0 1090 lbs (495kg)

Bore: C6 56mm
   C0 and MC0 57mm
Stroke: C6 74mm
   C0 and MC0 77 mm
Number of cylinders: 6
Capacity: C6 1094cc
   C0 and MC0 1096cc

BHP: C6 62 at 5600 rpm
  C0 83 at 6000 rpm
MC0 107 at 6750 rpm
Cylinder head: Detachable cast iron (C6)
  Cast iron integral with block C0 & MC0)
Valve no: 2 per cylinder
Valve angle: 100°
Cylinder block: Cast iron
Carburettor: C6 and C0: Solex 40
  MC0 Solex downdraught
Supercharger: Roots
Ignition: Bosch magneto
Plugs no: 1 per cylinder
Crankcase: Light alloy split on centre line of
  crankshaft
Crankshaft: One piece
Main bearing no: 7
Main bearing type: C6 plain
  C0 plain
  MC0 roller
Big end type: C6 plain
  C0 and MC0 roller

Lubrication: Dry sump
Camshaft no: 2
Camshaft location: In head driven by gear train
  from rear of crankshaft
Clutch: Single plate dry
Gearbox and location: 4 speed. In unit with
  engine
Transmission: Torque tube to bevel drive rear
  axle. (90 mm offset to left of frame in MC0)
Frame: Channel
Front suspension: Semi elliptic
Rear suspension: Quarter elliptic
Shock absorber type: Hartford friction
Brake system: Amilcar mechanical
Wheel type: Rudge
Number produced: C6 30/40 approximately
  C0 13
  MC0 3
Price: C6 £695

AUSTIN (*The Austin Motor Company Ltd., Longbridge, Birmingham.*)

Between 1919 and 1939, the Austin Motor Co. was one of the major manufacturers of the British motor industry and the Austin Seven had the distinction of being produced in more numbers than any other British car before the 1939/45 War. The Seven was introduced in 1923 and immediately the competition potential of this remarkable car was appreciated. Works and works-supported cars raced regularly during the 1920s, and in 1928, the famous Ulster sports racing model was produced; this dominated the 750cc sports and racing car classes in unsupercharged and supercharged form until surpassed by the Montlhery MG in 1931. At that time, maufacturers could gain much kudos by capturing international class records, and in 1930 and 1931, there was great rivalry between Austin and MG in the 750cc class, as both firms sought to be the first to exceed 100 mph in that class. This honour finally fell to MG. In pursuit of the goal, a special single seater Austin was built at the direction of Lord Austin. This used a developed version of the production, side-valve, four cylinder engine, installed in a production frame, with off-set transmission. This car was raced with some success and during 1931, the design was developed and a team of three cars was built which became known, because of their appearance, as the "Dutch Clogs" or "Rubber Ducks". Although these cars were raced principally at Brooklands, two of them went to the Avusennen in May 1932 and showed that they were quite capable of holding their own in a European voiturette field. Barnes finished second overall in the 1500 race, after winning a race-long duel with Steinweg's C6 Amilcar, while Goodacre was

1935: The first twin-cam 750cc Austin takes shape in the competition workshop at Longbridge. One of the Austin "Grasshopper" trials car is behind.

fourth. These cars did not race abroad again, but in 1933, Lord Austin approached Murray Jamieson, who was gaining a considerable reputation as a racing designer and expert on supercharging, and commissioned a new car which was intended to be the ultimate supercharged side valve 750. This car was successful and a road racing chassis was built for the engine, which developed 69 bhp at 8000 rpm. The car was raced during 1934, and a second example was built for the 1935 season. One of these cars was loaned to Ernst Burggaller who took the International 750cc class record for the standing start mile and kilometre with it, but despite its remarkable performance for a side valve, it did not appear in voiturette races. The team was scratched from the Mannin Beg race in the Isle of Man in 1935 and the cars were kept only for sprints, and short races at Brooklands and Donington.

While the side valve car was being raced, Murray Jamieson was busily engaged on a much more ambitious project which Sir Herbert (about to become Lord) Austin had commissioned. This was to be a car intended to dominate the 750 class and to be designed and built regardless of cost. The only restraint placed upon Jamieson was apparently the insistence of Austin that the suspension of the new racing car should bear some resemblance to the current production Austin Seven, which relied upon a beam front axle, with a transverse leaf spring with quarter elliptic springs supporting a live rear axle. The design was completed, and three cars were finished, for the beginning of the 1936 season. The engine was a 60mm x 64mm, 744cc unit with two overhead camshafts; these were driven by a train of gears from the rear of the crankshaft while the Jamieson-Roots supercharger was driven from the front. In road racing trim, as announced, the engine developed 90 bhp at 7600 rpm, while

172

The engine of the twin ohc 750cc Austin. The transverse starting handle is below the exhaust manifold.

for sprint work, 114 bhp was produced at 9400 rpm. It was intended that with steady development this remarkable engine would finally be taken up to 14000 rpm with safety. The team of three cars were raced almost exclusively in British & Irish National events and their appearances in International voiturette races were few. A car was driven by Charlie Dodson in the RAC Isle of Man race in 1936, and was running fourth, amidst the 1500 ERAs, when it was stopped by a broken sparking plug insulator, caused by a flying stone. One of the cars was lent to the German, Walter Baumer, who finished fifth in the 1936 Eifelennen and sixth in the Prix de Berne. In both races, the little Austin finished in front of a number of competitive 1500s and was not out-classed in any way. After 1937, the Austins made no further forays in voiturette racing. Lord Austin's desire to make the ultimate 750 was understandable as a means of gaining useful publicity for the production Austin Seven, although by the time the car appeared, public interest in such small production cars was waning. It is a great pity that Jamieson was not engaged to develop a full 1500 voiturette as such a car would have been formidable. Jamieson was probably the best racing designer in Britain in the 1930s and the Austin Motor Co. had the ability to produce a fine machine as the finish and quality of the 750s showed. Each twin-cam car is reputed to have cost Lord Austin £3,000 and an Austin 1500 would probably have cost little more and could well have picked up the torch of English prestige as it fell from the hands of ERA at the end of 1937.

AUSTIN 750cc o.h.c.

Designer: T. MURRAY JAMIESON
Wheelbase: 6' 10" (2.08m)
Front track: 3' 11" (1.19m)
Rear track: 3' 11" (1.19m)
Unladen weight: 1000 lbs approx (454 kg)
Bore: 60.3 mm

Stroke: 65.1 mm
Number of cylinders: 4
Capacity: 744 cc
BHP: 116
RPM: 8500
Cylinder head: Detachable light alloy

Valve no: 2 per cylinder
Valve angle: 90°
Cylinder block: Light alloy in unit with
  crankcase
Carburettor: S.U.
Supercharger: Roots-type Murray Jamieson
Ignition: Scintilla magneto
Plugs no: 1 per cylinder
Crankshaft: 1 piece
Main bearings no: 1 plain centre
  2 roller
Big ends type: Plain
Lubrication: Dry sump
Camshaft no: 2
Crankshaft location: In head driven by gear train
  from rear of crankshaft

Clutch: Single plate
Gearbox and location: 4 speed. In unit with
  engine
Transmission: Open propeller shaft with centre
  bearing to bevel drive rear axle with double
  reduction gears
Frame: Channel
Front suspension: Transverse leaf rigid axle
Rear suspension: Quarter elliptic
Shock absorber type: Jamieson friction
Brake system: Mechanical cable operated
Wheel type: Rudge
Number produced: 3

BUGATTI (*Ettore Bugatti, Molsheim, Bas-Rhim*)

Ettore Bugatti and his products probably hold a unique place in the history of
the motor car. No other cars and their maker are accorded the reverence,
bordering on idolatry, given to those produced in the little factory at Molsheim
in Alsace-Lorraine. Ettore Bugatti was born in Milan in 1881, the son of an
artist, Carlo Bugatti; as a youth, he studied sculpture, but at seventeen he began
an engineering apprenticeship and a year later, in 1899, he entered and drove a
motor tricycle of his own creation in the Paris-Bordeaux Race. In 1900, he built
his first car and when this was exhibited at the Milan Show, the design was
bought by the De Dietrich company and Bugatti moved to the German-held
province of Alsace to supervise its manufacture. In 1908, after working for a
while in Cologne, Bugatti moved to Molsheim, in Alsace, and became a car
manufacturer in his own right.

He immediately began to produce competition cars, and by 1914 had
established an enviable reputation. After the 1914-18 War, the province of
Alsace was returned to France and Bugatti, who was a great Francophile, and
had produced aero engines in Paris during the War, found that his factory was
now in French territory. The small concern again supported racing enthusiastically and Bugatti entered the grand prix field, although the type 30, which ran
in the French G.P. in 1922 and 1923, was, even by the standards of the time, not
a pretty car. The chrysalis of the T.30, broke open a year later however, and at
Lyons in 1924, Bugatti produced his T.35, the classic and immortal design with
which his name has become synonomous. The car, with its overhead camshaft 8
cylinder engine and alloy wheels, its horseshoe radiator and ideally propor-
tioned body was the basis of Bugatti racing car production for the next nine
years. The T.35 was supercharged in 1926 as the T.35C, and when the grand
prix formula was changed to 1500cc in 1926, the stroke of the T.35 engine was
reduced to 66mm, and the T.39 and T.39A (the supercharged version) appeared.
Although overshadowed by the contemporary 1500 Delage, the T.39 had its

a. The T37A Bugatti engine.

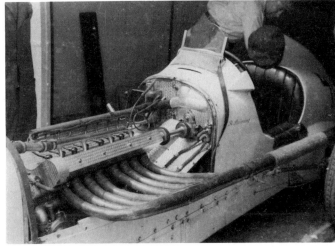

b. The engine of the Burggaller/Steinweg T51A Bugatti which was fitted with a single seater body.

moments in the formula of 1926/27. Bugatti was essentially a car manufacturer and realising the need for a production racing car, he took the T.35 chassis and installed in it what was virtually half a T.35 engine. This 4 cylinder unit, of almost identical layout to the T.35, had the classic 1500cc dimensions of 69mm x 100mm. Thus the T.37 was born in 1927 and became the backbone of 1500 racing in the late 1920s and early 1930s. A light car, with superb handling, it was easy for an amateur driver to maintain. At £700 it was not particularly cheap but enough were made for a ready second-hand market to be established very quickly and it was a car on which almost every continental amateur driver of the late 1920s learned his trade. In supercharged form, as the T.37A, the car was fast, as Chris Staniland's Brooklands lap at 122mph emphasised.

One of the great advantages of the GP Bugatti was the easy interchangeability of parts. The chassis design remained unaltered from the original T.35, apart from the appearance of larger brakes in 1927/28. The engine however, was a different matter. An American, called variously Leon Duray or George Stewart appeared in Europe in 1929 with two Miller 122s which he entered in some GP events as Packard Cable Specials. At the end of the season, Duray needed money to return to the United States so he exchanged the Millers with Ettore Bugatti in return for a pair of T.43 Bugattis. For Bugatti, the attraction of the Millers was the twin overhead camshaft engine which was a particularly fine example of its type. A year later, profiting by his study of the American cars, Bugatti introduced the T.51 which appeared early in 1931. This had the same chassis as the T.35 and the crankcase was similar, but the head, though still integral with the cylinder block had two overhead camshafts and showed evidence of the Miller ancestry. The T.51 was an immediate success and a short stroke 66mm version was produced for 1500 racing as the T.51A. This model was extremely successful between 1932 and 1934 and Pierre Veyron with a works supported car, gained many victories.

With the T.51, Bugatti's attitude to grand prix racing changed; he seemed to lose interest in the sport, perhaps because he realised that the T.59 which succeeded the T.51, had no hope of beating the German teams which now dominated Grand Prix racing. As a result, when the T.51A was surpassed by newer British & Italian voiturettes, the Molsheim factory did nothing to replace the design with a new 1500. With no new model, Bugatti, like its French confrères Amilcar and Salmson, became an also-ran in voirturette racing, although until 1939, some stalwarts still raced their ageing T.37s and T.51As, though with no hope of victory. In 1935 and 1936, there were many rumours that a new 1500 Bugatti was being built, but nothing appeared. At the end of the War, an ailing Ettore Bugatti declared his intention of making cars again and showed a new blown 1500 engine, the T.73C which was a four cylinder twin cam design. Although there is no evidence on the matter the T.73C had all the looks of a mid-thirties voiturette engine, so perhaps the original ideas which led to this design, also led to the rumours of the new car in 1935 and 1936.

Ettore Bugatti died on 21st August, 1947 and the marque effectively died with him.

T.37 AND T37A BUGATTI

Designer: ETTORE BUGATTI
Wheelbase: 7' 10" (2.38m)
Front track: 4' 01" (1.24m)
Rear track: 3' 11" (1.19m)
Unladen weight: 1560 lbs (709kg)
Bore: 69 mm
Stroke: 100 mm
Number of cylinders: 4
Capacity: 1496cc
BHP: 60 at 5000 rpm (T37)
   90 at 5000 rpm (T37A)
Cylinder head: Integral with block
Valve no: 2 inlet 1 exhaust per cylinder

Valve angle: Vertical
Cylinder block: Cast iron
Carburettor: Single Solex (T37)
   Single Zenith (T37A)
Supercharger: Roots (T37A)
Ignition: Coil (T37)
   S.E.V. Magneto (T37A)
Plugs no: 1 per cylinder
Crankcase: 2 piece light alloy split on centre line
Crankshaft: One piece
Main bearing no: 5
Main bearing type: Plain
Big end type: Plain

Lubrication: Wet sump
Camshaft no: One
Camshaft location: In head driven by bevel gears and vertical shaft from front of crankshaft.
Clutch: Multi plate cast iron and steel disc.
Gearbox and location: 4 speed. Separate from engine
Transmission: Open shaft to bevel drive rear axle.

Frame: Channel
Front suspension: Semi-elliptic
Rear suspension: Quarter elliptic
Shock absorber type: Bugatti friction
Brake system: Chain and cable mechanical
Wheel type: Rudge (some T37As had cast alloy)
Number produced: 209 T37
    78 T37A
Price: £700 (T37A in 1931)

T39A AND T51A BUGATTI

Designer: ETTORE BUGATTI
Wheelbase: 7' 10" (2.38m)
Front track: 4' 01" (1.24m)
Rear track: 3' 11" (1.19m)
Unladen weight: 1650 lbs (750 kg)
Bore: 60mm
Stroke: 66mm
Number of cylinders: 8
Capacity: 1492 cc
BHP: 120 bhp at 5500 rpm (T39A)
    150 bhp at 5500 rpm (T51A)
Cylinder head: Integral with block
Valve no: 2 inlet 1 exhaust per cylinder (T39A)
    1 inlet 1 exhaust per cylinder (T51A)
Valve angle: Vertical (T39A)
    96° (T51A)
Cylinder block: Cast iron in two blocks of four
Carburettor: Zenith
Supercharger: 3 lobe Roots
Ignition: Bosch or Scintilla Magneto
Plugs no: 1 per cylinder
Crankcase: 2 piece light alloy split on centre line

Crankshaft: Built-up
Main bearing no: 5
Main bearing type: Ball
Big end type: Roller
Lubrication: Wet sump
Camshaft no: 1 (T39A)
    2 (T51A)
Camshaft location: In head driven by bevel gears and vertical shaft from front of crankshaft.
Clutch: Multi plate cast iron and steel disc.
Gearbox location: 4 speed. Separate from engine
Transmission: Open shaft to bevel drive rear axle
Frame: Channel
Front suspension: Semi elliptic
Rear suspension: Quarter elliptic
Shock absorber type: Bugatti friction
Brake system: Chain and cable mechanical
Wheel type: Cast alloy
Number produced: 5 T39A
    7 T51A★
Price: £1,475 (T51A)

★ This is the factory figure for the number of T51As produced. Several T35 B and C and T51s were believed to have been converted to T51A specification.

DELAGE (*Automobiles Delage, Courbevoie-sur-Seine*)

Of the countless racing cars that have been built, some have achieved fame, many have declined into obscurity and a handful have been destined to become legends, revered and respected by all motor racing enthusiasts for their achievements and the manner in which these were attained. Such a car is the 1500cc straight 8 Delage.

Louis Delage was a flamboyant manufacturer who was born in 1874 and began building cars in a factory at Courbevoie-sur-Seine in 1906. From the first, Delage raced his cars, initially in the voiturette races of the pre-1914 era, then

177

The 8 cylinder Delage engine in 1927 trim.

graduating to the ultimate test of Grand Prix racing, and he made no secret of his ambition to build the fastest and finest racing cars in the world. When racing began again after the 1914-18 War, Delage was there and his V12 car produced for the 2 litre formula of 1922/25 and designed by Planchon was probably the most complex Grand Prix machine of that time.

For the 1500cc formula which followed in 1926, Louis Delage turned to Albert Lory who had previously worked for the Salmson Company and had now joined Delage. Lory was commissioned to design a car capable of defeating the principal French rivals of Bugatti and Talbot-Darracq, and to achieve this aim he produced an engine which, although a basically simple, twin overhead camshaft straight 8, had the remarkable technical feature of 62 ball and roller races aimed at reducing friction to a minimum. This engine, with its cast iron cylinder block and integral head, had the most remarkable capacity for high revolutions as it could be taken up to 8000 rpm in complete safety and this figure was often exceeded without mishap.* This robust quality, combined with a remarkable high power output, made the car unbeatable by its contemporaries, and it is quite rightly regarded as the pinnacle of racing design of the vintage years.

This remarkable engine was fitted in a low, but conventional chassis, with a two-seater body, as the GP regulations required, and the handling and road holding were probably as good as any of its contemporaries. Initially, when the car appeared in 1926, a small defect was manifest as the exhaust manifold, on the off-side of the engine, led into a pipe which was alongside the cockpit and the resultant heat in the cockpit made the car virtually un-drivable. This cost the

---

* The only car which remains in its original 1927 specification is now in the Briggs Cunningham Automobile Museum, Los Angeles, USA. The car was visited in the early 1970s by two former Delage mechanics, who told John Burgess, the Museum director, that the works drivers frequently exceeded 9000 rpm in the heat of a race without harming the engine. Burgess however, had already proved this inadvertently when the throttle of the car jammed open while it was being exercised and he subsequently estimated that the engine had exceeded 10,000 rpm momentarily without any damage! (John Burgess in conversation with the author, April 1979.)

Delage team victory in its debut in the Spanish Grand Prix at San Sebastian, and the hot, bothered and burned drivers only just managed to bring a shared car home to win the subsequent British G.P. at Brooklands. During the following winter, Lory rectified the defect by transfering the exhaust valves and manifold to the near side of the head. The transmission was now off-set and the car assumed a low purposeful look for which it became renowned. In 1927, the revised car was unbeatable except for a minor failure at La Baule and the engine was developing 170 bhp with a new and enlarged supercharger driven from the front of the crankshaft. At the end of the 1927 season, the team was sold, and Delage retired from racing. Of the four cars, one went to the USA while two cars came to England. One was bought by Earl Howe*, who raced it regularly between 1931 and 1935, eventually fitting larger brakes and an ENV preselector gearbox. At the end of 1931, Howe also bought from Robert Sénéchal, the only car which had remained in France and with these two machines, Howe gained victories at Dieppe in 1931, Avus in 1932 and Nurburg in 1933. His original car was written off in a crash at Monza in 1932 but the engine was saved and between 1931 and 1935 Howe was a very consistent voiturette competitor who gained many places with the surviving Delage.

During the 1935 season, Richard Seaman who was then one of the most successful drivers of the new ERA, was seeking a car which would be capable of beating the works ERA team and the rumoured new 6 cylinder Maserati in 1936. His cars were prepared by Giulio Ramponi, the former Alfa Romeo team driver, and to Seaman's astonishment, Ramponi suggested that the Delage was the car for which Seaman was looking. He dismissed the idea as he felt the Delage was too old, but Ramponi persisted, pointing out that the design had untapped potential and could be developed into a car that would be better than anything ERA or Maserati could produce. Ramponi's arguments prevailed upon Seaman who then himself persuaded Earl Howe to sell the car. Ramponi set to work with two aims, to increase the power and to reduce the weight. The former was achieved by fitting higher compression pistons and increasing the supercharger pressure from $7^{1}2$ to 12 lbs per sq. in.; it was found that either by accident or design the timing gears were incorrectly marked and there had been an appreciable power loss during Earl Howe's ownership. These changes now resulted in an output of 185 bhp at 7500 rpm, although below 4500 rpm the engine was "flat". A second engine assembled by Ramponi later gave another 10 bhp. The car, which had weighed about 1900 lbs (864 kg) when bought from Earl Howe was lightened by about 250 lbs (114 kg) by fiitting alloy wheels, an alloy radiator and a fuel tank which comprised the whole of the rear bodywork, while the heavy ENV preselector gearbox was discarded and replaced by a 5-speed box from a 1925 2 litre GP Delage.

Ramponi's judgement was totally vindicated, for the modified Delage won its first major voiturette race, the RAC event in the Isle of Man in May 1936. After this fine start, Seaman then had some worrying setbacks and the car gained no successes in June or July, but in August Seaman and the black Delage made a

---

* One of these cars was advertised by Thomson & Taylor for £1200 in the June 1930 issue of Motor Sport.

a. The Delage in the Donington Paddock on its first appearance with Seaman.

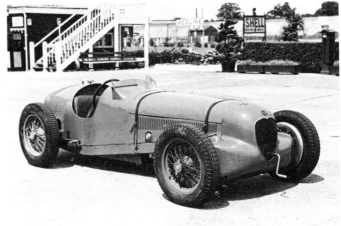

b. The Delage after the Chula modifications with its new chassis and front suspension, seen here being tested at Brooklands.

triumphant comeback and won three major races in fourteen days, the Coppa Acerbo at Pescara, the Prix de Berne and the JCC 200 at Donington Park. In doing so, Seaman trounced the works ERAs and Maseratis and the best of the private entrants, and proved that the ten year old car was superior to any 1500 that had been produced since. This feat was even more remarkable when it is realised that during the course of this triumphant progress from Pescara to Donington, the Delage only received the barest minimum of routine maintenance.

As far as Seaman was concerned the Delage had served its purpose and with the prospect of a Mercedes-Benz contract, he sold the car and all its spares to Prince Chula who thought, understandably, that if the car had been so effective in 1936, with further modifications it should have been equally superior in 1937, particularly when driven by Bira. Chula also bought the second Delage in England from Capt. J.C. Davis and decided that as the engine was already up-rated, the chassis now needed similar treatment and made the obvious and sensible move of going back to Albert Lory to design a 1937 chassis, to replace the 1926 original. Perhaps Lory had lost some of his skill, or perhaps, he was really only an engine designer, but all he could produce for Prince Chula was a frame which was almost identical with the original but with transverse-leaf independent front suspension fitted to it, which came straight from a current production Delage or Delahaye. As a result, the Siamese team had a car with an engine which was still competitive (although surpassed on power output by the 225 bhp of the 1937 C-type ERA) but with a chassis that was little advance on the original design. When Lord Howe heard of the proposed new chassis design, he commented that independent suspension was an unnecessary luxury on the Delage, as the original frame had flexed so much the effect was almost as good as independent suspension!* The Delage proved to be a financial disaster for Prince Chula and he stated that it cost him £7,836.** The change of chassis had obviously broken the magic spell and in Chula's ownership the car did not finish a voiturette race, let alone win one. It was a sad end to a magnificent car which was years ahead of its rivals in 1926-27, though it did perhaps show that the overall standard of voiturette design in 1936 was not as high as some people were pretending; nothing however, that happened in 1937 can diminish the glory of its feats between 1926 and 1936.

* Sidney Maslin, Lord Howe's mechanic in conversation with the author November 1978.
** "Blue and Yellow": Prince Chula 1947.

G. P. DELAGE 1927

Designer: ALBERT LORY
Wheelbase: 8' 2½" (2.50m)
Front track: 4' 5" (1.34m)
Rear track: 4' 5" (1.34m)
Unladen weight: 1900 lbs (863 kg)
   1650 lbs (1936) (750 kg)
Bore: 55.8 mm
Stroke: 76.0 mm
Number of cylinders: 8
Capacity: 1488 cc
BHP: 170 at 8000 rpm.
RPM: 185 at 7500 rpm (1936)
Cylinder head: Integral with block
Valve no: 2 per cylinder
Valve angle: 100°
Cylinder block: Cast iron
Carburettor: Zenith
Supercharger: Roots
Ignition: Bosch magneto
Plugs no: 1 per cylinder
Crankcase: 2 piece light alloy split on centre line
   of crankshaft

Crankshaft: One piece
Main bearing no: 10
Main bearing type: Roller
Big end type: Roller
Lubrication: Dry sump
Camshaft no: 2
Camshaft location: In head driven by train of
   gears from the crankshaft
Clutch: Multi plate
Gearbox and location: In unit with engine ENV
   preselector (1931/35) 5 speed manual (1936)
Transmission: Open propellor shaft to bevel
   drive rear axle
Frame: Channel
Front suspension: Semi elliptic
Rear suspension: Semi elliptic
Shock absorber type: Hartford friction
Brake system: Lockheed hydraulic (1936)
Wheel type: Rudge
Number produced: 4

ERA (*English Racing Automobiles Limited, Bourne, Lincolnshire.*)

The ERA was born of the ambition of two men to build a successful British voiturette. Raymond Mays had been one of the leading competitors in British sprints and hillclimbs in the 1920s and early 1930s, and his particular ambition in 1932 had been to regain the outright record for the Shelsley Walsh Hillclimb, which had been captured by Hans Stuck with an Austro-Daimler in 1930. Although Mays had gained many successes with the Vauxhall-Villiers and with an Invicta sports car, his early reputation had been built upon his many victories with AC, Bugatti and Hillman all of which were 1500s. As a result, he had a particular desire to regain the Shelsley record with a 1500cc car. In 1932, the Riley Company, which was supporting sports car racing most enthusiastically, produced a 1500cc 6-cylinder sports car which ran in some long distance races with moderate success. Mays felt that this car could be the basis for a Shelsley contender and could perhaps be developed into a successful voiturette. As recounted in his autobiography, "Split Seconds", Mays put his proposition to Victor Riley who responded enthusastically with financial aid and material support.

For many years, much of the development work on Mays' sprint cars had been done by his friend and associate, Peter Berthon, and when a 1500 Riley Six was supplied to Mays, Berthon went to work on the engine, carrying out the design work necessary to supercharge it, and produce the 150 bhp estimated as essential for the project. The engine was fitted with a supercharger of Roots pattern, designed by Murray Jamieson, who was a recognised expert in that field and had also developed a 750cc racing car for the Austin Motor Co. Berthon and Jamieson did their work well, and Mays regained the Shelsley record in September 1933 with the Riley which was known as the "White Riley", and before the end of the 1933 season, he had also captured the 1500cc class lap record for the Brooklands Mountain circuit.

Mays' exploits had been noted by Humphrey Cook, a rich amateur driver who raced in the 1920s, and often competed against Mays in sprints and hillclimbs. Cook wrote to Mays suggesting that he should finance the construction of a voiturette based on the "White Riley", with the intention that there should be a works team and cars should also be offered for sale. Cook's confessed aim was to produce a car that would enhance British prestige, and enable British drivers to compete in the growing voiturette class with a chance of success.

With Mays' energy and enthusiasm, and Cook's money, a new company, English Racing Automobiles Limited was formed and the prototype car completed in an astonishingly short time. Cook approached Mays in September 1933, and the first completed car was shown to the Press in March 1934. Berthon and Jamieson had continued the development of the engine, and Mays engaged Reid Railton of Thomson & Taylor Limited, the Brooklands engineers and tuners, to design a new chassis. Railton produced a simple conventional chassis with semi-elliptic springs all round, which owed much to the 8CM

182

a. The engine of Seaman's B-type ERA. This has the early type rocker boxes.

b. The Zoller supercharged ERA engine. This is Mays' car at the J.C.C. 200 mile race in 1936. The supercharger leaves little room for the driver in the cockpit.

Maserati, and Tipo B Alfa Romeo. Like the Maserati, the frame passed over the rear axle, thus giving the driver a high seating position and excellent visibility at the cost of an increase in frontal area. Railton decided against an underslung chassis which he felt could give unpredictable handling. He was influenced in this decision by the accident which had occurred to Sammy Davis at Brooklands in 1931, which had been attributed to the handling characteristics of the low chassis Invicta he had been driving.

The ERA first appeared in the Isle of Man for the Mannin meeting in May 1934, and after some teething troubles it gained its first victory, driven by Humphrey Cook, at the Brooklands August Bank Holiday meeting. The season finished with a most encouraging win at Donington in the Nuffield Trophy. During the winter of 1934, production began of the B-type which had a stiffer frame and altered spring rates. The first four cars produced were then designated as A-types. Unaccountably, sales of the B-type were slow and only two were sold to customers in 1935. However the six cars that had been built dominated voiturette racing during the season and were unbeaten in their class. As early as the Mannin Beg race in May 1935, Mays and Berthon had begun experiments to increase the power output by using a Zoller vane supercharger.

In 1936, the ERA was not quite as successful as it had been the previous year, although in 1936, seven cars were sold to customers who realised that it offered excellent value at £1800. There were several reasons for the slight setback. the opposition was stiffer, as the new 6CM Maserati, when driven by Trossi, was hard to beat, and the rejuvenated GP Delage when going properly, was more than the ERA could cope with. In addition, the ERA challenge was blunted by the very poor preparation of the works team which won no races during the season. Mays and Berthon persisted in using the Zoller supercharger which gave a power output that was greater than the connecting rods could stand, but even the factory-maintained Jamieson-blown cars were unreliable. The Zoller supercharger had to be placed behind the engine, on top of the gearbox, unlike the Jamieson which was driven vertically from the front of the crankshaft. This upset the weight distribution and made the car under-steer excessively. An increase in the size of the fuel tank, to enable the cars to go through a long distance race without refuelling, also had the same effect.

During the winter of 1936, Cook, who was apparently becoming slightly disillusioned by the cost of the unsuccessful works team, and the sale of each car at a loss, was persuaded by Mays and Berthon that the solution lay in stronger connecting rods and a revised chassis. Cook agreed, and a new car, the C-type, was evolved which used the Zoller supercharger with new connecting rods. This developed 225 bhp, a great increase on the 180/190 bhp of the B-type. A new chassis was designed using Porsche independent front suspension with trailing links and torsion bars, and new brakes were fitted. The faith of Mays and Berthon was justified and the C-type, after initial problems with the brakes, completely dominated the 1500 class in 1937 although the increased power from the engine began to show weaknesses in the transmission. The C-type was not offered for sale, which was perhaps understandable as it would merely have increased expenditure, but neither was any consideration given to marketing a kit to uprate the B-type, which might have been a more profitable venture.

184

Despite the reliance of the little company on Humphrey Cook's backing, no attempt was made to turn the considerable technical expertise that had been amassed, or the reputation of the marque, to commercial advantage, apart from a tentative proposal for a sports car which came to nothing. This had its repercussions when a decision was taken to develop a car to compete in the 3-litre GP formula which began in 1938. Only one C-type was retained by the factory for 1938 and this was slightly modified and became the D-type, but there was not enough money available now to produce a new car and to prepare and race this one works car in voiturette races, so the decline of the marque was swift. After the triumphs of 1937, only one International 1500 race was won by ERA in 1938. Murray Jamieson who had been designing the sports ERA had been killed tragically while watching a race at Brooklands in May 1938, so the design of the new GP car was being executed by Peter Berthon who was now joined by Arthur Barratt. Cook and Mays now realised that the little firm had no hope of offering any challenge to the German teams in GP racing and in September 1938, the decision was made that the car would be developed as a voiturette to oppose the recently announced Tipo 158 Alfa and the new model promised by Maserati.

Lack of money and resources slowed down the building of the car, and much work was contracted out to suppliers who had little incentive to do the work, now that large and lucrative armaments contracts were available. The car was eventually finished in March 1939 and became known as the E-type. Although the chassis design was advanced, the 6-cylinder engine was not wholly convincing, as it still retained the Riley system of push rods and developed its alleged 260 bhp by the use of a large Zoller supercharger with a high boost. Within a few weeks of the car's completion, Cook made the decision that he could not go on, and announced that ERA Limited would close. Mays and Berthon left the Company, and Cook, who had hoped that the whole venture would be taken over by the British Motor Racing Trust, announced he would continue until the end of the 1939 season. The E-type had been withdrawn from several British National events after mechanical problems in practice and it was obvious that apart from the shortcomings of the design, the workmanship probably left much to be desired. Arthur Barratt had now also left ERA Ltd. which suggested that other problems now beset the company which had left Bourne and moved to Donington Park in May 1939. The E-type finally raced at Albi in July 1939 and retired while in the lead as related elsewhere. This was the end of the racing activities of ERA Ltd. prior to the outbreak of war. In 1946, there was a further attempt to make the E-type raceworthy but the car ended its days as an inglorious failure, having broken the hearts and the pockets of all who owned it. Humphrey Cook sold his interests in the company to Leslie Johnson and severed all his connections with the sport, while Raymond Mays and Peter Berthon went on to be the driving force behind BRM.

The ERA gave British prestige a tremendous filip at a time when competitive British racing cars did not exist. Between 1935 and 1937 the marque dominated 1500 racing although it is perhaps fair to say that the opposition was not particularly strong. The dictum of Laurence Pomeroy that "The palm of victory goes more often to the designer who avoids foolishness than to the one who shows the greatest ingenuity"* defines the reason for the success of the B/C type ERA and the subsequent decline in 1938 and 1939 was a sad and unworthy end to a fine venture.

Only one ERA has ever been written off. The rest survive and many are still very active in the events of the Vintage Sports Car Club thus giving later generations a chance to appreciate the sight, the sound and smell of a 1930s voiturette in full cry.

* "The Grand Prix Car", Volume 1, 1954.

E.R.A A & B TYPE

Designers: PETER BERTHON
    REID RAILTON
Wheelbase: 8′ 0″ (2.44m)
Front track: 4′ 4½″ (1.33m)
Rear track: 4′ 0″ (1.22m)
Unladen weight: 1624 lbs (738 kg)
Bore: 57.5 mm
Stroke: 95.2 mm
Number of cylinders: 6
Capacity: 1488 cc
BHP: 180
RPM: 6500
Cylinder head: Aluminium detachable
Valve no: 2 per cylinder
Valve angle: 90°
Cylinder block: Cast iron with integral crankcase
Carburettor: S.U.
Supercharger: Roots type Jamieson
Ignition: Lucas magneto
Plugs no: 1 per cylinder
Crankshaft: One piece
Main bearing no: 3

Main bearing type: 1 centre roller
    2 plain
Big end type: Plain
Lubrication: Dry sump
Camshaft no: 2
Camshaft location: High in cylinder block operating valves by push rods and rockers
Gearbox and location: In unit with engine 4 speed Armstrong-Siddeley preselector
Transmission: Torque tube and bevel drive rear axle
Frame: Channel
Front suspension: Semi elliptic
Rear suspension: Semi elliptic
Shock absorber type: Hartford friction
Brake system: Girling mechanical
Wheel type: Rudge
Number produced: 4 A-type
    13 B-type
Price: £1,800.
    (B-type with 1500cc engine)

E.R.A. C TYPE

Designer: PETER BERTHON
Wheelbase: 8′ 0″ (2.44m)
Front track: 4′ 4½″ (1.33m)
Rear track: 4′ 0″ (1.22m)
Unladen weight: 1624 lbs (738 kg)
Bore: 57.5 mm
Stroke: 95.2 mm
Number of cylinders: 6
Capacity: 1488 cc
BHP: 225
RPM: 7500
Cylinder head: Aluminium detachable
Valve no: 2 per cylinder

Valve angle: 90°
Cylinder block: Cast iron with integral crankcase
Carburettor: S.U.
Supercharger: Zoller
Ignition: Lucas magneto
Plugs no: 1 per cylinder
Crankshaft: One piece
Main bearing no: 3
Main bearing type: 1 centre roller
    2 plain
Big end type: Plain
Lubrication: Dry sump
Camshaft no: 2

Camshaft location: High in cylinder block operating valves by push rods and rockers
Gearbox and location: In unit with engine 4 speed Armstrong-Siddeley preselector
Transmission: Torque tube and bevel drive rear axle
Frame: Box section

Front suspension: Porsche trailing arms with transverse torsion bars
Rear suspension: Semi elliptic
Shock absorber type: Girling hydraulic
Brake system: Lockheed hydraulic
Wheel type: Rudge
Number produced: 3 (B types converted)

ERA E TYPE

Designer: PETER BERTHON
    ARTHUR BARRATT
Wheelbase: 8' 7½" (2.62 m)
Front track: 4' 4" (1.32 m)
Rear track: 4' 4" (1.32 m)
Unladen weight: 1456 lbs (661 kg)
Bore: 63.0 mm
Stroke: 80.5 mm
Number of cylinders: 6
Capacity: 1487 cc
BHP: 260
RPM: 7000
Cylinder head: Detachable light alloy
Valve no: Two per cylinder
Valve angle: 90°
Cylinder block: Cast iron
Carburettor: SU
Supercharger: Zoller
Ignition: Lucas magneto
Plugs no: 1 per cylinder
Crankcase: Integral with block

Crankshaft: One piece
Main bearing no: Three
Main bearing type: Plain
Big end type: Plain
Lubrication: Wet sump
Camshaft no: 2
Camshaft location: Set high in block operating valves by push rods & rockers
Clutch: Dry multi plate
Gearbox and location: In unit with final drive 4 speed synchromesh
Transmission: Open propeller shaft with reduction gears
Frame: Tubular
Front suspension: Porsche trailing arms with transverse torsion bars
Rear suspension: DeDion with torsion bars
Shock absorber type: Hydraulic
Brake system: Lockhead hydraulic
Wheel type: Rudge
Number produced: 1★

★ A second car was produced in 1946.

MASERATI (*Officine Alfieri Maserati, Sp.A. Bologna*)

If the Bugatti is regarded as the product of paternalism then the Maserati was the outcome of a fraternity. Initially, there were six brothers Alfieri, Bindo, Carlo, Ettore, Ernesto and Mario. The brothers were the sons of a locomotive engineer from Voghera. Alfieri, who was born in 1887, began working for Isotta-Fraschini at fifteen and rode as mechanic in the winning Isotta in the 1908 Targa Florio. In 1914, with Ettore and Ernesto he opened a repair shop in Bologna. At this little shop, a business gradually grew up making sparking plugs and this enabled the Maserati brothers to start constructing specials based on Isotta-Fraschini and Diatto. Alfieri was commissioned to design a series of racing cars for the Diatto concern in Turin and when Diatto decided to withdraw from racing in 1925, Alfieri took over the 2-litre straight 8 GP car

187

which had been built in the Maserati factory at Bologna. This Diatto with modifications became the first Maserati in 1926, the Tipo 26 with a 1500 cc twin ohc supercharged engine and was the basis for the Maserati GP cars and voiturettes from 1926 to 1931. The Tipo 26 was produced as a 1500 and as an 1100, the Tipo 26C; a rather heavy car, the Tipo 26 was very fast and was still winning races as late as 1932 when the cars driven by Pierre Veyron and Armand Joly were probably the most successful 1500s of the 1932 season.

At the Monza GP in 1931 a new car, the 4CTR/1100, appeared, this being a two seater, with the chassis based on the old Tipo 26. The engine, designed by Alfieri Maserati, was, however, a complete breakaway, being a neat 4 cylinder supercharged twin ohc unit, the forerunner of the Maserati voiturette engines for the remainder of the decade. In 1932, a single seater was produced which was a much lighter and more agile machine than the Tipo 26. This car, using the supercharged 4 cylinder engine in 1100 and 1500 form, became known as the 4 CM; it was one of the principal competitors in voiturette racing between 1932 and 1936 and examples continued to appear in smaller events until the outbreak of War. Although it did not dominate the class, the 4 CM was a worthy opponent and scored many successes, particularly in Italian events.

Alfieri Maserati died in 1932 as the result of injuries he had received in the Coppa Messina in 1927, but the surviving brothers led by Ernesto carried on the business and Ernesto also drove the works cars in some events. By 1935 the voiturette 4 CM had been outclassed by the new ERA, while the Maserati GP cars were unable to cope with the two German teams. The factory team was taken over by Luigi Della Chiesa and Gino Rovere in 1935 who ran it as the Scuderia Subalpina and Rovere put some capital into the Maserati firm. In January 1936 Rovere became President of Maserati and provided further financial support. Ernesto Maserati had realised during 1935 that a new car was needed to replace the hard used 4 CM voiturette and the outcome was the 6 CM. This was a supercharged twin ohc six of 65mm x 75mm and it broke new ground in having independent front suspension using double wishbones and torsion bars, becoming the first of a new generation of voiturettes which was to leave the vintage image behind. Maserati had already used this torsion bar suspension on the 1935 V8 GP car and although this was an unsuccessful machine, the early successes of the 6 CM must be largely attributed to the improved road holding and cornering that the new suspension gave the car. The 6 CM was not as powerful as the ERA and even in the hands of such drivers as Trossi and Luigi Villoresi it found the best of the British cars difficult to beat after its initial success in the Eifelrennen in May 1936. In Italian events, however, the 6 CM was invincible and it found a ready market; by the end of 1936 four had been delivered to private entrants and a further twelve were delivered to buyers in 1937. At a price of 95,000 lire (£1050), ex-factory, it was arguably a better bargain than the ERA, which sold at £1,800, particularly when backed by the enthusiastic support that the Bologna works gave to private entrants. Another attraction was the ability of the car to keep its tune and to require the minimum of attention between races. This was a notable feature of all the Maserati voiturettes.

In the winter of 1936/37, Ernesto Maserati, realising the need for a more

The engine of Armand Hug's 4CM Maserati.

competitive voiturette, revised the old 4CM engine. This had already been boosted to give 200 bhp in a streamlined car used by Giuseppe Furmanik to break international class "F" records. The principal modification to the engine was an increase in the size of the supercharger from 115 mm to 130 mm and the record breaking car, with normal racing body work and new quarter-elliptic rear suspension in the 6 CM chassis, came second in its first race at Florence in 1937. Four of these 4CMs were produced in 1937/38 and were notably successful in the short circuit Italian events and one, driven by Armand Hug, gained a conspicuous success, beating the works ERAs at Berne in 1938.

While the 4 CM was having a renaissance, the 6 CM had not been neglected and was the mainstay of the works team in 1938, with support from the private Italian teams, notably the Scuderia Ambrosiana, which had strong links with the Bologna factory. The 1938 6 CM had quarter elliptic rear suspension and a lower, more streamlined body. The engine had been developed and the power increased from 155 bhp to 175 bhp; a car was produced for Viloresi at Livorno in 1938 with a light alloy cylinder block. The Maserati factory now had to cope with the new Tipo 158 Alfa Romeo but the 1938 6 CM was nearly as quick as the first Alfa Corse voiturettes and managed to beat them at Pescara and Modena.

Despite these successes Ernesto Maserati realised that the 6 CM design would be inadequate to continue the battle against the Alfa Romeos. Early in 1938 the small company had been bought by Commendatore Adolfo Orsi, a rich industrialist. With the backing of Orsi who retained the Maserati brothers and gave them a free hand, a new 1500 was designed in the autumn of 1938. This was the 4 CL model which had a "square" 78mm x 78mm engine and four valves per cylinder. The car was lower and more streamlined than the 6 CM although the chassis layout was the same as the later 6 CMs with torsion bar front suspension and quarter elliptic springs at the back.

As a parallel development a 24 valve head was designed for the 6 CM but although this was raced twice, the idea was not pursued.

The new 4 CL was manufactured as a car for the private entrant, as well as the factory team, and its first race appearance was at Brooklands where the first customer's car was driven by R.E. Tongue in the J.C.C. International Trophy in May 1939. The next day the Works team raced in the Tripoli GP and all were eliminated on the first lap with piston failure. For the rest of the 1939 Season, the 4 CL cars were unbeatable when the T158 Alfas were not running, and there was little to choose between the performance of the works cars and the best private entrants. When racing against the Alfas, the works cars were dogged by poor preparation and team management, although in Villoresi's hands the 4 CL was nearly a match for the best Alfa. In terms of maximum speed the 4 CL was probably the faster car and Villoresi was timed at Pescara at 147 mph, while a fully streamlined 4 CL exceeded 170 mph at Tripoli, but the car was handicapped by its less sophisticated rear suspension.

The Maserati factory moved from Bologna to Modena in the winter of 1939/40 but by the beginning of 1940 the Alfa Romeo had found more speed and the 4 CL Maserati was beginning to look inadequate, although it had the distinction of winning the Targa Florio in May 1940, the last 1500 race to be run in Europe before the War stopped all racing. After the War, the 4 CL continued to play an important part in the new formula 1 until superseded by the later 4 CLT/48 model.

It is unlikely that the Maserati brothers ever made money from their racing cars, but they had the great advantage over ERA, their principal voiturette rival of the mid-1930s, in possessing the reasonably firm economic base of the successful sparking plug business. The intervention of Gino Rovere in 1935/36 gave timely support to the factory racing team, but the firm would probably have survived, making racing cars and sparking plugs. The Maserati voiturette was produced in surprisingly small numbers and when the results the cars gained are considered, it must be appreciated that the cars produced were very hard-worked. The many voiturette races in Italy between 1936 and 1940 were almost exclusively Maserati affairs and the drivers who contested those events produced some fine and fierce racing. It is fair to say that throughout the decade of the 1930s, the Maserati was the backbone of voiturette racing and the small concern gave tremendous support to the private entrant for whom the latest models were always available over-the-counter fully ready to race.★ This was probably the principal reason for the enormous success of the Maserati voiturettes and their tremendous popularity; the cars were produced by enthusiastic mechanics/drivers who knew exactly what the racing driver needed.

★ The 4 CL was supplied by the works in full race trim and ready to go to the starting line in every respect (letter from R.E. Tongue to the author November 1978).

190

MASERATI TIPO 26 (1500 cc) AND TIPO 26C (1100 cc)

Designer: ALFIERI MASERATI
Wheelbase: 8' 5$\frac{1}{2}$" (2.58 m)
Front track: 4' 4$\frac{1}{2}$" (1.34 m)
Rear track: 4' 5$\frac{1}{2}$" (1.36 m)
Unladen weight: 1716 lbs (780 kg)
Bore: 60 mm (51 mm T26C)
Stroke: 62 mm
Number of cylinders: 8
Capacity: 1493 cc-1077 cc (T26C)
BHP: 128 at 6000 rpm (T26)
    105 at 6000 rpm (T26C)
Cylinder head: Cast iron detachable
Valve no: 2 per cylinder
Valve angle: 90°
Cylinder block: Aluminium or cast iron
Carburettor: Weber (T26C) Memini (T26)
Supercharger: Roots
Ignition: Bosch or Scintilla magneto (T26)
    Scintilla magneto (T26C)
Plugs no: 1 per cylinder
Crankcase: Electron split on centre line of
    crankshaft
Crankshaft: One piece

Main bearing no: 5
Main bearing type: Centre roller
    Outside plain
Big end type: Plain white metal
Lubrication: Dry sump
Camshaft no: 2
Camshaft location: In head driven by gear train
    from front of crankshaft
Clutch: Multi-plate dry
Gearbox and location: 4 speed. In unit with
    engine
Transmission: Torque tube to bevel drive rear
    axle
Frame: Channel
Front suspension: Semi-elliptic
Rear suspension: Semi-elliptic
Shock absorber type: Hartford friction
Brake system: Perrot Mechanical
Wheel type: Rudge
Number produced: 11 (T26)
    4 (T26C)
Price: £1100 (T26C chassis only)

MASERATI 4 CM 1100 AND 1500 (1932/36)

Designer: ERNESTO MASERATI
Wheelbase: 7' 10" (2.40 m)
Front track: 3' 11" (1.20 m)
Rear track: 3' 11" (1.20 m)
Unladen weight: 1276 lbs (580 kg)
Bore: 69 mm (65 mm – 1100)
Stroke: 100 mm (82 mm – 1100)
Number of cylinders: 4
Capacity: 1496 cc (1088 cc)
BHP: 130 at 5600 rpm – (1500)
    : 125 at 6000 rpm – (1100)
Cylinder head: Cast iron detachable
Valve no: 2 per cylinder
Valve angle: 90°
Cylinder block: Cast iron
Carburettor: Weber
Supercharger: Roots
Ignition: Scintilla magneto★
Plugs no: 1 per cylinder
Crankcase: Light alloy split on centre line of
    crankshaft
Crankshaft: One piece

Main bearing no: 3
Main bearing type: Plain
Big end type: Plain
Lubrication: Dry sump
Camshaft no: 2
Camshaft location: In head driven by gear train
    from front of crankshaft
Clutch: Single plate dry
Gearbox and location: 4 speed. In unit with
    engine
Transmission: Open propeller shaft to bevel
    drive rear axle
Frame: Channel section
Front suspension: Semi-elliptic
Rear suspension: Semi-elliptic
Shock absorber type: Hartford friction
Brake system: Hydraulic
Wheel type: Rudge
Number produced: 13: 4 CM
    (also 12: 4 CS with wide chassis and 2
    seater body)
Price: £887 (4 CM/1100)★★ in November 1934

★ Scuderia Subalpina cars were fitted with Bosch magnetos.
★★55000 lire converted at exchange rate then current.

MASERATI 6 CM

Designer: ERNESTO MASERATI
Wheelbase: 8' 3½" (2.53 m)
Front track: 4' 0" (1.22 m)
Rear track: 4' 0" (1.22 m)
Unladen weight: 1430 lbs (650 kg)
Bore: 65 mm
Stroke: 75 mm
Number of cylinders: 6
Capacity: 1493 cc
BHP: 175 (1938 model)
RPM: 6600
Cylinder head: Cast iron integral with cylinders
Valve no: 2 per cylinder
Valve angle: 90°
Cylinder block: Cast iron in pairs
Carburettor: Weber
Supercharger: Roots
Ignition: Scintilla magneto
Plugs no: 1 per cylinder
Crankcase: Light alloy split on central line of crankshaft
Crankshaft: One piece

Main bearing no: 5
Main bearing type: Plain
Big end type: Plain
Lubrication: Dry sump
Camshaft no: 2
Camshaft location: In head driven by gear train from front of crankshaft
Clutch: Single plate dry
Gearbox and location: 4 speed. In unit with engine
Transmission: Torque tube with bevel drive axle
Frame: Box section
Front suspension: Double wishbones and torsion bars
Rear suspension: Semi-elliptic (quarter elliptic 1938)
Shock absorber type: Friction
Brake system: Hydraulic
Wheel type: Rudge
Number produced: 27
Price: £1050 ex factory★

★ This figure is based on the lire/sterling exchange rate in 1937. This fluctuated considerably. The works quoted 95000 lire in November 1936.

MASERATI 4 CM/1500 (1937/38)

Designer: ERNESTO MASERATI
Wheelbase: 7' 11" (2.42 m)
Front track: 4' 0" (1.22 m)
Rear track: 4' 0" (1.22 m)
Unladen weight: 1276 lbs (580 kg)
Bore: 69 mm
Stroke: 100 mm
Number of cylinders: 4
Capacity: 1496 cc
BHP: 150
RPM: 6100
Cylinder head: Cast iron detachable
Valve no: 2 per cylinder
Valve angle: 90°
Cylinder block: Cast iron
Carburettor: Weber
Supercharger: Roots
Ignition: Scintilla Magneto
Plugs no: 1 per cylinder
Crankcase: Light alloy split on centre line of crankshaft
Crankshaft: One piece

Main bearing no: 3
Main bearing type: Plain
Big end type: Plain
Lubrication: Dry sump
Camshaft no: 2
Camshaft location: In head driven by gear train from front of crankshaft
Clutch: Single plate dry
Gearbox and location: 4 speed. In unit with engine
Transmission: Open propeller shaft to bevel drive rear axle
Frame: Box section
Front suspension: Double wishbones and torsion bars
Rear suspension: Semi elliptic (Quarter elliptic 1938)
Shock absorber type: Friction
Brake system: Hydraulic
Wheel type: Rudge
Number produced: 4★

★ 4 Cars were constructed as 4 CMs Trossi's 1937 car was apparently a converted 6 CM.

MASERATI 4 CL

Designer: ERNESTO MASERATI
Wheelbase: 8' 4" (2.54 m)
Front track: 4' 2" (1.27 m)
Rear track: 4' 3" (1.29 m)
Unladen weight: 1386 lbs (630 kg)
Bore: 78 mm
Stroke: 78 mm
Number of cylinders: 4
Capacity: 1491 cc
BHP: 220
RPM: 8000
Cylinder head: Cast iron integral with cylinders
Valve no: 4 per cylinder (2 inlet, 2 exhaust)
Valve angle: 90°
Cylinder block: Cast iron in pairs
Carburettor: Weber
Supercharger: Roots
Ignition: Scintilla Magneto
Plugs no: 1 per cylinder
Crankcase: Magnesium alloy split horizontally on line of crankshaft
Crankshaft: One piece

Main bearing no: 3
Main bearing type: Plain
Big end type: Plain
Lubrication: Dry sump
Camshaft no: 2
Camshaft location: In head gear driven from front of crankshaft
Clutch: Multi-plate
Gearbox and location: 4 speed. In unit with engine
Transmission: Torque tube with reduction gears to bevel drive rear axle
Frame: Box section
Front suspension: Double wishbone with torsion bars
Rear suspension: Quarter elliptic
Shock absorber type: Friction (front) Hydraulic (rear)
Brake system: Hydraulic
Wheel type: Rudge
Number produced: 9 (1939-1940)
Price: £1750 ex-works★

★ Price at mid-1939 sterling-lire exchange rate

MERCEDES-BENZ *(Daimler-Benz A-G, Unterturkheim, Stuttgart.)*

When the German teams entered Grand Prix racing at the beginning of the 750 kg formula in 1934, rumours began to fly about the possibility of Daimler-Benz building and racing a 1500. As it transpired, these were only rumours and apparently there was no consideration given to building a voiturette Mercedes-Benz. However, the Daimler-Benz engineers were fully aware of what was happening in the 1500 class and when Robert Kohrausch bought the 750cc M.G. Magic Midget, this car found its way to Unterturkheim where great interest was shown in its engine, and particularly in its Zoller vane supercharger, which seemed to offer a greater output than a Roots type of comparable size. An experimental Mercedes-Benz engine was equipped with a vane supercharger but the project was abandoned as it was decided that a vane blower was not sufficiently reliable to justify the greater power.★

During the summer of 1938, it was announced that the Tripoli Grand Prix, the fastest road race in the world would be restricted to 1500s in 1939. This was a challenge that Daimler-Benz could not resist, especially when it seemed likely that 1500cc would be the new G.P. formula limit in 1941, after the expiry of the

★ Letter from Dr. Rudolf Uhlenhaut to the author, February 1979.

193

The W165 Mercedes-Benz partly dismantled at Unterturkheim. The car is in 1940 trim with 2-stage supercharging.

3-litre formula, so it would be a chance to try out a 1500 Mercedes-Benz. The decision to go ahead was taken on 18th November 1938 and the design was executed and three chassis and engines were built in six months, which was a remarkable achievement, even though Daimler-Benz had a vast store of experience to draw upon and the ability and facilities to establish what would, and would not work, before any construction started. The cars were tested at Hockenheim early in April 1939 and it was then announced to an astonished motor racing world that the cars were in being, and would be entered for the Tripoli Grand Prix in May. The cars went to Tripoli, and driven by Lang and Caracciola, they dominated the race, finishing first and second and utterly humiliating the Italian teams, who had expected the race to be their especial domain.

After Tripoli, the cars were put away, and despite rumours of impending appearance during the rest of the 1939 season, they were never raced again. It was the intention of Daimler-Benz that the cars would appear at Tripoli in 1940, and much development was carried out to ensure that the 1939 win was repeated, but the War intervened and there was no possibility of the cars going to Tripoli again.

Technically, the W165 owed much to the current W163 3-litre GP car, and there was a similarity in appearance which gave rise to the oft-told story of the journalist who, when invited to inspect the new car, looked at it and asked when the new car would appear, being convinced that the car he had inspected was a W163.

The advent of the W165 brought a new standard into voiturette racing, or perhaps, more accurately, showed how the design of the 1500 racing car had stagnated between 1934 and 1938. With the possible exception of the Tipo 158

Alfa Romeo, the W165 made all its rivals obsolete and also pointed the path into the future with its V8 engine. In 1940, the Italians were determined not to be caught napping again, so Alfa Romeo did much work on the Tipo 158, which, as a result broke the race and lap record established by the W165 in 1939. It has been suggested that if Mercedes Benz had raced at Tripoli in 1940, a victory would have been harder to achieve than in the previous year, but this would probably have been unlikely. In 1940, Daimler-Benz had already begun a new chapter in the development of the voiturette with 2-stage supercharging, and the 278 bhp achieved at Unterturkheim in the winter of 1939/40 was not seen at Portello until 1947.

MERCEDES-BENZ W165

Designer: MAX WAGNER and ALBERT HEESS under direction of MAX SAILER
Wheelbase: 8' 0½" (2.45 m)
Front track: 4' 4¾" (1.34 m)
Rear track: 4' 2½" (1.28 m)
Unladen weight: 1582 lbs (719 kg)
Bore: 64 mm
Stroke: 58 mm
Number of cylinders: 8 (Vee 90°)
Capacity: 1493 cc
BHP: 246
RPM: 7500
Cylinder head: Welded construction integral with cylinders
Valve no: 2 inlet 2 exhaust per cylinder
Valve angle: 56°
Cylinder block: Welded steel
Carburettor: Solex
Supercharger: Roots (two stage projected for 1940)
Ignition: Bosch magneto
Plugs no: 1 per cylinder
Crankcase: Silumin split below centre line of crankshaft

Crankshaft: One piece
Main bearing no: 5
Main bearing type: Roller
Big end type: Roller
Lubrication: Dry sump
Camshaft no: 4 (2 per head)
Camshaft location: In head: gear driven from rear of crankshaft
Clutch: Single plate
Gearbox and location: 5 speed in unit with final drive
Transmission: Open propeller shaft Z F differential and open half shafts
Frame: Large section steel tube
Front suspension: Double wishbone and coil spring
Rear suspension: De Dion with torsion bar
Shock absorber type: Hydraulic
Brake system: Hydraulic with turbo finned drums
Wheel type: Rudge
Number produced: 2★

★ Parts for a third car were produced but it was not assembled.

M.G. (*The MG Car Co. Ltd., Abingdon*)

The initials MG, stand for Morris Garages. This small concern was the start of William Morris' (later Lord Nuffield) venture in the world of the motor car. When Morris Motors was founded, Morris Garages became the local Morris distributors in Oxford, and in 1923, the general manager, Cecil Kimber, began to market Morris touring cars fitted with sporting bodies built in the Morris Garage premises. These Morris sports tourers were soon marketed as MGs and

195

so the MG car came into being. During the 1920s the firm produced medium sized cars but in 1928, Morris announced his Morris Minor with an 847cc engine. This was an unusual economy car because the engine had an overhead camshaft operated by a vertical drive from the front of the engine. The engine was originally designed by the Wolseley Company, which was taken over by Morris in 1927, and probably had its origins in the Hispano Suiza aero engines built by Wolseley under licence during the 1914/18 War.

As soon as the Morris Minor appeared, Kimber produced an MG sporting version, the M-type, and in the winter of 1930/31, a new model was designed for sports car racing, which was derived from the original M type, and developed through the medium of a special car produced to capture 750cc International class records for MG. The new model was the 746cc Montlhery C-type. Initially, it had a short stroke M-type engine but soon sported a cross flow head, and following a remarkable run of successes in long distance sports car races in 1931, a supercharged version was produced. The chassis of the C type followed current racing practice having an underslung frame with semi-elliptic springs which were mounted in sliding trunnions in the best GP Bugatti style. The stripped C-type was quite a fast car in supercharged form, and gained some voiturette successes in the 750cc and 800cc classes, notably at the German GP in 1932 and at the Avus in 1933. The aim of MG was to sell sports cars; so the C-type was the basis of the next production model, the J2. This was introduced in August 1932, and was quickly followed by a full competition car, the J4 which had larger brakes and a longer chassis than the original C-type, but still used the basic engine and chassis design. The original ohc engine was particularly responsive to supercharging, and the J4 developed a power output which took the performance of the car beyond the limits of the chassis.

While the M-type had been developing into the C-type, the Abingdon factory had been producing another sports touring car, the F-type 6 cylinder Magna. This had a 1271cc ohc engine which it shared with the Wolseley Hornet. As a serious competition car, the F-type Magna had little future, being limited by its brakes and cylinder head design. The car was attractive though and amongst its owners were Earl Howe, Prince Bira, Dick Seaman and Charles Martin. At the 1932 Motor Show, a new MG was announced, the K-type Magnette which was a direct development of the F-type. This had all that was needed to make a successful racing car and during the winter of 1932/33 an outright competition version, the 1087cc supercharged K3 was developed. After a successful debut in the 1933 Mille Miglia, it was marketed at £695 and became an immediate success. By the end of the 1933 season the K3 had shown it was the fastest car in the 1100 class, and had won its first continental victory at Pescara, driven by Whitney Straight. A number of drivers removed the sports bodywork and converted their cars to single-seaters including Hugh Hamilton. In 1934, the K3 was given improved brakes, a pointed tailed two seater body in the place of the slab tank of the 1933 model, and a Marshall 85 supercharger replaced the Powerplus No 9 of the earlier model. So well did the K3 go, that by the middle of 1934, it was capable of beating not only the other 1100s but also the 1500 4CM Maserati and the T51A Bugatti as Cecchini and Seaman demonstrated, which was not bad going for a car developed from a production sports car and

196

Buxton
Derbyshire ENGLAND

BENTLEY DRIVERS CLUB
GOLDEN JUBILEE
1st–5th July, 1986

NEWSLETTER No. 3

Saturday, 28th June—Kensington Gardens Concours.

Sunday, 29th June—Brooklands Society Reunion at Brooklands Surrey.

Monday, 30th June—Snowball Runs from the Regions. Details to be published in February Notes Jubilee 'Newsletter'.

PROGRAMME

Tuesday, 1st July—Snowball Runs by the Regions (co-ordinated by Bryan and Robin Downes) to end between 10.00 a.m. and 4.00 p.m. at the Palace Hotel, Buxton, Derbyshire. All Registered Entrants to collect an information pack, individually numbered Jubilee Rally Numbers for fixing onto car, Jubilee Programme, etc., etc.

6.30 p.m.—CIVIC RECEPTION (by courtesy of Buxton Council) organised by Johnnie Green.

Wednesday, 2nd July—Chatsworth House—CONCOURS, DRIVING TESTS and tour of Chatsworth House organised by Charles Teal.

FREE EVENING with meal at your own hotel.

INTER-REGIONAL SWIMMING at the Palace Hotel organised by Heather Barraclough.

Thursday, 3rd July—Scenic Run to OULTON PARK for light-hearted regularity runs. Stanley Mann Trophies for winners.

8.00 p.m. LIVE THEATRE in Buxton.

Interval Drinks.

Pre-Theatre Supper or after Theatre Buffet/Barbecue.

Friday, 4th July—FREE DAY or lighthearted Navigational/ Scavenger/Scatter Rally, organised by Roger Collings.

FREE EVENING with meal at your own hotel.

FILM SHOW at Palace Hotel during the evening organised by Jim Medcalf.

Saturday, 5th July—Morning BENTLEY JUMBLE organised by Brian Fenn.

SCENIC RUN organised by Tom and Di Threlfall. Buffet/Packed Lunch.

Pre-GALA BALL RECEPTION (by courtesy of Richardson Hosken).

GALA BALL at Pavilion Gardens, Buxton.

Trophy presentations, speeches, dancing, etc.

As we are actively seeking sponsorship for the Jubilee Week which is still some nine months away—all the above programme is subject to change and we cannot guarantee, at this stage, that exact times will be adhered to.

The Regional Snowball Runs will be published in February and all registered entrants will receive an application form for tickets for all events/meals and security parking, etc.

OVERSEAS VISITORS

Overseas members who wish to visit the UK for the Golden Jubilee and require coach facilities in the Jubilee Week are asked to notify Club Office by RETURN so that arrangements can be put in hand and costings assessed.

A non-returnable deposit will be required shortly.

A 1934 Q-type MG

sharing major components with its humbler brethren.

While the K3 was being developed, the 750cc class was not being neglected. A new car, the Q-type, used the K3 chassis and body (with a narrower track) and an engine which was very closely related to the production P-type car. The Q-type had a three bearing crankshaft which was a great improvement on the two bearing crank of the J4. In its final form with a 38 lb boost using a Zoller supercharger, the Q type gave 146 bhp at 7500 rpm or 194 bhp per litre which was an enormous output for such a small engine and was a figure unsurpased by any racing car before the Second World War. Like the J4, the Q-type was too fast and powerful for its chassis and to remedy this the Abingdon factory developed a car of revolutionary design during the winter of 1934. The new car, designed by H.N. Charles, had independent suspension on all four wheels using double wishbone and torsion bars, while the frame was a "Y" shaped steel fabrication with the engine mounted between the arms of the Y. The Q-type engine was used with further modifications and the new car, called the R-type looked most promising although it was clear when the car began to race that it needed some further development. MGs had great hopes of the R-type and a larger 1100 cc version was intended to replace the K3, which had ceased production at the end of 1934, after 33 had been built. Looking further ahead, a new 1500 was also planned and had already been given the provisional label of the S-type.

The policy of MG had always been to sell production sports cars and to operate as an economically sound part of Lord Nuffield's empire. To this end, the racing MGs used a remarkably large number of parts from the production cars, but by the Spring of 1935 it was clear to Lord Nuffield that the Abingdon factory was not making enough money and this was attributed to the emphasis on competitions. In June 1935, therefore, it was decreed that racing would cease overnight. The competition department was closed and the production of racing models and the development of new racing designs stopped for ever. All the remarkable talents of the competitions department were to be directed to the improvement of production models and the development of new designs. While this was probably sound business sense, it was heartbreaking to motor racing enthusiasts and to the competition staff, as a full 1500 racing MG would certainly have been a formidable machine. MG had encountered the problem that eventually confronts all large firms who go motor racing; once success is achieved, it is expected by the public as a matter of course, and the publicity returns diminish. Failure can mean disaster and further success means more and more outlay. The only solution is to withdraw gracefully. With the factory backing gone, the MG customers quickly changed to other marques and within a season, those MGs still racing were back at the rear of the starting grids along with the Salmsons and Amilcars, as a reminder of failed glories. This was a great pity, as the competition department at Abingdon gave more support and help to its customers then any other voiturette manufacturer.* The MG was a remarkable example of how careful and painstaking development can produce results that belie the humble origins of a car.

* Letter from R.E. Tongue to the author: November 1978.

M.G. C-TYPE MONTLHERY 1931-32

Designer: H.N. CHARLES and M.G.
    DESIGN TEAM
Wheelbase: 6' 9" (2.05m)
Front track: 3' 6" (1.06m)
Rear track: 3' 6" (1.06m)
Unladen weight: 1200 lbs approx. (500kg)
Bore: 57 mm
Stroke: 73 mm
Number of cylinders: 4
Capacity: 746 cc
BHP: 52 at 6500 rpm
Cylinder head: Cast iron detachable
Valve no: 2 per cylinder
Valve angle: Vertical
Cylinder block: Cast iron
Carburettor: SU
Supercharger: Powerplus No. 6
Ignition: Coil
Plugs no: 1 per cylinder
Crankcase: Integral with block

Crankshaft: One piece
Main bearing no: 2
Main bearing type: 1 Ball 1 Plain
Big end type: Plain
Lubrication: Wet sump
Camshaft no: 1
Camshaft location: In head driven by bevel gears
    and vertical shaft from front of crankshaft
Clutch: Single plate dry
Gearbox location: 4 speed in unit with engine
Transmission: Open propeller shaft to bevel
    drive rear axle
Frame: Channel
Front suspension: Semi-elliptic
Rear suspension: Semi-elliptic
Shock absorber type: Hartford friction
Brake system: Cable mechanical
Wheel type: Rudge
Number produced: 44
Price: £575 (sports specification)

M.G. K3 MAGNETTE 1933/34

Designer: H.N. CHARLES and MG DESIGN
    TEAM

Wheelbase: 7' 10" (2.38 m)
Front track: 4' 0" (1.22 m)

Rear track 4' 0" (1.22 m)
Unladen weight: 1735 lbs (789 kg) in racing trim
Bore: 57 mm
Stroke: 71 mm
Number of cylinders 6
Capacity: 1086 cc
BHP: 120
RPM: 6500
Cylinder head: Cast iron detachable
Valve no: 2 per cylinder
Valve angle: Vertical
Cylinder block: Cast iron
Carburettor: SU
Supercharger: Powerplus No. 9 (1933)
   Marshall 85 (1934)
Ignition: BTH magneto
Plugs no: 1 per cylinder
Crankcase: Integral with block
Crankshaft: One piece
Main bearing no: 4

Main bearing type: Plain
Big end type: Plain
Lubrication: Wet sump
Camshaft no: 1
Camshaft location: In head driven by vertical
   shaft and bevel gears from front of crank-
   shaft
Gearbox and location: 4 speed ENV preselector.
   In unit with engine
Transmission: Open propeller shaft to bevel
   drive rear axle
Frame: Channel
Front suspension: Semi-elliptic
Rear suspension: Semi-elliptic
Shock absorber type: Hartford friction
Brake system: Cable mechanical
Wheel type: Rudge
Number produced: 33
Price: £795 (sports trim)

M.G. J4 1933–34

Designer: H.N. CHARLES and M.G. DESIGN
   TEAM
Wheelbase: 7' 2" (2.18m)
Front track: 3' 6" (1.06m)
Rear track: 3' 6" (1.06m)
Unladen weight: 1200 lbs approx (500kg)
Bore: 57 mm
Stroke: 73 mm
Number of cylinders: 4
Capacity: 746 cc
BHP: 72 at 6000 rpm
Cylinder head: Cast iron detachable
Valve no: 2 per cylinder
Valve angle: Vertical
Cylinder block: Cast iron
Carburettor: SU
Supercharger: Powerplus No. 7
Ignition: Coil
Plugs no: 1 per cylinder
Crankcase: Integral with block

Crankshaft: One piece
Main bearing no: 2
Main bearing type: 1 Ball 1 Plain
Big end type: Plain
Lubrication: Wet sump
Camshaft no: 1
Camshaft location: In head driven by bevel gears
   and vertical shaft from front of crankshaft
Clutch: Double plate dry
Gearbox location: 4 speed in unit with engine
Transmission: Open propeller shaft to bevel
   drive rear axle
Frame: Channel
Front suspension: Semi-elliptic
Rear suspension: Semi-elliptic
Shock absorber type: Hartford friction
Brake system: Cable mechanical
Wheel type: Rudge
Number produced: 9
Price: £445

M.G. Q-TYPE 1934–35

Designer: H.N. CHARLES and M.G. DESIGN
   TEAM
Wheelbase: 7' 10" (2.38m)
Front track: 3' 9" (1.14m)
Rear track: 3' 9" (1.14m)
Unladen weight: 1350 lbs (614kg)

Bore: 57 mm
Stroke 73 mm
Number of cylinders: 4
Capacity: 746 cc
BHP: 113 at 7200 rpm
Cylinder head: Cast iron detachable

Valve no: 2 per cylinder
Valve angle: Vertical
Cylinder block: Cast iron
Carburettor: SU
Supercharger: Zoller: Q4
Ignition: Lucas Magneto
Plugs no: 1 per cylinder
Crankcase: Integral with block
Crankshaft: One piece
Main bearing no: 3
Main bearing type: Plain
Big end type: Plain
Lubrication: Wet sump
Camshaft no: 1
Camshaft location: In head driven by bevel gears and vertical shaft from front of crankshaft

Gearbox location: ENV 4 speed preselector in unit with engine
Transmission: Open propeller shaft to bevel drive rear axle
Frame: Channel
Front suspension: Semi-elliptic
Rear suspension: Semi-elliptic
Shock absorber type: Hartford friction front Luvax hydraulic rear
Brake system: Cable mechanical
Wheel type: Rudge
Number produced: 8
Price: £750

M.G. R-TYPE 1935

Designer: H.N. CHARLES and M.G. DESIGN TEAM
Wheelbase 7' 6" (2.28m)
Front track: 3' 10" (1.16m)
Rear track: 3' 9" (1.14m)
Unladen weight: 1230 lbs (559 kg)
Bore: 57 mm
Stroke: 73 mm
Number of cylinders: 4
Capacity: 746 cc
BHP: 113 at 7200 rpm
Cylinder head: Cast iron detachable
Valve no: 2 per cylinder
Valve angle: Vertical
Cylinder block: Cast iron
Carburettor: SU
Supercharger: Zoller: Q4
Ignition: Lucas Magneto
Plugs no: 1 per cylinder
Crankcase: Integral with block

Crankshaft: One piece
Main bearing no: 3
Main bearing type: Plain
Big end type: Plain
Lubrication: Wet sump
Camshaft no: 1
Camshaft location: In head driven by bevel gears and vertical shaft from front of crankshaft
Gearbox location: 4 speed pre-selector in unit with engine
Transmission: Open propeller shaft to chassis mounted differential with open drive shaft
Frame: Y-shaped box section
Front suspension: Independent with torsion bars
Rear suspension: Independent with torsion bars
Shock absorber type: Luvax hydraulic
Brake system: Cable mechanical
Wheel type: Rudge
Number produced: 10
Price: £750

RILEY *(Riley (Coventry) Ltd., Coventry.)*

The Riley company was one of the oldest in the British industry and came to voiturette racing largely by accident, rather than design, although the basic Riley design had a tremendous influence on the history of the 1500 class in the mid-1930s. Until 1926, Rileys had been respectable touring cars, apart from a side-valve sports car, the Redwing, but at the London Motor Show in 1926, the Riley 9 was introduced and it was clear that this was a car quite out of the ordinary as a touring saloon. The significant feature was the 4 cylinder engine

200

which, despite a two bearing crankshaft, had two camshafts set high in the cylinder block, operating valves in a hemispherical head by short push-rods and rockers. The ports and combustion chambers were in accordance with the best current racing design, so it was appreciated immediately that the car had competition possibilities. The legendary Parry Thomas was enlisted to develop a sports version of the car and he was engaged in this task when he was killed at Pendine Sands in March 1927. Thomas's work was taken over by Thomson and Taylor at Brooklands and with the technical supervision of Reid Railton, a modified shortened chassis was produced with a neat two seater body. Success at Brooklands, encouraged Riley to develop the car and with a new and very low chassis it was marketed in 1928 as the Riley Speed Model, soon to be known as the redoutable Brooklands Riley which was to dominate the 1100 class in sports car races between 1928 and 1933. With its touring equipment removed, the Brooklands Riley was a businesslike racing car and the factory began an extensive racing programme. The works cars differed from the production model in many ways, although superficially similar, with special cylinder heads, stronger crankshafts★ and extensive use of light alloys in the chassis, although it was possible for a keen private owner to develop a Brooklands Riley into a highly competitive car in the 1100 class, as a number of entrants showed in British events. The only voiturette race in which a works car was entered, was the 1931 German Grand Prix, and the speed of this car surprised its opponents who were outpaced. When Scaron had trouble with his supercharged MC0 Amilcar, the unsuperchared Riley, driven by Dudley Froy, won. The only other success scored by the Brooklands Riley in voiturette racing, was the win by Freddie Dixon in the 1933 Mannin Beg, in the Isle of Man. Once again, the unsupercharged Riley was capable of keeping up with its supercharged rivals. With such a fast car available it is a great pity that more British drivers did not take Rileys to European voiturette races between 1931 and 1933 as with competent drivers they would surely have found success.

In 1932, Rileys produced a 1500cc, 6 cylinder sports racing car and continued to run this in suitable sports car races in 1933. The potential of this 6 cylinder engine was seen by Raymond Mays and formed the basis of the ERA. Rileys continued to run factory entries in British events until the firm had financial difficulties in 1938; the final version of the 1500 6-cylinder, in supercharged form, was almost a match for its cousin, the ERA, particularly when driven by Percy Maclure, but the car made very rare appearances in 1500 scratch races and never crossed the English Channel. Freddie Dixon also turned his attention to the Six but apart from entries in the Isle of Man races, and the Nuffield Trophy the Dixon cars were not driven in voiturette events.

RILEY "BROOKLANDS" 9 1931-33

Designer: PERCY RILEY (engine)
   PARRY THOMAS and REID RAILTON
   (chassis)
Wheelbase: 8' 0" (2.43m)
Front track: 3' 11" (1.19m)
★2" (51mm) journals instead of 1¹¹₁₆" (43mm)

Rear track: 3' 11" (1.19m)
Unladen weight: 1300 lbs approx in racing trim
   (590 kg)
Bore: 60.3 mm
Stroke: 95.2 mm

Number of cylinders: 4
Capacity: 1087 cc
BHP: 70
RPM: 6000
Cylinder head: Cast iron detachable
Valve no: 2 per cylinder
Valve angle: 90°
Cylinder block: Cast iron
Carburettor: 2 SU or 4 Amal
Supercharger: None
Ignition: Lucas or BTH Magneto
Plugs no: 1 per cylinder
Crankcase: Integral with block
Crankshaft: 1 piece
Main bearing no: 2
Main bearing type: Plain
Big end type: Plain

Lubrication: Wet sump
Camshaft no: 2
Camshaft location: High in block operating valves by push rods and rockers
Clutch: Single plate dry
Gearbox and location: 4 speed. In unit with engine
Transmission: Torque tube and bevel drive rear axle
Frame: Channel
Front suspension: Semi-elliptic
Rear suspension: Semi-elliptic
Shock absorber type: Hartford friction
Brake system: Cable operated mechanical
Wheel type: Bolt on wire or Rudge
Number produced: 93 (sports models)
Price: £420 (sports specification)

SALMSON (*Société des Moteurs Salmson, Billancourt*)

Until 1921, the Société des Moteurs Salmson had been, amongst other things, manufacturers of aero engines and also aeroplanes in their factory at Billancourt. With the decline in demand for their aeronautical products at the end of the 1914/18 War, the Société looked around for other sources of business and solved the problem by becoming motor manufacturers. The first Salmson was the English GN built under licence. The GN was a chain driven cyclecar with an air cooled twin cylinder engine and from these humble but lively beginnings, the Salmson soon grew into a comparatively sophisticated small car with the pace being set by the Société's support for competition motoring. By mid-1921, Emil Petit had designed a twin ohc 4-cylinder racing engine, and with steady development, this became the basis for a production sports car and in full race trim, a formidable machine in the 1100cc class. By 1927, it had become the "Grand Prix" model fitted with the Cozette blown 8 plug San Sebastian engine. Seventeen of these cars were produced and were still competitive in the 1100cc class in the early 1930s. The car was fast enough to enable Raymond Chambost to beat a field of 1500s at the Nimes GP as late as 1933. Not quite a match for the contemporary roller-bearing MC0 1100 Amilcar, the GP Salmson could cope with the production C6 Amilcar, but its days were numbered when such cars as the 4C 1100 Maserati appeared and the Salmsons disappeared as the 1100 class declined in 1933/34.

Not content with the success of the 4 cylinder twin cam engine, Emil Petit, who had formerly worked with Ballot and had perhaps come under the influence of the great Ernest Henry, designed a new engine in 1927. This followed the very best current Grand Prix practice, as it was a straight-8 with a bore and stroke of 49.9mm and 70mm. This 1085cc engine was supercharged by two Cozettes driven from the central timing gears, while an unusual feature was

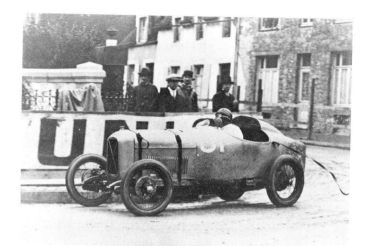

The San Sebastian G.P. Salmson seen here at Boulogne in 1926 driven by Casse.

The 8 cylinder G.P. Salmson with Armand Girod at the wheel.

semi-desmodromic (positive closing) valve operation, a system which had been used on the 1922 4 cylinder racing engine. The 8-cylinder engine was installed in a modified GP chassis, with a single seater body, but the car was not particularly successful and after initial troubles, the factory abandoned the project at the end of the 1928 racing season. In 1932, the two cars which had been built, passed into the hands of a Paris garage proprietor, Armand Girod. His only major change was to fit a Cotal electrical gearbox and in this form, Girod ran the cars in several voiturette races between 1933 and 1935. His greatest success was to win the 1100 class in the GP de France meeting at Montlhery in 1934. After 1935, the cars disappeared from the voiturette scene.

SALMSON GRAND PRIX (SERVICE DE COURSE) 1927/29

Designer: EMIL PETIT
Wheelbase: 8' 2" (2.49m)
Front track(3' 7" (1.09m)
Rear track: 3' 7" (1.09m)
Unladen weight: 960 lbs (436 kg)
Bore: 62.2 mm
Stroke: 90.0 mm
Number of cylinders: 4
Capacity: 1097 cc
BHP: 64 (standard model)
RPM: 5000
Cylinder head: Cast iron detachable
Valve no: 2 per cylinder
Valve angle: 90°
Cylinder block: Cast iron with steel water jacket
Carburettor: Cozette
Supercharger: Cozette No. 8
Ignition: Salmson Magneto
Plugs no: 2 per cylinder
Crankcase: Light alloy
Crankshaft: One piece

Main bearing no: 3
Main bearing type: Ball bearing
Big end type: Plain
Lubrication: Wet sump
Camshaft no: 2
Camshaft location: On head in separate cam-boxes driven by vertical shaft and skew gears from front of crankshaft
Clutch: Single plate dry.
Gearbox and location: 4 speed. Separate from engine
Transmission: Torque tube to pressed steel axle: No differential
Frame: Channel
Front suspension: Semi-elliptic
Rear suspension: Quarter-elliptic
Shock absorber type: Hartford friction
Brake system: Perrot mechanical
Wheel type: Rudge
Number produced: 17
Price: £475

SALMSON GRAND PRIX 8 C

Designer: EMIL PETIT
Wheelbase: 8' 2" (2.49m)
Front track: 3' 7" (1.09m)
Rear track: 3' 7" (1.09m)
Bore: 49.9 mm
Stroke: 70.0 mm
Number of cylinders: 8
Capacity: 1085 cc
BHP: 140
RPM: 8000
Cylinder head: 2 cast iron detachable per 4 cylinder
Valve no: 2 per cylinder
Valve angle: 90°
Cylinder block: Cast iron in two blocks of four
Carburettor: 2 Cozette
Supercharger: 2 Cozette No. 7
Ignition: Salmson magneto
Plugs no: 2 per cylinder

Crankcase: Light alloy barrel
Crankshaft: 2 piece
Main bearing no: 2 roller 4 ball
Big end type: Roller
Lubrication: Wet sump
Camshaft no: 2
Camshaft location: In head (semi-desmodromic operation) driven by gear train from centre of crankshaft
Clutch: Single plate dry
Gearbox and location: 4 speed in unit with engine
Transmission: Torque tube to bevel rear axle.
Frame: Channel
Front suspension: Semi-elliptic
Rear suspension: Quarter-elliptic
Shock absorber type: Hartford friction
Brake system: Perrot mechanical
Wheel type: Rudge
Number produced: 2

TALBOT *(Automobiles Talbot, Suresnes)*

The French Talbot sprang from one of the earliest international motor company amalgamations. In 1903 the English firm of Clement-Talbot was founded by

Adolphe Clement and the Earl of Shrewsbury, and produced the Talbot, which had a high reputation as a quality car and achieved immortality when Percy Lambert drove one at Brooklands in 1913, and became the first man to achieve the magic target of 100 miles in one hour. In 1919 Clement-Talbot acquired the old established French firm of Alexandre Darracq, and a year later, in June 1920, the respected English firm of Sunbeam joined the group to form the STD combine. By 1914, Sunbeam had established itself as the principal British manufacturer in motor racing, and under the control of Louis Coatalen, the marque re-entered grand prix racing in 1921, as the STD representative. When the grand prix formula was changed to a 2-litre limit in 1922, STD prepared new cars, and achieved its greatest success, with Segrave's victory in the French GP at Tours in 1923. The GP Sunbeams were built at Wolverhampton, but the active 1500 class was not neglected, and STD voiturettes were built in the old Darracq factory at Suresnes outside Paris and raced as Talbot-Darracq. These Talbot-Daracq voiturettes were virtually invincible and when the 1500cc GP formula was introduced in 1926, the STD combine decided to produce a suitable car, and perhaps feeling that the Talbot-Derracq factory knew more about 1500s than Wolverhampton, the new cars were built and developed at Suresnes. The new cars were designed by Vincent Bertarione, an Italian who had already collaborated with Ernest Henry and Louis Coatalen in the design of the successful 2 litre Sunbeam, and had also been a co-designer of the 1922 GP Fiat. Bertarione produced a machine for STD that was the height of GP fashion; a supercharged straight-8 with offset transmission in a very low chassis.

The new cars were not ready for the 1926 French GP at Miramas but made their first appearance in England for the British GP at Brooklands, where, in honour of the STD parentage, they were painted green. The three Talbots led the race in the early stages but then fell back and retired, leaving victory to the 8-cylinder Delages which were busy burning their driver's feet. The Talbot team returned to Brooklands, seven weeks later, for the JCC 200 and this time, with the Delage team absent, the new cars finished first, second and fourth. The season finished with another victory in the Coupe du Salon at Montlhery where the cars were now painted blue.

The British GP had shown that although Talbot was the faster car, it lacked the brakes and road holding of the Delage. The brakes were improved during the winter of 1926/27, but to no avail, and in the first appearance of the Talbot in the opening meeting at Montlhéry in March, a single car was no match for its Delage rival. A full team of three cars appeared for the French GP at Montlhéry in July, but the result was the same; a clean sweep for Delage and failure for the Talbots with one car finishing a poor fourth.

It was clear that the STD combine could not afford to race the team or probably even to prepare it properly. Their entries were scratched from the Spanish GP, and at the end of 1927, the four cars which had been built were sold to an Italian, Emilio Materassi, who had been a Bugatti works driver in 1927. Materassi formed the Scuderia Materassi and the cars were modified and painted red, and then raced in Italian events with some success throughout the 1928 season. Sadly at the end of the season, Materassi was killed driving one of the cars in the Italian GP at Monza, when he crashed into the crowd killing twenty-

205

26th August, 1934: Prix de Berne: Enrico Platé's 8C Talbot behind the pits.

two spectators. Despite this disaster the Scuderia continued and the cars appeared again in 1929 and 1930 driven by such notable drivers as Nuvolari, Brivio, Biondetti and Pintacuda. Sadly, Count Brilli-Peri, who had become a member of the team, was killed during practice for the Tripoli GP in 1930 and at the end of the season at least two of the cars were bought by Gigi Platé.

Platé now modified the cars again, and for the remainder of the decade, until 1939, he entered them in voiturette races all over Europe, the cars reaching a point where they were named Platé Specials. He drove the cars himself and was occasionally joined by Count Castelbarco but the cars were too slow, and lacked a Giulio Ramponi to get the best out of them. A third car came to England in 1937 and was modified by Thomson & Taylor for Anthony Powys-Lybbe who hoped "to do a Seaman" with it but his efforts were unsuccessful. Platé's best result with one of the cars, was a third place at Albi, in 1938.

Never as good as the Delage, the Talbot fell on harder times than it deserved during the 1930s, whereas with money and development it could perhaps have been quite a competitive car during the earlier years of the decade. When the STD combine broke up in 1934 the French Talbot assets were acquired by Anthony Lago and from this basis came the Lago Talbot which represented France in Grand Prix racing in the later 1940s and early 1950s.

TALBOT 1500/8C G.P.

Designer: VINCENT BERTARIONE
Wheelbase: 8' 7" (2.60m)
Front track: 4' 1½" (1.25m)
Rear track: 4' 1½" (1.25m)
Unladen weight: 1570 lbs (715 kg)
Bore: 56 mm
Stroke: 75.5 mm
Number of cylinders: 8
Capacity: 1485cc
BHP: 160 at 7200 rpm

Cylinder head: Steel welded construction integral with cylinder block
Valve no: 2 per cylinder
Valve angle: 90°
Cylinder block: Steel welded construction in two blocks of 4
Carburettor: Solex
Supercharger: Roots
Ignition: 2 Bosch magneto
Plugs no: 1 per cylinder

Crankcase: Two piece light alloy
Crankshaft: Two piece
Main bearings no: 9
Main bearings type: Roller
Big ends type: Roller
Lubrication: Dry sump
Camshaft no: 2
Camshaft location: In head driven by gear train from rear of crankshaft
Clutch: Wet multi plate

Gearbox location: 4 speed in unit with engine
Transmission: Torque tube with reduction gears to bevel drive rear axle
Frame: Girder lattice
Front suspension: Semi-elliptic
Rear suspension: Semi-elliptic
Shock absorber type: Talbot friction
Brake system: Perrot-Piganeau mechanical
Wheel type: Rudge
Number produced: 3

THE DRIVERS

(who had three or more voiturette victories 1931-1940)

Prince Birabongse Bhanutej Bhanubandh (B. Bira). Born in Thailand in 1914, a member of the Thai Royal Family.★ Bira came to England in 1927 and was educated at Eton. Supported by his cousin, H.R.H Prince Chula Chakrabongse, Bira began racing in 1935 with a Riley Imp and a K3 MG Magnette, and showed sufficient promise for Chula to buy an ERA for him. He finished second in his first race with this car at Dieppe, in July 1935, and followed this with another second place at Berne. In April 1936, he gained his first voiturette victory in the Coupe de Prince Rainier at Monaco, and during the 1936 season, Bira was the most successful ERA driver as he had further victories at Peronne and Albi; without his efforts, the results of the ERA marque in 1936 would have been very disappointing.

After the successes of the previous year, 1937 was a setback, as Bira and Chula tackled a programme of events which strained the resources of their White Mouse Stable to the utmost, particularly as the team was endeavouring, without success, to develop and rebuild the 1500 Delage bought from Richard Seaman at the end of the 1936 season. As a result, the preparation of Bira's cars suffered and he only won a single international voiturette race, the RAC event in the Isle of Man. This was perhaps his finest voiturette drive, as he beat the works ERAs with a two year old car, and emphasized his geat sensitivity as a driver under adverse conditions.

In 1938, Chula abandoned the Delage project and bought an ex-works 1937 C-type ERA. With this car, Bira was the equal of the works D-type ERA, and more than a match for the best of the 4CM and 6CM Maseratis, but the team made fewer forays to the European mainland, and raced mainly in British events, as Chula admitted that the venture of 1937 had caused financial worries. With the C-type ERA, Bira won at Cork, one of the only two voiturette victories achieved by the ERA marque in 1938. In the final season before the 1939-45 War, Bira started well by winning the Nuffield Trophy at Donington with the C-type ERA. This car was subsequently damaged badly, however, when Bira crashed in practice at Rheims and escaped with slight injuries. He and Chula were now finding that the ERA was outclassed by the new 4CL Maserati, and his last voiturette event in the 1939 season was at Albi where he finished

---

★ Bira was a grandson of King Mongkut the hero of the musical "The King and I".

third behind the Maseratis of Wakefield and Tongue.

Bira resumed racing after the War and gained a number of successes driving Maserati, Osca and Gordini in the 1500ccS, 4500cc U/S GP formula of 1947/51 and in the subsequent 2 litre formula of 1952/53, and in the early days of the $2^1{}_2$ litre formula of 1954. Although it seemed that some of his pre-war speed had gone he was one of the most prominent private entrants and was always a force to be reckoned with in minor GP events. Bira's last victory was the 1955 New Zealand GP driving a 250 F Maserati and he retired from racing at the end of that season. He now lives in retirement in Thailand. In addition to his racing successes, Bira has also been acknowledged as an accomplished sculptor.★

Despite the slight physical handicap of extreme short sight, (he always raced in spectacles or goggles with corrective lenses), between 1936 and 1939, Bira was the most consistently successful private entrant in 1500 racing and the efficiency of the Bira/Chula team was such, that it was regarded as an equal by the factory teams of ERA and Maserati. If the German GP teams had not been committed by Nazi doctrines to the policy of engaging Aryan drivers, it is probable that Bira would have been offered a trial, as he was a superior driver to most of the second and third strings of the German teams. Nello Ugolini, manager of the Scuderia Ferrari, described Bira, in 1938, as "A fine driver and very correct, but not always quite as fast as he should be", which was probably a very fair assessment.

Franco Cortese. Born at Oggebbio, near Turin, in 1903. He began his career in 1926, driving an Itala, and over the next four years gained a considerable reputation driving Alfa Romeos in sports car races, although he also competed with Alfa Romeo and Bugatti in GP events.

In 1930, he joined the Scuderia Ferrari, driving the 1750 Alfa and then the 2.3 model. With this, he finished second at Le Mans in 1932 and in the same position in the 1933 Mille Miglia. In 1934, he scored the first of five successive victories in the Targa Abbruzo, the long distance sports car event on the Pescara circuit.

In 1937, Alfa Romeo's activity in sports car races had diminished so Cortese decided to enter the voiturette class and bought a 6CM Maserati from the factory in April 1937. After retiring at Turin, he made a considerable impact in his next race with the car at Naples, where he led a high quality field for the first five laps, before being forced to stop for plugs. Obviously the class suited him, for a few weeks later he had a tough battle with Dreyfus' works 6CM at Tripoli and only conceded victory to his opponent after a hard fight over the 278 mile course. For the rest of the season he drove consistently and was always well placed, coming third at Milan and Pescara, and fourth at Berne, behind the faster ERAs.

Cortese had made his mark in 1937, for at the beginning of the 1938 season he joined the Maserati team. During the season he fully justified his "promotion", his first success was a victory in the Circuit of Varese in July, and by September, when the T158 Alfa Romeo had become the car to beat, Cortese still did his

★ The bronze bas-relief on the Pat Fairfield Memorial Fountain in the Silvertsone Paddock is Bira's work.

210

best, by finishing second at Lucca, and then coming fourth behind the Alfa team at Monza. His best performance of the season came at the end of the month, when he survived the war of attrition between the Alfa and Maserati teams at Modena and won, his sports car experience possibly enabling him to save his car while the others fell out. The 1939 season began equally well, for Cortese accompanied Luigi Villoresi to South Africa and finished second behind his team-mate in the South African Grand Prix, and then won the Grosvenor Grand Prix. This was his last victory with the faithful 6CM for the Maserati team now had the new 4CL. The whole team retired at Tripoli, but later in the season, Cortese came second at Carnaro and Livorno and was third at Naples. In the abbreviated 1940 season, he supported Villoresi, taking fifth place at Tripoli behind the much improved and faster Alfas, and completed his pre-war motor racing with a second place in the Targa Florio.

With the War over, Cortese returned to the sport, and scored a number of victories in Italian events. To him fell the honour, in May 1947, of being the first to drive a Ferrari car to victory on the Caracalla circuit at Rome. Thereafter, he raced the new marque regularly and successfully in sports car and formula races, but in 1951, he forsook Ferrari and drove a Frazer Nash in the Targa Florio, gaining a remarkable and unexpected victory for the small British firm. Now a veteran, Cortese continued racing until the end of 1953 and then retired from the sport. After giving up racing he pursued his business interests and became an agent for a number of foreign motor component manufacturers in Italy where he now lives in retirement.

Louis Decaroli. Born in Nice in 1898. He began his racing career driving Salmsons in the 1920s, and in 1930 he bought two new GP models and with these cars he became a regular competitor in the 1100 racing class. In his first season he had a number of minor successes, the principal one being a third place in the 1100 class of the GP du Comminges. The next year, 1931, he blossomed out and his first success came in June when he finished second behind Scaron at the Prix Royal inaugural meeting on the Littorio Circuit outside Rome. Better things were to come, for he won his class at the Freiburg Hill Climb in the Black Forest on 26th July, and then went on to Berlin to finish second at the Arus meeting on 2nd August. As soon as the Berlin meeting was over, Decaroli set off on the long journey to Pescara, but this effort was justified, as he won the Coppa Acerbo Vetturette race on the 16th August.

In 1932 he appeared once again with the two Salmsons and made another journey to Rome in April where he beat the new single seater Maserati to win the 1100 class of the Prix Royale in wet and slippery conditions. This was the only road racing success he had in the season, but he continued to run the Salmsons in hill climbs.

In 1933 Decaroli abandoned the faithful Salmsons and acquired a T37A Bugatti, but he only raced this infrequently and was unfortunate when he crashed at Brno in the appalling conditions in which the Czech GP was run. The Bugatti was rebuilt after the Brno crash and he brought it out again in 1934 with a single-seater body. In this form Decaroli gained another notable victory when he won the Picardie GP in May, beating several potential faster T51As.

This was his last success and he then retired from racing, although in 1936 his name was associated with the Rocatti, a supercharged 8 cyl. 1500 with all-independent suspension which was being built at Neuilly, but nothing came of the project.

Decaroli died at Nice in 1968.

P.G. (Pat) Fairfield. Born in Liverpool in 1908, but went to live in South Africa as a child, where his father had extensive interests in fruit farming. He returned to England when he went up to Cambridge and in 1933, became associated with Freddie Dixon, driving Dixon's Riley in a number of British events and gained the reputation of being an erratic driver, nicknamed "Skidder". In 1935, Fairfield was the first customer for an ERA, and with his white painted A-type, fitted with an 1100 engine, he gained the first victory for the new marque in an International race with his win in the Mannin Beg race in the Isle of Man. This was followed by a victory at Dieppe, which was a remarkable feat against a field of 1500s and showed that Fairfield had matured into a fast but very steady driver.

After the successes of 1935, the following season was a disaster for Fairfield. At the beginning of the season he raced as a private entrant, but was dogged by petty misfortunes that prevented him from achieving satisfactory results. Half through the season, he was invited by Raymond Mays to join the works ERA team which meant that his car was taken over by ERA Ltd. and prepared at Bourne. No improvement in his fortunes came from this change, as his ERA was then subject to the same inferior preparation as the other works cars in 1936. Fairfield became so discouraged by the setback that he was considering the

Pat Fairfield

possibility of giving up motor racing, though he was able to show that his ability was not impaired, by such feats as the fastest practice lap at Berne.

At the beginning of the 1937 season he decided to stay with the ERA team and with the introduction of the C-type ERA and with better preparation of the works cars at Bourne, his luck changed. The season started very well with victories in the Nuffield Trophy Handicap at Donington, and in the Coronation Trophy, the first race on the new Crystal Palace circuit. The future looked bright indeed, for the new C-type was now the fastest voiturette, and a reliable one. As a diversion, Fairfield agreed to drive a works 328 BMW at Le Mans. Shortly after the start, there was a multiple crash at White House Corner and Fairfield suffered very severe injuries to which he succumbed two days later on the 21st June.

Fairfield's death was a great loss to the ERA team, for with maturity, he had become a fast and reliable driver who still retained the ability to fight tenaciously when required.

Giuseppe Farina. Born in Turin in 1906, a son of one of the founders of the coachbuilding firm of that name. He qualified as a doctor of engineering then began his motor racing career driving a 1500cc sports Alfa Romeo in the Aosta-Grand St. Bernard hillclimb in 1932. The debut was not auspicious, as he crashed. After gaining more experience in hillclimbs and raillies, Farina began racing a 1500 4CM Maserati towards the end of the 1934 season. With this car, he showed that he was a driver of uncommon ability, for he won the 1500cc class of the Circuit of Biella in September and proved himself capable of keeping up with cars running in the GP class of this race. At the end of that month, he gained his first outright victory, in Czechoslovakia, when he came first in the voiturette race preceding the Czech Grand Prix at Brno, having led all the way from the start. The 1934 season finished with a second place at Modena after a race-long battle with Cecchini. For the 1935 season, Farina joined Gino Rovere in the Scudera Subalpina, to race the ex-Furmanik record breaking Maserati, now fitted with a 1500 engine, but he only had a few outings with this car for his talents had already been recognised, and he was engaged in 1936 to drive for the Scuderia Ferrari in Grand Prix events.

Farina did not drive a voiturette again for three seasons, as he was fully occupied with bigger things, but with Italian fortunes in decline his successes were few and he was one of the also-rans to the all-conquering German teams. He gained a number of successes in minor Formula GP events when the Germans did not run, the most important being a victory at Naples in 1937.

When Ferrari amalgamated with Alfa Corse in 1938, Farina went too, and thus found himself heading the team of Tipo 158 Alfa Romeos, and back in a voiturette again. After the initial humiliation of the Alfas at Tripoli in 1939, Farina had a convincing win at Livorno, and followed this with a third place at Pescara. The best was to come though, for at Berne, he had an easy win in the 1500 heat of the Swiss GP, and then driving his Alfetta in the main event with the full 3-litre GP cars, he held a remarkable second place for much of the race and eventually finished sixth. The War then intervened but before Italy joined the conflict, Farina managed one more victory for Alfa Romeo in the 1940 Tripoli GP. When the War finished Farina, rejoined the Alfa Romeo team and was victorious in the GP des Nations at Geneva in 1946. In 1947 and 1948 he left the Alfa team and drove a 4CLT Maserati as an independent winning the Monaco GP in 1948. When Alfa Romeo returned to racing in 1950, Farina was back in the team again and his career reached its pinnacle when he won the 1950 World Championship. After this high point his fortunes declined somewhat although he won the 1951 Belgian Grand Prix, and was runner-up in the World Championship in 1952, and gained his last Grand Prix victory at the Nurburgring in 1953, driving for Ferrari. Farina's last Grand Prix event was the 1955 Belgian race where he finished third, and he retired from racing at the end of the 1955 season.

After his retirement, Farina became the Jaguar agent for Italy and later was a main agent for Alfa Romeo. He was killed in a road accident in France in June, 1966. He was undoubtedly one of the best drivers to race voiturettes in the 1930s and carried this ability through the War years to gain the 1950 Championship. At his peak, he was a fast and most stylish driver, and his extended-arm driving position set a new fashion in racing technique which became universal in the generations of drivers that followed him.

H.C. (Hugh) Hamilton. Born in Ireland in 1905, and came to England in 1922. He began his competitive career on motor cycles and after some successes with cars in reliability trials, he began motor racing in 1930 when he drove a Riley in the Double-12 at Brooklands. As he worked as a salesman for University Motors, the London distributors of MG⋆, it was understandable that he would drive the marque when it became established in motor racing. His first voiturette success was in the 800cc class of the German GP in 1932, at the Nurburgring, where he had a runaway victory driving a works C-type MG. He repeated this success in the following year with a new supercharged works J4 model in the Eifelrennen but was unlucky with this car for the rest of the season, when victory eluded him in the Ulster TT, and he crashed and was injured while leading the 1500 class of the Masaryk GP at Brno in Czechoslovakia, competing against cars of double the capacity of the MG.

In 1934, Hamilton bought a K3 MG Magnette which was fitted with an off-set single seater body. With this car, he again suffered misfortunes, but gained a notable victory in the Coppa Acerbo Junior at Pescara. By then, he was recognised as one of the most competent and promising British drivers, and he was driving regularly for Whitney Straight who was running a team of 8CM Maseratis in Grand Prix events. Driving one of these cars, Hamilton skidded off the course on the last lap of the 1934 Swiss Grand Prix and was killed instantly when his car struck a tree.

Earl Howe. At the age of forty-four, most racing drivers, if they are still racing, are considering retirement from the sport and the possibility of taking up a more sedentary pastime. Francis, 5th Earl Howe, had different ideas however. Earl Howe was born in 1884, and although a keen motorist, he did not take part in any competition motoring in his youth but followed a life of public service. He

---

⋆ Earl Howe was a director of University Motors.

Hugh Hamilton.

commanded a battalion in the Royal Naval Reserve Division in France in the 1914-18 War with distinction, and in 1919 he was returned to Parliament as the Member for Battersea South. He held the seat until 1929, when he succeeded to the earldom on the death of his father, but a year earlier, when forty-four years old, he had started motor racing, at first, with a T43 Bugatti sports car and then with a 38/250 sports Mercedes-Benz.

By 1931 he was regarded as one of the leading British drivers and he had widened his activities and bought a new T51 Bugatti for Grand Prix events and the 1500cc 8 cylinder GP Delage to run in the voiturette class. With the Delage, Lord Howe soon showed his ability and won the 1500 class of the 1931 Dieppe GP. During the 1931 season he gained his most notable victory when he shared the wheel of the winning Alfa Romeo at Le Mans with Sir Henry Birkin. At the end of the 1931 season, another Delage was purchased from Robert Sénéchal, and both cars were used during the 1932 season, when the 1500 class was won at the Avusrennen, and he finished fourth in the 1500 class of the German Grand Prix, after losing ground with falling fuel pressure. At the end of the season, Lord Howe had a remarkable escape in the Formula Libre Monza GP, when the throttle of his original Delage apparently jammed open, and the car left the track and was bent 360° around a tree. His comment on walking away unhurt was, "I am afraid I have one car less".

The surviving Delage was raced again in 1933, and once more Lord Howe did well in German events, finishing third at the Avus with a stiff engine and a week later gaining victory, in what he described as the hardest race of his career, when he won a race-long battle with Burggaller's Bugatti in the Eifelrennen, and finished a length in front after 212 miles. A fine performance for a man who had just celebrated his forty-ninth birthday. Later in the season, Lord Howe entered a new K3 MG Magnette for the Coppa Ciano at Livorno, and had another narrow escape when the car overturned in practice.

Although fully committed to racing Maseratis and Bugattis in GP events, Lord Howe brought out the veteran Delage again in 1934, and finished fifth at Berne and fourth in the Nuffield Trophy at Donington. By 1935, the going was getting harder for the old car, as the ERAs were now racing but the veteran driver and car still had a good season finishing second at Albi and third at Berne. At Berne, Lord Howe was approached by Richard Seaman who wanted to buy the Delage, and in November, a sale was arranged. Perhaps Lord Howe did not share the faith of Giulio Ramponi in the potential of the old car and maybe, after five seasons, he wanted a change while as a most patriotic man, he wanted to race an ERA.

A new ERA was bought for the 1936 season, and perhaps, disastrously for Howe, he agreed with Raymond Mays to join the works team using his own car which was prepared at the Bourne factory. The standard of preparation of the works cars in 1936 was poor, and although while the car was running well, he was a formidable opponent for his younger rivals, a fifth place at Monaco, a third at Peronne and a fourth at Berne did his ability less than full credit. The best performance of the season came in August, in the JCC 200 at Donington, where Howe fought a magnificent battle with Seaman driving the Delage and finished second. For 1937, the ERA was being prepared again by his own mechanics, and the prospects looked much brighter, but on May 1st his fifty third birthday, he crashed at Brooklands while leading the Campbell Trophy, the inaugural event on the new Campbell circuit and suffered very serious injuries. After that, most men would have accepted the inevitable and given up, but Earl Howe, who made a miraculous recovery, was racing again in August, in the JCC 200, where he narrowly escaped another accident when the ERA's brakes failed.

In 1938, Howe was again invited to join the works ERA team, and his car was up-rated to full C-type specification. The works ERAs made fewer forays in international voiturette racing in 1938, but Howe showed that he had lost none of his skill, by finishing second in his heat at Peronne, but was eliminated in the final with supercharger failure. At Berne, it looked as if he was to gain a well deserved victory, but after holding the lead he dropped back to fourth place in the final with a misfire. The season finished on a better note with another second place in JCC 200 on the Campbell circuit. In May 1939, at the age of fifty-five, Lord Howe decided to retire, and his last race was the JCC International Trophy at Brooklands.

With the outbreak of war, he served again with the Royal Naval Reserve in the rank of Commodore, and after the war in 1945 he resumed his interests in the sport, and became deeply involved in its international administration, as Vice President of the C.S.I., for many years. He died in 1964.

Any driver would have been satisfied with Lord Howe's record but for a man of his age it was remarkable. He had the speed and courage of a driver of half his years and his sportsmanship was legendary; he was one of the most colourful and outstanding personalities in motor racing in the 1930s.

Armand Hug. Born in Lausanne in 1915, the son of a rich *haute couturier*. His

216

23rd April, 1938: Cork G.P.: Armand Hug in his new 4CM Maserati at the pits.

first success was a class win at the Kesselberg hillclimb in 1934 with a 2.3 Bugatti. In 1936 he bought a new T51A Bugatti and gained his first success in voiturette racing when he finished fifth in the Avus race, in 1937, with this car. For 1938, Hug bought a new 4CM Maserati, with the latest quarter-elliptic rear suspension, and with this car came a measure of support from the Maserati factory. 1938 was a full season for him; he had his first race with the Maserati at Cork, where he came fifth, and followed this with sixth place at Tripoli. Hug's driving was improving rapidly, and by the middle of June, he was capable of holding second place at Peronne until brake failure intervened. At Albi, he showed that he was as good as the best of his contemporaries, by winning the second heat ahead of Luigi Villoresi, having been eliminated by an oil leak in the first heat. On the form he was showing, a victory seemed inevitable, and fittingly, he won the Prix de Berne in August in front of his fellow countrymen. A week later, Hug scored again, with a win in the minor meeting at La Baule and finished the season in the "Lion's Den" of Italian 1500 racing, with a third place at Monza, and a second at Modena.

For 1939, it seemed that Hug would join the Maserati team, but the Italian Government directed that Italian works cars should only be driven by Italian drivers. Hug was forced to continue with his 4CM and gained a fifth place in the titanic event at Tripoli in May and then perhaps as a consolation received a new 4CL engine from the factory to fit into his older car. With this engine he came first at Rheims at the beginning of July, but a week later, he went to Albi and while practising for the GP, on a wet road, he skidded and overturned. In the crash, he received very severe head injuries and was partially paralysed. Sadly, these injuries caused permanent brain damage and for the rest of his life, Hug was incapacitated, living as an invalid in Switzerland. He died in the late 1960s.

The best Swiss driver to emerge between the wars, by 1938 Hug was one of the most able voiturette drivers, and with the Albi crash his career came to a particularly sad end.

Raymond Mays. Born at Bourne in Lincolnshire, in 1899. He was commissioned in the Grenadier Guards in 1918 and served in France during the last months of the 1914/18 War. He began his racing career with a 1500cc Hillman in 1921 while still a Cambridge undergraduate and won his first race at Brooklands with this car. During the 1920s, Mays specialised in hillclimbs and sprints and was probably the most successful driver of the decade in these events. Until he purchased the 3-litre TT Vauxhaull in 1928, Mays' racing had been confined almost entirely to 1500cc cars, the Hillman, Bugattis and ACs and this was to have a considerable influence on his future career.

The Vauxhall, with the help of Amherst Villiers, became the Vauxhall-Villiers, and then the Villiers Special, and by 1931 had become the fastest sprint car in England. As related previously, Mays had an overwhelming ambition to regain the course record at Shelsley Walsh, captured by Hans Stuck in 1930 and furthermore, he wanted to do this with a 1500cc car. The outcome was the "White" Riley built with the aid of Victor Riley and developed by Peter Berthon. With the sponsorship of Humphrey Cook, in 1934 the Riley grew into the ERA, built in the grounds of Mays' house at Bourne. As one of the co-founders of the ERA marque, Mays became the principal driver of the cars entered by the little company between 1934 and 1938 and his driving ability wholly justified this role. After some preliminary events in Great Britain in 1934, the ERA won its first Continental international voiturette race at the Nurburgring in 1935 and Mays had the fitting honour of driving the car to this first victory. After this splendid start, it was astonishing that Mays was unable to gain another victory in an international 1500cc race for two years. This was no reflection on his ability, although he was a hard driver who expected the utmost from his cars. The reason for the lack of success lay in the continuous attempts by Mays and Berthon to make the ERA engine give more power, and also in the poor preparation of the cars at the Bourne factory, where the resources were insufficient to build new cars for sale and maintain a works team.

The manufacture and sale of cars finished at the end of 1936, and Mays and Berthon were also getting power with reliability with the C-type ERA introduced at the beginning of the 1937 season. The improvement in Mays' fortunes was dramatic, and during the 1937 season he won at Peronne, Albi and Dublin, and was second at the Isle of Man and Berne. The C-type ERA was acknowledged as the unofficial 1500 champion of Europe in 1937, and a similar honour was perhaps due to Mays as its principal driver. As the ERA marque declined, so once again did Mays' fortunes as a voiturette driver. In 1938, the car was becoming obsolete, and his only victory was at Peronne. Shortage of money and policy differences brought a breach between Mays and Cook in April 1939, and he left to drive as an independent using his faithful D-type ERA; in a limited season, he picked up a second place in the Nuffield Trophy at Donington.

When racing resumed in 1946 Mays was a regular competitor and was still unsurpassed in British sprints and hillclimbs although making relatively few appearances in races. Just as he had been the driving force in establishing ERA in the 1930s, Mays was now fully engaged in promoting BRM as the British representative in Grand Prix racing. As a result, he had no time to continue racing and retired from circuit racing at the end of 1949; his last race was the International Trophy at Silverstone in August 1949. Despite the disappointments of the BRM in the 1950s, Mays' faith in the car remained unshaken and this faith was finally justified in 1962 when BRM won the Formula 1 Constructors' Championship and gave Graham Hill the World Drivers' Championship.

A lifetime of service to British motor racing was recognised by the award of a CBE to Mays in 1978. He died at Bourne in January 1980. As a driver Mays was very fast and competitive although hard on his cars, all probably legacies of his years of apprenticeship in sprints and hillclimbs. Although he had relatively little road racing experience when he began driving ERAs, he drove like an experienced veteran; it was notable that he rarely had an "off" day and was also a remarkably safe driver and never had any significant accidents. Despite his qualities as a driver, Mays will always be associated with the promotion and development of the ERA; it was largely due to the strong element of competition brought by ERA to voiturette racing, that the class assumed such importance in the late 1930s and for this, much credit must go to Raymond Mays.

Giovanni Rocco. Born in Naples, he began his racing career in 1934 driving a Tipo 26B Maserati and had his first success with this car in the Criterium di Roma. At the end of the 1934 season, Rocco bought an early 4CS 1500 Maserati and used this car in sports trim for the 1935 and 1936 seasons in Italian national events. In February 1937, Rocco bought a new 6CM Maserati from the Bologna factory. With this car he soon showed he was a driver of ability when he outpaced all the Italian voiturette stars and led the Targa Florio on the Favorita circuit until a valve burnt out. His next notable drive was at Genoa when he finished third in the Circuito della Superba and on the form he was now showing, it was clear that a win would not be long in coming. This was achieved in August in the unfortunate Coppa Acerbo meeting at Pescara, when Rocco profited by the misfortunes of the other drivers and came through to win. To drive home the point that he was now one of the leading "Millecinquecentisti" he finished by winning the last event of the season on the tiny circuit at Campione d'Italia.

Rocco's abilities were recognised at the beginning of the 1938 season when he was invited to join the Maserati works team with Trossi and Marazza. He lived up to factory expectations by coming second at Tripoli after a fierce battle with Taruffi and a week later, he won the Targa Florio. Despite these results, Rocco's place in the works team was taken by Luigi Villoresi at the end of July for the Livorno meeting; his appearances were sporadic for the rest of the season and his best place was fifth at Lucca in September. In the spring of 1939 he was back in a works Maserati at Tripoli and retired with piston failure like his team-mates. Perhaps the edge had now gone from Rocco's driving for his best circuit result of the season was a third at the small meeting at Carnaro, although he did lead at Naples until he had engine bothers and won the 1500 class at the Frieburg hillclimb. His season finished with a fifth place at Berne, running ostensibly as a

219

20th August, 1939: Prix de Berne: Giovanni Rocco in his 4 CL Maserati.

private entrant. The very last voiturette race to be run before war engulfed Europe, the 1940 Targa Florio, saw Rocco take third place. This was his last race, as he did not return to the sport when racing resumed after the end of the War. Such was the intensity and profusion of 1500 races in Italy in the three seasons preceding the war, that Rocco, apart from his trips to Tripoli, only raced outside Italy on three occasions. These excursions were to the Freiburg and Grossglockner hillclimbs and to Berne in 1939. Despite the rather limited scope of his racing, Rocco's ability made him one of the leading voiturette competitors during that time.

José Scaron. Born in Brussels in 1895. He became a French national on his enlistment in the French army in August 1914. He remained in France at the end of the 1914-18 war and his first motor race was the 1922 Bol d'Or a 24 hour event on the Vaujours Circuit in the Forest of St. Germain, driving a CC Amilcar, a marque to which he remained faithful for the next eleven years. His debut was not particularly auspicious, as he crashed. During the next four years Scaron continued to drive Amilcars in competitions and he became the agent for the marque in Le Havre.

In 1926, the C6 Amilcar was announced and Scaron had one of the first production models for the 1927 season. His principal success with that car during its first season was a victory in the GP de la Baule. The next year, there were more successes with victories at La Baule again, Rheims and Boulogne. For the 1929 season, the factory supplied Scaron with a racing roller bearing engine to replace the standard plain bearing unit he had used previously in the C6. More good fortune now came Scaron's way, as André Morel, who had been the principal works driver, had a disagreement with the Amilcar factory, and departed, so the two single seater MCO Amilcars which had been used by Morel were now provided for Scaron. With this profusion of equipment, he gained victories at Antibes, Lyons, Tunis and Dieppe and came second at

Comminges. Scaron maintained this form in 1930 with major successes at Dieppe, Grenoble, Comminges and Algiers. By now, Scaron was virtually unbeatable in the 1100 class and with one of the MO0s running with a 1270cc engine, he was one of the fastest competitors in the 1500 class as well, so it was no surprise that he maintained his form in 1931, apparently, by now, owning the two cars but racing them with works support. Among the many successes he gained in 1931, probably the most outstanding was his runaway win at Monza when he outpaced the best 1100s in Europe and won by nearly two minutes. The Amilcar factory was now beset with economic problems and this was reflected in fewer victories for Scaron in 1932; the rivals were getting quicker and there was probably now little scope for further development of the MC0 design. His best result was a good win at Pescara, but this was virtually the end of his efforts with Amilcars and in 1933, his successes were limited to hillclimbs. At the end of the 1933 season, Scaron made a break with Amilcar and also with voiturette racing and sold both cars. During the next few seasons, he made occasional appearances with Bugatti and Alfa Romeo cars in minor GP events, but in 1938, at the age of 43, be began a new chapter in his racing career when he formed an association with Amédee Gordini who was racing competition versions of the Simca, the French-built Fiat. With the Simca-Gordini, Scaron raced in several sports car events in 1938/39 and won the Biennial Cup at Le Mans in 1939. By now, he had become the Simca agent in Le Havre.

At the end of the War, the veteran Scaron raced again, and won the 1100 class in the Spa 24 hour race in 1948, co-driving with his old voiturette rival, Pierre Veyron. In 1949 Scaron had a remarkable drive in the French GP, at Comminges, which was held for sports cars that year, and finished third with a 1500 Gordini beating many larger cars. By now, perhaps the years were beginning to tell but he continued racing, and his last event was a drive in a Gordini at Le Mans in 1952, when he was 57.

After his retirement from racing, Scaron continued his business activities in Le Havre; and his achievements were recognised by his appointment as a Chevalier of the Legion of Honour in 1954, he died in 1975. His numerous victories for Amilcar in the late 1920s and early 1930s showed him to be a driver of undoubted talent and if a voiturette championship had been held in 1931 and 1932, the title would certainly have been his. There are few drivers who can claim an active racing career spanning 30 years, and are still capable of racing in International events at the age of 57.

R.J.B. (Dick) Seaman. Born in London in 1913, the son of rich parents. He was educated at Rugby and Cambridge, and while an undergraduate, began his motor career in 1931 with a Riley, and then with a T35A Bugatti. It was his parents' wish that he should enter the diplomatic service, but he left Cambridge at the beginning of 1934 with the avowed aim of being a professional racing driver. Encouraged by Whitney Straight, whom he had met at Cambridge, Seaman bought the black K3 MG Magnette that Straight had raced in 1933, although, to mollify his parents, Seaman announced that the car was still owned by Straight and was being entered by him as part of his team. With the MG,

Seaman, after some early setbacks, finished third in the Coppa Acerbo at Pescara, and then followed this with an impressive victory in difficult conditions at Berne, where he beat all the best 1500 drivers. He completed the 1934 season by taking second place overall and winning the 1100 class in the Nuffield Trophy at Donington Park.

Seaman had already admitted to his close friends his eventual ambition was to be a professional GP driver, and he realised that to achieve this, he would have to dominate 1500 racing. His next step, and an act of faith, was to buy a new 1500 ERA, but he had the car prepared at the ERA factory at Bourne under contract. This was a mistake, as the factory had enough problems building cars for sale and preparing a factory team; as a result, Seaman's car was ill-prepared for the early events of the 1935 season and he was forced to retire from several races when strongly placed. He terminated the arrangement with ERA and had the car prepared by his own mechanics, and victories at Pescara, Berne and Brno followed.

For 1936, Seaman wanted a car that could beat the Zoller supercharged works ERAs, and as previously recounted, he was persuaded by Giulio Ramponi to buy Lord Howe's 1927 GP Delage. When re-built by Ramponi, this car, despite some failures, gave Seaman four major victories in the Isle of Man, at Pescara, Berne and Donington; at the end of the 1936 season, Seaman was acknowledged as the leading 1500 driver in Europe. A contract with Mercedes-Benz followed and Seaman matured into a successful Grand Prix driver as evidenced by his victory in the German Grand Prix in 1938. Tragically, his career was cut short when he crashed while leading the Belgian Grand Prix on 26th June 1939 and he died of his injuries.

As the only British driver who had attained full Grand Prix status in the 1930s, he was deeply mourned. He had a natural ability that enabled him to match the best of his Grand Prix contemporaries although that perceptive observer of form, Nello Ugolini, had described him in 1938 as "fast, but a trifle too risky". Much of Seaman's success as a voiturette driver stemmed from his intelligent and professional approach to his racing, which was in marked contrast to the casual attitude of many of his rivals. In this respect, he was a generation ahead of his time.

Count Carlo Felice Trossi. Born in 1908 of an aristocratic family, he lived at Biella, north of Milan, where he owned a medieval castle. Supported by his interests in the woollen industry, he began his competition career in 1931 in hillclimbs and rallies, driving Mercedes-Benz and Bugatti, but his talents were soon recognised by the Scuderia Ferrari and in his first race, the 1932 Mille Miglia, he finished second. He became a regular competitor in GP events, driving an Alfa Romeo, and he gained a number of successes in 1934, notably at Montreux, Vichy and in his home town of Biella.

At the beginning of the 1936 season, Trossi was offered the wheel of the new 1500 6CM Maserati by his friend Gino Rovere, and in his first drive with this works prepared car at the Eifelrennen, he gained a notable victory beating the works ERA team and giving the 6CM its first success. After this, Trossi drove the car mainly in Italian events for the rest of the season and had wins at Milan,

Livorno, Modena and Lucca, with a second place at Pescara. Despite its initial promise, the 6CM Maserati was not as fast as the ERA or Seaman's Delage, but his victories gave Trossi the Italian 1500cc Championship for 1936.

Trossi began the 1937 season with a win at Naples, then the Maserati brothers prepared a new car for him; a 6CM chassis with a 4C engine. Trossi first drove this car at Florence and although much faster than the opposition, he was forced to hand it over to Rovere as he felt unwell, and it finished second. He was not quite as active in the 1500 class as he had been in 1936 but he won again at Lucca with the new 4CM and ended the season by losing the Italian 1500 Championship to Ettore Bianco, by a narrow margin. Trossi's health was perhaps a problem, because he made few appearances in voiturette races in 1938, and while in the lead at Naples, he was forced to retire because he was unwell. He still remained faithful to Maserati despite the advent of the Tipo 158 Alfa Romeo and drove the new 4CL Maserati at Tripoli, in 1939 though he retired on the first lap.

Perhaps adopting the adage "if you can't beat them, join them", Trossi joined the Alfa Romeo team for its only outing in 1940, and finished third at Tripoli. After that, the War intervened and as an experienced aviator, he joined the Regia Aeronautica, where he served with distinction as a fighter pilot. With the return of the Tipo 158 Alfa Romeo to racing in 1946, Trossi was at the wheel again and scored a major victory in the Italian GP. He stayed with the team in 1947 and 1948 but by now he was a very sick man. His last race was the Monza GP in October 1948 where he was second. His health then deteriorated rapidly, and he died of cancer in May 1949.

With his victories in 1936 and 1937, Trossi made it evident that he was as good as any of his rivals in the 1500 class, and contemporary reporters were inclined to regard him as the best voiturette driver in the 1500 class at that time. This is probably true, and his post war successes when he was a sick man, showed that he was a driver of considerable skill; without the handicap of illness he could perhaps have laid claim to be regarded as among the very best of his generation.

Pierre Veyron. Born in the French department of Lozere in 1903. He began his racing career in 1930, driving an EHP in the Mont Ventoux hillclimb, and his first voiturette success came in 1931 when he won the 1500 class at Geneva in a T37A Bugatti. Veyron was receiving some support from Andre Vagniez, an industrialist from Amiens, and in 1932, Vagniez bought a 1500cc Tipo 26 Maserati. With this car, Veyron won at Casablanca, Comminges and Nancy and finished second at Oran and Brno.

Veyron's driving during 1932 made a very favourable impression on Jean Bugatti, and at the beginning of 1933, he was invited to work as a test driver for Bugatti and to race a factory-entered T51A Bugatti in voiturette races. Two golden years were to follow for Veyron; in 1933 he won at Albi, Avus and Lwow, and the following year he repeated the Albi and Avus victories. While Veyron's ability was undiminished, the same unfortunately could not be said for the T51A Bugatti which, by 1935, was being surpassed by younger designs and particularly ERA. Veyron's only successes were to complete a hat-trick of Albi victories and to win the voiturette class at Nancy but he pursued the ERAs valiantly at Dieppe and Brno, taking second place at both events. With the obsolete T51A Bugatti, the best that Veyron could achieve in 1936, was second place at his hunting ground of Albi and he drove voiturettes no more after the end of the 1936 season, principally because Bugatti could no longer provide a modern car. All the rumours of a new 1500 Bugatti came to naught, and Veyron found himself driving Bugatti sports cars instead. In these, he now gained his greatest victory, sharing the wheel of the winning T57SC with Jean-Pierre Wimille at Le Mans in 1939.

At the outbreak of war Veyron was called to the colours as an army reservist and served as a quartermaster in an artillery regiment until the fall of France in 1940. He then joined the Resistance and was decorated with the Croix de Guerre for distinguished service. At the end of the war, with Bugatti now defunct, Veyron turned to Gordini and raced for France once more in sports car events, winning his class in the Spa 24 hours and the Montlhéry 12 hours in 1948 sharing the wheel with his old voiturette rival José Scaron. After some unsuccessful drives at Le Mans for the Nash Healey team, Veyron retired; his last race was at Le Mans in 1954. With his racing career ended, Veyron became engaged with his own company in research for the petroleum industry. He died at Cap d'Eze in November 1976.

Luigi Villoresi. Born in Milan in 1909 he began his competition career in 1931 driving a Lancia Lambda in minor events. His first important race was the 1933 Mille Miglia when he finished fifth in the 1100 class driving a Balilla Fiat with his younger brother Emilio and his first voiturette race was the 1935 Coppa Ciano at Livorno where he came third with the Fiat. So successful was Villoresi with this car that at the end of the 1935 season he was declared to be the 1100cc sports car champion of Italy.

At the beginning of 1936, he bought a 4CM Maserati and in his first race with this car he finished sixth at Monaco after a fast drive, interrupted by an abrupt contact with a wall. The car soon recovered and he finished third at Livorno once again. By now, Villoresi was recognised as one of the leading 1500 drivers in Italy and he was sharing the 4CM with Emilio, some four years younger, who had returned to the sport after completing his compulsory military service. For 1937, Luigi had a new 6CM Maserati racing with the Scuderia Ambrosiana of Milan and throughout the season he was one of the most active competitors racing as far afield as the Isle of Man and Tripoli. Once again, he gained a number of places and was generally recognised as one of the fastest competitors, although an outright victory eluded him until the very last voiturette race of the season, when he drove a well-judged race at Brno in Czechoslovakia and beat the ERA opposition.

Brno was the turning point, for in 1938, Villoresi became 1500 champion of Italy. He began the season racing his 6CM with the Scuderia Ambrosiana and won at Albi, but the new Tipo 158 Alfa Romeos appeared in August and were clearly faster cars than the Maseratis, so Villoresi was recruited into the Maserati works team for the Livorno race and then proved that he could beat the rival marque with an excellent victory at Pescara. He followed this up with another win at Lucca. His brother Emilio was now his biggest rival, as a member of the Alfa Romeo team, and it was inevitable that comparisons were drawn between the brothers and some observers suggested that despite Luigi's results, Emilio possessed the greater talent. At the beginning of the 1939 season, Luigi Villoresi stayed with the Maserati works team to drive the new 4CL, having already won the South African Grand Prix with a 6CM, and perhaps as a demonstration of the abundance of his talent, he made fastest practice lap at Tripoli with the new car. The race was an Italian disaster but Villoresi atoned the next week, by winning the Targa Florio with a 6CM. There was now tragedy, for Emilio was killed at Monza on 20th June, testing a Tipo 158 Alfa Romeo. Obviously deeply affected by the loss, Luigi continued to race and had another win in a small meeting at Abazzia in July.

With the outbreak of war, racing was curtailed, but in the short Italian season in 1940, before Italy entered the conflict, Villoresi repeated his 1939 victory in the Targo Florio and provided the principal opposition to the faster Alfa Romeos at Tripoli.

At the end of the war, Villoresi resumed racing again, driving 1500 Maseratis but now as full Grand Prix racing cars. He gained many successes between 1946 and 1948 and was Italian champion in 1946 and 1947. He won the British GP in 1948 and during this time he was carefully nurturing the talents of his protegé, Alberto Ascari. Villoresi and Ascari joined the new Ferrari team in 1949 and he gained a major success in winning the Dutch GP at Zandvoort. He was probably now past his best, but was still a driver to be reckoned with by the post-war generation. He remained with the Ferrari team until the end of the 1953 season, and then accompanied Ascari to the new Lancia team, but this venture was cut short with the death of Ascari in May 1955. Villoresi was now forty-six and the death of his team-mate affected him greatly. In 1956, he returned to his first love, Maserati, but after some appearances with a works 250F he retired after a bad accident in the Rome GP.

Now living in retirement in Italy, Villoresi still maintains an active interest in motor racing and attends many race meetings. In terms of victories, he was the most successful voiturette driver of the late 1930s; as a driver he was perhaps more of a skilled craftsman than an artistic genius but in the immediate pre-war and post-war years, he was a formidable opponent.

J.P. (Johnnie) Wakefield. Born in London in 1915, the son of a rich Westmoreland explosives manufacturer. After some preliminary work in motor cycle races, he began racing cars in 1936 using a 1500cc Alta and gained his first win in a Mountain Handicap at the August Bank Holiday Meeting at Brooklands. As the Alta was a rather unreliable car Wakefield bought a new 6CM Maserati for the 1937 season and soon became recognised as a fast but rather erratic driver. With this car, he was second at Peronne and Phoenix Park but he had a setback when he crashed the Maserati at Cork in April 1938 and was slightly injured. During this race he had shown he had the ability to keep up with Luigi Villoresi who was driving a similar, but works supported car.

Following the destruction of the Maserati, Wakefield bought the only B/C type ERA to be built and with this car he had a fine win in the JCC 200 at

Brooklands in August 1938. Appreciating the obsolescence of the ERA, Wakefield bought a new 4CL Maserati for the 1939 season, and in his first race in this car, he beat the works 4CLs and gained a notable victory at Naples. This was followed by further victories at Peronne and Albi, which ensured that he was the most successful private entrant during the 1939 season, and confirmed him as the most promising British driver and perhaps, following Richard Seaman's death, the most able. In addition to his motor racing activities, Wakefield was also an accomplished skiier and had competed in international events for England.

On the outbreak of war, Wakefield was commissioned in the Fleet Air Arm and became a pilot. He was killed in a flying accident at Wargrave near Henley in April 1942. His death was a great loss to British motor racing, as a driver of his calibre was sorely needed in the lean years of the late 1940s.

THE RESULTS

Results of the principal voiturette races 1931 to 1940

(Author's note: I have given the fullest results available. Fastest laps have been omitted as the information available is often uncertain. The results are for 1500cc events unless stated otherwise. Maps are shown of the principal circuits but are not of a uniform scale.)

BELGIUM

G.P. DES FRONTIÈRES, Chimay (6.75m (10.87km) lap)

1933 (4 June)

1100 class. 10 laps 67.5m (108.7km) 3 starters
1. Bennart (Rally) 1 hr 34' 8.2" 43.4 mph (69.87kph)

1500 class 15 laps 101m (163km) 5 starters
1. Legat (Bugatti) 1hr 23' 59" 72.7mph (117.04kph)
2. Gé (Bugatti) 1 hr 33' 32"

1934 (20 May)

1100 class 8 laps 54m (87km)
1. Rouleau (Amilcar) 64.73mph (104.21kph)
2. des Ormes (Amilcar)
3. Chevallier (Chevallier)

CZECHOSLOVAKIA

CZECHOSLOVAK G.P. (1500cc Class), Masaryk circuit, Brno. (18m (29km) lap)

1931 (27 September)

17 laps 308m (492km)
1. Schmidt (Bugatti) 61.94mph (99.72kph)
2. Arco (Amilcar)

3. Sojka (Bugatti)

1932 (4 September)

15 laps 272m (437km)
1. Burggaller (Bugatti) 4hr 31' 28" 60.02mph (96.63kph)
2. Veyron (Maserati) 4hr 45' 44".
3. Sojka (Bugatti) 4hr 47' 59"
4. Hartmann (Bugatti) 4hr 48' 42"
5. Maserati (Maserati) 5hr 10' 16"
6. Macher (DKW) 5 hr 11' 13"
7. Szczyzcki (Wikow) 5hr 12' 18"
8. Konechnik (Wikow) 5hr 24' 41"

1933 (17 September)

15 laps 272m (437km) 15 starters
1. Burggaller (Bugatti) 4hr 32' 50" 59.73mph (96.16kph)
2. Sojka (Bugatti)
3. Ruesch (Alfa Romeo)
4. Ripper (Bugatti)

1934 (30 September)

15 laps 272m (437km) 20 starters
1. Farina (Maserati) 3hr 58' 49" 68.26mph (109.89kph)
2. Burggaller (Bugatti) 3hr 59' 32"
3. Sojka (Bugatti) 3hr 59' 44"
4. Eyston (MG) 3hr 59' 47"
5. Seaman (MG) 4hr 1' 32"

1935 (29 September)

15 laps 272m (437km)
1. Seaman (ERA) 3hr 48′ 04″ 71.32mph (114.82kph)
2. Veyron (Bugatti) 3hr 51′ 58.6″
3. Sojka (Bugatti)

1937 (26 September)

5 laps 90m (145km) 12 starters
1. L. Villoresi (Maserati) 1hr 10′ 19.8″ 77.6mph (124.93kph)
2. Martin (ERA) 1hr 10′ 19.8″
3. Hartmann (Maserati) 1hr 11′ 06′
4. Bira (ERA)
5. Sojka (Bugatti)

FRANCE

G.P. d'ALBIGEOIS, Albi (5.5m (8.9km) lap)

1933 (27 August)

12 laps 66m (106.8km)

1. Veyron (Bugatti) 51′ 44.6″ 79.51mph (127.96kph)
2. Vagniez (Maserati)
3. Durand (Bugatti)
4. Mme. Itier (Bugatti)
5. Guilbaut (Bugatti)

1934 (22 July)

18 laps 100m (161km)
1. Veyron (Bugatti) 1hr 14′ 48.6″ 79.94mph (128.70kph)
2. Abad (Bugatti) 1hr 15′ 05″
3. Durand (Bugatti) 1hr 17′ 04″
4. Saugé (Bugatti)
5. Rey (Bugatti)

1935 (14 July)

2 heats of 20 laps 110m (178km) Result from aggregate time of both heats 17 starters

Heat 1.
1. Barbieri (Maserati) 1hr 16′ 30.8″ 86.26mph (138.87kph)
2. Veyron (Bugatti) 1hr 17′ 34.2″
3. Leoz (Bugatti)
4. Durand (Bugatti)
5. Howe (Delage)

Heat 2.
1. Veyron (Bugatti) 1hr 17′ 35.8″ 85.06mph (136.94kph)
2. Howe (Delage)

3. Durand (Bugatti)
4. Maillard Brune (MG)

Final placing
1. Veyron
2. Howe
3. Durand
4. Maillard Brune

1936 (12 July)

2 Heats of 20 laps 110m (178km) Result from aggregate time of both heats 13 starters

Heat 1.
1. Bira (ERA) 1hr 11′ 02″ 92.98mph (149.66kph)
2. Lehoux (ERA) 1hr 11′ 39″
3. Fairfield (ERA) 1hr 13′ 33″
4. Bianco (Maserati) 1hr 13′ 42″
5. Veyron (Bugatti) 19 laps
6. Hartmann (Maserati) 19 laps
7. Ruesch (Maserati) 18 laps
8. Tongue (ERA) 16 laps

Heat 2.
1. Bira (ERA) 1hr 13′ 8.4″ 90.23 mph (145.28kph)
2. Veyron (Bugatti) 19 laps
3. Ruesch (Maserati) 19 laps

Final placing.
1. Bira
2. Veyron
3. Ruesch

1937 (11 July)

2 heats of 20 laps, 110m (178km) Result from aggregate time of both heats.

Heat 1.
1. E. Villoresi (Maserati) 1hr 12′ 58″ 90.25mph (145.30kph)
2. Tongue (ERA) 1hr 14′ 16″
3. Cook (ERA) 1hr 14′ 56″
4. L. Villoresi (Maserati)
5. Righetti (Maserati)
6. Martin (ERA)
7. Gollin (Maserati)
8. Bassadonna (Maserati)
9. De Puy (Maserati)

Heat 2.
1. Mays (ERA) 1hr 11′ 46″ 92.48mph (148.89kph)
2. Martin (ERA) 1hr 13′ 51″
3. Righetti (Maserati) 19 laps
4. Tongue (ERA)
5. De Graffenried (Maserati)
6. Gollin (Maserati)
7. L. Villoresi (Maserati)
8. Bassadonna (Maserati)

Final placing.
1. Mays & Cook
2. Martin
3. Tongue
4. Righetti
5. L. Villoresi
6. Gollin
7. Bassadonna
8. De Graffenried

1938 (10 July)

2 heats of 20 laps, 110m (178km) Result from aggregate time of both heats

Heat 1.
1. L. Villoresi (Maserati) 1hr 12' 31.2" 91.01mph (146.52kph)
2. Teagno (Maserati) 19 laps
3. Soffietti (Maserati) 19 laps
4. Berg (Maserati) 18 laps
5. Platé (Talbot) 15 laps

Heat 2.
1. Hug (Maserati) 1hr 13' 5.4" 90.30mph (145.38kph)
2. L. Villoresi (Maserati) 1hr 14' 38"
3. Soffietti (Maserati) 1hr 16' 55"
4. Platé (Talbot) 17 laps

Final placing
1. L. Villoresi
2. Soffietti
3. Platé

1939 (16 July)

2 heats of 20 laps, 110m (178km) Result from aggregate of both heats 15 starters

Heat 1.
1. Wakefield (Maserati) 1hr 10' 22" 94.32mph (151.84kph)
2. Tongue (Maserati) 1hr 11' 52"
3. Bira (ERA) 1hr 13' 42"
4. Abecassis (Alta) 19 laps
5. Dipper (Maserati) 19 laps
6. Brooke (Brooke Special) 19 laps
7. Sommer (Maserati) 18 laps
8. De Graffenried (Maserati) 18 laps
9. Horvilleur (Maserati) 18 laps
10. Contet (Maserati) 18 laps
11. Herkuleyns (MG) 16 laps
12. Delorme (Bugatti) 14 laps

Heat 2.
1. Wakefield (Maserati) 1hr 10' 58.8" 93.50mph (150.53kph)
2. Tongue (Maserati) 1hr 11' 18"
3. Bira (ERA) 19 laps
4. Dipper (Maserati) 19 laps
5. Sommer (Maserati) 19 laps

6. De Graffenried (Maserati) 18 laps
7. Herkuleyns (MG) 15 laps
8. Delorme (Bugatti) 15 laps
9. Horvilleur (Maserati) 14 laps

Final placing
1. Wakefield
2. Tongue
3. Bira
4. Dipper
5. Sommer
6. De Graffenried
7. Horvilleur
8. Herkuleyns
9. Delorme

G.P. DE COMMINGES, St. Gaudens (16.34m (26.3km) lap)

1931 (19 August)

1100 class 10 laps 163m (263km) 6 starters
1. Lemoine (Caban) 2hr 27' 58" 66.70mph (107.38kph)
2. Rougieras (BNC) 2hr 36' 06"
3. Demazel (Salmson) 2hr 39' 00"

1500 class 12 laps 196m (315km) 10 starters
1. Joly (Maserati) 2hr 32' 49" 76.57mph (123.30kph)
2. Veyron (Bugatti) 2hr 36' 06"
3. Antonio (Maserati) 2hr 44' 39"
4. Rey (Bugatti) 2hr 47' 33"
5. Ragot (Bugatti) 2hr 52' 44"

1932 (31 July)

12 laps 196m (315km)
1. Veyron (Maserati) 2hr 35' 15.6" 75.50mph (121.55kph)
2. Dourel (Amilcar) 2hr 41' 40"
3. Antonio (Maserati) 2hr 44' 09"
4. Guilbaut (Bugatti) 2hr 45' 33"

G.P. DE CASABLANCA (4.21m (6.77km) lap)

1931 (17 May)

55 laps 231m (371km) 12 starters
1. Scaron (Amilcar) 2hr 58' 45" 77.49mph (124.75kph)
2. Galba (Bugatti) 3hr 00' 25"
3. Platé (Alfa Romeo) 3hr 24' 40"
4. Dourel (Amilcar)
5. Capello (Alfa Romeo)
6. Saint-Genies (Bugatti)
7. Hiercourt (Bugatti)

1932 (22 May)

70 laps 294m (474km)
1. Veyron (Maserati) 3hr 42' 29" 79.38mph (127.83kph)
2. Durand (Bugatti)
3. Scaron (Amilcar)
4. Maddeler (Bugatti)
5. Galba (Bugatti)

G.P. DE DIEPPE (5.06m (8.15km) lap)

1931 (26 July)

4hrs duration 16 starters
1. Howe (Delage) 471kms 73.12mph (117.75kph)
2. Delorme (Bugatti) 406kms
3. Vagniez (Bugatti)
4. Chevallier (Chevallier)

1935 (20 July)

2 hrs duration 19 starters
1. Fairfield (ERA) 243.94kms 75.7mph (121.97kph)
2. Bira (ERA) 242.09kms
3. Veyron (Bugatti) 241.50kms
4. Cook (ERA) 238.85kms
5. Berrone (Maserati) 237.54kms
6. Rayson (Bugatti) 232.81kms
7. Hertzberger (MG) 230.22kms
8. Rovere/Farina (Maserati) 228.12kms
9. Guilbaut (Bugatti) 219.80kms
10. Dubois (Bugatti) 163.00kms

CIRCUIT DAUPHINE, Grenoble

1931 (2 August)

1100 class 134m (217km)
1. Scaron (Amilcar) 2hr 35' 53" 62.74mph (101.04kph)
2. Martinatti (Salmson)
3. Dourel (Amilcar)
4. Girard (BNC)

1500 class 144m (233km)
1. Toselli (Bugatti) 2hr 18' 30" 64.97mph (104.63kph)
2. Ralph (Bugatti)
3. Veyron (Bugatti)
4. Mme Itier (Bugatti)
5. Joly (Maserati)
6. Angwerd (Bugatti)
7. Mlle Helle-Nice (Bugatti)

CIRCUIT DE LA GAROUPE, Antibes

1932 (11 September)

62m (101km) 6 starters
1. Toselli (Bugatti) 1hr 16' 3.6" 49.28mph (79.38kph)
2. Chambost (Salmson) 1hr 19' 24.2"
3. Martinatti (Salmson) 1hr 20' 35.2"
4. Mme Orsini (Maserati)

G.P. DE LA BAULE (1.8m (3km) lap)

1933 (13 August)

68 laps 126 m (204km) 3 starters
No finishers.

1938 (28 August)

40 laps 74m (120km)
1. Hug (Maserati) 1hr 05' 16" 68.49mph (110.30kph)
2. Berg (Maserati) 39 laps
3. Delorme (Bugatti) 37 laps
4. Mestivier (Amilcar) 35 laps
5. Gordini (Fiat) 35 laps
6. Guerin (Bugatti) 34 laps
7. Breillet (Fiat) 34 laps
8. Corsi (Maserati) 34 laps
9. Grignard (Amilcar) 33 laps

G.P. DE FRANCE, Montlhéry (1934 3.1m (5.0km) (1935 3.8m (6.2km) lap)

1934 (9 September)

750 s/c and 1100 u/s class 14 laps 43.4m (70km)
1. Herkuleyns (MG) 37' 20.4" 69.85mph (112.48kph)
2. Dhome (Darmont) 37' 54"
3. Maillard-Brune (MG) 38' 44.4"
4. Debille (Salmson) 13 laps
5. Boussin (Amilcar) 13 laps

1100 s/c and 1500 u/s class 16 laps 49.6m (81.6km) 7 starters
1. Girod (Salmson) 40' 40.4" 86.85mph (139.86kph)
2. Mestivier (Amilcar) 40' 48.2"
3. Toni (Bugatti) 14 laps

1935 (2 June)

750 s/c and 1100 u/s class 11 laps 42m (69km)
1. Maillard Brune (MG) 34' 40" 74.25mph (119.57kph)
2. Gaudichet (Sandford) 10 laps
3. Pacheco (Robail) 10 laps
4. Hup (BNC) 9 laps

5. Lemaitre (EHP) 8 laps
6. Demarchi (Caban) 8 laps
7. Danvignes (Danvignes) 8 laps

1100 class 12 laps 46m (75km)
1. Mestivier (Amilcar) 36' 18.6" 77.36mph (124.58kph)
2. Sandford (Sanford) 11 laps
3. Venot (La Pintade) 10 laps
4. Malivoir (BNC) 10 laps

G.P. DE LORRAINE, Nancy (Seichamps) (3.4m (5.5km) lap)

1932 (26 June)

23 laps 79m (127km) 20 starters
1. Veyron (Maserati) 1hr 18' 07" 60.70mph (97.72kph)
2= Guilbaut (Bugatti) = 1hr 20' 56"
   Lister (Bugatti)
4. Valette (Maserati) 1hr 21' 15"

1935 (30 June)

3 hours 5 starters
1. Veyron (Bugatti) 276.60km 55.39mph (89.20kph)
2. Cholmondeley-Tapper (Bugatti) 256.46km
3. Miss Ellison (Bugatti) 199.17km

G.P. DE NICE (2m (3.2km) lap)

1932 (24 July)

750 class 10 laps 20m (32km)
1. Lebas (Lebas) 26' 40" 45.10mph (72.63kph)
2. Calmes (Rosengart)
3. Labbay (Mathis)

1100 class 10 laps 20m (32km)
1. Chambost (Salmson) 22' 57.6" 52.37mph (84.34kph)
2. Reveiller (Amilcar 23' 07"
3. Martinatti (Salmson) 23' 23"

1500 class 10 laps 20m (32km)
1. Toselli (Bugatti) 22' 24" 53.17mph (85.62kph)
2. Veyron (Maserati) 23' 04"
3. Leurquin (Amilcar) 23' 31"

G.P. DE NIMES (Trophees de Provence) (1.8m (2.9km) lap reduced to 1.62m (2.61km) in 1933)

1932 (17 May)

750 s/c & 1100 u/s 15 laps 27m (43km) 4 starters

1. Chambost (Salmson) 29' 30.2" 55.04mph (88.64kph)
2. de la Rochette (Rosengart) 29' 32.6"
3. Labbay (Mathis) 12 laps

1100 s/c 26 laps 46m (75km) 5 starters
1. Scaron (Amilcar) 38' 28" 70.19mph (113.04kph)
2. Marret (Salmson) 23 laps

1500 class 30 laps 54m (87km) 7 starters
1. Mme Itier (Bugatti) 46' 12.4" 70.15mph (112.97kph)
2. Cousinie (Bugatti) 47' 11'
3. Jamy (Bugatti) 29 laps
4. Moulin (Bugatti) 29 laps
5. Roux (Bugatti) 29 laps

1933 (4 June)

1100 class 40 laps 64m (104km) 5 starters
1. Chambost (Salmson) 1hr 04' 11" 59.07mph (95.13kph) for 39 laps★
2. Reveillet (Amilcar)

1500 class 40 laps 64m (104km) 9 starters
1. Vagniez (Maserati) 1hr 03' 24" 56.77mph (91.42kph) for 37 laps
2. Ralph (Bugatti)
3. Arnaud (Bugatti)

★ Note: both classes ran with the 2000cc class and were flagged off when the winner of that class had covered the distance.

G.P. d'ORANIE, Oran

1932 (24 April)

1100 class 3 hours duration
1. Scaron (Amilcar) 196.32m (316.14km) 65.44mph (105.38kph)
2. Boucly (Salmson)
3. Vanoni (Amilcar)

1500 class 3 hours duration
1. Joly (Maserati) 218.47m (351.81km) 72.38mph (117.27kph)
2. Veyron (Maserati)
3. Miquel (Bugatti)

CIRCUIT d'ORLEANS (2.24m (3.61km) lap)

1935 (26 May)

1100 class 25 laps 56m (90km)
1. Mestivier (Amilcar) 54' 10" 62.09mph (99.99kph)
2. Maillard Brune (MG) 54' 56"
3. Hertzberger (MG) 54' 59"

4. Gilbert (BNC) 21 laps

1500 class 25 laps 56m (90km)
1. Leoz (Bugatti) 54' 42" 61.49mph (99.02kph)
2. Césure (Bugatti) 24 laps
3. Saugé (Bugatti) 22 laps

G.P. DE PICARDIE, Peronne (5.97m (9.625km) lap)

1932 (5 June)

1100 class 11 laps 65m (105km) 14 starters
1. Girod (Lombard) 65.63mph (105.68kph)
2. Druck (Amilcar)
3. Treumet (BNC)

1500 class 25 laps 149m (240km)
1. Lister (Bugatti) 67.04mph (107.96kph)
2. Guilbaut (Bugatti)
3. Robaut (Bugatti)

1933 (21 May)

15 laps 90m (144km) 8 starters
1. Mme Itier (Bugatti) 1hr 15' 56.2" 72.20mph (116.24kph)
2. Vagniez (Maserati) 1hr 23' 32"
3. Devaud (Maserati) 1hr 29' 49"
4. Gé (Bugatti) 1hr 33' 26"
5. Guilbaut (Bugatti) 14 laps

1934 (27 May)

20 laps 119m (191km) 7 starters
1. Decaroli (Bugatti) 1hr 46' 28" 68.34mph (110.05kph)
2. Girod (Salmson) 1hr 42' 32.6"
3. Mme Itier (Bugatti) 1hr 48' 41"
4. Guilbaut (Bugatti) 1hr 53' 06"
5. Barowski (Bugatti) 18 laps
6. Melinaut (Bugatti) 18 laps

1936 (21 June)

2 heats of 10 laps 60m (96km) & final of 15 laps 90m (144km)

Heat 1.
1. Trossi (Maserati) 43' 47" 82.22mph (132.38kph)
2. Fairfield (ERA) 43' 55"
3. Bira (ERA) 43' 57"
4. Lehoux (ERA)
5. Durand (Maserati)
6. Chambard (Bugatti)
7. Mme Itier (Bugatti)
8. Blot (Amilcar)

Heat 2.
1. Seaman (Delage) 44' 43" 80.50mph (129.61kph)

2. Howe (ERA) 44' 49.4"
3. Tongue (ERA) 45' 43"
4. McEvoy (Maserati)
5. Villeneuve (Bugatti)
6. Guilbaut (Bugatti)
7. Mrs. Stewart (Derby)
8. De Gavardie (Amilcar)

Final
1. Bira (ERA) 1hr 03' 43" 85.70mph (137.93kph)
2. Fairfield (ERA) 1hr 04' 14"
3. Howe (ERA) 1hr 04' 38"
4. McEvoy (Maserati)

1937 (27 June)

2 heats of 10 laps 60m (90km) & final of 15 laps 90m (144km)

Heat 1.
1. Dreyfus (Maserati) 41' 34.2" 86.60mph (139.42kph)
2. Hanson (Maserati) 45' 36"
3. De Puy (Maserati) 47' 41"
4. Mme Itier (Bugatti)

Heat 2.
1. Mays (ERA) 41' 30.6" 86.72mph (139.61kph)
2. de Graffenreid (Maserati) 45' 12"
3. Wakefield (Maserati) 46' 41"
4. Herkuleyns (MG)
5. Gollin (Maserati)

Final
1. Mays (ERA) 59' 47.6" 93.28mph (150.18kph)
2. Dreyfus (Maserati) 1hr 01' 30.6"
3. Wakefield (Maserati) 1hr 03' 52"
4. de Graffenried (Maserati)
5. Gollin (Maserati)
6. Hanson (Maserati)
7. Herkuleyns (MG)
8. Mme Itier (Bugatti)

1938 (12 June)

2 heats of 10 laps 60m (90km) & final of 15 laps 90m (144km) 15 starters

Heat 1
1. Bira (ERA) 39' 45.8" 94.10mph (151.50kph)
2. Howe (ERA) 38' 59"
3. Bianco (Maserati) 9 laps
4. Soffietti (Maserati) 9 laps
5. Herkuleyns (MG) 7 laps

Heat 2.
1. Mays (ERA) 40' 53" 89.07mph (143.40kph)
2. Wilson (ERA) 44' 47.2"
3. Lanza (Maserati) 9 laps

232

4. De Burnay (MG) 8 laps
5. Hug (Maserati) 8 laps
6. Villeneuve (Bugatti) 8 laps

Final
1. Mays (ERA) 1hr 00' 33" 90.94mph (146.41kph)
2. Bianco (Maserati) 1hr 02' 26.6"
3. Soffietti (Maserati) 14 laps
4. Wilson (ERA) 14 laps
5. Lanza (Maserati) 14 laps
6. Villeneuve (Bugatti) 12 laps
7. De Burnay (MG) 11 laps

1939 (11 June)

A 10 lap heat 60m (90km) & a 15 lap final 90m (144km) 10 starters

Heat
1. Wakefield (Maserati) 81.20mph (130.73kph)
2. Hug (Maserati)
3. Tremoulet (Amilcar)
4. Grignard (Amilcar)
5. Herkuleyns (MG)
6. Horvilleur (Maserati)

Final
1. Wakefield (Maserati) 1hr 06' 33" 82.03mph (132.07kph)
2. Sommer (Maserati) 13 laps
3. Horvilleur (Maserati) 13 laps
4. Roumani (Bugatti) 13 laps
5. Tremoulet (Amilcar) 13 laps
6. Herkuleyns (MG) 12 laps

G.P. DE LA MARNE, Rheims (4.85m (7.815km) lap)

1931 (5 July)

50 laps 242.5m (390.75km)
1. Auber (Bugatti) 3hr 19' 1.4" 74.36mph (121.32kph)
2. Delorme (Bugatti) 3hr 22' 5.2"
3. Mme Itier (Bugatti) 49 laps
4. Devaud (Amilcar) 45 laps

COUPE DE LA COMMISSION SPORTIF, Rheims (4.85m (7.815km) lap)

1939 (9 July)

38 laps 184m (297km) 11 starters
1. Hug (Maserati) 1hr 58' 21.6" 93.55mph (150.61kph)
2. Wakefield (Maserati) 2hr 00' 18.4"
3. Dipper (Maserati) 36 laps
4. Gordini (Simca) 32 laps

5. Contet (Simca) 31 laps
6. Paul (Simca) 31 laps

G.P. DE TUNISIE, Bardo Circuit, Carthage (7.89m (12.7km) lap)

1931 (29 March)

37 laps 292m (470km) 15 starters
1. E. Maserati (Maserati) 3hr 40' 02" 79.93mph (128.68kph)
2. Veyron (Bugatti) 3hr 51' 20"
3. Scaron (Amilcar) 3hr 53' 38"
4. Giraud-Cabantous (Caban) 4hr 01' 20"
5. Roux (Bugatti) 4hr 02' 38"
6. Vagniez (Bugatti)
7. Mme Itier (Bugatti)
8. Dourel (Amilcar)

1932 (3 April)

37 laps 292m (470km) 9 starters
1. Joly (Maserati) 3hr 34' 32" 81.40mph (131.05kph)
2. Veyron (Maserati) 3hr 37' 15"
3. Castelbarco (Bugatti) 3hr 38' 56"
4. Scaron (Amilcar) 3hr 45' 10"
5. Mme Itier (Bugatti) 35 laps
6. Mme Mareuse (Bugatti) 34 laps

GERMANY

AVUSRENNEN., Avus, Berlin (12.2m (20km) lap)

1931 (2 August)

750 class 5 laps 61m (99km)
1. Macher (DKW) 49' 14" 74.66mph (120.24kph)
2. Kohlrausch (BMW) 49' 16"

1500 class 10 laps 122m (198km) 12 starters
1. Lewy (Bugatti) 1hr 18' 26" 93.24mph (150.18kph)
2. Decaroli (Salmson) 1hr 23' 28"

1932 (22 May)

10 laps 122m (198km) 17 starters
1. Howe (Delage) 110.00mph (177.10kph)
2. Barnes (Austin)
3. Steinweg (Amilcar)
4. Goodacre (Austin)
5. Pohl (Bugatti)

1933 (21 May)

1500 class 10 laps 122m (198km) 9 starters

233

1. Veyron (Bugatti) 1hr 04' 54.8" 112.67mph (181.39kph)
2. Burggaller (Bugatti) 1hr 04' 59.2"
3. Howe (Delage) 1hr 08' 24.2"
4. Ruesch (Alfa Romeo) 1hr 16' 14"
5. Seibel (Bugatti) 1hr 26' 09"

800 class 10 laps 122m (198km) 7 starters
1. Horton (MG) 1hr 21' 03"
2. Barnes (Austin) 1hr 21' 42"
3. Macher (DKW) 1hr 22' 13.6"
4. Goodacre (Austin) 1hr 23' 48"
5. Delius (BMW) 1hr 26' 12.2"

1934 (27 May)

10 laps 122m (198km) 16 starters
1. Veyron (Bugatti) 1hr 04' 36" 113.52mph (182.76kph)
2. Burggaller (Bugatti) 1hr 05' 9.1"
3. Castelbarco (Maserati) 1hr 08' 8.4"
4. Simons (Bugatti) 1hr 12' 16.1"
5. Fork (MG) 1hr 12' 16.2".
6. Briem (Amilcar) 1hr 13' 46"
7. Seibel (Bugatti) 1hr 21' 59.1"
8. Brudes (MG) 1hr 22' 12" (winner special 800cc prize)

1937 (30 May)

7 laps 85m (136km) 11 starters
1. Martin (ERA) 42' 13" 119.67mph (192.55kph)
2. Plate (Maserati) 46' 05"
3. Teagno (Maserati) 46' 30"
4. Uboldi (Maserati) 46' 37"
5. Hug (Bugatti) 47' 15"
6. Basadonna (Maserati)
7. Bjornstadt (ERA)

EIFELRENNEN, Nurburgring (14.17m (22.8km) lap)

1932 (29 May)

1500 class 14 laps 198m (319km)
1. Tauber (Alfa Romeo) 3hr 07' 24" 63.49mph (102.24kph)
2. Hartmann (Bugatti) 3hr 17' 59"
3. Seibel (Bugatti) 3hr 28' 52"

800 class 10 laps 141.7m (228km)
1. Macher (DKW) 2hr 40' 59" 52.95mph (85.28kph)
2. Simon (DKW) 2hr 48' 37"
3. Stoll (DKW) 3hr 30' 56"

1933 (28 May)

800 class 12 laps 170m (273km)

1. Hamilton (MG) 2hr 50' 15" 59.30mph (95.5kph)
2. Kohlrausch (Austin) 3hr 14' 32"

1500 class 15 laps 212m (342km)
1. Howe (Delage) 3hr 17' 42" 64.39mph (103.7kph)
2. Burggaller (Bugatti) 3hr 17' 43"
3. Veyron (Bugatti) 3hr 23' 36"

1934 (4 June)

1500 class 12 laps 170m (273km)
1. Castelbarco (Maserati) 2hr 36' 23" 65.17mph (104.92kph)
2. Schmidt (Bugatti) 2hr 36' 42"
3. Burggaller (Bugatti) 2hr 37' 30"
4. Simons (Bugatti) 2hr 39' 04"
5. Sojka (Bugatti) 2hr 45' 14"
6. Seibel (Bugatti) 2hr 44' 33.4"
7. Mme Itier (Bugatti) 2hr 53' 30.3"
8. Stoewer (DKW) 3hr 00' 35.4"
9. Durand (Bugatti) 3hr 11' 01.4"
10. Vagniez (Maserati) 3hr 21' 29.3"

800cc class
1. Brudes (MG) 2hr 50' 19.2". Only finisher

1935 (16 June)

1500cc 8 laps 113m (182km) 17 starters
1. Mays (ERA) 1hr 38' 33" 69.03mph (111.10kph)
2. Ruesch (Maserati) 1hr 39' 02.1"
3. Rose-Richards (ERA) 1hr 40' 15.1"
4. Seaman (ERA) 1hr 40' 18.3"
5. Cook (ERA) 1hr 41' 8.4"
6. Sojka (Bugatti) 1hr 43' 22"
7. Kessler (Maserati) 1hr 43' 28.4"
8. Castelbarco (Maserati)

800cc 8 laps 113m (182km)
1. Kohlrausch (MG) 1hr 50' 22" 61.64mph (99.00kph)
2. Wren (MG) 1hr 54' 39.2"
3. Brudes (MG) 1hr 56' 13"

1936 (14 June)

8 laps 113m (182km) 16 starters
1. Trossi (Maserati) 1hr 37' 17.6" 69.90mph (112.53kph)
2. Tenni (Maserati) 1hr 38' 3.8"
3. Bira (ERA) 1hr 40' 13.2"
4. Lehoux (ERA) 1hr 40' 29.6"
5. Baumer (Austin) (winner special 800cc prize)
6. Hartmann (Maserati)
7. Kautz (Maserati)
8. Howe (ERA)
9. L. Villoresi (Maserati)

10. Mays (ERA)
11. Embiricos (ERA)
12. Gessner (Maserati)

GERMAN G.P. Nurburgring (14.17m (22.8km) lap)

1931 (19 July)

1100cc 18 laps 256m (413km) 14 starters
1. Froy (Riley) 4hr 23' 56" 58.03mph (93.34kph)
2. Arco (Amilcar) 4hr 32' 18"
3. Scaron (Amilcar) 4hr 34' 52"
4. Rouleau (Amilcar) 5hr 07' 52"
5. Samuelson (MG) 5hr 09' 52"
6. Macher (DKW) 5hr 13' 50"
7. Thiessen (DKW) 5hr 24' 18"

1932 (17 July)

800 class 19 laps 269m (433km) 7 starters
1. Hamilton (MG) 4hr 33' 29" 59.03mph (95.03kph)
2. Kohlrausch (BMW) 4hr 46' 00.8"
3. Baumer (Austin)

1500 class 23 laps 326m (524km) 15 starters
1. Tauber (Alfa Romeo) 4hr 54' 46.4" 66.36mph (106.83kph)
2. Hartmann (Bugatti) 5hr 07' 22.2"
3. E. Maserati/Ruggieri (Maserati) 5hr 13' 46.4"
4. Howe (Delage) 5hr 15' 03.8"
5. Wagner (Bugatti) 5hr 15' 44"
6. Sigrand (Bugatti)
7. Scaron (Amilcar)
8. Seibel (Bugatti)
9. Simons (Bugatti)
10. Mme Itier (Bugatti)

GREAT BRITAIN

CAMPBELL TROPHY, (1500cc Class) Brooklands (2.26m (3.63km) lap)

1937 (1 May)

100 laps 226m (363km) 11 starters
1. Rayson (Maserati) 3hr 19' 24.4" 68.25mph (109.88kph)
2. Scribbans (ERA) 3hr 27' 07"
3. Tongue (ETA) 98 laps
4. Fairfield/Mays (ERA) 92 laps
5. Hanson (Maserati) 91 laps

CORONATION TROPHY, Crystal Palace, London (2.0 m (3.22km) lap)

1937 (24 April)

2 heats of 20 laps 40m (64km) and 30 lap final 60m (96km) 15 starters

Heat 1
1. Fairfield (ERA) 45' 37" 52.63mph (84.73kph)
2. Brackenbury (Maserati) 46' 59.1"
3. Aitken (Frazer Nash) 47' 29.9"
4. Maclure (Riley) 47' 48.2"

Heat 2
1. Mays (ERA) 45' 40.9" 52.55mph (84.60kph)
2. Dobson (ERA) 45' 42.1"
3. Whitehead (ERA) 45' 59.6"
4. Wilkinson (Riley) 46' 20"
5. Hanson (Maserati) 47' 21.1"

Final
1. Fairfield (ERA) 1hr 07' 8.8" 53.70mph (86.45kph)
2. Dobson (ERA) 1hr 7' 57.2"
3. Hanson (Maserati) 1hr 09' 25.2"
4. Maclure (Riley) 1hr 10' 18.1"
5. Whitehead (ERA) 1hr 13' 45"

JCC 200 MILE RACE (1500cc Class) Donington Park 1936 & 1937: 2.55m (4.10km; lap: Brooklands, Campbell Circuit, 1938 2.26m (3.63km) lap)

1936 (29 August)

77 laps 197m 317km 11 starters
1. Seaman (Delage) 2hr 50' 14.6" 69.28mph (111.54kph)
2. Howe (ERA) 2hr 51' 06"
3. Briault/Evans (ERA) 2hr 57' 19.6"
4. Mays (ERA) 72 laps
5. Parnell (MG) 71 laps
6. MacRobert/Faulkner (MG) 62 laps

1937 (28 August)

77 laps 197m (317km) 11 starters
1. Dobson (ERA) 2hr 49' 12.4" 69.67mph (112.16kph)
2. Whitehead (ERA) 2hr 54' 45"
3. Wakefield (Maserati) 2hr 56' 36"
4. Brackenbury (ERA) 3hr 01' 16"
5. Parnell (MG) 73 laps

1938 (27 August)

1500 class 88 laps 199m (321km) 13 starters
1. Wakefield (ERA) 2hr 48' 37" 70.97mph (114.26kph)

2. Howe (ERA) 86 laps
3. Tongue (ERA) 83 laps
4. Rolt (ERA) 82 laps
5. Rayson (Maserati) 78 laps

1100 class 88 laps 199m (321km) 6 starters
1. Cuddon-Fletcher (MG) 82 laps completed 65.92mph (106.13kph)
2. Wilson (ERA) 81 laps
3. Smith (MG) 80 laps
4. Woolley/Monkhouse (MG) 79 laps

MANNIN BEG, Douglas, Isle of Man (1933 4.6m (7.6km) lap: 1934 3.7m (5.95km) lap: 1935 4.04m (6.50km) lap)

1933 (12 July) 1100cc s/c 1500cc u/s

50 laps 230m (370km) 14 starters
1. Dixon (Riley) 4hr 13′ 35″ 54.41mph (87.60kph)
2. Mansell (MG) 4hr 28′ 30″
3. Ford (MG) 4hr 34′ 09″

1934 (30 May) 1100cc s/c 1500cc u/s

50 laps 183m (294km) 19 starters
1. Black (MG) 2hr 34′ 37″ 70.99mph (114.29kph)
2. Dodson (MG) 2hr 36′ 20″
3. Eyston (MG) 2hr 36′ 57″
4. Martin (MG) 2hr 41′ 05″
5. Eccles (MG) 2hr 44′ 22″
6. Paul (Riley) 2hr 44′ 25″
7. Horton (MG) 2hr 44′ 54″
8. Everitt (MG) 2hr 48′ 03″

1935 (20 May) 1100cc s/c 1500cc u/s

50 laps 202m (325km) 13 starters
1. Fairfield (ERA) 2hr 59′ 54″ 67.29mph (108.33kph)
2. Dixon (Riley) 3hr 08′ 46″
3. Hall (MG) 48 laps
4. Baird (MG) 41 laps

RAC INTERNATIONAL LIGHT CAR RACE, Douglas, Isle of Man (1936: 4m (6.44km) lap. 1937 3.89m (6.26km) lap)

1936 (28 May)

50 laps 200m (322km) 18 starters
1. Seaman (Delage) 2hr 52′ 01″ 69.76mph (112.31kph)
2. Bira (ERA) 2hr 53′ 18″
3. Paul (ERA) 2hr 55′ 02″
4. Fairfield (ERA) 2hr 55′ 23″
5. Lehoux (ERA) 2hr 55′ 47″
6. Manby-Colegrave/Featherstonhaugh

(ERA) 3hr 04′ 57″
7. Everitt (ERA) 47 laps
8. Dodson (Austin) 44 laps
9. Briggs (MG) 43 laps

1937 (3 June)

50 laps 194.5m (313.1km) 15 starters
1. Bira (ERA) 2hr 45′ 34″ 70.69mph (113.81kph)
2. Mays (ERA) 2hr 46′ 16″
3. Fairfield (ERA) 2hr 46′ 53″
4. Tongue (ERA) 2hr 48′ 05″
5. Whitehead/Walker (ERA) 2hr 50′ 30″
6. de Graffenreid (Maserati) 49 laps
7. A.C. Dobson (ERA) 48 laps
8. Austin Dobson (Maserati) 48 laps
9. Hanson (Maserati) 48 laps
10. Maclure (Riley) 48 laps
11. Connell (ERA) 45 laps
12. Parnell (MG) 35 laps

NUFFIELD TROPHY Donington Park (1934-1937: 2.55m (4.10km) lap. 1938-1939: 3.125m (5.30km) lap)

1934 (7 October)

Class handicap 40 laps 102m (164km) 17 starters
1. Mays (ERA) 1hr 41′ 08″ 61.51mph (99.03kph)
2. Seaman (MG) 1hr 44′ 41.6″
3. Evans (MG) 1hr 45′ 18″
4. Howe (Delage)
5. Cook (ERA)
6. Martin (MG)
7. Horton (MG)
8. Cholmondley-Tapper (Bugatti)

1935 (13 July)

Class handicap 60 laps 153m (246km) 20 starters
1. Fairfield (ERA) 2hr 25′ 10″ 63.67mph (102.47kph)
2. Maclure (Riley) 2hr 26′ 23″
3. Briault (MG) 2hr 29′ 39″
4. Dixon (Riley) 2hr 30′ 25″
5. Bira (MG) 2hr 34′ 54″
6. Miss Evans (MG) 2hr 36′ 04″

1936 (4 July)

Class handicap 60 laps 153m (246km) 21 starters
1. Martin (ERA) 2hr 25′ 06″ 68.50mph (110.28kph)
2. Dobson (ERA) 2hr 25′ 44″
3. Whitehead/Walker (ERA) 2hr 26′ 35″

4. Dobbs (Riley) 2hr 27' 1.2"
5. Bira (Austin) 2hr 27' 28.2"
6. Howe (ERA) 2hr 28' 27"
7. Briault (ERA) 2hr 31' 25"

1937 (12 June)

Class handicap 60 laps 153m (246km) 17 starters
1. Fairfield (ERA) 2hr 28' 43" 65.89mph (106.08kph)
2. Dobson (ERA) 2hr 29' 29"
3. Mays (ERA) 2hr 29' 53"
4. Maclure (Riley) 2hr 31' 02"
5. de Graffenreid (Maserati) 2hr 33' 45"
6. Martin (ERA)

1938 (9 July)

Class handicap 64 laps 200m (322km) 22 starters
1. Bira (ERA) 2hr 53' 58" 72.74mph (117.11kph)
2. Hadley (Austin) 2hr 54' 20"
3. Dobson (ERA) 63 laps
4. Dodson (Austin) 63 laps
5. Rolt (ERA) 62 laps
6. Connell/Evans (ERA) 61 laps
7. Nickols (MG) 60 laps
8. Wilson (ERA) 60 laps
9. Aitken (Maserati) 59 laps
10. Woolley (MG) 58 laps
11. Hyde (Riley) 58 laps
12. Gerard (Riley) 58 laps
13. Hanson (Maserati) 56 laps
14. Maclure (Riley) 48 laps

1939 (10 June)

64 laps 200m (322km) 17 starters
1. Bira (ERA) 2hr 38' 10" 75.87mph (122.15kph)
2. Mays (ERA) 2hr 39' 48"
3. Whitehead (ERA) 63 laps
4. Ansell (ERA) 62 laps
5. Dodson (Maserati) 59 laps
6. Pollock (ERA) 59 laps
7. Aitken (ERA) 59 laps
8. Hadley (Austin) 58 laps
9. Gerard (Riley) 56 laps

IRELAND

CORK G.P., Carrigrohane Circuit, Cork (6.08m (9.79km) lap)

1938 (23 April)

12 laps 73m (117.5km) 11 starters

1. Bira (ERA) 47' 55" 91.47mph (147.26kph)
2. Dobson (ERA) 49' 35.2"
3. L. Villoresi (Maserati) 49' 35.4"
4. Wilson (ERA) 52' 48"
5. Hug (Maserati) 53' 28"
6. Soffietti (Maserati) 11 laps

PHOENIX PARK, Dublin (4.25m (6.84km) lap)

1937 (11 September)

24 laps 102m (164km) 10 starters
1. Mays (ERA) 59' 38.2" 102.90mph (165.66kph)
2. Wakefield (Maserati) 1hr 01' 50"
3. Cotton (ERA) 1hr 02' 34.4"
4. Hanson (Maserati) 23 laps

ITALY

CIRCUIT OF PIETRO BORDINO, Alessandria (5.00m (8.00km) lap)

1931 (26 April)

1100 class 35 laps 175m (281km)
1. Comotti (Salmson) 2hr 31' 44" 69.20mph (111.41kph)
2. Benoit (Amilcar) 32 laps
3. Carnevali (Rally) 31 laps

CIRCUIT OF BIELLA (1.36m (2.2km) lap)

1934 (2 September)

3,25 laps heats 34m (54km) 40 lap final 45m (88km)

Final classification
1. Farina (Maserati) 1hr 03' 44" 51.45mph (82.86kph)
2. Lurani (Maserati)
3. Castelbarco (Maserati)
4. Bianchi (Bugatti)

1935 (9 June)

23 laps 31m (50km) 4 starters
1. Lurani (Maserati 39' 11.6" 47.53mph (76.54kph)
2. Castelbarco (Maserati) 39' 26.2"
3. Rovere (Maserati) 20 laps
4. Siena (Maserati) 13 laps

CIRCUIT OF CAMPIONE D'ITALIA (0.7m (1.11km) lap)

1937 (26 September)

3 40 lap heats 27m (44km) & 50 lap final 34m (55km) 14 starters

Heat 1
1. Bianco (Maserati) 31' 46.4" 53.34mph (85.90kph)
2. Marazza (Maserati) 31' 55.8"
3. Minetti (Maserati) 32' 25.2"

Heat 2
1. Rocco (Maserati) 31' 36.4" 52.62mph (84.74kph)
2. Lurani (Maserati) 31' 51.4"
3. Teagno (Maserati) 31' 53.4"
4. Basadonna (Maserati) 39 laps
5. Caspani (Maserati) 28 laps

Heat 3
1. Trossi (Maserati) 31' 18.4" 53.12mph (85.55kph)
2. Severi (Maserati) 31' 21.6"
3. Righetti (Maserati) 34 laps

Final
1. Rocco (Maserati) 39' 09.4" 53.09mph (85.50kph)
2. Severi (Maserati) 39' 30.2"
3. Lurani (Maserati) 39' 43"

CIRCUIT OF CARNARO Abbazia (3.72m (6.00km) lap)

1939 (9 July)

25 laps 93m (150km) 9 starters
1. L. Villoresi (Maserati) 1hr 10' 51.2" 78.45mph (127.14kph)
2. Cortese (Maserati) 1hr 11' 3.4"
3. Romano (Maserati) 1hr 18' 17.3"
4. Rocco (Maserati) 24 laps

G.P. OF FLORENCE (2.04m (3.3km) lap)

1937 (13 June)

70 laps 143m (231km) 19 starters
1. Dreyfus (Maserati) 2hr 03' 00" 70.55mph (113.58kph)
2. Trossi/Rovere (Maserati) 69 laps
3. Bianco/Rocco (Maserati) 69 laps
4. Cortese (Maserati) 69 laps
5. Tongue (ERA)
6. Dusio (Maserati)
7. Severi (Maserati)
8. Whitehead (ERA)
9. Marazza (Maserati)

10. Wakefield (Maserati)

CIRCUITO DELLA SUPERBA, Genoa (1.86m (3.00km lap)

1937 (30 May)

40 laps 74m (120km) 11 starters
1. Marazza (Maserati) 1hr 21' 00" 55.86mph (89.95kph)
2. Severi (Maserati) 1hr 21' 18.2"
3. Belmondo (Maserati) 1hr 21' 19"
4. Barbieri (Maserati) 39 laps
5. Lurani (Maserati) 38 laps (1st 1100)
6. Azzi (Maserati) 32 laps
7. Nespoli (Amilcar) 29 laps

G.P. OF ITALY, 1500cc class Monza (6.21m (10.0km) lap)

1931 (24 May)

10 hr duration 5 starters
1. Pirola/Lurani (Alfa Romeo) 1290.243km
2. Ruggeri/Balestrero (Talbot) 1290.00km

CIRCUIT OF LUCCA (Coppa Edda Ciano) (1.45m (2.35km) lap)

1936 (7 September)

30 laps 43m (70km)
1. Trossi (Maserati) 46' 14.6" 56.80mph (91.47kph)
2. Belmondo (Maserati) 46' 57.4"
3. Barbieri (Maserati) 47' 26.8"
4. Bianco (Maserati) 29 laps

1937 (19 September)

60 laps 87m (141km) 13 starters
1. Trossi (Maserati) 1hr 30' 40" 57.94mph (93.308kph)
2. L. Villoresi (Maserati) 59 laps
3. Rocco (Maserati) 59 laps
4. Righetti (Maserati) 57 laps
5. Teagno (Maserati) 57 laps
6. Severi (Maserati) 54 laps
7. Bertani (Maserati) 51 laps (special prize 1st 1100)

1938 (4 September)

60 laps 87m (141km) 11 starters
1. L. Villoresi (Maserati) 1hr 36' 02.2" 54.70mph (88.09kph)
2. Cortese (Maserati) 1hr 36' 52.2"
3. Pietsch (Maserati) 1hr 37' 05.4"
4. Taruffi (Maserati) 59 laps

5. Rocco (Maserati) 59 laps
6. Barbieri (Maserati) 58 laps
7. Baruffi (Maserati) 57 laps*
8. Ruggieri (Maserati) 54 laps
9. Corsi (Maserati) 51 laps
10. Brezzi (Maserati) 50 laps

*Pino Baruffi is sometimes confused with the much better known Piero Taruffi. Baruffi formed a small scuderia with Gigi Soffietti in 1937/38, the Gruppo Volta di Como.

COPPA CIANO, Livorno (1931–1935, Montenero circuit (12.5m (20.1km) (1936–1939, Livorno, (1936 4.34m (7.00km) lap: 1938 & 1939, 3.6m (5.8km) lap)

1931 (2 August)

1100 class 8 laps 100m (160km) 5 starters
1. Premoli (Salmson) 2hr 14' 03.4" 44.48mph (71.63kph)
2. Ferrari (Talbot) 2hr 14' 05"
3. Matrullo (Salmson) 2hr 16' 39"
4. Pratesi (Salmson) 2hr 16' 55"
5. Cioni (Fiat) 2hr 27' 51"

1932 (31 July)

1100 class 8 laps 100m (160km) 5 starters
1. Cerami (Maserati) 2hr 09' 29.2" 49.50mph (79.71kph)
2. Matrullo (Maserati) 2hr 10' 01.6"
3. Pratesi (Salmson) 2hr 13' 35"
4. Del Re (Fiat Lombard) 2hr 24' 24.8"

1933 (30 July)

1100 class 8 laps 100m (160km) 6 starters
1. Barbieri (Maserati) 2hr 01' 38.8" 47.44mph (76.40kph)
2. Landi (Maserati) 2hr 02' 32.2"
3. Furmanik (Maserati) 2hr 16' 15.6"
4. Dourel (Amilcar) outside time limit

1934 (22 July)

1100 class 8 laps 100m (160km) 13 starters
1. Malaguti (Maserati) 2hr 09' 39" 46.81mph (75.38kph)
2. Matrullo (Maserati) 2hr 12' 05"
3. Mallucci (Fiat) 2hr 14' 10"
4. Toti (Maserati) 2hr 19' 11"
5. Nencioni (Rocca) 2hr 28' 46"
6. Corrado (Fiat) 2hr 34' 05"

1935 (5 August)

1100 class 8 laps 100m (160km) 10 starters
1. Tuffanelli (Maserati) 1hr 59' 06.6" 50.05mph (80.59kph)

2. Bianco (Maserati) 2hr 00' 52.8"
3. L. Villoresi (Fiat) 2hr 11' 06"
4. Ferrara (Fiat) 2hr 15' 35.6"

1936 (26 July)

15 laps 65m (105km) 15 starters
1. Trossi (Maserati) 58' 05" 67.30mph (108.45kph)
2. Embiricos (ERA) 59' 03.8"
3. L. Villoresi (Maserati) 59' 13.4"
4. Hartmann (Maserati) 1hr 01' 14.4"
5. Rovere (Maserati) 1hr 01' 58"
6. Seaman (Delage) 1hr 02' 37"
7. Bergamini (Maserati) 14 laps
8. McEvoy (Maserati) 14 laps
9. Prosperi (Maserati) 14 laps
10. Plate (Talbot) 13 laps
11. De Sanctis (Fiat) 12 laps

1938 (7 August)

25 laps 90m (145km) 16 starters
1. E. Villoresi (Alfa Romeo) 1hr 05' 21.6" 86.66mph (133.10kph)
2. Biondetti (Alfa Romeo) 1hr 05' 23.8"
3. Marazza (Maserati) 1hr 06' 22.2"
4. Cortese (Maserati) 1hr 06' 42.8"
5. Barbieri (Maserati) 24 laps
6. Ruggieri (Maserati) 24 laps
7. Severi (Alfa Romeo) 23 laps
8. Corsi (Maserati) 23 laps

1939 (30 July)

60 laps 216m (348km) 11 starters
1. Farina (Alfa Romeo) 2hr 30' 10.4" 86.32mph (139.00kph)
2. Cortese (Maserati) 59 laps
3. Pintacuda/Biondetti (Alfa Romeo) 57 laps
4. Taruffi (Maserati) 56 laps
5. Biondetti/Severi (Alfa Romeo) 52 laps

"Juniors" 20 laps 72m (116km) 12 starters
1. Teagno (Maserati) 56' 29.6" 76.55mph (123.28kph)
2. Lami (Maserati) 56' 30"
3. Brezzi (Rocca) 57' 49.8"
4. Lanzi (Maserati) 19 laps
5. Corsi (Maserati) 17 laps

CIRCUIT OF MILAN (1.6m (2.57km) lap)

1936 (28 June)

40 laps 64m (103km)
1. Trossi (Maserati) 1hr 09' 17.2" 55.45mph (89.28kph)
2. E. Villoresi (Maserati) 1hr 10' 35.2"
3. Belmondo (Maserati) 1hr 10' 52.4"

4. Bianco (Maserati) 39 laps
5. Rovere (Maserati) 38 laps (1st 1100)
6. Gilera (Maserati) 37 laps
7. Plate (Maserati) 37 laps
8. Rosa (Maserati) 37 laps
9. Baronessa Avanzo (Maserati) 34 laps
10. Bianchi (Maserati) 33 laps

1937 (20 June)

50 laps 80m (123km) 20 starters
1. Siena (Maserati) 1hr 13′ 02.9″ 61.24mph (98.59kph)
2. Marazza (Maserati) 1hr 13′ 35.6″
3. Cortese (Maserati) 1hr 13′ 44.3″
4. Tongue (ERA) 1hr 14′ 50.3″
5. Belmondo (Maserati) 1hr 15′ 39.3″
6. L. Villoresi (Maserati) 1hr 17′ 08.5″
7. Severi (Maserati)
8. Whitehead (ERA) 1hr 17′ 35.3″
9. Righetti (Maserati)
10. Wakefield (Maserati)
11. Lurani (Maserati) (1st 1100)
12. Taruffi (Maserati)

CIRCUIT OF MODENA, (2m (3.2km) lap)

1934 (14 October)

25 laps 50m (80km) 10 starters
1. Cecchini (MG) 50′ 12.6″ 59.28mph (95.44kph)
2. Farina (Maserati) 50′ 18.4″
3. Malaguti (Maserati) 24 laps
4. Balzacchi (Rocca) 22 laps
5. Matrullo (Maserati) 22 laps
6. Lami (PE) 22 laps

1935 (15 October)

25 laps 50m (80km) 10 starters
1. Berrone (Maserati) 49′ 40″ 60.41mph (97.26kph)
2. Tuffanelli (Maserati) 49′ 54″ (1100 class winner)
3. Bergamini (Maserati) 24 laps
4. Plate (Talbot) 23 laps
5. Taruffi (Maserati) 23 laps

1936 (21 September)

25 laps 50m (80km) 10 starters
1. Trossi (Maserati) 47′ 13.2″ 63.03mph (101.65kph)
2. Biondetti (Maserati) 49′ 01.8″
3. Righetti (Maserati) 24 laps
4. Prosperi (Maserati) 24 laps
5. Bergamini (Maserati) 23 laps (1st 1100)
6. Plate (Talbot) 23 laps
7. Degner (Maserati)

8. Carnevali (Bugatti)
9. Baruffi (Maserati)
10. Meroni (P.P.)

1938 (18 September)

55 laps 110m (176km) 19 starters
1. Cortese (Maserati) 1hr 43′ 54″ 63.10mph (101.62kph)
2. Hug (Maserati) 54 laps
3. Dobson (ERA) 52 laps
4. Plate (Maserati) 48 laps

MONZA G.P. (1931: 4.26m (6.86km) lap. 1938: 4.34m (6.99km) lap)

1931 (6 September)

1100cc class 20 laps 85m (137km) 15 starters
1. Scaron (Amilcar) 1hr 00′ 47.4″ 85.40mph (135.43kph)
2. Premoli (Salmson) 1hr 03′ 06.4″
3. Arco (Amilcar) 1hr 03′ 27″
4. Cabantous (Caban) 1hr 04′ 18.4″
5. Klinger (Maserati) 1hr 05′ 4.2″
6. Dourel (Amilcar) 1hr 06′ 25.2″
7. Plate (BNC) 1hr 07′ 47.4″
8. Pratesi (Salmson) 1hr 08′ 48.6″
9. Boucly (Salmson) 1hr 13′ 38.6″
10. Macher (DKW) 1hr 15′ 42.4″

1938

25 laps 108m (174km) 20 starters
1. E. Villoresi (Alfa Romeo) 1hr 11′ 4.2″ 91.65mph (147.59kph)
2. Severi (Alfa Romeo) 1hr 11′ 5.4″
3. Hug (Maserati) 1hr 14′ 05″
4. Cortese (Maserati) 24 laps
5. Marazza (Maserati) 24 laps
6. Bianco (Maserati) 24 laps
7. Castelbarco (Maserati) 23 laps
8. Barbieri (Maserati) 25 laps
9. De Teffe (Maserati) 23 laps
10. Sommer (Alfa Romeo) 23 laps
11. Garagnani (Maserati) 22 laps
12. Pelassa (Maserati) 22 laps

COPPA PRINCIPESSA DI PIEMONTE, Naples, Posillipo circuit (2.54m (4.1km) lap)

1937 (25 April)

30 laps 76m (123km) 21 starters
1. Trossi (Maserati) 1hr 14′ 41.4″ 61.21mph (98.81kph)
2. Bira (ERA) 1hr 15′ 40.6″
3. Bjornstadt (ERA) 1hr 16′ 10.6″

4. Prosperi (Maserati) 1hr 16′ 45″
5. Bianco/Rocco (Maserati) 29 laps
6. De Graffenried (Maserati) 29 laps
7. Tongue (ERA) 29 laps
8. Gessner (Maserati) 28 laps
9. Lurani (Maserati) 28 laps (1st 1100)
10. Moradei (Maserati) 28 laps
11. Bassadonna (Maserati) 27 laps
12. Chambord (Bugatti) 26 laps
13. Leuzinger (   ) 26 laps

1938 (26 June)

60 laps 152m (246km) 18 starters
1. Marazza (Maserati) 2hr 26′ 08.6″ 62.71mph
   (100.9kph)
2. L. Villoresi (Maserati) 2hr 26′ 36.2″
3. Pelassa/Dusio (Maserati) 59 laps
4. Bianco/Belucci (Maserati) 58 laps
5. Hug (Maserati) 58 laps
6. Soffietti (Maserati) 58 laps
7. Lanza (Maserati) 56 laps
8. Pietsch (Maserati) 56 laps
9. De Teffe (Maserati) 56 laps
10. Teagno (Maserati) 55 laps
11. Raph/Ghersi (Maserati) 53 laps
12. Trossi/Rocco (Maserati) 51 laps

1939 (28 May)

60 laps 152m (246km)
1. Wakefield (Maserati) 2hr 24′ 50.8″
   63.62mph (102.43kph)
2. Taruffi (Maserati) 2hr 25′ 45″
3. Cortese (Maserati) 2hr 27′ 26″
4. L. Villoresi (Maserati) 2hr 28′ 39″
5. Bianco (Maserati) 59 laps
6. Barbieri (Maserati)
7. Bellucci (Maserati)
8. Romano (Maserati)
9. Plate (Maserati)
10. Rocco (Maserati)
11. Corsi (Maserati)

COPPA ACERBO, Pescara: (15.9m (25.6km) lap)

1931 (16 August)

1100 class 4 laps 63m (102km) 10 starters
1. Decaroli (Salmson) 56′ 10.6″ 67.69mph
   (108.94kph)
2. Ferrari (Talbot) 56′ 56″
3. Matrullo (Salmson) 58′ 26.6″
4. Plate (BNC) 1hr 02′ 45.4″
5. Ardizzone (Ardizzone) 1hr 09′ 04.1″

1932 (14 August)

1100 class 4 laps 63m (102km) 13 starters

1. Scaron (Amilcar) 51′ 39″ 73.79mph
   (118.75kph)
2. Chambost (Salmson) 52′ 04″
3. Matrullo (Maserati) 52′ 08″
4. Cerami (Maserati) 54′ 43″
5. Martinatti (Salmson) 56′ 34″
6. Decaroli (Salmson) 57′ 30.4″
7. Del Re (Lombard) 57′ 31″
8. Moradei (Talbot)

1933 (15 August)

1100 class 63m (102km) 8 starters
1. Straight (MG) 50′ 23.23″ 75.91mph
   (121.74kph)
2. Barbieri (Maserati) 50′ 33.4″
3. Furmanik (Maserati) 51′ 04.6″
4. Malaguti (Maserati) 51′ 59.8″
5. Cecchini (Fiat) 56′ 57.2″
6. Dourel (Amilcar) 1hr 02′ 06.2″

1934 (15 August)

4 laps 63m (102km) 8 starters
1. Hamilton (MG) 52′ 24.2″ 73.4mph
   (118.16kph)
2. Cecchini (MG) 53′ 22.6″
3. Seaman (MG) 54′ 34.6″
4. Furmanik (Maserati) 55′ 06.2″
5. Felizzola (Maserati) 56′ 04.2″
6. Beccaria (Fiat) 58′ 33.6″
7. Matrullo (Maserati) 1hr 00′ 56.4″

1935 (15 August)

4 laps 63m (102km) 12 starters
1. Seaman (ERA) 48′ 42.4″ 78.99mph
   (127.28kph)
2. Bianco (Maserati) 49′ 52.2″
3. Steinweg (Bugatti) 51′ 19.2″
4. Ghersi (Maserati) 51′ 47.6″ (1100 class
   winner)
5. Bergamini (Maserati) 51′ 57.4″
6. Plate (Talbot) 55′ 32.8″
7. Tongue (MG) 56′ 07.2″
8. Carnevali (Bugatti) 56′ 51.4″

1936 (15 August)

6 laps 96m (154km) 10 starters
1. Seaman (Delage) 1hr 14′ 25.2″ 77.55mph
   (124.08kph)
2. Trossi (Maserati) 1hr 15′ 04.8″
3. Ruesch (Maserati) 1hr 19′ 38″
4. McEvoy (Maserati) 1hr 20′ 45″
5. Bergamini (Maserati) 1hr 24′ 08″

1937 (15 August)

6 laps 96m (154km) 15 starters
1. Rocco (Maserati) 1hr 14′ 12.4″ 77.59mph
   (124.91kph)

241

2. Bianco (Maserati) 1hr 14′ 18.1″
3. Cortese (Maserati) 1hr 14′ 43.2″
4. Severi (Mascrati) 1hr 16′ 04″
5. Baruffi (Maserati) 1hr 25′ 38.5″
6. Teagno (Maserati) 1hr 27′ 04.6″

1938 (14 August)

6 laps 96m (154km) 11 starters
1. L. Villoresi (Maserati 1hr 10′ 49″ 82.06mph (132.11kph)
2. Pietsch (Maserati) 1hr 13′ 29″
3. Barbieri (Maserati) 1hr 16′ 46″
4. Severi (Alfa Romeo) 1hr 18′ 12.2″
5. Libbeccio (Maserati) 1hr 19′ 57.1″
6. Plate (Talbot) 1hr 27′ 44.2″
7. Baruffi (Maserati) 1hr 28′ 59.2″

1939 (13 August)

14 laps 223m (357km) 10 starters
1. Biondetti (Alfa Romeo) 2hr 41′ 38.1″ 83.31mph (134.07kph)
2. Pintacuda (Alfa Romeo) 2hr 43′ 37.1″
3. Farina (Alfa Romeo) 2hr 43′ 56.2″
4. Severi (Alfa Romeo) 2hr 45′ 16.4″
5. Pollock (ERA) 2hr 50′ 13.3″

"Juniors" 4 laps 63m (102km)
1. Barbieri (Maserati) 50′ 59″ 75.49mph (121.51kph)
2. Teagno (Maserati) 53′ 34″
3. Lami (Maserati) 54′ 49″
4. Plate (Maserati)
5. Corsi (Maserati)

PRIX ROYAL, Rome
(Littorio circuit (2.4m (3.9km) lap)

1931 (7 June)

1100cc class 25 laps 60m (96km)
1. Scaron (Amilcar) 45′ 53.6″ 81.70mph (131.53kph)
2. Decaroli (Salmson) 49′ 12″
3. Ardizzone (Ardizzone) 50′ 59″
4. Comotti (Salmson)

1932 (24 April)

1100cc class 25 laps 60m (96km) 9 starters
1. Decaroli (Salmson) 46′ 58.8″ 79.30 mph (127.70kph)
2. Tuffanelli (Maserati) 49′ 25.8″
3. Matrullo (Salmson) 51′ 32.2″

CIRCUIT OF SAN REMO (1.15m
(1.86km) lap)

1937 (25 July)

3 heats of 25 laps 29m (46.5km) Final of 30 laps 34m (55km) 17 starters

Heat 1
1. Dusio (Maserati) 30′ 29.4″
2. E. Villoresi (Maserati) 32′ 01″
3. Villa (Bugatti) 20 laps
4. Bianco (Maserati) 18 laps

Heat 2
1. Varzi (Maserati) 29′ 06″
2. Ermini (Maserati) 24 laps
3. Righetti (Maserati) 24 laps

Heat 3
1. Rocco (Maserati) 29′ 36″
2. Lurani (Maserati) 31′ 31″ (incl 1′ penalty)

Final
1. Varzi (Maserati) 34′ 39.6″ 60.05mph (96.69kph)
2. Dusio (Maserati) 32′ 26.4″
3. Rocco (Maserati) 35′ 31″
4. Ermini (Maserati) 29 laps

G.P. OF TRIPOLI (1500cc Class) (Mellaha
circuit (8.1m (13.1km) lap)

1937 (15 May)

34 laps 276m (448km) 11 starters
1. Dreyfus (Maserati) 2hr 33′ 55.7″ 107.95mph (173.79kph)
2. Cortese (Maserati) 2hr 36′ 51.3″
3. Severi (Maserati) 30 laps
4. L. Villoresi (Maserati) 39 laps
5. Dusio (Maserati) 27 laps

1938 (15 May)

40 laps 325m (524km)
1. Taruffi (Maserati) 2hr 57′ 47″ 109.79mph (177.02kph)
2. Rocco (Maserati) 2hr 57′ 56″
3. Lurani (Maserati) 3hr 03′ 37″
4. Bianco (Maserati) 39 laps
5. Raph (Maserati) 38 laps
6. Hug (Maserati) 29 laps

1939 (7 May)

30 laps 244m (393km) 30 starters
1. Lang (Mercedes-Benz) 1hr 59′ 12.3″ 122.90mph (197.86kph)
2. Caracciola (Mercedes-Benz) 2hr 02′ 49.6″
3. E. Villoresi (Alfa Romeo) 2hr 07′ 00″
4. Taruffi (Maserati) 2hr 12′ 31″
5. Hug (Maserati) 2hr 17′ 05.6″
6. Brezzi (Maserati) 2hr 20′ 15.6″
7. Dipper (Maserati) 2hr 35′ 14.8″
8. Lanza (Maserati) 28 laps

9. Teagno (Maserati 28 laps
10. Castelbarco (Maserati) 27 laps
11. Balestrero (Maserati) 27 laps
12. Plate (Maserati) 26 laps

1940 (12 May)

30 laps 244m (393km) 22 starters
1. Farina (Alfa Romeo) 1hr 54' 16.4"
   128.21mph (206.41kph)
2. Biondetti (Alfa Romeo) 1hr 54' 45.9"
3. Trossi (Alfa Romeo) 1hr 55' 09.3"
4. Villoresi (Maserati) 1hr 55' 23.5"
5. Cortese (Maserati) 2hr 02' 41.5"
6. Pintacuda (Alfa Romeo) 2hr 02' 53.3"
7. Brezzi (Maserati)
8. Taruffi (Maserati)
9. Ascari (Maserati)
10. Rocco (Maserati)

CIRCUIT OF TURIN (Valentino Park 1.81m (2.92km) lap)

1937 (18 April)

40 laps 72m (117km) 16 starters
1. Bjornstadt (ERA) 1hr 18' 12.5" 55.78mph
   (89.80kph)
2. Dreyfus (Maserati) 1hr 18' 27.2"
3. Tongue (ERA) 1hr 18' 33.8"
4. Bianco/Rovere (Maserati) 1hr 19' 30.4"
5. Dusio (Maserati) 1hr 20' 25.1"
6. Gabardi (Maserati) 39 laps
7. Basadonna (Maserati) 38 laps
8. Lurani (Maserati) 36 laps (1st 1100)

TARGO FLORIO (1935: short Madonie circuit; 44.5m (72km) lap: 1937–40 Favorita Park Palermo, 1937: 3.26m (5.26km) 1938–1939: 3.55m (5.72km) lap)

1935 (28 April)

1100 class 6 laps 267m (430km)
1. Toia (Fiat) 6hr 36' 39" 40.43mph
   (65.09kph)
2. Ferrari (Fiat) 6hr 41' 33"

1937 (23 May)

60 laps 196m (315km) 12 starters
1. Severi (Maserati) 2hr 55' 49" 66.88mph
   (107.70kph)
2. Lurani (Maserati) 58 laps (1st 1100)
3. Bianco (Maserati) 55 laps
4. Barbieri (Maserati) 54 laps
5. Bertani (Maserati) 51 laps
6. Belmondo (Maserati) 51 laps
7. Sciandra (Fiat) 41 laps

1938 (22 May)

30 laps 107m (171km) 16 starters
1. Rocco (Maserati) 1hr 30' 04.6" 70.98mph
   (114.30kph)
2. Raph (Maserati) 1hr 32' 15"
3. L. Villoresi (Maserati) 1hr 34' 09.4"
4. Battaglia (Maserati) 1hr 35' 56.4"
5. Soffietti/Baruffi (Maserati) 1hr 36' 15"
6. De Teffe (Maserati) 29 laps

1939 (14 May)

40 laps 141m (227km) 14 starters
1. L. Villoresi (Maserati) 1hr 40' 15.4"
   83.78mph (134.88kph)
2. Taruffi (Maserati) 1hr 42' 05.8"
3. Barbieri (Maserati) 1hr 45' 56.4"
4. Pietsch (Maserati) 1hr 48' 30.6"
5. Capelli (Maserati) 1hr 50' 16.6"
6. Plate (Maserati) 38 laps
7. Teagno (Maserati)
8. Galinari (Maserati)

1940 (23 May)

40 laps 141m (227km) 15 starters
1. L. Villoresi (Maserati) 1hr 36' 08.6"
   88.40mph (142.32kph)
2. Cortese (Maserati) 1hr 37' 23.6"
3. Rocco (Maserati) 1hr 37' 40"
4. Bianco (Maserati) 1hr 38' 45"
5. Ruggieri (Maserati) 1hr 39' 30.2"
6. Barbieri (Maserati) 1hr 39' 54.2"
7. Palmieri (Maserati) 37 laps
8. "Pimpiricchio" (Maserati) 37 laps
9. Plate (Maserati) 36 laps
10. Balestrero (Maserati) 36 laps
11. Corsi (Maserati) 36 laps

CIRCUIT OF VARESE (2.23m (3.6km) lap)

1938 (17 July)

2 heats of 15 laps 33m (54km) Final 30 laps 67m (108km)

Heat 1
1. Marazza (Maserati) 30' 57" 65.00mph
   (104.68kph)
2. Teagno (Maserati)
3. Soffietti (Maserati)

Heat 2
1. L. Villoresi (Maserati) 30' 08.2" 66.76mph
   (107.51kph)
2. Cortese (Maserati)
3. Pietsch (Maserati)

Final
1. Cortese (Maserati) 59' 35.2" 67.53mph (108.74kph)
2. Marazza (Maserati) 1hr 01' 03.6"
3. Ghersi (Maserati) 1hr 01' 08.4"
4. Pietsch (Maserati) 29 laps
5. Teagno (Maserati)
6. Barbieri (Maserati)
7. Lanza (Maserati)
8. Soffietti (Maserati)

MONACO

COUPE PRINCE RAINIER (1.95m (3.14km) lap)

1936 (11 April)

50 laps 97m (157km) 18 starters
1. Bira (ERA) 1hr 51' 51.5" 52.99mph (85.31kph)
2. Lehoux (ERA) 1hr 53' 56.3"
3. Embiricos (ERA) 49 laps
4. Kautz (Maserati) 49 laps
5. Howe (ERA) 48 laps
6. L. Villoresi (Maserati) 46 laps

POLAND

G.P. OF LWOW (1.88m (3.04km) lap)

1932 (12 June)

65 laps 123m (197km)
1. Hartmann (Bugatti) 47.60mph (76.63kph)
2. Ripper (Bugatti)
3. Holuj (Bugatti)

1933 (11 June)

100 laps 188m (304km) 10 starters
1. Veyron (Bugatti) 3hr 52' 44.1" 49.06mph (78.98kph)
2. Burggaller (Bugatti) 3hr 54' 20"
3. Landi (Maserati) 3hr 55' 36"
4. Ripper (Bugatti)
5. Mme Itier (Bugatti)
6. Mme Kozmian (Bugatti)

SOUTH AFRICA

GROSVENOR GRAND PRIX (4.61m (7.42km) lap)

1939 (14 January)

44 laps 203m (326km)
1. Cortese (Maserati) 76.80mph (123.64kph)
2. Aitken (ERA)
3. Chiappini (Maserati)
4. Hesketh (ERA)

SOUTH AFRICAN GP (Prince George circuit, East London (11m (17.7km) lap)

1939 (2 January)

18 laps 198m (318km)
1. L. Villoresi (Maserati) 1hr 59' 26" 99.66mph (128.74kph)
2. Cortese (Maserati) 2hr 00' 56"
3. Massacuratti (Maserati) 2hr 01' 50"
4. Hesketh (ERA)
5. Howe (ERA)
6. Hug (Maserati)
7. Aitken (ERA)
8. Chiappini (Maserati)

SWITZERLAND

GP DE GENEVA (Meyrin circuit (6.2m (9.98km) lap)

1931 (7 June)

1100 class 20 laps 124m (200km)
1. Benoit (Amilcar) 1hr 47' 30" 69.23mph (111.46kph)
2. Romano (Bugatti) 1hr 50' 00"
3. Dourel (Amilcar) 1hr 55' 45"

1500 class eliminating heat 15 laps 93m (150km)
1. Veyron (Bugatti)
2. Roux (Bugatti)
3. Kessler (Alfa Romeo)
4. Avondet (Bugatti)
5. Lurani (Alfa Romeo)
6. Wimille (Bugatti)
7. Angwerd (Bugatti)

1500 clas final (with GP cars) 25 laps 155m (250km)
1. Kessler (Alfa Romeo) 2hr 04' 02.5" 74.97mph (120.70kph)
2. Pirola (Alfa Romeo) 2hr 05' 24"

PRIX DE BERNE: Bremgarten circuit (4.5m (7.28km) lap)

1934 (26 August)

14 laps 63m (102km) 22 starters
1. Seaman (MG) 50' 43.4" 74.91mph (120.60kph)
2. Veyron (Bugatti) 51' 05.6"
3. Burggaller (Bugatti) 51' 11.4"
4. Sojka (Bugatti) 51' 41"
5. Howe (Delage) 51' 53"
6. Castelbarco (Maserati)
7. Girod (Salmson)
8. Cholmondley-Tapper (Bugatti)
9. Mme Itier (Bugatti)
10. Mme Kozmian (Bugatti)

1935 (25 August)

20 laps 90m (145km) 18 starters
1. Seaman (ERA) 1hr 05' 21" 80.07mph (128.91kph)
2. Bira (ERA) 1hr 06' 15.7"
3. Howe (Delage) 1hr 07' 16.2"
4. Tuffanelli (Maserati) 1hr 07' 31.8"
5. Ghersi (Maserati) 1hr 07' 35"
6. Ruesch (Maserati) 1hr 07' 47.6"
7. Mays (ERA) 1hr 08' 17.5"
8. Steinweg (Bugatti) 19 laps
9. Kessler (Maserati) 19 laps
10. Cholmondley-Tapper (Bugatti) 19 laps
11. Evans (MG) 19 laps
12. Leiningen (ERA) 18 laps
13. Veyron (Bugatti) 17 laps
14. Herkuleyns (MG) 16 laps
15. Mrs Stewart (Derby) 15 laps

1936 (23 August)

28 laps 127m (203km) 16 starters
1. Seaman (Delage) 1hr 26' 30" 87.84mph (141.42kph)
2. Embiricos (ERA) 1hr 27' 54"
3. Tongue (ERA) 1hr 29' 44"
4. Howe (ERA) 27 laps
5. Ruesch (Maserati) 27 laps
6. Baumer (Austin) 27 laps
7. McEvoy (Maserati) 27 laps
8. Plate (Talbot) 23 laps
9. Herkuleyns (MG) 23 laps
10. Bianco (Maserati) 21 laps

1937 (22 August)

2 heats of 14 laps 63m (101km) Final of 21 laps 95m (152km)
Heat 1
1. E. Villoresi (Maserati) 42' 40"
2. Mays (ERA) 42' 42"
3. Martin (ERA) 43' 23"
4. Hartmann (Maserati)

Heat 2
1. Dobson (ERA) 43' 03"
2. Cortese (Maserati) 43' 20"
3. Bira (ERA) 43' 21"
4. Berg (Maserati)
5. Marazza (Maserati)

Final
1. Dobson (ERA) 1hr 09' 5.6" 82.60mph (132.98kph)
2. Mays (ERA) 1hr 09' 5.8"
3. Bira (ERA) 1hr 09' 52.4"
4. Cortese (Maserati) 1hr 10' 22"
5. Martin (ERA) 1hr 10' 23.4"
6. Marazza (Maserati) 1hr 11' 04.8"
7.
8. Minetti (Maserati) 20 laps
9. L. Villoresi (Maserati) 20 laps
10. Hanson (Maserati) 20 laps
11. Hertzberger (MG) 19 laps
12. Gollin (Maserati) 10 laps

1938 (21 August)

2 heats of 14 laps 63m (101km) Final of 21 laps 95m (152km)
Heat 1
1. Pietsch (Maserati) 48' 56.6"
2. Wilson (ERA) 52' 17.8"
3. Wakefield (ERA)
4. Ghersi (Maserati)
5. Plate (Talbot)
6. Bircher (Bugatti)
7. Herkuleyns (MG)

Heat 2
1. Mays (ERA) 46' 30"
2. Howe (ERA)
3. Rolt (ERA)
4. Bianco (Maserati)
5. Hug (Maserati)
6. de Teffe (Maserati)
7. Hanson (Maserati)
8. Teagno (Maserati)
9. Pollock (ERA)
10. Plate (Maserati)

Final 14 starters
1. Hug (Maserati) 1hr 10' 00.5" 81.88mph (131.82kph)
2. Bianco (Maserati) 1hr 11' 40.8"
3. Wakefield (ERA) 1hr 11' 41.8"
4. Howe (ERA) 1hr 12' 00.8"
5. de Teffe (Maserati) 1hr 13' 00.6"

6. Wilson (ERA) 20 laps
7. Teagno (Maserati) 20 laps
8. Pollock (ERA) 20 laps
9. Rolt (ERA) 19 laps
10. Herkuleyns (MG) 19 laps

1939 (20 August)

20 lap heat 90m (145km) for all cars 30 lap final 135m (217km) with GP cars

Heat
1. Farina (Alfa Romeo) 56′ 28″ 96.30mph (155.04kph)
2. Biondetti (Alfa Romeo) 57′ 05″
3. Wakefield (Maserati) 57′ 36.9″
4. Rocco (Maserati) 58′ 14.9″
5. Pietsch (Maserati) 19 laps
6. Ansell (ERA) 19 laps
7. Joa (Maserati) 18 laps
8. Pollock (ERA) 17 laps

Final
1. Farina (Alfa Romeo) (29 laps only) 1hr 26′ 21.6″
2. Biondetti (Alfa Romeo) 28 laps
3. Wakefield (Maserati) 26 laps
4. Ansell (ERA) 25 laps

Maps

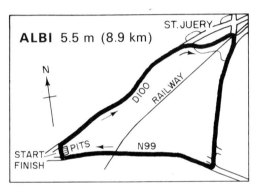

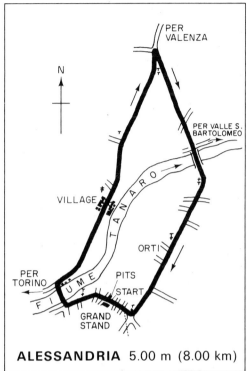

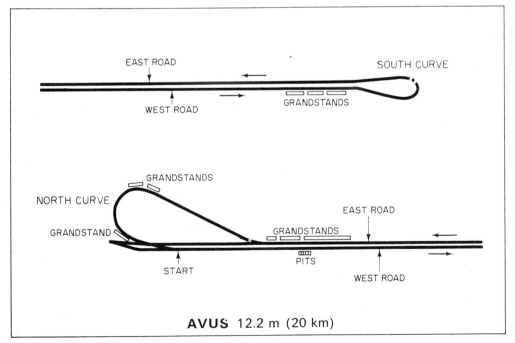

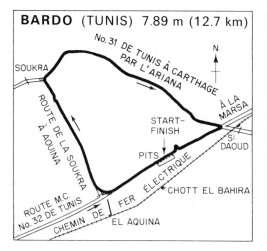
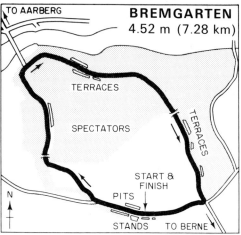
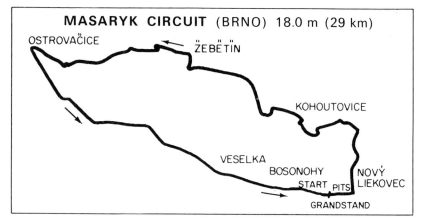
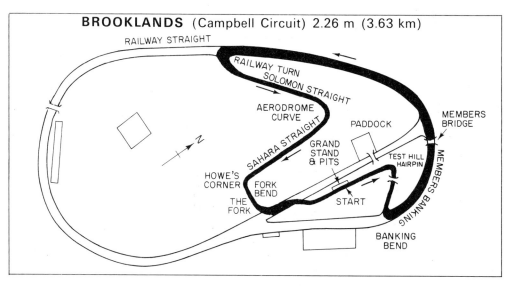

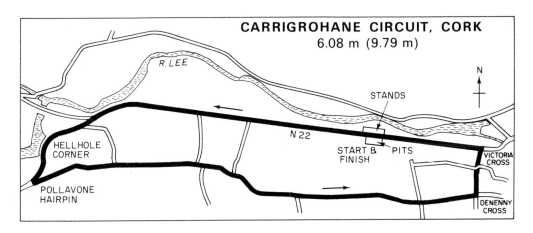

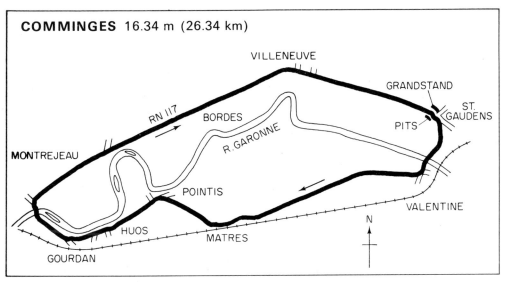

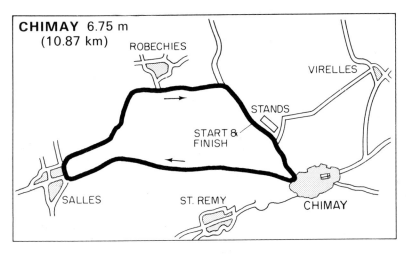

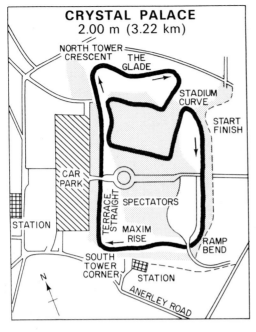

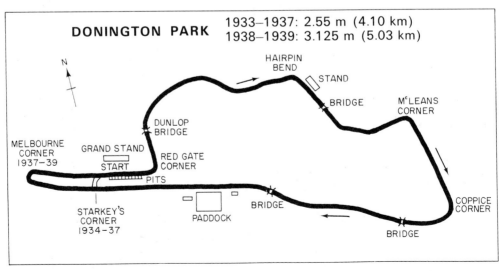

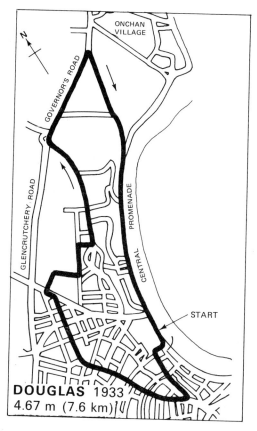
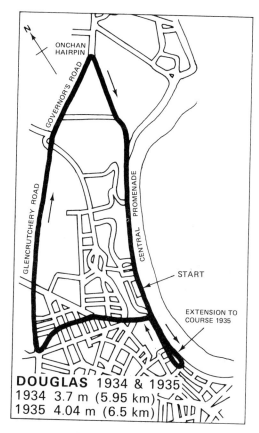
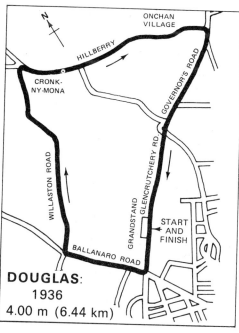
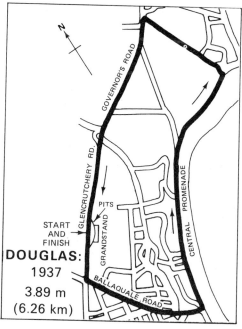

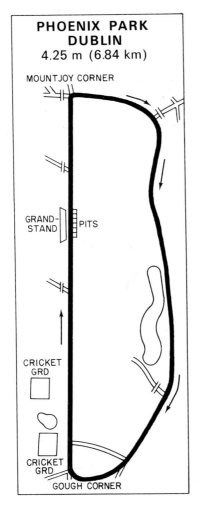
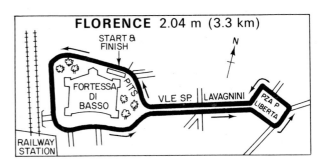
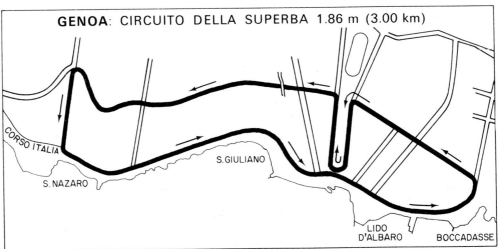

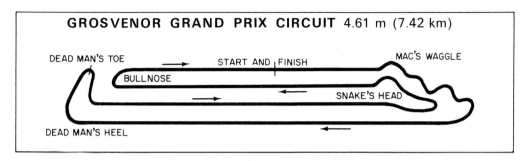

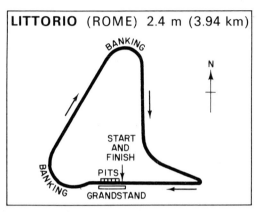

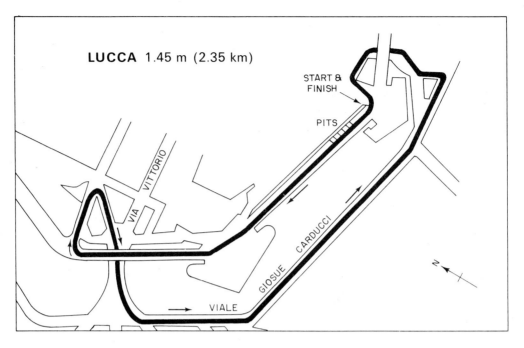
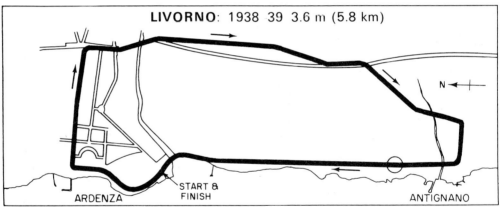
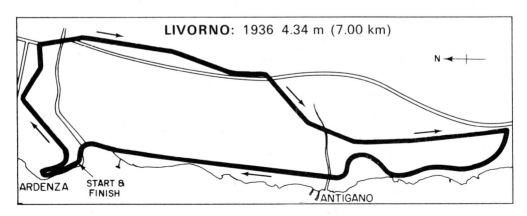

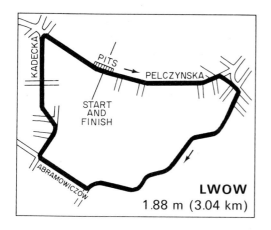

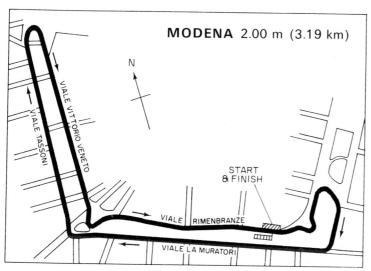

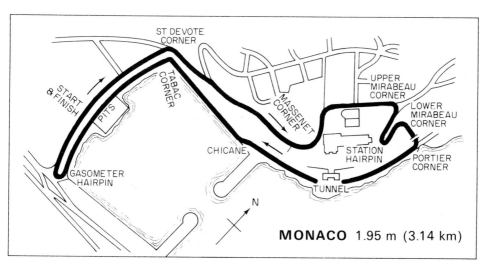

255

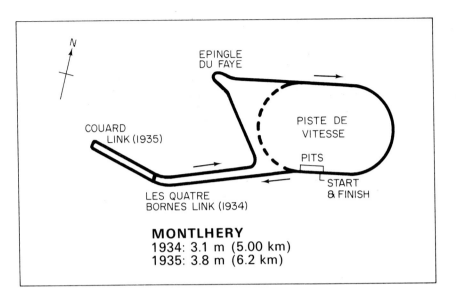

MONTLHERY
1934: 3.1 m (5.00 km)
1935: 3.8 m (6.2 km)

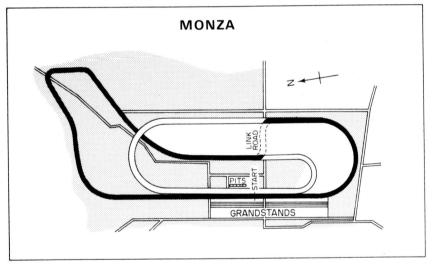

Italian Grand Prix 1931
6.21 m (10.00 km)

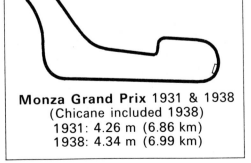

Monza Grand Prix 1931 & 1938
(Chicane included 1938)
1931: 4.26 m (6.86 km)
1938: 4.34 m (6.99 km)

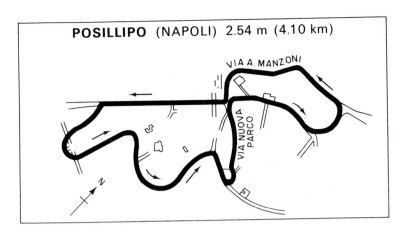

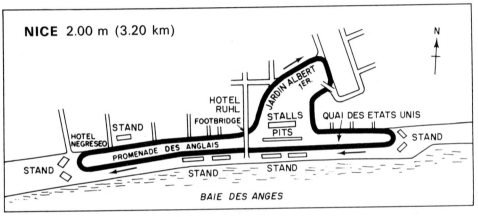

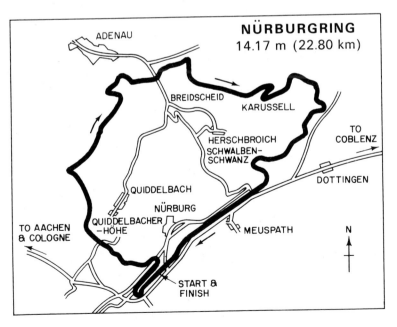

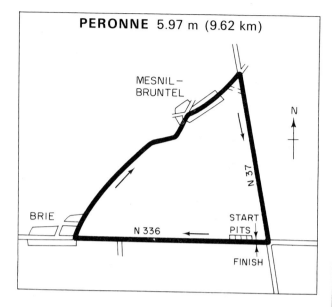
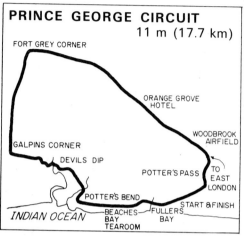
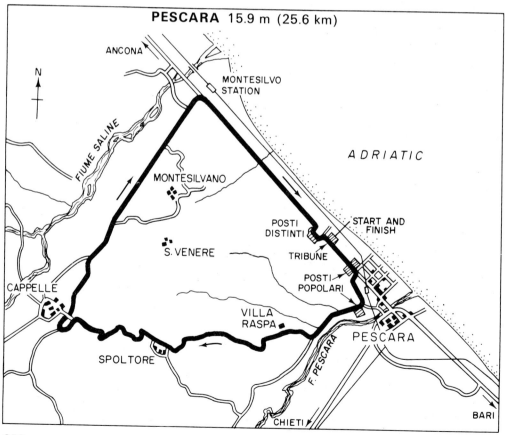

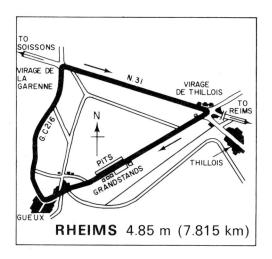

RHEIMS 4.85 m (7.815 km)

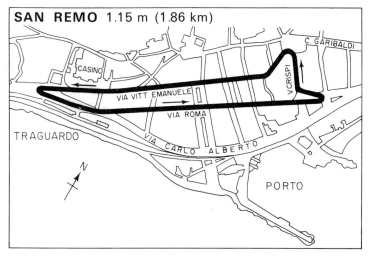

SAN REMO 1.15 m (1.86 km)

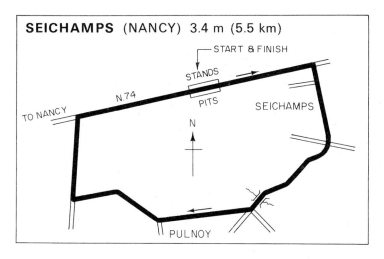

SEICHAMPS (NANCY) 3.4 m (5.5 km)

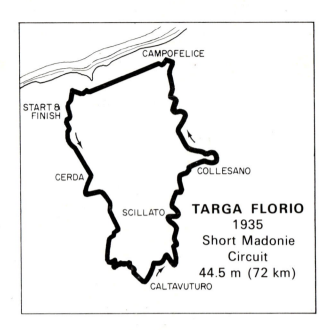

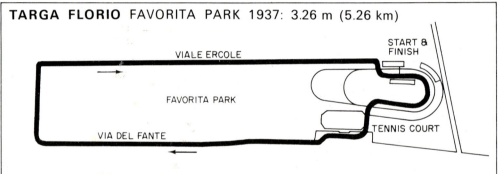

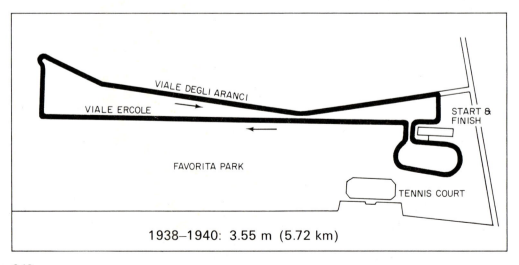

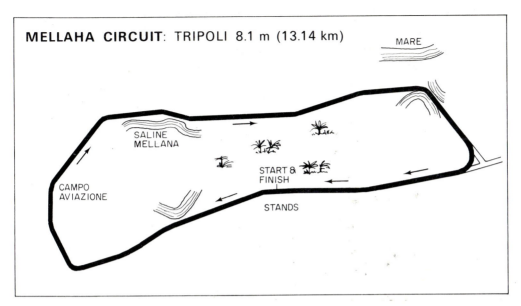
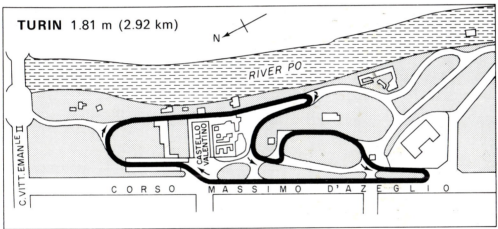

BIBLIOGRAPHY

Books

Amateur Racing Driver: T.P. Cholmondeley Tapper, Foulis, 1954
Alfa Romeo: Peter Hull & Roy Slater, Cassel, 1964
The Alfa Romeo Type 158/159: David Hodges, Profile Publications 1967
The Austin Seven: R.J. Wyatt, Macdonald 1968
Austin Racing History: R.C. Harrison, Motor Racing Publications 1949
Bits and Pieces: Prince Birabongse of Thailand, Foulis 1942
Blue & Yellow: Prince Chula of Siam, Foulis 1947
The Story of Brooklands: W. Boddy, Grenville Publishing Co. 1950
Etorre Bugatti: W.F. Bradley, Motor Racing Publications 1948
Bugatti: H.G. Conway, Foulis, 1963
Grand Prix Bugatti: H.G. Conway, Foulis 1968
Combat: Barre Lyndon, Heinemann 1933
Circuit Dust: Barre Lyndon, John Miles 1934
Das Autobuch: Hans Stuck & Ernst Burggaller, Dreimastenverlag, Berlin, 1933
The History of English Racing Automobiles Ltd: David Weguelin, White
    Mouse Editions 1980
The Chain Drive Frazer Nash: David Thirlby, Macdonald 1965
The German Grand Prix: Cyril Posthumus, Temple Press 1966
German High Performance Cars: Jerrold Sloniger & Hans-Heinrich van Fersen,
    Batsford 1965
Grand Prix: Barre Lyndon, John Miles 1935
The Grand Prix Car Vol. 1 & 2: Laurence Pomeroy, Temple Press 1954
Grand Prix Racing Facts and Figures: George Monkhouse, Foulis 1950
Maintaining the Breed: John Thornley, Motor Racing Publications 1950
Maserati: Richard Crump & Rob de la Rive Box, Haynes 1973
Maserati: Luigi Orsini & Franco Zagari, Emmeti Grafica 1980
The Mercedes-Benz Racing Cars: Karl Ludvigzen, Bond/Parkhurst Books 1971
M.G. Story: Wilson McComb, Osprey 1979
Monza Year Books 1962 & 1963
Motor Races: George Monkhouse, George Newnes 1937
Motor Racing with Mercedes-Benz: George Monkhouse, Foulis 1949
Motor Sport Racing Car Review: D.S. Jenkinson, Grenville Publishing Co.
    1947

262

The Power and the Glory: William Court, Macdonald 1966
A Pictorial Survey of Racing Cars 1919-1939: T.A.S.O. Mathieson, Motor Racing Publications 1963
Racing Round the World: Count Giovanni Lurani, Foulis 1950
Racing Voiturettes: Kent Karslake, Motor Racing Publications 1950
Riley: The production and competition history of the pre-1939 Riley motor car, Dr A.T. Birmingham, Foulis 1965
Road Racing 1936: Prince Chula of Siam, Foulis 1946
Road Star Hat Trick: Prince Chula of Siam, Foulis 1941
The Salmson Story: Chris Draper, David & Charles 1974
La Scuderia Ferrari 1929-1939: Luigi Orsini & Franco Zagari, Editoriale Olimpia 1979
Dick Seaman Racing Motorist: Prince Chula of Siam, Foulis 1941
Shelsley Walsh: C.A.N. May, Foulis 1945
Split Seconds: Raymond Mays, Foulis 1951
La Favolosa Targa Florio: Giovanni Canestrini, Editrice de l'Automobile 1966
The Two Hundred Mile Race: W. Boddy, Grenville Publishing Co. 1947
Wheels at Speed: Prince Chula of Siam, Foulis 1946
Works Driver: Piero Taruffi, Temple Press 1964

Periodicals

The Autocar
L'Automobiliste
Autosport
Bugantics
Classic & Sports Car
Figaro
La Fanatique de l'Automobile
Frankfurter Zeitung
La Gazetta dello Sport
Il Giornale d'Italia
Light Car
Moteurs
The Motor
Motor Racing
Motor Sport
Omnia
Speed
Thoroughbred and Classic Car
Trident
La Vie Automobile